SCHOOL OF THEOLOGY AND MINISTRY
SEATTLE UNIVERSITY
900 BROADWAY
SEATTLE, WASHINGTON 98122-4340

Hispanic Christianity within

Mainline Protestant Traditions

A Bibliography

Paul Barton and David Maldonado, Jr.
editors

Perkins School of Theology
Southern Methodist University
Dallas, Texas

Asociación para la Educación Teológica Hispana
(AETH)
Decatur, Georgia
1998

Hispanic Christianity Within Mainline Protestant Traditions
A Bibliography
Editors: Paul Barton & David Maldonado, Jr.
Publisher: AETH Books

ISBN Number: 0-965-7839-3-6

The following have generously given permission to include part or all of their bibliographic materials in this bibliography.

Atkinson, Ernest E. *A Selected Bibliography of Hispanic Baptist History*. Nashville, TN: Historical Commission, Southern Baptist Convention, 1981.

Fernandez-Calienes, Raul. "Bibliography of the Writings of Orlando E. Costas." *Missiology: An International Review* 17, no 1 (1989): 87-105, 2nd. ed. Denver, CO: Editorial Génesis, 1995.

Table of Contents

Abbreviations

ABHMS	American Baptist Home Mission Society
AETH	Asociación para la Educación Teológica Hispana
APHILA	Academia para la Historia de la Iglesia Latina
BTI	Boston Theological Institute
CEHILA	Comisión de Estudios de Historia de la Iglesia en Latinoamérica
CELAM	Consejo Episcopal Latinoamericano
CELEP	Centro Evangélico Latinoamericano de Estudios Pastorales
CLAI	Consejo Latinoamericano de Iglesias
CUPSA	Casa Unida de Publicaciones, S.A.
DEI	Departamento Ecuménico de Investigaciones
FTL	Fraternidad Teológica Latinoamericana
ICDC	Iglesia Cristiana (Discípulos de Cristo) in Puerto Rico
ISAL	Iglesia y Sociedad en América Latina [World Council of Churches]
LAMAG	Latin American Methodist Action Group
MARCHA	Metodistas Asociados Representando la Causa de los Hispano Americanos/Methodists Associated Representing the Cause of Hispanic Americans
SEBILA	Seminario Bíblico Latinoamericano [currently, Universidad Bíblica Latinoamericana]
WABHMS	Woman's American Baptist Home Mission Society

Introduction to the Bibliography
David Maldonado, Jr.

This bibliography is part of a larger project focusing on Hispanic Christianity within mainline traditions. With generous support from the Lilly Endowment, the project set out to contribute toward the definition and understanding of Hispanic Protestantism in the United States. Of special interest were U.S. Hispanics within the "old-line" or "historic" churches. A fundamental purpose of the project was to define what is "Protestant" about Hispanic Protestants and what is "Hispanic" about Hispanic Protestants. The methodology utilized the notion of doing theology *"en conjunto."* This is grounded in Justo L. González's insight that Hispanic theology tends to be guided by a sense of community. Thus, this project was designed as a communal endeavor through which invited participants shared and developed their respective contributions in dialogue with the whole. The spirit of sharing was an important element that contributed to the working of the group and provided for mutual influence and relationship among the various contributions. It is in that spirit of sharing, with a wider circle of Latinos and Latinas and other colleagues who share a common interest in Hispanic Christianity, that this bibliography has been designed and disseminated.

The need for a bibliography focused on U.S. Hispanic Protestantism was recognized from the very beginning. Several factors contributed toward the necessity for this bibliography.

First, we recognized that much has already been written by and about Hispanic Protestants in United States. Important pioneering work needs to be acknowledged and made known. This includes work by early Anglo American missionaries as well as Hispanic Protestants themselves. For example, the writings of Thomas Harwood regarding his work in New México and the descriptions of personal experiences of early Hispanic Protestants in Texas by José Policarpo Rodriguez offer insights to the early days of Hispanic Protestantism in the Southwest. The spirit of *conjunto* calls us to know and be informed by the writings of those who precede us and shaped the early days of Hispanic Christianity in the United States.

Another important factor was the need to identify archives and other sources of information, data, and historical records. Protestant denominations, which played major a role in the emergence of Hispanic Protestant Christianity, possess key archival resources and records. They generated literature as part of their missionary efforts and continue to produce important documentation. Certain libraries, private collections, and schools of theology need to be highlighted as significant depositories for research. The need to identify and make known these bibliographic resources was an important factor in producing this bibliography.

In addition, we recognized that there are a number of Latinas and Latinos who are actively writing about the Hispanic Protestant reality. Many of them publish in mainstream journals and have publications produced by established publishing houses. For example, Justo L. González is a highly respected author and is sought by major publishing houses. However, many Hispanics publish their work through smaller and less known avenues. For example, *Apuntes: Reflexiones Teológicas desde el Margen Hispano* is a Hispanic theological journal that has been published by the Mexican American Program of the Perkins School of Theology for over a decade. It is known throughout Latin America and among U.S. Hispanics. Yet, *Apuntes* is little known beyond these circles. This bibliography is an effort to make known and to share these Hispanic resources with a wider audience.

We also realize that Anglo American and Catholic colleagues have contributed important insights on the Hispanic religious reality, including the Protestant experience. The bibliography could not be restricted to Hispanic authors or to Hispanic Protestants. We have taken the liberty to include selected writings by Hispanic Catholics and Anglos as well. The study of Hispanic Protestantism would be incomplete without the views and perspectives from the broader Hispanic and religious communities.

Producing a bibliography such as this one reminds us how little we really know, and how much there is yet to learn about U.S. Hispanic Christianity within the historic traditions. The bibliography reflects areas in which important work has been initiated. For example, Justo L. González has been an important contributor in the area of history and theology. Harold Recinos has made impressive contributions in the areas of urban anthropology and immigration. Orlando Costas made pioneering contributions in evangelism and missiology. As important as these authors' works have been, they are but beginnings for U.S. Hispanic contributions to these fields.

With regard to the other fields of study such as theology, Biblical studies, ethics, systematic theology, sociology, and especially in the practical and ministry fields, such as Christian education, homiletics, pastoral counseling, sacred music and social ministry, much still needs to be done at the initial level by mainline Hispanic Protestants. There has been some work done recently in these areas, but some have come out after the cutoff date for the bibliography. Some promising work is being done by such Protestant writers as Ismael García, Pablo Jiménez, Daisy Machado, José David Rodríguez, David Traverso, and Luis Pedraja, for example. The contributions of Rubén Armendáriz, Jorge Lara Braud, Jorge González, Francisco Garcia-Treto continue to be worthy of recognition.

The interest in Hispanic Christianity in its various manifestations and the need for a bibliography on U.S. Hispanic Protestantism illustrates the increased significance of the Hispanic population in the United States for the many religious denominations ministering with Hispanics, and especially for theological education which seeks to prepare future pastors for an increasingly diverse society. The U.S. Hispanic population has expanded numerically and in proportion to the general population. It can no longer be ignored or treated as a mere "home mission." This comes at a time when many mainline Protestant denominations are struggling to maintain their current membership levels and many local Anglo Protestant congregations are suddenly surrounded by a community of Latinos and Latinas. In many cases, Hispanics are already part of Anglo church structures and present new and challenging situations. This bibliography seeks to contribute toward a more informed understanding of this particular population.

An important motivational factor for producing this bibliography is also the need to provide Hispanic Protestants with resources helpful in their journeys toward greater self understanding. As Hispanics and Protestants they are a minority in both their ethnic and religious communities. Hispanic Protestants are an ethnic minority within their denominational bodies, and they are a religious minority within their traditionally Catholic Hispanic community. Self understanding and clarity of identity are important to Hispanic Protestants. This bibliography seeks to guide them to a valuable body of literature that represents and speaks to their experience and perspectives. It is the documentation and expression of their story.

However, the primary purpose for this bibliography is the need and desire to provide a bibliographic resource and tool for those interested in studying Hispanic Protestantism in the United States. It is designed as a research tool for students, instructors, researchers, and church leaders. No such resource is known to exist at this time, yet the demand for the bibliography is great. Hispanic Christianity is rapidly growing and has become a central point of much discussion. Hopefully, this bibliography will contribute toward a more informed discussion.

Like all other bibliographies, this bibliography is not a finished task. The challenge of finding new items, archival sources and other material continues. Likewise, new publications appear every year. May this bibliography inspire others and serve as an invitation to search for new sources and make them known *en conjunto* to the rest of the community.

On a personal note, I want to give special thanks to Craig Dykstra, Olga Villa Parra, Jeanne Knoerle, Paul Barton, and others who contributed to this project. Craig provided wise counsel and vision to the project and has been a friend to this project. Olga was then a consultant to the Lilly Endowment and served as liaison between the Endowment and the project. She was a fountain of encouragement and support. Her wise counsel and moral support will always be appreciated. The authors who contributed the introductory essays on the various fields of study also provided counsel on the availability of literature. Assistants on the project, Ary Bolaños, Teresa Santillana, and Martin Stemerick provided much help in the compilation and editing of the bibliography. Paul Barton served as research assistant while working on his Ph.D. at Southern Methodist

University. He played a major role in producing the bibliography and contributed many hours and much energy towards its production. As a result, not only do we have a bibliography, but we also have in Paul an important resource who knows the literature well.

The Bibliography: Criteria, Methodology and Usage
Paul Barton

Like a spelunker exploring a cave, investigation into Hispanic Protestantism led us to new and exciting findings that had heretofore remained in the dark. To our surprise and delight, the amount of materials we eventually collected for this bibliography greatly exceeded our original expectations. When we first started working on the bibliography in August, 1994, six months seemed like an adequate time for collecting all of the materials. After early research revealed a vast amount of literature available, we extended the deadline to a year's worth of research, and yet again to one-and-a-half years. Many materials are not included only because time constraints limited our ability to continue collecting materials for the bibliography. We have not traversed all of the passageways of this "cave" called Hispanic Protestantism; we cannot claim to have amassed all available materials in this field of study. Rather, the bibliography is an attempt to compile as many resources on Hispanic Protestantism as possible within a limited amount of time and present them in an arrangement that is most helpful for researchers.

Research for the bibliography began with a review of Hispanic professors' and Bridwell Library's collections at Perkins School of Theology. These works provided a solid basis for searching other works in other theological libraries. Some of the most productive bibliographic sources include the *Dissertation Abstracts International* by UMI, the *ATLA Religion Database on CD-ROM, Apuntes: Reflexiones Teológicas desde el Margen Hispano,* and *Journal of Hispanic/Latino Theology.* Other sources of information came from contributions by dozens of professors and other individuals, bibliographies submitted by Hispanic Protestant scholars, denominational archives, periodicals, and various other bibliographies. We also queried theological libraries, especially those accessible by computer. Roberts Library at Southwestern Baptist Theological Seminary in Forth Worth, Texas provided much material on Hispanic Baptists. Letters were sent to theological libraries across the country requesting them to provide basic information on their holdings in this field. Likewise, requests for bibliographies were sent to all known Hispanic (mainline) Protestant professors and scholars. Our appreciation goes to the staff of those libraries and to those scholars who responded to our inquiries.

There are some sources that remain untapped for this project, such as newspapers, some periodicals, indexes, and collections in other theological libraries that could not be accessed by computer.

The Criteria for Selecting Materials
The criteria for including materials in the bibliography are

straightforward: either the work deals with, or touches on, Hispanic Protestantism or it is written by a Hispanic Protestant. The work may be directly about Hispanic Protestantism, or some aspect of it, or it may focus on another subject but contains some material about, or references to, Hispanic Protestantism. References by Hispanic Protestant authors may address subjects that do not have anything to do with Hispanic Protestantism. These were included so that the researcher might appreciate the broad range of interests and activity of Hispanic Protestant professors, scholars, ministers, and laity.

As much as possible, we have endeavored to allow the stated criteria to inform decisions about inclusion or exclusion of materials. The criteria stated above helps to offset the temptation to determine the inclusion or exclusion of certain materials based upon the bibliographer's personal judgments about the value of those materials. Judgments about the value and usefulness of each reference are left to the reader. What one person might consider worthless or insignificant another person might find valuable and helpful. Additionally, the inclusion of works generally considered less significant helps the researcher, and especially the historian, examine the trends and common perspectives of a particular period.

The Latino Character of the Bibliography—Transcending Limits and Boundaries

Having just stated the policy for selecting and including materials in the bibliography, it is necessary now to state the exceptions to that policy. Indeed, these exceptions manifest the Latino pattern to eschew rules and measures that constrict our freedom, movement, and customs. This is the case with the bibliography as well.

This bibliography exhibits some of the characteristics of the fluidity and multi-textured quality of the Latino condition. For instance, the dichotomy between Catholic and Protestant is less distinct than in years past. Some of the works in this bibliography reveal the blurring of boundaries that have existed between Catholics, Protestants, and Pentecostals. While the criteria for the bibliography is clearly defined (works dealing with Hispanic Protestantism or written by Hispanic Protestants), the Latino reality challenges us to transcend these denominational borders. In this regard the bibliography reflects the arbitrary nature of borders that Latinos/as have experienced for centuries.

Just as Latinos/as have disregarded borders and boundaries for centuries, so we at times have also disregarded some of the borders we established for the bibliography. For example, we include some works by Catholic and Pentecostal authors that are gradually attaining the status of "classic." The rationale for this is to provide a sampling of some of the most significant works by Hispanic Pentecostal and Catholic scholars to a wide audience. For instance, the bibliography includes a sampling of works on Women's Studies by Catholic women; this compensates for the lack of material on Hispanic Protestant women and written by Hispanic Protestant women. Another rationale for the inclusion of some works that transcend the limits set for this project is the desire to maintain an ecumenical orientation in Hispanic American Christianity.

Similarly, the bibliography has crossed the boundaries set by its criteria by including some general materials that can assist the researcher as background or statistical information. These demographic and a social-scientific materials on Hispanics include works such as Stanford University's *The Mexican American: A Selected and Annotated Bibliography*. These references do not deal directly with Hispanic Protestantism, but they provide helpful background information that might aid the researcher as he or she studies Hispanic Protestantism.

The time limits imposed on the compilation of materials prohibited the compilation of materials past 1995. Yet, as the project moved into the current year, it became evident that researchers would benefit from the most recent publications. For this reason, we have trespassed yet another criteria and included an addendum that includes a very partial list of works produced in 1996 and 1997.

Features of the Bibliography

As is evident from the Table of Contents, the bibliographic material is arranged according to five fields of study (Theology, Biblical Studies, Sociology and Anthropology, History, and Congregational Studies) and a section on archives. References within each section are ordered alphabetically; those without authorship appear at the end of each section. This structure benefits the researcher by allowing him or her to view alphabetically all of the materials in one field of study; it is intended to provide the easiest access to works for scholars working in one of the above fields of study.

As you use the bibliography, you might find that some references might not yield the desired information within that particular field of study. Certainly, subjective decisions about the inclusion of references in the various fields of study comes into play at this point. Some materials did not fit well within any of the fields of study, so they were placed in a field of study that approximates the subject matter of the work. Given the above mention, if you do not find a work that you expect to find within a particular field of study, consider looking for it in another field of study.

Another advantage of the bibliography is cross-referencing. Because some authors write from an inter-disciplinary orientation, combining theological considerations with Biblical studies, for example, their works encompass several fields of study. Other authors intentionally consider the multi-dimensional reality of Hispanic Christianity, and so their works also are included in more than one field of study. There are approximately 1,000 references in the bibliography that appear in two or more fields of study.

Initially, we decided to omit authors' names from the keywords; doing so would obviate the Author's Index. However, as we came across Raúl Fernández-Calienes' bibliography on Orlando E. Costas, and when we received Justo L. González' bibliography, we were struck by the prolific contributions each has made to Hispanic Protestantism. Indeed, their works increasingly serve as foundations for a younger generation of Hispanic Protestant scholars. Recognizing the special importance of these two authors, we decided to include their names in the keywords list. The bibliography incorporates a revised version of a copyrighted bibliography on Orlando E. Costas prepared by Raúl Fernández-Calienes, titled "Bibliography of the Writings of Orlando E. Costas." This bibliography includes over 200 of Costas' writings as well as writings about Costas. The bibliography also includes 157 references by Justo L. González.

The bibliography also includes references to 15 bibliographies, some of which are found in authors' works and others of which are independent bibliographies. Over 100 references from Ernest A. Atkinson's *A Selected Bibliography of Hispanic Baptist History* have been incorporated into this bibliography with permission from the author and the Baptist Historical Commission. Another significant bibliography is Anthony M. Stevens-Arroyo and Segundo Pantoja's *Discovering Latino Religion: A Comprehensive Social Science Bibliography.* Stevens-Arroyo and Pantoja's bibliography and this bibliography contain a number of the same Protestant works, but *Discovering Latino Religion* emphasizes Roman Catholic authors and contexts. It also maintains a social-scientific emphasis.

In addition to the bibliographies just mentioned, this bibliography contains titles of 64 hymnals and songbooks, 48 Doctor of Ministry Projects, 56 Masters' theses, and 58 doctoral dissertations.

Seeking to mitigate the lack of information available to researchers about archival collections, we have attempted to compile a preliminary listing of archives, collections, and periodicals. Many of the listings refer to minutes of annual meetings of Hispanic Protestant organizations, denominational and regional periodicals, Hispanic Protestant organizations and institutions, archival locations, and archival collections of denominations, organizations, and individuals. These listings are found in the Archives section toward the end of the bibliography. The references in this section are also indexed according to keywords and authors. If you are searching for a particular periodical, you might find it in the Archives section. We have attempted to determine which volumes are available and where the periodicals are located.

Another helpful tool of the bibliography is the Authors and Keywords indices, which are designed to assist researchers to find references with the greatest of ease.

Some Suggestions on Using the Bibliography

Because of the use of accent marks, researchers should try searching for an author's name with and without accent marks. For example, if the reader does not find an author under "Martínez," he or she should look under "Martinez," and vice versa.

Every attempt has been made to provide references that are as complete as possible. Despite our best efforts, some references did not yield complete bibliographic information. We deemed it more important to include references lacking some bibliographical elements rather than to omit them for the sake of professional style.

Every attempt has been made to follow the *Chicago Manual of Style*, 14th edition. This has required adapting the bibliographical information we received to this style. Sometimes, it was not always possible to do so exactly according to *Chicago Manual of Style's* format. Every effort has been made to achieve a consistency in style, whether or not it conformed to the *Chicago Manual of Style*.

With over 2,000 original references, I am certain readers will find some errors in the information provided. I hope that they will notify us of these errors so they can be corrected as the occasion warrants. As we are hoping to add a supplement to this volume in the future, we encourage readers to inform us of works omitted from this bibliography and of new literature that continues to be produced.

Acknowledgments

Finally, this bibliography represents a communal effort; it is the fruit of labor provided by many individuals. The staff at Perkins School of Theology's Bridwell Library provided considerable assistance. James Powell spent untold days providing us with materials through the inter-library loan system. Page Thomas also assisted with Methodist historical materials. Mary Ann Marshall and Daniel Griswold lent their technical expertise when computer-related complications arose. The authors of the introductions to the fields of study, in addition to contributing their written essays, also contributed their knowledge of the literature within their fields of expertise. Finally, David Maldonado provided the vision, guidance, and experience to keep the project on course. All of this is to say that we did not explore this profound "cave" alone; it was done *en conjunto*.

Characteristics of Latino Protestant Theology
Justo L. González

A general bibliography by its very nature represents a wide variety of perspectives, concerns, and authors. Thus, any general comments about the section that follows must be understood to be no more than precisely that: a generalization—and therefore fairly accurate if taken to apply to the list as a whole, but not necessarily applicable to each of its members. On that basis, and with that caveat, there are some general statements that may help the reader navigate through the list that follows.

First of all, this list shows that Latino mainline Protestant theology is widely ecumenical. In years past, that ecumenism was generally limited to other mainline Protestant denominations. The reason for this should be obvious: when Protestants were a minuscule minority within Hispanic circles, often pressed both by a pre-conciliar Roman Catholicism as well as by racial and cultural prejudice, it was natural for all Protestants to work together, and to minimize denominational distinctions. In more recent decades, that ecumenical stance has widened both in the direction of Roman Catholics and in the direction of Pentecostals. The rapprochement with Roman Catholics has been greatly facilitated by the Second Vatican Council and the changes that have taken place in that church since that time. The growing partnership—it is more than a dialogue—with Pentecostals has been facilitated both by the enormous numeric growth of that body of believers and by their increasing interest in the theological tradition of the entire church catholic. Also, a greater awareness on the part of all Hispanics of our common cultural heritage and our common cultural and social struggle has led to an even greater rapprochement. Thus, Hispanic mainline Protestant theology, which in the first decades of the twentieth century had little use for either Roman Catholic or Pentecostal theology, now finds itself in constant dialogue and collaboration with both. For that reason, although by far the majority of the authors listed do belong to mainline Protestant denominations, their own work would not be properly understood without reference to Roman Catholics on one side, and Pentecostals on the other. Among the Roman Catholics included in the pages that follow are such names as María Pilar Aquino, Arturo Bañuelas, Stephen Bevans, Allan Figueroa Deck, Virgilio Elizondo, Felipe Estévez, Dorothy Folliard, Sixto J. García, Roberto Goizueta, Andrés Guerrero, Ada María Isasi-Díaz, Gloria Inés Loya, Verónica Méndez, Ana María Pineda, Ricardo Ramírez, Fernando Segovia, and Antonio M. Stevens-Arroyo. Among the Pentecostals, the names of Samuel Solivan and Eldin Villafañe stand out. It is impossible to understand the work of the rest of us who comprise this bibliography without taking into account the works of these colleagues and friends from other Christian traditions.

Secondly, Hispanic theology is in constant dialogue with Latin American theology, both Protestant and Catholic. For that reason, the reader should not be surprised to find in this list names such as Mortimer Arias, Plutarco Bonilla, Rafael Cepeda, Guillermo Cook, José Míguez Bonino, Elsa Támez, and others. Furthermore, for many of us this dialogue is also an internal dialogue. Many of us were either born or have spent a substantial part of our lives in Latin America. Thus, while we are keenly aware of the differences between the Latin American situation and that of Latinos and Latinas in the United States, in many ways we are both. For most of us this has entailed a long process of varying self-definitions as that inner dialogue progresses. For many Puertorricans, that inner dialogue also takes the form of political and social struggle, as the island seeks to define itself. In any case, although there are clearly significant differences between Latino theology in the United States and the various theologies coming out of Latin America, there are also many points in common.

Thirdly, our theology tends to be highly contextual. That context includes two fundamental dimensions: the society in which we live, and the church in that society. Being contextual in the present society means that ours is a theology that must take seriously such matters as race, social class, gender, economic status, etc. We find ourselves constantly struggling to be heard in a society where our language and/or our accent are not welcome. We find ourselves constantly struggling to be seen in a society that only sees in terms of white and black—whereas we are brown, black, white, yellow, red, and all sort of mixtures thereof. In the church, similar situations are common. Most of us belong to denominations that wish to have a Hispanic ministry, but at the same time leave little room for our own self-expression. The churches most of us attend are poor churches with a rich ministry in poor communities. All of this is reflected in most of the bibliographical entries that follow. Also, since many of the writings in this list are addressed to that church, many are what more "sophisticated" scholars might consider "popular." They are not, however, simply popularizing what others have said, but rather saying what needs to be said to our churches in our context and in our idiom.

Fourth, as mainline Protestants we place great stress on Scripture. Therefore, many of the works in this section could just as easily have been listed in the section on Biblical Studies—and vice versa. Indeed, the user of this bibliography will find that many of the names listed in this section are also listed under "Biblical Studies" and under "History." We refuse to separate these, which in the actual life of the church always go together.

Fifth, Latino mainline Protestantism has always had a deep sense of mission. It is no coincidence that one of the authors with the most entries in this section is the late Orlando E. Costas, whose formal field of training and research was missiology. In a very real sense, most of our theology is missiology. Again, that is the reason why many of the names listed in this section on "Theology" will also be found in the sections on "Social Science" and "The Church and Its

Ministry."

Sixth, the reader who examines the list of names in this section will note that very few women are listed—and many of those who are listed are Roman Catholic. This is perhaps the greatest shortcoming of the Hispanic Protestant church. Partly as a result of the sexism of our own culture, partly out of the manner in which the Protestant message and ecclesiology were taught to our ancestors, and partly due to the obstacles that women must overcome in this society as well as in many others before they are recognized as intellectual and theological leaders, the number of Protestant Latinas writing in the field of theology is tragically low. This is something we must all seek to correct.

Finally, it is necessary to explain how Latino Protestant theology seeks to be contextual, and how it understands its relationship to more traditional theologies. The reader who knows the authors in the following section will know that most of them are at once very loyal to and very critical of their denominations and Christian tradition in general. Their particular context leads them to be critical, for they see things in a different manner. Yet, Protestant Latino theologies are not sectarian. They do not seek to create a theology from a Latino experience, about the Latino experience, and solely for Latinos and Latinas. On the contrary, Latino Protestant theologies tend to see themselves as part of the ongoing dialogue that has always characterized the intellectual life of the church, but at the same time to bring into that dialogue nuances and insights that others might not see. Thus, the purpose of such theologies is not so much to undermine traditional theologies and to create a new one, as it is to enrich the theological tradition of the church. For this reason, most of the theologians whose works are listed in the following pages will appear to outsiders as at times quite radical and at times quite conservative. They tend to be radical in their insistence in claiming their own culture and experience as the place from which they must do their theology. This will lead them to be quite critical of the church's involvement in the racist, sexist, classist, and consumerist character of the dominant culture—which will lead many to consider them radical. But on the other hand they will then do this on the basis of Scriptural authority, or in the name of orthodox Christian doctrine and faith—which will seem quite conservative from the perspective of the same people who consider them radical in other matters. For us, however, it is not a matter of being conservative or radical; it is rather a matter of being faithful to the very old Gospel in all its contemporary radicality.

Theology Bibliography

1. **Alvarez, Carmelo.** "Protestantismo y Misión: Hacia una Ubicación Histórico-Teológica del Pensamiento de Orlando E. Costas en América Latina y el Caribe." Puerto Rico. 1989. Mimeographed.

2. **Aponte, Edwin D.** "Popular Theology in Song: A Hispanic Case Study." Paper presented at "The Church Speaks to the CHURCH," a theological symposium held at Moravian Theological Seminary, February 1994.

3. **Aquino, María Pilar.** "The Challenge of Hispanic Women." *Missiology* 20, no. 2 (1992): 261-68.

4. **Aquino, María Pilar.** "Directions and Foundations of Hispanic/Latino Theology: Toward a *Mestiza* Theology of Liberation." *Journal of Hispanic/Latino Theology* 1, no. 1 (1993): 5-21.

5. **Aquino, María Pilar.** "El 'Des-cubrimiento' Colectivo de la Propia Fuerza: Perspectivas Teológicas desde las Mujeres Latinoamericanas." *Apuntes: Reflexiones Teológicas desde el Margen Hispano* 13, no. 1 (1993): 86-103.

6. **Arbaugh, William.** "American Lutheranism, Hispanics and Liberation Theology." Master's thesis. Pacific Lutheran Theological Seminary, 1985. [183] pp.

7. **Arbaugh, William** "The Lutheran Church and Hispanic People in the Perspective of Liberation Theology." D.Min. Project Report. Pacific Lutheran Theological Seminary, 1985.

8. **Arias, Mortimer.** "In Search of a New Evangelism (En Búsqueda de una Nueva Evangelización)." *Perkins Journal* 32 (Winter 1979): English: 1-39; Spanish: 40-71.

9. **Arias, Mortimer.** *Announcing the Reign of God: Evangelization and the Subversive Memory of Jesus.* Philadelphia, PA: Fortress Press, 1984. 155 pp.

10. **Armendáriz, Rubén P.** "Necessary Factors for an Indigenous Theology." Paper presented at the Hispanic Symposium of the United Presbyterian Church of the USA, held in El Paso, TX, 1980.

11. **Armendáriz, Rubén P.** "Las Posadas." *Reformed Liturgy and Music* 22, no. 3 (1988): 142-43.

12. **Arrastía, Cecilio.** "La Iglesia como Comunidad Hermenéutica."

Apuntes: Reflexiones Teológicas desde el Margen Hispano 1, no. 1 (1981): 7-13.

13. **Arrastía, Cecilio.** "The Eucharist: Liberation, Community, and Commitment." *Apuntes: Reflexiones Teológicas desde el Margen Hispano* 4, no. 4 (1984): 75-81.

14. **Baert, María Luisa Santillán.** "The Church and Liberation." *Apuntes: Reflexiones Teológicas desde el Margen Hispano* 1, no. 1 (1981): 14-18.

15. **Bañuelas, Arturo.** "U.S. Hispanic Theology." *Missiology* 20, no. 2 (1992): 275-300.

16. **Bañuelas, Arturo J., ed.** *Mestizo Christianity: Theology from the Latino Perspective.* Maryknoll, NY: Orbis Books, 1995. 278 pp.

17. **Benavidez, Marta.** "My Mother's Garden is a New Creation." In *Inheriting Our Mothers' Gardens: Feminist Theology in Third World Perspective,* edited by Letty M. Russell, *et al.* 123-42. Philadelphia, PA: Westminster Press, 1988.

18. **Benko, Stephen.** *Los Evangélicos, los Católicos y la Virgen María.* 4th ed. El Paso, TX: Casa Bautista de Publicaciones, 1993. 165 pp.

19. **Besançon-Spencer, Aida, et al.** *The Goddess Revival.* Grand Rapids, MI: Baker Book House, 1995. 320 pp.

20. **Besançon-Spencer, Aida and William David Spencer.** *Joy through the Night: Biblical Resources for Suffering People.* Downers Grove, IL: Intervarsity Press, 1994. 252 pp.

21. **Bevans, Stephen and Ana María Pineda, eds.** "Columbus and the New World: Evangelization or Invasion?" *Missiology* 20, no. 2 (1992): 133-300.

22. **Bongers, Harvey.** "Congregations Responding to Transitional Neighborhoods." D.Min. Project Report. Austin Presbyterian Theological Seminary, 1994. 158 pp.

23. **Bonilla, Plutarco A.** "Viaje de Ida y Vuelta: Evangelización y Misión—Apuntes Sobre el Pensamiento Misionológico de Orlando E. Costas." Puerto Rico. 1989. Mimeographed.

24. **Boots, Nora.** "La Iglesia Hispana en los Estados Unidos y su Relación con la Iglesia en Latinoamérica." In *La Iglesia Hispana en Misión,* edited by Conrado G. Soltero. 30-39. New York: National Program Division of the General Board of Global Ministries, The United Methodist Church, 1992.

25. **Boots, Nora Quiroga.** "Response." *Apuntes: Reflexiones Teológicas desde el Margen Hispano* 7, no. 3 (1987): 61-65.

26. **Bosch, David J.** "'Ecumenicals' and 'Evangelicals': A Growing Relationship?" *The Ecumenical Review* 40, nos. 3-4 (1988): 472.

27. **Butterfield, Robert A.** "Los Natán de Esta Epoca Somos Nosotros." *Apuntes: Reflexiones Teológicas desde el Margen Hispano* 10, no. 3 (1990): 70-72.

28. **Caloca-Rivas, Rigoberto.** "Hermeneutics for a Theology of Integration: Components for an Understanding of the Role of the Hispanic Church in the United States." Master's thesis. Graduate Theological Union, 1982.

29. **Canales, Ferrer.** "Perfil del Ensayista Domingo Marrero." *Revista de Estudios Hispánicos* 1, nos. 3-4 (1971): 69-74.

30. **Candelaria, Michael.** "Justice: Extrapolations from the Concept *Mishpat* in the Book of Micah." *Apuntes: Reflexiones Teológicas desde el Margen Hispano* 3, no. 4 (1983): 75-81.

31. **Caraballo, José A.** "A Certificate Program for Hispanic Clergy and Lay Leaders in an Accredited Theological Seminary: A Case Study with Projections." D.Min. Project Report. Drew University, 1983. 239 pp.

32. **Carcaño, Minerva Garza.** "Una Perspectiva Bíblico-Teológica Sobre la Mujer en el Ministerio Ordenado." *Apuntes: Reflexiones Teológicas desde el Margen Hispano* 10, no. 2 (1990): 27-35.

33. **Carmona, Juan A.** "The Liberation of Puerto Rico: A Theological Perspective." D.Min. Project Report. Colgate Rochester Divinity School/Bexley Hall/Crozer Theological Seminary, 1982. 93 pp.

34. **Carson, Keith.** "The Mission of the Church according to Orlando Costas: A Biblical and Historical Evaluation." Master's thesis. Trinity Evangelical Divinity School, 1984. 104 pp.

35. **Castuera, Ignacio.** "The Theology and Practice of Liberation in the Mexican American Context/La Teología y Práctica de Liberación en el Contexto México Americana." *Perkins Journal* 29, no. 1 (1975): English: 2-11; Spanish: 43-53.

36. **Castuera, Ignacio.** "The Best Administrator is a Poet: Towards a Theology of Administration." *Apuntes: Reflexiones Teológicas desde el Margen Hispano* 3, no. 2 (1983): 33-45.

37. **Catalá, Rafael.** "Liberation Theology: A Cultural Synthesis." *Apuntes: Reflexiones Teológicas desde el Margen Hispano* 6, no. 4 (1986): 75-80.

38. **Cepeda, Rafael.** *José Martí: Perspectivas Eticas de la Fe Cristiana.* San José, Costa Rica: DEI, 1991.

39. **Chávez, Guillermo.** "Los Signos de los Tiempos: Una Mirada hacia el Futuro desde la Perspectiva Latinoamericana y Caribeña." *Apuntes: Reflexiones Teológicas desde el Margen Hispano* 13, no. 1 (1993): 104-17.

40. **Chávez, Tomás, Jr.** "The Theological Basis for a 'Serviglesia'." *Apuntes: Reflexiones Teológicas desde el Margen Hispano* 6, no. 2 (1986): 44-47.

41. **Chinula, Don.** "Liberation, Praxis, and Psychotherapy." *Apuntes: Reflexiones Teológicas desde el Margen Hispano* 5, no. 4 (1985): 87-95.

42. **Collinson-Streng, P. and Ismael de la Tejera.** "Bible and Mission in a Hispanic Congregation." In *Bible and Mission: Biblical Foundations and Working Models for Congregational Ministry,* edited by Wayne Stumme. 129-37. Mission in the U.S.A. Minneapolis, MN: Augsburg Publishing House, 1986.

43. **Conde-Frazier, Elizabeth.** "Hispanic Ministry: Teaching and Healing." In *Hidden Stories: Unveiling the History of the Latino Church,* edited by Daniel R. Rodríguez-Díaz and David Cortés-Fuentes. 131-39. Decatur, GA: AETH, 1994.

44. **Cone, James.** "Theologies of Liberation among U.S. Racial-Ethnic Minorities." In *Convergences and Differences,* edited by Leonardo Boff and Virgilio Elizondo. 54-64. Concilium, vol. 199. Edinburgh: T & T Clark, 1988.

45. **Consulta Latinoamericana de Iglesia y Sociedad.** *Social Justice and the Latin Churches.* Translated by Jorge Lara-Braud. Richmond, VA: John Knox Press, 1969. 137 pp.

46. **Cook, A. William.** "The Power and the Powerlessness: The Pastoral Vocation of the Hispanic Church in the USA." *Evangelical Review of Theology* 9, no. 2 (1985): 156-65.

47. **Cook, Guillermo.** "Protestant Mission and Evangelization in Latin America: An Interpretation." In *New Face of the Church in Latin America: Between Tradition and Change,* edited by Guillermo Cook. 41-55. American Society of Missiology Series, no. 18. Maryknoll, NY: Orbis Books, 1994. References to Orlando Costas on pp. 53, 55, 280.

48. **Cortez, Ernest.** "Response." *Apuntes: Reflexiones Teológicas desde el Margen Hispano* 7, no. 3 (1987): 66-70.

49. **Costa, Ruy O., ed.** *One Faith, Many Cultures: Inculturation, Indigenization, and Contextualization.* Vol. 2 of Boston Theological Institute Annual Series. Cambridge, MA: Boston Theological Institute; Maryknoll, NY: Orbis Books, 1988. 162 pp.

50. **Costa, Ruy O.** "Toward a Latin American Protestant Ethic of Liberation: A Comparative Study of the Writings of Rubem Alves and José Miguez Bonino from the Perspective of the Sources and Substance of their Social Ethics." Ph.D. diss., Boston University, 1990.

51. **Costas, Orlando E.** "Contextualization and Incarnation." *Journal of Theology for Southern Africa* 29, no. 29 (1979): 23-30.

52. **Costas, Orlando E.** "Evangelism from the Periphery: The Universality of Galilee." *Apuntes: Reflexiones Teológicas desde el Margen Hispano* 2, no. 4 (1982): 75-84.

53. **Costas, Orlando E.** "Contextualization and Incarnation." San José, Costa Rica. Separatas de CELEP, n.d. 8 pp.

54. **Costas, Orlando E.** "Educación Teológica y Misión." N.p., n.d. 20 pp. Mimeographed.

55. **Costas, Orlando E.** "El Mensaje de los Profetas y la Evangelización de las Naciones." San José, Costa Rica. Seminario Bíblico Latinoamericano, n.d. 7 pp. Mimeographed.

56. **Costas, Orlando E.** "La Evangelización en los Años Setenta: La Búsqueda de Totalidad." N.p., n.d. 24 pp. Mimeographed.

57. **Costas, Orlando E.** "La Iglesia como Agente de Dios para la Evangelización." San José, Costa Rica. Seminario Bíblico Latinoamericano, n.d. 18 pp. Mimeographed.

58. **Costas, Orlando E.** "La Misión Cristiana en las Américas." San José, Costa Rica. CELEP, n.d. 20 pp. Mimeographed separatas del CELEP.

59. **Costas, Orlando E.** "A Strategy for Third World Christians." San José, Costa Rica. Seminario Bíblico Latinoamericano, n.d. 15 pp. Mimeographed.

60. **Costas, Orlando E.** "Baptist Ecclesiology in the 17th Century." Master's thesis. Winona Lake School of Theology, 1967.

61. **Costas, Orlando E.** "El Culto en Su Perspectiva Teológica." San José, Costa Rica. Publicaciones INDEF, 1971. 25 pp. Mimeographed.

62. **Costas, Orlando E.** "Latin American Revolutions and the Church." *Foundations* 14, no. 2 (1971): 116-27.

63. **Costas, Orlando E.** "A Postscript to 'Basic Presuppositions in the Theological and Methodological Thought of McGavran.'" San José, Costa Rica. 1971. 17 pp. Mimeographed.

64. **Costas, Orlando E.** "Presuposiciones Básicas en el Pensamiento Teológico y Metodológico de Donald A. McGavran." N.p., 1971. Mimeographed.

65. **Costas, Orlando E.** "Teología y Evangelización." *En Marcha Internacional* 18 (1971): 14-15.

66. **Costas, Orlando E.** "La Iglesia como Agente Movilizador." Paper presented at a meeting of the Fraternidad Teológica Latinoamericana, held in Cuernavaca, México, 1972.

67. **Costas, Orlando E.** *La Realidad de la Iglesia Evangélica Latinoamericana a través de su Expresión Cultural.* San José, Costa Rica: Seminario Bíblico Latinoamericano, 1972.

68. **Costas, Orlando E.** "Aspectos Sobresalientes del Ministerio de Jesús y Sus Implicaciones para la Evangelización." In *Hacia una Teología de la Evangelización,* edited by Orlando E. Costas. 35-44. Buenos Aires, Argentina: Editorial La Aurora, 1973.

69. **Costas, Orlando E.** "Church Growth as a Goal of In-Depth Evangelism." San José, Costa Rica. Institute of In-Depth Evangelism, 1973.

70. **Costas, Orlando E.** "El Culto como Índice de la Realidad que Vive la Iglesia." *Vida y Pensamiento,* vol. 1, no. 1 (1973).

71. **Costas, Orlando E.** "El Llamamiento de Israel y la Evangelización de las Naciones." In *Hacia una Teología de la Evangelización,* edited by Orlando E. Costas. 19-23. Buenos Aires, Argentina: Editorial La Aurora, 1973.

72. **Costas, Orlando E.** "El Mensaje de los Profetas y la Evangelización." In *Hacia una Teología de la Evangelización,* edited by Orlando E. Costas. 25-33. Buenos Aires, Argentina: Editorial La Aurora, 1973.

73. **Costas, Orlando E.** "La Centralidad de Jesucristo en la Evangelización." In *Hacia una Teología de la Evangelización,* edited by Orlando E. Costas. 115-29. Buenos Aires, Argentina: Editorial La Aurora, 1973.

74. **Costas, Orlando E.** "La Iglesia como Agente Evangelizadora." In *Hacia una Teología de la Evangelización,* edited by Orlando E. Costas. 131-56. Buenos Aires, Argentina: Editorial La Aurora, 1973.

75. **Costas, Orlando E.** "Mission Out of Affluence." *Missiology* 1, no. 4 (1973): 405-23.

76. **Costas, Orlando E.** *¿Qué Significa Evangelizar Hoy?* San José, Costa Rica: INDEF, 1973. 56 pp.

77. **Costas, Orlando E.** "Revelación, Gracia y Creación: Presuposiciones Básicas de la Evangelización." In *Hacia una Teología de la Evangelización,* edited by Orlando E. Costas. 101-13. Buenos Aires, Argentina: Editorial La Aurora, 1973.

78. **Costas, Orlando E.** *The Church and Its Mission: A Shattering Critique from the Third World.* Wheaton, IL: Tyndale House Publishers; London: Coverdale House Publishers, 1974. 313 pp.

79. **Costas, Orlando E.** "Evangelism and the Gospel of Salvation." In *Evangelisation im Ökumenischen Gespräch: Beiträge eines Symposiums (Genf 1973),* edited by Walter Arnold. Band 29. Erlanger Tashenbücher. Erlangen, West Germany: Verlag der Ev. Luth. Mission, 1974. Also published in *International Review of Mission* 63 (249 January 1974): 24-37; *Testimonio Cristiano* (Buenos Aires, Argentina) No. 4 (March 1974): 4-12.

80. **Costas, Orlando E.** *Messages sur Evangélization Totale.* Brussels: Comité de Literature, Evangélization Totale en Belgique, 1974.

81. **Costas, Orlando E.** "Depth in Evangelism: An Interpretation of 'In-Depth Evangelism' Around the World." In *Let the Earth Hear His Voice: Official Reference Volume: International Congress on World Evangelization, Lausanne, Switzerland,* edited by James Dixon Douglas. 675-94. Minneapolis, MN: World Wide Publications, 1975.

82. **Costas, Orlando E.** *El Protestantismo en América Latina Hoy: Ensayos del Camino (1972-1974).* San José, Costa Rica: Publicaciones INDEF, 1975. 175 pp.

83. **Costas, Orlando E.** "In-Depth Evangelism in Latin America." In *Let the Earth Hear His Voice: Official Reference Volume: International Congress on World Evangelization, Lausanne, Switzerland,* edited by James Dixon Douglas. 211-12. Minneapolis, MN: World Wide Publications, 1975.

84. **Costas, Orlando E.** "Missiology in Contemporary Latin America." *EFMS Bulletin* (December 1975). Also published as "Missiology in Contemporary Latin America: A Survey." *Missiology* 5, no. 1 (1977): 89-114.

85. **Costas, Orlando E.** *Introducción a la Evangelización I.* San José, Costa Rica: Editorial SEBILA, 1976. 42 pp. Second printing titled *Introducción a la Comunicación.*

86. **Costas, Orlando E.** "Nuestra Misión y el Crecimiento de la Iglesia: Hacia una Misionología de Masas y Minorías." *Ensayos Ocasionales [de CELEP]* 3, no. 2 (1976): 2-28. Also published as "Our Mission and Church Growth: Towards a Missiology of Masses and Minority Groups." *Theological Fraternity Bulletin* 4 (1976): 3-24.

87. **Costas, Orlando E.** "Socialism and the Christian Witness: An Interview with Orlando Costas." *The Other Side* 12, no. 1 (1976): 27-30, 39-43.

88. **Costas, Orlando E.** "Theology of the Crossroads in Contemporary Latin America: Missiology in Mainline Protestantism, 1969-1974." D.Th. diss., Free University of Amsterdam, 1976.

89. **Costas, Orlando E.** "Evangelism as a Total Task: A Look into Jesus' Evangelistic Ministry." 1977. 39 pp. Mimeographed.

90. **Costas, Orlando E.** "Evangelism in a Latin American Context." *Occasional Essays [of CELEP]* 4, nos. 1-2 (1977): 3-15. Also published in *Evangelical Review of Theology* (Exeter, England) 3, no. 1 (1979): 52-67; *Latin American Pastoral Issues* (San José, Costa Rica) 1, no. 16 (1989): 33-48.

91. **Costas, Orlando E.** "Evangelism in the 70's: The Quest for Totality." N.p., 1977. 28 pp. Mimeographed.

92. **Costas, Orlando E.** "A Latin American Theologian Looks at the Charismatic Movement—Pros & Cons." *Latin America Evangelist* 57, no. 3 (1977): 10-14.

93. **Costas, Orlando E.** "Responding to the Challenge of Change (Acts 16:8ff)." Audio recording. Pasadena, CA: Fuller Theological Seminary, 1977.

94. **Costas, Orlando E.** "Tradition and Reconstruction in Mission: A Latin American Protestant Analysis." *Occasional Bulletin of Missionary Research* 1, no. 1 (1977): 4-8. Also published in *IAMS Newsletter* (Leiden, The Netherlands) 10 (March 1977): 7-13; as "Tradition und Wiederaufbau in der Mission in Lateinamerika: Ein protestantischer Versuch." *Zeitschrift für Mission* (Basel-Korntal, West Germany) 2, no. 4 (1976): 191-98; "Tradition and Reconstruction in Mission in Latin America: A Protestant Approach." *Ekumenisk Orientering.* Mission and Evangelism 3 (1976): 2-7; "Tradición y Reconstrucción en Misión: Un Análisis Latinoamericano Protestante." *Ensayos Ocasionales [de CELEP]* (San José, Costa Rica) 4, nos. 1-2 (1977); "Tradition och ateruppbyggnad mission Latinamerika." *Svensk Missionstidskrift* (Uppsala, Sweden) 65 (1977): 10-16.

95. **Costas, Orlando E.** "El CELEP y la Pastoral." *Pastoralia* 1, no. 1

(1978): 1-12. Also published in *Pastoralia* 6, nos. 12-13 (1984): 81-90, and as "CELEP and Ministry." *Occasional Essays [of CELEP]* 12, no. 2 (1985): 118-28.

96. **Costas, Orlando E.** "Liberation Theology: A Solution?" *The Mennonite* 93, no. 27 (1978): 433-35.

97. **Costas, Orlando E.** "Christ's Lordship and the New Humanity." Audio Recording. Richmond, VA: Union Theological Seminary, 1979.

98. **Costas, Orlando E.** "Christian Mission in the Américas." *Occasional Essays [of CELEP]* 6, nos. 1-2 (1979): 24-37.

99. **Costas, Orlando E.** *Compromiso y Misión.* Colección CELEP. Miami, FL: Editorial Caribe; San José, Costa Rica: Editorial Caribe: 1979. 159 pp.

100. **Costas, Orlando E.** "Conversion as a Complex Experience: A Personal Case Study." In *Gospel & Culture: The Papers of a Consultation on the Gospel and Culture, Convened by the Lausanne Committee's Theology and Education Group,* edited by John Stott and Robert T. Coote. 240-62. Pasadena, CA: William Carey Library, 1979. Also published in *Occasional Essays [of CELEP]* 5, no. 1 (1978): 21-44. Revised editions published in Robert T. Coote and John R. Stott, eds., *Down to Earth: Studies in Christianity and Culture: The Papers of the Lausanne Consultation on Gospel and Culture* (Grand Rapids, MI: William B. Eerdman's Publishing Co., 1980), 173-91; *Gospel in Context* 1, no. 3 (1978): 14-24, with reactions and responses on pages 36-39; *Latin American Pastoral Issues* (San José, Costa Rica) 16, no. 1 (1989): 8-32.

101. **Costas, Orlando E.** *The Integrity of Mission: The Inner Life and Outreach of the Church.* San Francisco: Harper & Row, 1979. 114 pp.

102. **Costas, Orlando E.** "What Belongs in a Future Ecumenical Creed?: A Free Church Answer." In *An Ecumenical Confession of Faith?,* edited by Hans Küng and Jürgen Moltmann. Translated by Paul Burns. 72-76. Concilium, vol. 118. New York: Seabury Press, 1979.

103. **Costas, Orlando E.** "Ecumenical Experiences of an Hispanic Baptist." *Journal of Ecumenical Studies* 17, no. 2 (1980): 118-24. Also published in William Jerry Booney and Glenn A. Ingleheart, eds., *Baptists and Ecumenism* (Valley Forge, PA: Judson Press, 1980).

104. **Costas, Orlando E.** "The Great Commission: History and Horizons." Audiotaped address at Union Theological Seminary, Richmond VA, 15 February 1980.

105. **Costas, Orlando E.** "The Nature and Mission of the Church: A Commentary on the Ecclesio-Missiology of EBTS' Doctrinal Basis." Paper presented at "The Theological Colloquium," held at Eastern Baptist Theological Seminary, Philadelphia, PA, December 1980.

106. **Costas, Orlando E.** "Pecado y Salvación en América Latina." In *América Latina y la Evangelización en la Década de los Años 80: Un Congreso Auspiciado por la Fraternidad Teológica Latinoamericana, noviembre de 1979,* edited by Pedro Savaga. 271-89. Cuernavaca, México: CLADE II, 1979. Reprint, Cuernavaca, México: Fraternidad Teológica Latinoamericana, 1980. Also published in *Pastoralia* 2, nos. 4-5 (November 1980): 211-34.

107. **Costas, Orlando E.** "A Strategy for Third World Missions." In *World Missions: Building Bridges or Barriers?,* edited by Theodore Williams. Bangalore, India: WEF Missions Commission, 1980. Reprint in D. Fraser, ed., *The Church in New Frontiers for Missions* (1983), pp. 223-34.

108. **Costas, Orlando E.** "The Whole Gospel for the Whole World." Inaugural Address as Thornly B. Wood Professor of Missiology and Director of Hispanic Studies at Eastern Baptist Theological Seminary, 20 February 1980.

109. **Costas, Orlando E.** "The Whole World for the Whole Gospel." *Missiology* 8, no. 4 (1980): 395-405.

110. **Costas, Orlando E.** "Christian Faith in the Third World." In *Educating for Christian Missions: Supporting Christian Missions through Education,* edited by Arthur Lonzo Walker, Jr. 73-84. Nashville, TN: Broadman Press, 1981. Originally published in Separatas del *CELEP,* San José, Cost Rica: CELEP, 1979.

111. **Costas, Orlando E.** "Christian Missions in the 80's: Crisis and Hope." Audiotaped address at Westminster Theological Seminary, Philadelphia, PA, 15 April 1981.

112. **Costas, Orlando E.** "Impressions of Melbourne." *International Review of Mission* 69, nos. 276-277 (1981): 529-31.

113. **Costas, Orlando E.** "A Radical Evangelical Contribution from Latin America [and Reply]." In *Christ's Lordship and Religious Pluralism,* edited by Gerald H. Anderson and Thomas F. Stransky. 133-56; 163-70. Maryknoll, NY: Orbis Books, 1981.

114. **Costas, Orlando E.** *Christ Outside the Gate.* Maryknoll, NY: Orbis Books, 1982. 238 pp.

115. **Costas, Orlando E.** "Evangelism as Story-Sharing." Audio recording. Alumnae Lectures. Atlanta GA: Protestant Radio and Television Center, 1982.

116. **Costas, Orlando E.** "The Hispanics Next Door." *The Christian Century* 99, no. 26 (1982): 851-56.

117. **Costas, Orlando E.** "La Misión como Discipulado." *Boletín Teológico* 6 (March-April 1982): 45-59.

118. **Costas, Orlando E.** "La Misión en el Pueblo de Dios en la Ciudad." *Boletín Teológico* 7 (July-September 1982): 85-96.

119. **Costas, Orlando E.** "Outside the Gate." *Brethren Life and Thought* 27, no. 2 (1982): 91-95.

120. **Costas, Orlando E.**, ed. *Predicación Evangélica y Teología Hispana.* San Diego, CA: Publicaciones de las Américas, 1982. 279 pp.

121. **Costas, Orlando E.** "Predicación Evangélica y Teología Hispana: Los Parámetros del Tema." In *Predicación Evangélica y Teología Hispana,* edited by Orlando E. Costas. 7-19. San Diego, CA: Publicaciones de las Américas, 1982.

122. **Costas, Orlando E.** "Proclamando a Cristo en los Dos Terceros Mundos." *Boletín Teológico* 8 (October-December 1982): 1-15. Also published as "Proclaiming Christ in the Two-Thirds World." *Theological Fraternity Bulletin* 3 (1982): 1-10.

123. **Costas, Orlando E.** "Christian Mission from the Periphery." *Faith and Mission* 1, no. 1 (1983): 1-14.

124. **Costas, Orlando E.** "Commentary on 'The Eye of the Needle.'" In *Human Rights: A Dialogue Between the First and Third World,* edited by Robert A. and Alice Frazer Evans. 144-50. Maryknoll, NY: Orbis Books; Surrey, England: Lutterworth Press, 1983.

125. **Costas, Orlando E.** "Commentary on 'To Bear Arms.'" In *Human Rights: A Dialogue Between the First and Third World,* edited by Robert A. and Alice Frazer Evans. 37-41. Maryknoll, NY: Orbis Books; Surrey, England: Lutterworth Press, 1983.

126. **Costas, Orlando E.** "Crecimiento Integral y Palabra de Dios." N.p. (1983).

127. **Costas, Orlando E.** "Ecumenics from the Periphery: A Minority Perspective of Vancouver '83." *Global Outreach,* vol. 2 (November 1983).

128. **Costas, Orlando E.** "Evangelical Theology in the Two-Thirds World."

Paper presented at the "Context and Hermeneutics" conference, held in Tlayacapan, México, November 1983.

129. **Costas, Orlando E.** *Evangelización Contextual: Fundamentos Teológicos y Pastorales.* San José, Costa Rica: Editorial SEBILA, 1983.

130. **Costas, Orlando E.** "Interpretación Misionológica del Ministerio." México, D.F. Iglesia Bautista Horeb, 1983. 17 pp. Mimeographed. Also published in *Encuentro y Diálogo* 1, no. 1 (1984): 43-56 and *Diálogo Teológico* no. 25 (1985): 96-115.

131. **Costas, Orlando E.** "Life before Death (Deut. 30:15-16)." Audiotaped address at Fuller Theological Seminary, Pasadena, CA, 26 January 1983.

132. **Costas, Orlando E.** "Los Hispanos en los Estados Unidos." *Misión* 2, no. 6 (1983): 6-11.

133. **Costas, Orlando E.** "Witnessing in a Divided World." *International Review of Mission* 72, no. 288 (1983): 631-35.

134. **Costas, Orlando E.** "Costas on Compassion." *The Wittenburg Door,* no. 77 (1984): 29-30.

135. **Costas, Orlando E.** "Iglecrecimiento, el Movimiento Ecuménico y el Evangelicalismo." *Misión* 3, no. 9 (1984): 56-60.

136. **Costas, Orlando E.** "Interpretación Misionológica del Ministerio." *Encuentro y Diálogo* 1, no. 1 (1984): 43-56. Also published in *Diálogo Teológico* no. 25 (1985): 96-115.

137. **Costas, Orlando E.** "Jesucristo el Hombre." In *Creencias Bautistas,* edited by Rolando Gutiérrez. 10-20. México: n.p., 1984.

138. **Costas, Orlando E.** "The Missiological Thought of Emilio Castro." *International Review of Mission* 73, no. 289 (1984): 86-97.

139. **Costas, Orlando E.** "Proclaiming Christ in the Two Thirds World." In *Sharing Jesus in the Two Thirds World: Evangelical Christologies from the Contexts of Poverty, Powerlessness and Religious Pluralism,* edited by Vinay Samuel and Chris Sugden. 1-11. Grand Rapids, MI: William B. Eerdmans Publishing Co, 1984.

140. **Costas, Orlando E.** "Evangelical Theology in the Two Thirds World." *TSF Bulletin* 9, no. 1 (1985): 7-12. Also published in *Evangelical Review of Theology* (Exeter, England) 11, no. 1 (1987): 65-77; Mark Lau Branson and C. René Padilla, *Conflict and Context: Hermeneutics in the Américas* (Grand Rapids, MI: William B. Eerdman's Publishing

Co., 1986); Joel R. Carpenter and Wilbert R. Shenk, *Earthen Vessels: American Evangelicals and Foreign Missions, 1880-1980* (Grand Rapids, MI: William B. Eerdmans Publishing Co., 1990). Published as "La Teología Evangélica en el Mundo de los Dos Tercios." *Boletín Teológico* 19, no. 28 (1987): 201-18.

141. **Costas, Orlando E.** "IV International Mission Studies Conference Convened in Zimbabwe." *The Judson Bulletin,* no. 5 (1985): 4-7. Also published as "IV Conferencia de la Asociación Internacional de Estudios Misionales." *Boletín Teológico* 19, no. 28 (1987): 201-18.

142. **Costas, Orlando E.** "Waiting on God." In *E. T. Earl Lectures. Sermon on Acts 16:6-10.* Video Recording. Berkeley, CA: Pacific School of Religion, 1985.

143. **Costas, Orlando E.** *Evangelización Contextual: Fundamentos Teológicos y Pastorales.* San José, Costa Rica: Editorial SEBILA, 1986. 119 pp.

144. **Costas, Orlando E.** "Hispanic Theology in North America." Paper presented at the "Liberation Theology Consultation" of Boston Theological Institute, held at Andover Newton Theological School, Newton Centre, MA, October 1986.

145. **Costas, Orlando E.** "La Iglesia como Comunidad Misionera en la Misionología del Movimiento de Iglecrecimiento." *Misión* 5, no. 2 (1986): 46-53.

146. **Costas, Orlando E.** "La Vida en el Espíritu." *Boletín Teológico* 18, nos. 21-22 (1986): 7-24.

147. **Costas, Orlando E.** "The Mission of Ministry." *Missiology* 14, no. 4 (1986): 463-72.

148. **Costas, Orlando E.** "Social Justice in the Other Protestant Tradition: A Hispanic Perspective." In *Contemporary Ethical Issues in the Jewish and Christian Tradition,* edited by Frederick E. Greenspahn. 205-29. Denver, CO: Center for Judaic Studies at the University of Denver; Hoboken, NJ: Ktav Publishing House, 1986.

149. **Costas, Orlando E.** "Woven Together in Life and Mission: A Theological Vision." *American Baptist Quarterly* 5, no. 4 (1986): 357-68.

150. **Costas, Orlando E.** "Choosing Life: The Path to Justice and Peace." *The Judson Bulletin,* n.s., 6, no. 2 (1987): 40-46. Also published as "Escoger la Vida: El Camino hacia la Justicia y la Paz." *Pastoralia* 10, nos. 20-21 (1988): 70-85.

151. **Costas, Orlando E.** "The Experience of God in the New China." *The Judson Bulletin,* n.s., 6, no. 1 (1987): 41-47.

152. **Costas, Orlando E.** "Liberating News!: A Theology of Contextual Evangelization." *Today's Ministry: A Report from Andover Newton. Special Issue,* vol. 5, no. 2 (1988).

153. **Costas, Orlando E.** "Mi Itinerario Teológico." *Misión* 7, no. 1 (1988): 17-23.

154. **Costas, Orlando E.** "The Subversiveness of Faith: Esther as a Paradigm for a Liberating Theology." *The Ecumenical Review* 40, no. 1 (1988): 66-78.

155. **Costas, Orlando E.** "Survival, Hope, and Liberation in the Other American Church: An Hispanic Case Study." In *One Faith, Many Cultures,* edited by Ruy O. Costa. 136-44. Boston Theological Institute Annual Series, vol 2. Maryknoll, NY: Orbis Books; Cambridge, MA: Boston Theological Institute, 1988.

156. **Costas, Orlando E.** "Conversion as a Complete Experience: A Hispanic Case Study." *Latin American Pastoral Issues* 14, no. 1 (1989): 8-32.

157. **Costas, Orlando E.** *Liberating News: A Theology of Contextual Evangelization.* Grand Rapids, MI: William B. Eerdmans Publishing Co., 1989. 182 pp.

158. **Costas, Orlando E.** "Liberation Theologies in the Américas: Common Journeys and Mutual Challenges." In *Yearning to Breathe Free: Liberation Theologies in the United States,* edited by Mar Peter-Raoul, et al. 28-44. Maryknoll, NY: Orbis Books, 1990.

159. **Costas, Orlando E.** "How do Liberation Theologians Approach the 'Doing of Theology' Today?" In *Doing Theology in Today's World: Essays in Honor of Kenneth S. Kantzer,* edited by Thomas McComisky and John Woodbridge. 377-96. Grand Rapids, MI: Zondervan Publishing House, 1991.

160. **Costas, Orlando E.** "Evangelism from the Periphery: The Universality of Galilee." In *Voces: Voices from the Hispanic Church,* edited by Justo L. González. 16-23. Nashville, TN: Abingdon Press, 1992.

161. **Costas, Orlando E.** "Hispanic Theology in North America." In *Struggles for Solidarity: Liberation Theologies in Tension,* edited by Lorine M. Getz and Ruy O. Costa. 63-74. Minneapolis, MN: Fortress Press, 1992.

162. **Costas, Orlando E.** "Teólogo en la Encrucijada." In *Hacia una Teología Evangélica Latinoamericana,* edited by C. René Padilla. San José, Costa Rica: Editorial Caribe, n.d.

163. **Cotto-Pérez, Irving.** "The Design and Implementation of a Strategy for a Congregational Mission in Hispanic Churches in the Eastern Pennsylvania Conference of The United Methodist Church." D.Min. Project Report. Eastern Baptist Theological Seminary, 1986. 240 pp.

164. **Deck, Allan Figueroa, S.J. ed.** *Frontiers of Hispanic Theology in the United States.* Maryknoll, NY: Orbis Books, 1992. 174 pp.

165. **Deck, Allan Figueroa, S.J.** "The Challenge of Evangelical/Pentecostal Christianity to Hispanic Catholicism." In *Hispanic Catholic Culture in the U.S.: Issues and Concerns,* edited by Jay P. Dolan and Allan Figueroa Deck, S.J. 409-39. Notre Dame, IN: University of Notre Dame Press, 1994.

166. **Deck, Allan Figueroa, S.J.** "Latino Theology: The Year of the 'Boom.'" *Journal of Hispanic/Latino Theology* 1, no. 2 (1994): 51-63.

167. **Delgado, Hector.** "A Strategy for Developing a More Effective Ministry to the Hispanic Community in Southern California." D.Min. Project Report. Fuller Theological Seminary, 1989. 385 pp.

168. **Díaz, Rey.** "La Liberación Hispana en U.S.A." *Apuntes: Reflexiones Teológicas desde el Margen Hispano* 9, no. 1 (1989): 13-19.

169. **Elizondo, Javier.** "The Use of the Bible in the Moral Deliberation of Liberation Theologians: An Examination of the Works of Leonardo Boff, José Miguez Bonino, and Porfirio Miranda." Ph.D. diss., Baylor University, 1988. 216 pp.

170. **Elizondo, Virgilio.** *Galilean Journey: The Mexican-American Promise.* Maryknoll, NY: Orbis Books, 1983. 147 pp.

171. **Elizondo, Virgil.** *The Future is Mestizo: Life When Cultures Meet.* Bloomington, IN: Meyer Stone Books, 1988. 111 pp.

172. **Elizondo, Virgilio P.** *Christianity and Culture: An Introduction to Pastoral Theology and Ministry for the Bicultural Community.* Huntington, IN: Our Sunday Visitor, Inc., 1975. 199 pp.

173. **Elizondo, Virgil P.** "A Theological Interpretation of the Mexican American/Una Interpretación Teológica de la Experiencia México Americana." *Perkins Journal* 29, no. 1 (1975): English: 12-21; Spanish: 54-65.

174. **Elizondo, Virgilio P.** *Mestizaje: The Dialectic of Cultural Birth and the Gospel.* San Antonio, TX: Mexican American Cultural Center, 1978.

175. **Erdman, Daniel.** "Liberation and Identity: Indo-Hispano Youth." *Religious Education* 78, no. 1 (1983): 76-89.

176. **Escamilla, Roberto.** "Toward a Hispanic Liturgy." Paper presented at the "Hispanic Symposium on Ministries of the Hispanic Church," held at Perkins School of Theology, Dallas, TX, November 1978.

177. **Escobar, J. Samuel.** "Conflict of Interpretations of Popular Protestantism." In *New Face of the Church in Latin America: Between Tradition and Change,* edited by Guillermo Cook. 112-34. American Society of Missiology Series, no. 18. Maryknoll, NY: Orbis Books, 1994. References to Orlando E. Costas on pp. 114, 134.

178. **Escobar, Samuel.** *"Forward in the Fullness of Mission": The 1988 CMS Annual Sermon Preached on 25 October 1988.* London: Church Missionary Society, 1988. 13 pp.

179. **Espinoza, H. O.** "Response to William H. Bently." In *Evangelical Affirmations,* edited by K. Kantzer and C. Henry. 335-42. Grand Rapids, MI: Academie Books, 1990. pp. 299-333.

180. **Estévez, Felipe J.** "The Hispanic Search beyond Biculturalism." *Theological Education* 20, no. 1 (1983): 58-64.

181. **Estrada, Leobardo F.** "Doctrine of the Trinity in Recent American and British Thought." Master's thesis. Southwestern Baptist Theological Seminary, 1954. 72 pp.

182. **Evangelista, Ramón A.** "A Theology of Liberation as a Basis for Ministry in the First Hispanic United Methodist Church of Buffalo." D.Min. Project Report. Drew University, 1987. 201 pp.

183. **Feliciano, Juan G.** "Gustavo Gutiérrez' Liberation Theology: Toward a Hispanic Epistemology and Theology of the Suffering of the Poor." *Apuntes: Reflexiones Teológicas desde el Margen Hispano* 13, no. 2 (1993): 151-61.

184. **Feliciano, Juan G.** "Suffering: A Hispanic Epistemology." *Journal of Hispanic/Latino Theology* 2, no. 1 (1994): 41-50.

185. **Folliard, Dorothy.** "Theological Literature of the USA Minorities." In *Convergences and Differences,* edited by Leonardo Boff and Virgilio Elizondo. 90-95. Concilium, vol. 199. Edinburgh: T & T Clark, 1988.

186. **Folliard, Dorothy.** "Sparks from the South: The Growing Impact of Liberation Theology on the United States Hispanic Church." *International Review of Mission* 78 (April 1989): 150-54.

187. **Garcia, Alberto L., with the collaboration of Enrique Carcas and Moraima Y. García.** *Conozca a Cristo.* St. Louis, MO: International Lutheran Laymen's League, 1977. 88 pp.

188. **Garcia, Albert L.** *Evangelismo y Liberación.* Ft. Wayne, IN: Concordia Theological Seminary Press, 1985. 64 pp.

189. **Garcia, Albert L.** "Curso de Cristología." Textbooks and audio cassettes. Fort Wayne, IN: Concordia Theological Seminary Press, [1982].

190. **García, Ismael.** "Theological Reflection in a Global Context: A View from the Underside of History." *Church and Society* 76, no. 1 (1985): 31-42.

191. **García, Ismael.** "Ethical Issues of the Mission of the Church." *Austin Seminary Bulletin* (October 1987): 25-36.

192. **García, Ismael.** "Reflections on the Ethics of AIDS." *Austin Seminary Bulletin* (Fall 1989): 37-45.

193. **García, Ismael.** "King and the Critique of North American Conceptions of Justice." Austin, TX. 1990. Manuscript.

194. **García, Ismael.** "Praxis." In *A New Handbook of Christian Theology,* edited by Donald W. Musser and Joseph L. Price. 377-79. Nashville, TN: Abingdon Press, 1992.

195. **García, Ismael.** "The Retrieval of a Church Centered Ethics." *Windows, A Publication of Austin Seminary* (February 1992).

196. **Garcia, Osvaldo.** "Ministry to the Hispanic Community of the Pomona Valley." D.Min. Project Report. Claremont School of Theology, 1982. 229 pp.

197. **García, Sixto J.** "Sources and Loci of Hispanic Theology." *Journal of Hispanic/Latino Theology* 1, no. 1 (1993): 22-43.

198. **Getz, Lorine M. and Ruy O. Costa, eds.** *Struggles for Solidarity: Liberation Theologies in Tension.* Minneapolis, MN: Fortress Press, 1992. 171 pp.

199. **Glaze, Michael S.** "A Pilot Study of Southern Baptists' Attitudes towards the Active Use of Art in the Church: A Prelude to Future Research." Ph.D. diss., Florida State University, 1993. 288 pp.

200. **Goizueta, Roberto S.** "Nosotros: Toward a U.S. Hispanic Anthropology." *Listening: Journal of Religion and Culture* 27, no. 1 (1992): 55-69.

201. **Goizueta, Roberto S.** "Rediscovering Praxis: The Significance of U.S. Hispanic Experience." In *We are a People! Initiatives in Hispanic American Theology,* edited by Roberto S. Goizueta. 51-77. Minneapolis, MN: Fortress Press, 1992.

202. **Goizueta, Roberto S.** "U.S. Hispanic Theology and the Challenge of Pluralism." In *Frontiers of Hispanic Theology,* edited by Allan F. Deck, S.J. 1-22. Maryknoll, NY: Orbis Books, 1992.

203. **Goizueta, Roberto S.,** ed. *We are a People! Initiatives in Hispanic American Theology.* Minneapolis MN: Fortress Press, 1992. 164 pp.

204. **Gómez, Roberto L.** "Pastoral Care and Counseling in a Mexican American Setting." *Apuntes: Reflexiones Teológicas desde el Margen Hispano* 2, no. 2 (1982): 31-39.

205. **González, Jorge A.** "The Offices of Christ: Prophet, Priest, King." *Response* 14, no. 11 (1982): 36-37.

206. **González, Justo L.,** ed. *Por la Renovación del Entendimiento: La Educación Teológica en América Latina. Ensayos.* Río Piedras, PR: Librería La Reforma, 1965. 152 pp.

207. **González, Justo L.** *Revolución y Encarnación.* 2nd ed. Río Piedras, PR: La Reforma, 1966.

208. **González, Justo L.** "Crisis y Promesa de la Misión Mundial." *El Boletín* (April-June 1967): 13-18.

209. **González, Justo L.** "Today's Mission in the Land of Mañana." *Encounter* 33, no. 3 (1972): 276-86.

210. **González, Justo L.** "Athens and Jerusalem Revisited: Reason and Authority in Tertullian." *Church History* 43, no. 1 (1974): 17-25. Reprinted in Everett Ferguson, David Scholer and Paul Corby Finney, eds., *The Early Church and Greco-Roman Thought.* Studies in Early Christianity, vol. 8 (New York: Garland Publishing, Inc., 1993).

211. **González, Justo L.** "Como Escogidos de Dios." In *Diversos Dones, Un Espíritu.* 3-4. Women's Division, General Board of Global Ministries, The United Methodist Church, 1974.

212. **González, Justo L.** "Cuida de Mis Ovejas." In *Diversos Dones, Un Espíritu.* 45-46. Women's Division, General Board of Global Ministries, The United Methodist Church, 1974.

213. **González, Justo L.** "Encarnación e Historia." In *Fe Cristiana y Latinoamérica,* edited by René Padilla. 151-67. Buenos Aires, Argentina: Ediciones Certeza, 1974.

214. **González, Justo L.** "Los Ministerios en la Iglesia Protestante." In *Ministerios Eclesiales en América Latina,* edited by CELAM. 106-20. Bogotá, Colombia: CELAM, 1974.

215. **González, Justo L.** "Ni Frío Ni Caliente." In *Diversos Dones, Un*

Espíritu. 31-32. Women's Division, General Board of Global Ministries, The United Methodist Church, 1974.

216. González, Justo L. "Un Cuerpo-Diferentes Funciones." In *Diversos Dones, Un Espíritu,* 13-14. Women's Division, General Board of Global Ministries, The United Methodist Church, 1974.

217. González, Justo L. *Itinerario de la Teología Cristiana.* Reprint, 1979. San José, Costa Rica: Editorial Caribe, 1975.

218. González, Justo L. *Jesucristo es el Señor.* San José, Costa Rica: Editorial Caribe, 1975.

219. González, Justo L. "The Forgiveness of Sins: A Theological Brief." In *Christian Theology: A Case Method Approach,* edited by Robert A. Evans and Thomas D. Parker. 221-24. New York: Harper & Row, 1976.

220. González, Justo L. "Inner and Outer Authority in St. Teresa of Avila." *Occasional Essays [of CELEP]* 4, no. 3 (1977): 29-39.

221. González, Justo L. "Interpreting the Scriptures from the Hispanic Perspective." *Engage/Social Action* 6, no. 6 (1978): 13-18.

222. González, Justo L. "Searching for a Liberating Anthropology." *Theology Today* 34, no. 4 (1978): 386-94.

223. González, Justo L. "Liberation Theology: Is It Scriptural?" *Presbyterian Survey* 69, no. 10 (1979): 14-17.

224. González, Justo L. "Theology 'From Below.'" *Directions in Hispanic American Theology,* vol. 10, no. 7 (1979).

225. González, Justo L. "Wanted: Minority Ministers: How Can the Church Expect to Reach the Whole World When Almost All Its Ministers are Alike?" *Presbyterian Survey* 70, no. 2 (1980): 43-44.

226. González, Justo L. "Celebrating Our Unity in Cultural Diversity." *The Interpreter* 25, no. 3 (1981): 8-10.

227. González, Justo L. "Prophets in the King's Sanctuary." *Apuntes: Reflexiones Teológicas desde el Margen Hispano* 1, no. 1 (1981): 3-6.

228. González, Justo L. "Towards a New Reading of History." *Apuntes: Reflexiones Teológicas desde el Margen Hispano* 1, no. 3 (1981): 4-14.

229. González, Justo L., ed. *Proclaiming the Acceptable Year: Sermons from a Perspective of Liberation.* Valley Forge, PA: Judson Press, 1982.

230. González, Justo L. "Espiritualidad Política." *Apuntes: Reflexiones Teológicas desde el Margen Hispano* 3, no. 1 (1983): 3-9.

231. **González, Justo L.** "Let the Dead Gods Bury Their Dead." *Apuntes: Reflexiones Teológicas desde el Margen Hispano* 4, no. 4 (1984): 91-95.

232. **González, Justo L.** "Sanctuary: Historical, Legal, and Biblical Considerations." *Apuntes: Reflexiones Teológicas desde el Margen Hispano* 5, no. 2 (1985): 36-47.

233. **González, Justo L.** "Sanctuary: Some Historical, Legal, and Theological Considerations." *Exodus,* vol. 3, no. 3 (1985).

234. **González, Justo L.** "The Apostles' Creed and the Sanctuary Movement." *Apuntes: Reflexiones Teológicas desde el Margen Hispano* 6, no. 1 (1986): 12-20.

235. **González, Justo L.** "I Believe...In Sanctuary." *Alternatives* 12, no. 2 (1986): 14-20.

236. **González, Justo L.** "Of Fishes and Wishes." *SEEDS,* Sprouts Edition (1986).

237. **González, Justo L.** "Hacia un Redescubrimiento de Nuestra Misión." *Apuntes: Reflexiones Teológicas desde el Margen Hispano* 7, no. 3 (1987): 51-60.

238. **González, Justo, L.** *A History of Christian Thought: Vol. I: From the Beginnings to the Council of Chalcedon.* 2nd ed. Nashville, TN: Abingdon, 1987.

239. **González, Justo L.** *A History of Christian Thought: Vol. II: From Saint Augustine to the Eve of the Reformation.* 2nd ed. Nashville, TN: Abingdon Press, 1987.

240. **González, Justo L.** *A History of Christian Thought: Vol. III: From the Reformation to the Present.* 2nd ed. Nashville, TN: Abingdon Press, 1987.

241. **González, Justo L.** "The Two Faces of Hispanic Christianity." *The Judson Bulletin* 6 (1987): 17-26.

242. **González, Justo L.** "Why Do Some Suffer and Others Not?" *SEEDS* 11 (1988): 32.

243. **González, Justo L.** *Christian Thought Revisited.* Nashville, TN: Abingdon Press, 1989. 185 pp.

244. **González, Justo L.** "Reading the Bible in Spanish." *Apuntes: Reflexiones Teológicas desde el Margen Hispano* 9, no. 2 (1989): 39-46.

245. **González, Justo L.** "El Pluralismo en la Iglesia." *El Intérprete* 28, no. 4 (1990): 12-13.

246. **González, Justo L.** *Faith and Wealth: A History of Early Christian Ideas on the Origin, Significance, and Use of Money.* San Francisco: Harper & Row, 1990. 240 pp.

247. **González, Justo L.** *Mañana: Christian Theology from a Hispanic Perspective.* Nashville, TN: Abingdon Press, 1990. 184 pp.

248. **González, Justo L.** "The Next Ten Years." *Apuntes: Reflexiones Teológicas desde el Margen Hispano* 10, no. 4 (1990): 84-86.

249. **González, Justo L.** "Pluralismo, Justicia y Misión: Un Estudio Bíblico Sobre Hechos 6:1-7." *Apuntes: Reflexiones Teológicas desde el Margen Hispano* 10, no. 1 (1990): 3-8.

250. **González, Justo L.** Prologue to *Jesús y los de Abajo,* edited by David White. 11-16. México: CUPSA, 1990.

251. **González, Justo L.** "Some Reflections on Faith and Wealth." *The Ellul Studies Forum,* no. 6 (1990): 5-6.

252. **González, Justo L.** "Where Frontiers End...And Borders Begin." *Basta!* (February 1990): 19-22.

253. **González, Justo L.** Foreword to *A Violent Evangelism: The Politicial and Religious Conquest of the Américas,* by Luis N. Rivera. Louisville, KY: Westminster/John Knox Press, 1992.

254. **González, Justo L.** Foreword to *A Vision Transformed,* by Bernard E. Quick. Ocean City, MD: Skipjack, 1992.

255. **González, Justo L.** *Historia del Pensamiento Cristiano: Vol II: Desde San Agustín Hasta las Vísperas de la Reforma.* 2nd ed. Miami, FL: Editorial Caribe, 1992.

256. **González, Justo L.** *Historia del Pensamiento Cristiano: Vol. I: Desde los Orígenes Hasta el Concilio de Calcedonia.* 2nd ed. Miami, Fl: Editorial Caribe, 1992.

257. **González, Justo L.** *Mentors as Instruments of God's Call.* Nashville, TN: General Board of Higher Education and Ministry, The United Methodist Church, 1992.

258. **González, Justo L.** *Out of Every Tribe and Nation: Christian Theology at the Ethnic Roundtable.* Nashville, TN: Abingdon Press, 1992. 128 pp.

259. **González, Justo L.** "Setting the Context: The Option for the Poor in Latin American Liberation Theology." In *Poverty and Ecclesiology: Nineteenth-Century Evangelicals in the Light of Liberation Theology,* edited by Anthony L. Dunnavant. 9-26. Collegeville, MN: Liturgical Press, 1992.

260. **González, Justo L., ed.** *Voces: Voices from the Hispanic Church.* Nashville, TN: Abingdon Press, 1992. 171 pp.

261. **González, Justo L.** "Espiritualidad Política." *El Faro* 108 (March-April 1993): 55-57.

262. **González, Justo L.** "Globalization in the Teaching of Church History." *ATS Theological Education* 29, no. 2 (1993): 49-71.

263. **González, Justo L.** *Historia del Pensamiento Cristiano: Tomo 3: Desde la Reforma Protestante Hasta el Siglo Veinte.* Miami, FL: Editorial Caribe, 1993. 491 pp.

264. **González, Justo L.** "Reading the Bible in Spanish." *Unidad Cristiana/Christian Unity* 1, no. 1 (1993): 5-9.

265. **González, Justo L.** "Confusion at Pentecost in Latin American Liberation Theology: Scripture as the Foundation for Freedom." In *The Bible in Theology and Preaching,* edited by Donald K. McKim. 146-49. Nashville, TN: Abingdon Press, 1994.

266. **González, Justo L.** *Historia del Cristianismo I y II.* Rev. ed. Miami, FL: Editorial Unilit, 1994.

267. **González, Justo L.** "In Remembrance of Me: Present, Past, and Future." In *Hidden Stories: Unveiling the History of the Latino Church,* edited by Daniel R. Rodríguez-Díaz and David Cortés-Fuentes. 159-65. Decatur, GA: AETH, 1994.

268. **González, Justo L.** "Voices of Compassion Yesterday and Today." In *New Face of the Church in Latin America,* edited by Guillermo Cook. 3-12. Maryknoll, NY: Orbis Books, 1994.

269. **González, Justo L.** *Bosquejo de Historia de la Iglesia.* Decatur, GA: AETH, 1995. 117 pp.

270. **González, Justo L.** "Hispanics in the New Reformation." In *Mestizo Christianity: Theology from the Latino Perspective,* edited by Arturo J. Bañuelas. 238-59. Maryknoll, NY: Orbis Books, 1995.

271. **González, Justo L.** "The Work of Christ in Saint Bonaventure's Systematic Works." *S. Bonaventura 1274-1974* (Rome) 4 (n.d.): 371-85.

272. **González, Justo L. and Catherine Gunsalus González.** *Rejoice in Your Savior: A Study for Lent-Easter.* Nashville, TN: Graded Press, 1979.

273. **González, Justo L. and Catherine Gunsalus González.** *Liberation Preaching: The Pulpit and the Oppressed.* Nashville, TN: Abingdon, 1980. 113 pp.

274. González, Justo L. and Catherine Gunsalus González. *Paul: His Impact on Christianity.* Nashville, TN: Graded Press, 1987.

275. González, Justo L. and Catherine Gunsalus González. "The Larger Context." In *Preaching as a Social Act: Theology and Practice,* edited by Arthur van Seters. 29-54. Nashville, TN: Abingdon Press, 1988.

276. González, Justo L. and Catherine Gunsalus González. "An Historical Survey." In *The Globalization of Theological Education,* edited by Alice F. Evans, Robert A. Evans, and David A. Roozen. 13-32. Maryknoll, NY: Orbis Books, 1993.

277. González, Justo L. and Catherine Gunsalus González. *The Liberating Pulpit.* Nashville, TN: Abingdon Press, 1994. 123 pp.

278. González, Justo L. and Catherine Gunsalus González. "Liberation Preaching." In *Concise Encyclopedia of Preaching,* edited by William H. Willimon and Richard Lischer. 307-8. Louisville, KY: Westminster/John Knox Press, 1995.

279. González, Justo L., Daniel Rodríguez-Díaz, and Eliseo Pérez Alvarez, eds. *Desde el Reverso: Materiales para la Historia de la Iglesia.* Chicago, IL: Publicaciones el Faro and APHILA, 1993. 141 pp.

280. González y Pérez, Belén. "A Reading of Orlando E. Costas on the Theology of Contextual Evangelization: A Galilean Perspective." Master's thesis. Lutheran Theological Seminary at Gettysburg, 1991. 51 pp.

281. Goris, Anneris. "Rites for a Rising Nationalism: Religious Meaning and Dominican Cultural Identity in New York City." In *Old Masks, New Faces,* edited by Anthony M. Stevens-Arroyo and Gilbert Cadena. 117-41. Vol. 2 of PARAL Studies Series. New York: Bildner Center for Western Hemisphere Studies, 1995.

282. Guerrero, Andrés G. *A Chicano Theology.* Maryknoll, NY: Orbis Books, 1987. 186 pp.

283. Hamid, Idris, ed. *Out of the Depths: Papers Presented at Four Missiology Conferences Held in Antigua, Guyana, Jamaica and Trinidad.* San Fernando, Trinidad & Tobago, W.I.: St. Andrew's Theological College, 1977. 261 pp.

284. Hawkins, Wayne R. "Hispanic and Anglo Christians: A Model for Shared Life." D.Min. Project Report. San Francisco Theological Seminary, 1985. 156 pp.

285. Hernandez, Edwin I. "Jesus the Galilean." *Adventist Review,* 16 April 1987, 8-9.

286. **Hernandez, Edwin I.** "The Social Ethics of the Coming Generation." Paper presented at the meeting of the Andrews Society for Religious Studies, San Francisco, CA, November 1992.

287. **Hernandez, Jose A.** "Training Hispanic Leaders in the United States: An Application of the Concept of Contextualization to Theological Education." Ph.D. diss., Southwestern Baptist Theological Seminary, 1985.

288. **Hernández, Lydia.** "La Mujer Chicana y la Justicia Económica." *Apuntes: Reflexiones Teológicas desde el Margen Hispano* 6, no. 4 (1986): 81-83.

289. **Herrera, Pedro G.** *Una Mirada a Cristo a través de la Teología Contemporánea: Sermones por Pedro G. Herrera.* San Antonio, TX: n.p., 1971. 188 pp.

290. **Hispanic Ecumenical Project.** "A Message to the Hispanic Community of the United States and Puerto Rico and the Christian People of North America from the Hispanic Ecumenical Theological Project." Mexican American Cultural Center, San Antonio, TX. Hispanic Ecumenical Theological Project, October 1978. 5 pp.

291. **Hispanic Ecumenical Theological Project.** "A Message to the Hispanic Community of the United States and Puerto Rico." *Mid-Stream: An Ecumenical Journal* 18, no. 2 (1979): 179-85.

292. **Isasi-Díaz, Ada María.** "'Apuntes' for a Hispanic Women's Theology of Liberation." *Apuntes: Reflexiones Teológicas desde el Margen Hispano* 6, no. 3 (1986): 61-71.

293. **Isasi-Díaz, Ada María.** "A Hispanic Garden in a Foreign Land." In *Inheriting Our Mothers' Gardens: Feminist Theology in Third World Perspective,* edited by Letty M. Russell and et al. 91-106. Philadelphia, PA: Westminster Press, 1988.

294. **Isasi-Díaz, Ada María.** "Mujeristas: A Name of Our Own." In *The Future of Liberation Theology,* edited by Marc H. Ellis and Otto Maduro. 410-19. Maryknoll, NY: Orbis Books, 1989.

295. **Isasi-Díaz, Ada María.** "The Bible and Mujerista Theology." In *Lift Every Voice: Constructing Christian Theologies from the Underside,* edited by Susan Brooks Thistlethwaite and Mary Potter Engel. 261-269. New York: Harper & Row, 1990.

296. **Isasi-Díaz, Ada María.** "Mujerista Theology's Method: A Liberative Praxis, a Way of Life." *Listening: Journal of Religion and Culture* 27, no. 1 (1992): 41-54.

297. **Isasi-Díaz, Ada María.** "¡Viva la Diferencia!" *Journal of Feminist Studies in Religion* 8, no. 1 (1992): 98-102.

298. **Isasi-Díaz, Ada María.** "Praxis: The Heart of *Mujerista* Theology." *Journal of Hispanic/Latino Theology* 1, no. 1 (1993): 44-55.

299. **Isasi-Díaz, Ada María, and others.** "Mujeristas: Who We are and What We are About." *Journal of Feminist Studies in Religion* 8, no. 1 (1992): 105-25.

300. **Isasi-Díaz, Ada María.** *En la Lucha-In the Struggle: A Hispanic Women's Liberation Theology.* Minneapolis, MN: Fortress Press, 1993. 226 pp.

301. **Isasi-Díaz, Ada María and Yolanda Tarango.** *Hispanic Women, Prophetic Voice in the Church.* San Francisco, CA: Harper & Row, 1988. Reprint, Minneapolis, MN: Fortress Press, 1992. 123 pp.

302. **Japas, Salim.** *Fuego de Dios en la Evangelización [God's Fire in Evangelization].* Mayagüez, PR: Departamento de Teología, Antillian Adventist College, 1971.

303. **Japas, Salim.** *Cristo en el Santuario: Su Intercesión por el Hombre.* 2nd ed. Bogota, Colombia: Asociación Publicadora Interamericana, 1988. 143 pp.

304. **Japas, Salim.** *Llama Divina: Respuesta al Problema de la Evangelización Contemporanea [Divine Flame: Answers to the Problem of Contemporary Evangelization].* Coral Gables, FL: Asociación Publicadora Interamericana, 1989. 122 pp.

305. **Jiménez, Pablo A.** "Creando una Nueva Humanidad: Reflexión Sobre la Tarea Educativa de la Iglesia Basada en Efesios 4:17-32." *Apuntes: Reflexiones Teológicas desde el Margen Hispano* 11, no. 4 (1991): 75-80.

306. **Jiménez, Pablo A.** "La Gran Comisión." *Apuntes: Reflexiones Teológicas desde el Margen Hispano* 12, no. 4 (1992): 150-61.

307. **Jiménez, Pablo A.** "In Search of a Hispanic Model of Biblical Interpretation." *Journal of Hispanic/Latino Theology* 3, no. 2 (1995): 44-64.

308. **Jiménez, Pablo A.** "The Use of the Bible in Hispanic Theology." D.Min. Project Report. Columbia Theological Seminary, 1995. 139 pp.

309. **Lara-Braud, Jorge.** "By Means of the Cross He United Both Races." *Austin Seminary Bulletin: Faculty Edition* 83, no. 7 (1968): 42-46.

310. **Lara-Braud, Jorge.** "Hispanic-Americans and the Crisis in the Nation." *Theology Today* 26, no. 3 (1969): 334-38.

311. **Lara-Braud, Jorge.** "Hispanic-Americans and the Crisis in the Nation: Background Paper." *Social Progress* 59, no. 6 (1969): 50-60.

312. **Lara-Braud, Jorge.** "Theological Reflection on Mexican Immigration." *JSAC [Joint Strategy and Action Committee] Grapevine,* vol. 11, no. 8 (1980).

313. **Lara-Braud, Jorge.** "El Salvador: Dilemma for Christian Conscience." *Church and Society* 72, no. 2 (1981): 7-14.

314. **Lara-Braud, Jorge.** "Monseñor Romero: Model Pastor for the Hispanic Diaspora." *Apuntes: Reflexiones Teológicas desde el Margen Hispano* 1, no. 3 (1981): 15-21.

315. **Lara-Braud, Jorge.** "Hispanic Christianity: Eccentricity and Synthesis." *Pacific Theological Review,* vol. 15, no. 3 (1982).

316. **Lara-Braud, Jorge.** "Reflexiones Teológicas Sobre la Migración." *Apuntes: Reflexiones Teológicas desde el Margen Hispano* 2, no. 1 (1982): 3-7.

317. **Lara-Braud, Jorge.** *What is Liberation Theology? Answers from within and Reflections from the Reformed Tradition.* Atlanta, GA: General Assembly Mission Board, Presbyterian Church in the United States, 1982. 45 pp.

318. **Lara-Braud, Jorge.** "The Role of North Americans in the Future of the Missionary Enterprise." *International Bulletin of Missionary Research* 7, no. 1 (1983): 2-5.

319. **Lara-Braud, Jorge.** "How Shall We Sing the Lord's Song in a Strange Land?" *Pacific Theological Review,* vol. 19, no. 1 (1985).

320. **Lara-Braud, Jorge.** "Latin-American Liberation Theology: Pastoral Action as the Basis for the Prophetic Task." In *The Pastor as Prophet,* edited by Earl E. Shelp and Ronald H. Sunderland. 135-68. New York: Pilgrim Press, 1985.

321. **Lara-Braud, Jorge.** "Authenticity before the Altar as Affirmation and Celebration of Cultural Diversity and Spiritual Oneness." *Church and Society,* vol. 76, no. 4 (1986).

322. **Lara-Braud, Jorge.** "Hispanic Ministry: Fidelity to Christ." *Pacific Theological Review,* vol. 19, no. 2 (1986).

323. **Lara-Braud, Jorge.** "Theology: Little Faith in Search of Large Pertinence." *Pacific Theological Review,* vol. 22, no. 2 (1989).

324. **Lara-Braud, Jorge.** "Reflections on Liberation Theology from the Reformed Tradition." In *Major Themes in the Reformed Tradition,*

edited by Donald K. McKim. 412-15. Grand Rapids, MI: William B. Eerdmans Publishing Co., 1992.

325. **Lee, Lewis E.** "Study of the Educative Process in Neo-Thomism and Evidences of its Similarities as Reflected in Baptist Adult Spanish Curriculum Materials, 1968-1971." Ed.D. thesis. Southwestern Baptist Theological Seminary, 1973.

326. **Lockwood, George F.** "Recent Developments in U.S. Hispanic and Latin American Protestant Church Music." D.Min. Project Report. Claremont School of Theology, 1981. 165 pp.

327. **López, Hugo.** "Toward a Theology of Migration." *Apuntes: Reflexiones Teológicas desde el Margen Hispano* 2, no. 3 (1982): 68-71.

328. **López, Hugo.** "El Divino Migrante." *Apuntes: Reflexiones Teológicas desde el Margen Hispano* 4, no. 1 (1984): 14-19.

329. **Loya, Gloria Inés.** "The Hispanic Woman: Pasionaria and *Pastora* of the Hispanic Community." In *Frontiers of Hispanic Theology in the United States,* edited by Allan Figueroa Deck, S.J. 124-33. Maryknoll, NY: Orbis Books, 1992.

330. **Luna, David.** "An Historical, Sociological, Theological Analysis of the Hispanic American Baptist in Southern California." D.Min. Project Report. American Baptist Seminary of the West, 1990. 96 pp.

331. **Machado, Daisy L.** "Roundtable Response Article." *Journal of Feminist Studies in Religion* 8, no. 1 (1992): 120-22.

332. **Machado, Daisy L.** "The Forest of Felled Trees: Hope in the Midst of Despair." In *Sisters Struggling in the Spirit, A Women of Color Theological Anthology,* edited by Rose Brewer. 147-50. Louisville, KY: Women's Ministries Program Area of the National Ministries Division, Presbyterian Church (U.S.A.), 1994.

333. **Machado, Daisy L.** "Being Ecumenical in the Barrio." *Journal of Hispanic/Latino Theology* 3, no. 2 (1995): 6-13.

334. **Madriz, Esther.** "Nuestra Responsabilidad Social Cristiana: ¿Opción o Mandato Bíblico?" In *La Iglesia Hispana en Misión,* edited by Conrado G. Soltero. 6-12. New York: National Program Division, General Board of Global Ministries, The United Methodist Church, 1992.

335. **Maldonado, David, Jr.** "Towards a Theology of Aging." *NICA Inform,* vol. 11, no. 1 (1985-86).

336. **Maldonado, David, Jr.** "Faith, Peace, and Courage." In *The Upper*

Room Disciplines, edited by Tom Page. 122-28. Nashville, TN: The Upper Room, 1987.

337. **Maldonado, David, Jr.** "Freedom from Barriers." In *Disciplines, 1993,* edited by Glenda Webb. 79-85. Nashville, TN: The Upper Room, 1993.

338. **Mark, Leslie David.** "The Role of Seminary Education in the Development of Spiritual Leadership in the Hispanic American Protestant Church." D.Min. Project Report. Fuller Theological Seminary, School of Theology, 1982.

339. **Marrero, Gilberto.** "Hispanic Americans and Liberation." *Church and Society* 62, no. 3 (1972): 25-34.

340. **Marrero Navarro, Domingo.** "Satre y el Concepto Cristiano de la Tragedia." *El Boletín* 16, no. 4 (1951): 3-4.

341. **Marrero Navarro, Domingo.** "Crítica de la Ciencia y Concepto de la Filosofía en Ortega." *Homenaje a Ortega, La Torre* 5, nos. 15-16 (1956): 285-303.

342. **Marrero Navarro, Domingo.** "Relaciones Esenciales Entre la Filosofía y la Teología." *La Nueva Democracia* 40, no. 3 (1960): 74-91.

343. **Marrero Navarro, Domingo.** *Los Fundamentos de la Libertad.* San Juan, PR: Talleres Gráficos Ineramericanos, 1970.

344. **Marrero Navarro, Domingo.** "Notas para Organizar el Estudio de las Ideas en Puerto Rico." *Revista de Estudios Generales* 1, no. 1 (1987): 18-39.

345. **Martell-Otero, Loida .** "Lifting Voices, Praising Gifts." *Apuntes: Reflexiones Teológicas desde el Margen Hispano* 13, no. 3 (1993): 171-79.

346. **Martell-Otero, Loida.** "Women Doing Theology: Una Perspectiva Evangélica." *Apuntes: Reflexiones Teológicas desde el Margen Hispano* 14, no. 3 (1994): 67-85.

347. **Martin, Carlos G.** "Evangelistic Strategies of Seventh-Day Adventists to Reach Recent Hispanic Immigrants to Texas: A Critical Evaluation." Ph.D. diss., Southwestern Baptist Theological Seminary, 1992. 300 pp.

348. **Martínez, Felipe.** "El Quinto Centenario: Perspectivas." *Apuntes: Reflexiones Teológicas desde el Margen Hispano* 11, no. 3 (1991): 51-61.

349. **Martínez, Jill.** "Worship and the Search for Community in the Presbyterian Church (U.S.A.): The Hispanic Experience." *Church and Society* 76, no. 4 (1986): 42-46.

350. **Martínez, Jill.** "In Search of an Inclusive Community." *Apuntes: Reflexiones Teológicas desde el Margen Hispano* 9, no. 1 (1989): 3-9.

351. **Martínez, Joel N.** "The People on the Go: The Church on the Way." *Apuntes: Reflexiones Teológicas desde el Margen Hispano* 15, no. 2 (1995): 58-71.

352. **Mata del Rio, Dinorah.** "The Cuban Woman in Church and in Theology." *Journal of the Interdenominational Theological Center* 15, nos. 1-2 (1987-1988): 187-91.

353. **Méndez, Verónica and Allan Figueroa Deck, S.J.** *An Annotated Bibliography on Hispanic Spirituality.* Berkeley, CA: The Jesuit School of Theology at Berkeley, 1989. 41 pp.

354. **Mercado, Maribel.** "Ser Puertorriqueño en el Pensamiento de Domingo Marrero." Paper presented for the "Seminario de Integración," Seminario Evangélico de Puerto Rico, held at the Seminario Evangélico de Puerto Rico, San Juan, PR, June 1988.

355. **Mergal, Angel M.** *Reformismo Cristiano y Alma Española.* Buenos Aires, Argentina: Editorial La Aurora, 1949.

356. **Mergal, Angel M.** "Evangelical Catholicism as Represented by Juan de Valdés." In *Spiritual and Anabaptist Writers: Documents Illustrative of the Radical Reformation,* edited by Angel M. Mergal. 297-319. The Library of Christian Classics, vol. 25. Philadelphia, PA: Westminster Press, 1957.

357. **Mergal, Angel M.** "Erasmo de Rotterdam (1465-1536)." *Educación* 12 (November 1962): 61-78.

358. **Mergal, Angel M.** *El Reino Permanente.* San Juan, PR: Iglesia Evangélica Unida de Puerto Rico, 1965.

359. **Mergal Llera, Angel M.** *El Agraz.* Río Piedras, PR: Seminario Evangélico, 1945. 106 pp.

360. **Míguez Bonino, José.** "Iglesia y Secta: Revisión de un Vocabulario." *Apuntes: Reflexiones Teológicas desde el Margen Hispano* 8, no. 3 (1988): 60-69.

361. **Miranda, Jesse.** "Los Nuevos Samaritanos: Un Sermón Modelo." In *Predicación Evangélica y Teología Hispana,* edited by Orlando E. Costas. 269-79. San Diego, CA: Publicaciones de las Américas, 1982.

362. **Moody, Linda A.** "Women's Expanding Conceptions of God: A Consideration of Feminist, Mujerista, and Womanist Theological Reflection on God in Light of U.S. Third World Feminist Critical Theory." Ph.D. diss., Graduate Theological Union, 1993. 291 pp.

363. **Mulligan, Joseph E.** "The Good News according to Paul: An Invitation to Community." *Apuntes: Reflexiones Teológicas desde el Margen Hispano* 3, no. 1 (1983): 15-20.

364. **Nieto, Leo D.** "The Chicano Movement and the Churches in the United States/El Movimiento Chicano y las Iglesias en Los Estados Unidos." *Perkins Journal* 29, no. 1 (1975): English: 32-41; Spanish: 76-85.

365. **Nieto, Leo D.** "Chicano Theology of Liberation." In *Mission Trends No. 4: Liberation Theologies,* edited by Gerald H. Anderson and Thomas F. Stransky. 277-82. New York: Paulist Press, 1979.

366. **Ortiz, Manuel.** "My Commitment to Intercultural Christian Community: An Hispanic Pilgrimage." *Urban Mission* 12, no. 2 (1994): 14-24.

367. **Ortiz, Manuel, ed.** "[Pastoral Needs of Hispanic American Churches]." *Urban Mission* 10, no. 4 (1993): 3-59.

368. **Ortíz, José.** "Un Trabajo Independiente: Teología de Liberación una Sinóptica Latinoamericana." Chicago, IL. 1976. 12 pp. Typescript.

369. **Ortíz, José.** "A Program Proposal for Spanish-Speaking Mennonite Theological Training." 1977. 12 pp. Typescript.

370. **Pagán, Samuel.** "El Significado de Esta Hora." *Apuntes: Reflexiones Teológicas desde el Margen Hispano* 3, no. 4 (1983): 83-88.

371. **Pagán, Samuel.** *La Resurrección de la Esperanza.* Bayamón: ICDC, 1983.

372. **Pagán, Samuel.** *Púlpito, Teología y Esperanza.* Miami, FL: Editorial Caribe, 1988.

373. **Pagán, Samuel.** "El Apocalipsis de Juan y la Iglesia Hispana." *Apuntes: Reflexiones Teológicas desde el Margen Hispano* 12, no. 1 (1992): 3-12.

374. **Pagán, Samuel.** *Su Presencia y la Ausencia.* Miami, FL: Editorial Caribe, 1992.

375. **Pagán, Samuel.** "Estudios Bíblicos: Pródigos, Profetas, Siervos y Mesías." *Apuntes: Reflexiones Teológicas desde el Margen Hispano* 13, no. 1 (1993): 4-29.

376. **Pagán, Samuel.** "Apocalyptic Poetry: Isaiah 24-27." *Apuntes: Reflexiones Teológicas desde el Margen Hispano* 15, no. 1 (1995): 14-27.

377. **Pazmiño, Robert W.** "Double Dutch: Reflections of an Hispanic North-American on Multicultural Religious Education." *Apuntes: Reflexiones Teológicas desde el Margen Hispano* 8, no. 2 (1988): 27-37.

378. **Pazmiño, Roberto W.** *Foundational Issues in Christian Education: An Introduction in Evangelical Perspective.* Grand Rapids, MI: Baker Book House, 1988. 264 pp.

379. **Pazmiño, Roberto W.** *Principles and Practices of Christian Education: An Evangelical Perspective.* Grand Rapids, MI: Baker Book House, 1992. 176 pp.

380. **Pazmiño, Robert W.** *By What Authority Do We Teach? Sources for Empowering Christian Educators.* Grand Rapids, MI: Baker Book House, 1994. 160 pp.

381. **Pazmiño, Robert W.** *Latin American Journey: Insights for Christian Education in North America.* Cleveland, OH: United Church Press, 1994. 170 pp.

382. **Pearce, Guy E.** "Latino, Come!" D.Min. Project Report. Austin Presbyterian Theological Seminary, 1993. 107 pp.

383. **Pedraja, Luis G.** "Dialogical Theology: Using the Trinity as a Bridge between Process Theology and Jüngel as Hispanic Methodology." Paper presented at the Fund for Theological Education Mini-Consultation, Pacific School of Religion, Berkeley, CA, 1992.

384. **Pedraja, Luis G.** "The Destruction of the 'Other' in the Conquest of Latin America." Paper presented at the annual meeting of the Mid-Atlantic Region, American Academy of Religion, Philadelphia, PA., 1993.

385. **Pedraja, Luis G.** "Infinity and Finitude: The Trinity in Process Theology and Eberhard Jüngel." Ph.D. diss., University of Virginia, 1994.

386. **Pedraja, Luis G.** "Infinity in the Thought of A. N. Whitehead and E. Jüngel." Paper presented at the annual meeting of the Pacific Northwest Region, American Academy of Religion, Portland, OR, 1994.

387. **Plaskow, Judith and Elisabeth Schussler Fiorenza, eds.** "Appropriation and Reciprocity in Womanist/Mujerista/Feminist Work." *Journal of Feminist Studies in Religion* 8 (Fall 1992): 91-122.

388. **Plowman, Edward E.** "Hispanic Christians in the United States." *Christianity Today* 30, no. 1 (1986): 44-45.

389. **Pope-Levison, Priscilla.** "Comprehensive and Contextual: The Evangelism of Orlando Costas." *Journal of the Academy for Evangelism in Theological Education* 4 (1988-1989): 4-14.

390. **Quiñones-Ortiz, Javier.** "The *Mestizo* Journey: Challenges for Hispanic Theology." *Apuntes: Reflexiones Teológicas desde el Margen Hispano* 11, no. 3 (1991): 62-72.

391. **Ramírez, Guillermo.** "Perspectivas Apocalípticas: Reto para Hoy." *Apuntes: Reflexiones Teológicas desde el Margen Hispano* 3, no. 3 (1983): 51-57.

392. **Ramírez, Johnny.** "Food and Religion." Paper presented at the annual meeting of the American Academy of Religion, Chicago, IL, 1994.

393. **Ramírez, Ricardo, Bishop.** "The Challenge of Ecumenism to Hispanic Christians." *Ecumenical Trends* 21, no. 8 (1992): 117/1, 127/11-130/14.

394. **Ramos, Jovelino, ed.** "Authenticity before the Altar: A Racial-Ethnic Colloquium." *Church and Society* 76, no. 4 (1986): 3-71.

395. **Ranck, Lee, ed.** "Hispanic Americans: A Growing Force/Los Hispano Americanos: Una Fuerza Cresciente." *Engage/Social Action [e-sa Forum, 99]* 11, no. 11 (1983): English: 9-49; Spanish: 50-72.

396. **Recinos, Hal.** "Militarism and the Poor." *Apuntes: Reflexiones Teológicas desde el Margen Hispano* 7, no. 4 (1987): 86-94.

397. **Recinos, Hal.** *Hear the Cry! A Latino Pastor Challenges the Church.* Louisville, KY: Westminter/John Knox Press, 1989. 156 pp.

398. **Recinos, Harold.** "Mission: A Latino Pastoral Theology." *Apuntes: Reflexiones Teológicas desde el Margen Hispano* 12, no. 3 (1992): 115-26.

399. **Recinos, Harold J.** "Militarism and the Poor." *The Other Side* 24, no. 4 (1988): 17.

400. **Recinos, Harold J.** "Walking with Christ in the Barrio." *The Other Side* 25, no. 2 (1989): 30-32.

401. **Recinos, Harold J.** "Cultura, Identidad y la Iglesia Latina." *El Intérprete* 28, no. 4 (1990): 8, 13.

402. **Recinos, Harold J.** "God's Sacred Place: The City." *Christian Social Action* 3, no. 6 (1990): 31-33.

403. **Recinos, Harold J.** *Jesus Weeps: Global Encounters on Our Doorstep.* Nashville, TN: Abingdon Press, 1992. 142 pp.

404. **Recinos, Harold J.** "Racism and Drugs in the City: The Church's Call to Ministry." In *Envisioning the New City,* edited by Eleanor Scott Meyers. 98-108. Louisville, KY: Westminster/John Knox Press, 1992.

405. **Recinos, Harold J.** "Commentary on the Changing Face of the Parish." In *Globalization of Theological Education,* edited by David A. Roozen, Robert A. Evans and Alice F. Evans. 84-89. Maryknoll, NY: Orbis Books, 1993.

406. **Recinos, Harold J.** "Mission: A Latino Pastoral Theology." In *Mestizo Christianity: Theology from the Latino Perspective,* edited by Arturo Bañuelas. 132-45. Maryknoll, NY: Orbis Books, 1995.

407. **Reyes, José A.** *The Hispanics in the United States.* Cleveland, TN: White Wing Publishing House and Press, 1991. 146 pp.

408. **Reyes, Ruben.** "Prolegomena to Chicano Theology." D.Min. Project Report. Claremont School of Theology, 1974.

409. **Rivas, Michael G.** "The Hispanic Church and the Future: A Discussion Starter." Paper presented at the annual meeting of Hispanic Instructors, Perkins School of Theology, Dallas, TX, December 1994. Published in *Apuntes: Reflexiones Teológicas desde el Margen Hispano* 15, no. 2 (1995): 72-79.

410. **Rivas, Yolanda.** "Confrontación y Reconciliación." *Apuntes: Reflexiones Teológicas desde el Margen Hispano* 2, no. 2 (1982): 40-47.

411. **Rivas-Druck, Michael G.** "The Challenge of Minority Identification and Enlistment of Ministry." *Apuntes: Reflexiones Teológicas desde el Margen Hispano* 5, no. 3 (1985): 51-57.

412. **Rivera, Alejandro García.** "Artificial Inelligence, 1992, and Las Casas: The Valladolid Connection." *Apuntes: Reflexiones Teológicas desde el Margen Hispano* 11, no. 2 (1991): 39-43.

413. **Rivera, Elí S.** "Desarrollo de una Congregación Misional Hispana." In *La Iglesia Hispana en Misión,* edited by Conrado G. Soltero. 1-5. New York: National Program Division, General Board of Global Ministries, The United Methodist Church, 1992.

414. **Rivera-Pagán, Luis N.** "Breves Reflexiones Sobre la Unidad de la Iglesia." *El Boletín* 32, no. 3 (1967): 15-23.

415. **Rivera-Pagán, Luis N.** "Unity and Truth: The Unity of God, Man, Jesus Christ, and the Church in Irenaeus." Ph.D. diss., Yale University, 1971.

416. **Rivera-Pagán, Luis N.** "Aportes del Marxismo." In *Pueblo Oprimido, Señor de la Historia,* edited by Hugo Assmann. 249-53. Montevideo, Uruguay: ISAL, 1972.

417. **Rivera-Pagán, Luis N.** "Teología y Praxis de Liberación." In *Pueblo Oprimido, Señor de la Historia,* edited by Hugo Assmann. 173-76. Montevideo, Uruguay: ISAL, 1972.

418. **Rivera-Pagán, Luis N.** "The Mission of the Church and the Development of a Caribbean Theology of Liberation." In *Out of the Depths: Papers at Four Missiology Conferences Held in Antigua, Guyana, Jamaica*

and Trinidad, 1975, edited by Idris Hamid. 249-61. San Fernando, Trinidad & Tobago, W.I.: St. Andrew's Theological College, 1977.

419. **Rivera-Pagán, Luis N.** "Praxis Cristiana y Producción Teológica en el Caribe." In *Praxis Cristiana y Producción Teológica,* edited by Jorge V. Pixley and Jean-Pierre Bastian. 137-62. Barcelona: Editorial Sígueme, 1979.

420. **Rivera-Pagán, Luis N.** "Christliche Neuorientierung in Lateinamerika und in der Karibik." *Standpunkt* 10, no. 7 (1982): 190-91.

421. **Rivera-Pagán, Luis N.** "La Utopía Bíblica, la Amenaza Nuclear y el Problema de la Paz." In *La Esperanza en el Presente de América Latina,* edited by Luis N. Rivera Pagán and Raúl Vidales. 383-407. San José, Costa Rica: DEI, 1983.

422. **Rivera-Pagán, Luis N.** "Educación y Libertad." *Cupey* 1, no. 1 (1984): 18-23.

423. **Rivera-Pagán, Luis N.** "El Derecho a la Vida y el Armagedón Nuclear." *Cupey* 2, no. 1 (1985): 7-47.

424. **Rivera-Pagán, Luis N.** "Las Armas Nucleares: Desafío a una Nueva Ética." *Apuntes: Reflexiones Teológicas desde el Margen Hispano* 5, no. 2 (1985): 27-35.

425. **Rivera-Pagán, Luis N.** "Ciencia, Nacionalismo Y Guerra." *Cupey* 3, no. 1 (1986): 67-86.

426. **Rivera-Pagán, Luis N.** "El Vaticano y la Teología de la Liberación." *Apuntes: Reflexiones Teológicas desde el Margen Hispano* 6, no. 3 (1986): 51-60.

427. **Rivera-Pagán, Luis N.** "Chernobyl: Reflexiones Críticas Sobre la Energía Nuclear." *Exégesis* 1, no. 3 (1987): 2-9. Also published in *Cupey* 4, no. 1 (1987): 102-19.

428. **Rivera-Pagán, Luis N.** *Domingo Marrero-La Paradoja de la Razón: Filosofía y Religión.* Guaynabo, PR: Editorial Sonador, 1987.

429. **Rivera-Pagán, Luis N.** "Idolatría Nuclear y Paz en el Mundo: Breves Reflexiones Teológicas." *Apuntes: Reflexiones Teológicas desde el Margen Hispano* 7, no. 4 (1987): 75-84.

430. **Rivera-Pagán, Luis N.** "La Cristianización de América: Reflexión y Desafío." *Apuntes: Reflexiones Teológicas desde el Margen Hispano* 7, no. 1 (1987): 14-19.

431. **Rivera-Pagán, Luis N.** "Las Instrucciones del Vaticano Sobre la Teología Latinoamericana de la Liberación." *Cupey* 3, no. 2 (1987):

97-113. Also published in *Pasos,* segunda época, 9 (January 1987): 10-17 and *Cuadernos de Teología* (Buenos Aires, Argentina) 8, no. 2 (1987): 183-96.

432. **Rivera-Pagán, Luis N.** "Respuesta: La Cristianización de América: Reflexión y Desafío." *Apuntes: Reflexiones Teológicas desde el Margen Hispano* 7, no. 1 (1987): 14-19.

433. **Rivera-Pagán, Luis N.** "La Religión Nuclear: Hacia una Teología de la Paz." *Revista de Estudios Generales* 2, no. 2 (1988): 141-70. Also published in *Cuadernos de Teología* (Buenos Aires, Argentina) 9, no. 1 (1988): 27-52.

434. **Rivera-Pagán, Luis N.** *A la Sombra del Armagedón: Reflexiones Críticas Sobre el Desafío Nuclear.* Río Piedras, PR: Editorial Edil, 1988. 335 pp.

435. **Rivera-Pagán, Luis N.** "La Utopía Bíblica de la Paz: Anotaciones Críticas a la Hermenéutica Latinoamericana." In *Hacia Una Fe Evangélica Latinoamericanista: Una Perspectiva Bautista,* edited by Jorge Pixley. 183-200. San José, Costa Rica: DEI, 1988. Also published as "Toward a Theology of Peace: Critical Notes on the Biblical Hermeneutic of Latin American Theology of Liberation," in Dow Kirkpatrick, ed., *Faith Born in the Struggle of Life: A Reading of Protestant Faith in Latin America* (Grand Rapids, MI: Wm. B. Eerdmans, 1988), pp. 52-77.

436. **Rivera-Pagán, Luis N.** "Liberación y Paz: Imperativos Evangélicos." In *Tercer Congreso Continental de Estudio y Asamblea Plenaria de la Conferencia Cristiana por la Paz para América Latina y el Caribe,* edited by Sergio Arce & Carlos Piedra. 11-24. Matanzas, Cuba: Centro de Información y Estudio "Augusto Cotto," 1988. Also published in Luis N. Rivera-Pagán, Nancy Cardoso Pereira, & Frei Betto, *Liberación y Paz: Perspectivas Teológicas desde América Latina* (Guaynabo, PR: Editorial Sonador, 1988), pp. 9-36.

437. **Rivera-Pagán, Luis N.** "War and Peace in the Third World and the Third World War." In *Towards a Theology of Peace: A Symposium,* edited by Stephen Tunniclife. 230-49. London: European Nuclear Disarmament, 1988. First published in *Towards a Theology of Peace: Preparatory Papers of the Second International Budapest Seminar,* (Budapest, Hungary: Reformed Theological Seminary, 1987), 76-95.

438. **Rivera-Pagán, Luis N.** *Senderos Teológicos: El Pensamiento Evangélico Puertorriqueño.* Río Piedras, PR: Editorial La Reforma, 1989. 197 pp.

439. **Rivera-Pagán, Luis N.** "Nuclear Apocalypse and Metanoia: Christian Theology in the Light of Hiroshima and Nagasaki." *Apuntes: Reflexiones Teológicas desde el Margen Hispano* 10, no. 3 (1990): 59-69. Also published in Justo L. González, ed., *Voces: Voices from the Hispanic Church* (Nashville, TN: Abingdon Press, 1992), pp. 101-11, and Roger Williamson, ed., *Images of the End & Christian Theology* (Uppsala, Sweden: Life and Peace Institute, 1990), pp. 41-52.

440. **Rivera-Pagán, Luis N.** "El Descubrimiento y la Conquista de América: Una Empresa Misionera Imperial." *Pasos* segunda época, no. 41 (May-June 1992): 1-10. Also published in *Casabe,* no. 4 (1992): 11-27.

441. **Rivera-Pagán, Luis N.** *Evangelización y Violencia: La Conquista de América.* 3rd ed. San Juan, PR: Ediciones Cemí, 1992.

442. **Rivera-Pagán, Luis N.** "A New Word and a New Church." *New Conversations* 14, no. 2 (1992): 16-20.

443. **Rivera-Pagán, Luis N.** "Prophecy and Patriotism: A Tragic Dilemma." *Apuntes: Reflexiones Teológicas desde el Margen Hispano* 12, no. 2 (1992): 49-64.

444. **Rivera-Pagán, Luis N.** *A Violent Evangelism: The Political and Religious Conquest of the Américas.* Louisville, KY: Westminster/John Knox Press, 1992. 357 pp.

445. **Rivera-Pagán, Luis N.** "Formation of a Hispanic American Theology: The *Capitulations of Burgos.*" In *Hidden Stories: Unveiling the History of the Latino Church,* edited by Daniel Rodríguez-Díaz and David Cortés-Fuentes. 67-97. Decatur, GA: AETH, 1994. Also published in Spanish as "Las Capitulaciones de Burgos: Paradigma de las Paradojas de la Cristiandad Colonial." *Apuntes: Reflexiones Teológicas desde el Margen Hispano* 13, no. 1 (1993): 30-48 and *Exégesis* (Colegio Universitario de Humacao, Puerto Rico) 6, no. 6 (1993): 2-11.

446. **Rivera-Pagán, Luis N.** "Migajas Teológicas: Breves Reflexiones Sobre la Producción Teológica Protestante Puertorriqueña." *El Boletín* Special Issue (October 1994): 4-18.

447. **Rivera-Pagán, Luis N.** "The Penitential Doctrine of Restitution: Its Use by Bartolomé de Las Casas to Liberate Popular Religiosity during the Conquest of America." In *An Enduring Flame: Studies on Latino Popular Religiosity,* edited by Anthony M. Stevens-Arroyo and Ana María Díaz-Stevens. 97-112. Vol. 1 of PARAL Studies Series. New York: Bildner Center for Western Hemisphere Studies, 1994.

448. **Rivera-Pagán, Luis N.** "Los Sueños del Ciervo: Justicia, Paz y

Esperanza Solidaria." *Pasos* segunda época, no. 58, (1995): 1-11. Also published in *Cristianismo y Sociedad* 33, no. 123 (1995): 19-39.

449. **Rivera-Pagán, Luis N.** *Los Sueños del Ciervo: Perspectivas Teológicas desde el Caribe.* San Juan, PR: Equipo de Historia y Sociología del Protestantismo en Puerto Rico; Programa de Educación y Teología del Concilio Evangélico de Puerto Rico, 1995. 103 pp.

450. **Rivera-Pagán, Luis N.** "Anotaciones Críticas a la Hermenéutica Bíblica de la Teología Latinoamericana de Liberación: Hacia una Teología de la Paz." *Talleres* 3, nos. 3-4 (n.d.): 93-108.

451. **Rivera-Pagán, Luis N., Nancy Cardoso Pereira, and Frei Betto.** *Liberación y Paz: Perspectivas Teológicas desde América Latina.* Guaynabo, PR: Editorial Sonador, 1988.

452. **Rivera-Pagán, Luis N. and Raúl Vidales, eds.** *La Esperanza en el Presente de América Latina.* San José, Costa Rica: DEI, 1983.

453. **Rodríguez, Angel Manuel.** *La Teología de la Epístola a los Hebreos.* Mayagüez, PR: Antillian College, 1983. 162 pp.

454. **Rodríguez, Angel Manuel.** "Nothing to Bring." *Adventist Review,* 24 June 1983, 8-11.

455. **Rodríguez, Angel Manuel.** "Sanctuary Theology in the Book of Exodus." *Andrews University Seminary Studies* 24, no. 2 (1986): 127-45.

456. **Rodríguez, Angel Manuel.** "Cristo: Mediador e Intercesor." *El Ministerio,* vol. 35, nos. 207-208 (1987).

457. **Rodríguez, Angel Manuel.** *Podemos Hablar con Dios.* Nampa, ID: Pacific Press, 1988. 7 pp.

458. **Rodríguez, Angel Manuel.** "Salvation by Sacrificial Substitution." *Journal of the Adventist Theological Society* 3, no. 1 (1992): 49-77.

459. **Rodríguez, Angel Manuel.** "Health and Healing in the Pentateuch." In *Health 2000 and Beyond: A Study Conference of Adventist Theology, Philosophy, and Practice of Health and Healing.* 17-29. Silver Spring, MD: Home Study International Press, 1994.

460. **Rodríguez, Angel Manuel.** *Stewardship Roots—Toward a Theology of Stewardship, Tithe and Offerings.* Silver Spring, MD: Church Ministries, 1994. 69 pp.

461. **Rodríguez, Angel Manuel.** *Esther: A Theological Approach.* Berrien Springs, MI: Andrews University Press, 1995. 162 pp.

462. **Rodríguez, José David.**"Theology from the Underside of History: The Perspective of Liberation Theology." *Lutheran Theological Seminary Bulletin* 68, no. 1 (1988): 16-30. Discussion on pp. 31-35.

463. **Rodríguez, José David.** "De 'Apuntes' a 'Esbozo': Diez Años de Reflexión." *Apuntes: Reflexiones Teológicas desde el Margen Hispano* 10, no. 4 (1990): 75-83.

464. **Rodríguez, José David.** "The Challenge of Hispanic Ministry (Reflections on John 4)." *Currents in Theology and Mission* 18, no. 6 (1991): 420-26.

465. **Rodríguez, José David.** "Breaking Down Barriers." *Apuntes: Reflexiones Teológicas desde el Margen Hispano* 13, no. 4 (1993): 203-12.

466. **Rodríguez, José David.** *Introducción a la Teología.* San José, Costa Rica: DEI, 1993.

467. **Rodríguez, José David.** "Hispanic Theology's Foundational Challenges." In *Hidden Stories: Unveiling the History of the Latino Church,* edited by Daniel R. Rodríguez and David Cortés-Fuentes. 125-29. Decatur, GA: AETH, 1994.

468. **Rodríguez, José D.** *Relectura de la Teología de Lutero desde el Contexto del Tercer Mundo.* México: Publicaciones El Faro, 1994.

469. **Rodríguez Rivera, José David.** *El Precio de la Vocación Profética.* México: Publicaciones El Faro, 1994.

470. **Rodríguez-Díaz, Daniel R. and David Cortés-Fuentes, eds.** *Hidden Stories: Unveiling the History of the Latino Church.* Decatur, GA: AETH, 1994. 165 pp.

471. **Rosado, Caleb.** "The Significance of Galilee to the Mission of the Hispanic Church." Presented at the "First Annual Hispanic Convocation Lectures," Hispanic Studies and Ministry Program, Eastern Baptist Theological Seminary, Philadelphia, PA, October 1983. pp. 13-25.

472. **Rosado, Caleb.** "Black and African Theologies of Liberation: Marxian and Weberian Perspectives." *Journal of Religious Thought* 42 (Spring-Summer 1985): 22-37.

473. **Rosado, Caleb.** "The Significance of Galilee." *Lake Union Ministerial Digest* 3, no. 2 (1985): 11-22.

474. **Rosado, Caleb.** "The Deceptive Theology of Institutionalism." *Ministry* 60, no. 11 (1987): 9-12.

475. **Rosado, Caleb.** "The Nature of Society and the Challenge to the Mission of the Church." *International Review of Mission* 77 (January 1988): 22-37.

476. **Rosado, Caleb.** "The Church, the City, and the Compassionate Christ." *Apuntes: Reflexiones Teológicas desde el Margen Hispano* 9, no. 2 (1989): 27-35. Also published in Justo L. González, ed, *Voces: Voices from the Hispanic Church.* (Nashville, TN: Abingdon Press, 1992), pp. 72-80.

477. **Rosado, Caleb.** "The Stewardship of Power." *Ministry* (July 1989): 18-20. Also published in *Health and Development* 11, no. 1 (1991): 20-33.

478. **Rosado, Caleb.** "Thoughts on a Puerto Rican Theology of Community." *Apuntes: Reflexiones Teológicas desde el Margen Hispano* 9, no. 1 (1989): 10-12.

479. **Rosado, Caleb.** *Women/Church/God.* Riverside, CA: Loma Linda University Press, 1990.

480. **Rosado, Caleb.** "Affluence and the Advent Hope." *Adventist Review,* 2 January 1992, 18-21.

481. **Rosado, Caleb.** "How Liberating is Theology?" *Message,* January-February 1992, 8-9.

482. **Rosado, Caleb.** "Jesus, the Political Activist." *Adventist Professional* 4, no. 2 (1992): 18-19.

483. **Rosado, Caleb.** "The Role of Liberation Theology on the Social Identity of Latinos." In *Twentieth-Century World Religious Movements in Neo-Weberian Perspective,* edited by W. Swatos, Jr. 195-209. Lewiston, NY: The Edwin Mellen Press, 1992. Also published in *Latino Studies Journal,* vol. 3, no. 3 (1992).

484. **Rosado, Caleb.** "Are You a Part of the Final Generation?" *Message,* March-April 1993, 10-12.

485. **Rosado, Caleb.** "El Papel de la Teología de la Liberación en la Identidad Social de los Latinos." *Cristianismo y Sociedad,* nos. 118-119 (1993-1994): 63-78.

486. **Rosado, Caleb.** "The Sin of Saint Peter—Racism." *Ministry* (June 1994): 7-9.

487. **Rosado, Caleb.** "God's Affirmative Action." *Christianity Today* 39, no. 13 (1995): 34-35. Also published as "Affirmative Action and the Gospel." *Message,* July-August 1995.

488. **Rosado, Caleb.** "United In Christ: Diversity and the Mission of the Church." *Adventist Review,* 22 June 1995, 8-12.

489. **Rosas, Carlos.** "La Música al Servicio del Reino." *Apuntes: Reflexiones Teológicas desde el Margen Hispano* 6, no. 1 (1986): 3-11.

490. **Rossing, John P.** "Mestizaje and Marginality: A Hispanic American Theology." *Theology Today* 45, no. 3 (1988): 293-304.

491. **Runyon, Theodore, ed.** *Wesleyan Theology Today: A Bicentennial Theological Consultation.* Nashville, TN: Kingswood Books, United Methodist Publishing House, 1985. 426 pp.

492. **Salomon, Esaul.** "The Role of Liturgy in Hispanic Lutheran Churches." *Lutheran Forum* 25, no. 2 (1991): 30-31.

493. **Sanchez, Daniel R.** "An Interdisciplinary Approach to Theological Contextualisation with Special Reference to Hispanic Americans." Ph.D. diss., Oxford Centre for Mission Studies, 1991. 466 pp.

494. **Sandín-Fremaint, Pedro A.** "Hacia una Teología Femenista Puertorriqueña." *Apuntes: Reflexiones Teológicas desde el Margen Hispano* 4, no. 2 (1984): 27-37.

495. **Santiago, William Fred.** "Un Hidalgo Iluminado." *Teología y Pastoral Puertorriqueña,* 21 January 1984, 23-28.

496. **Santillana, Fernando.** "¿Refugiados Económicos, o Víctimas?" *Apuntes: Reflexiones Teológicas desde el Margen Hispano* 5, no. 4 (1985): 81-85.

497. **Schipani, Daniel S.** *La Angustia y la Dimensión Trascendente.* Buenos Aires, Argentina: La Aurora, 1969. 153 pp.

498. **Schipani, Daniel S.** *Conscientization and Creativity: Paulo Freire and Christian Education.* Lanham, MD: University Press of America, 1984.

499. **Schipani, Daniel S., ed.** *Los Niños y el Reino.* Bogotá, Colombia: CAEBC, 1987.

500. **Schipani, Daniel S., ed.** *Freedom and Discipleship: Liberation Theology in an Anabaptist Perspective.* Maryknoll, NY: Orbis Books, 1989. 188 pp.

501. **Schipani, Daniel S.** *El Reino de Dios y el Ministerio Educativo de la Iglesia.* San José, Costa Rica, Editorial Caribe, 1983. Reprint, Miami, FL: Editorial Caribe, 1992.

502. **Schipani, Daniel S.** *Theology in the Context of "New World Order."* Amsterdam: Freje Universiteit, 1992.

503. **Schipani, Daniel S.** *Teología del Ministerio Educativo: Perspectivas*

Latinoamericanas. Grand Rapids, MI: William B. Eerdmans Publishing Co.; Buenos Aires, Argentina: Nueva Creación, 1993.

504. **Schipani, Daniel S.** "Liberation Theology and Christian Religious Education." In *Theologies of Religious Education,* edited by Randolph C. Miller. 286-313. Birmingham AL: Religious Education Press, 1995.

505. **Schipani, Daniel S. and Paulo Freire.** *Educación, Libertad y Creatividad.* San Juan, PR: Universidad Interamericana de Puerto Rico; Elkhart, IN: IMS, 1992.

506. **Schkade, Landon.** "The Hispanic Lutheran Cultus: A Bilingual Exposition of Its Biblical-Theological Bases within a Cultural Setting." Master's thesis. Concordia Theological Seminary, 1984. 93 pp.

507. **Segovia, Fernando F.** "A New Manifest Destiny: The Emerging Theological Voice of Hispanic Americans." *Religious Studies Review* 17, no. 2 (1991): 102-9.

508. **Segovia, Fernando F.** "Hispanic American Theology and the Bible: Effective Weapon and Faithful Ally." In *We are a People! Initiatives in Hispanic American Theology,* edited by Roberto S. Goizueta. 21-49. Minneapolis, MN: Fortress Press, 1992.

509. **Segovia, Fernando F., ed.** "Hispanic Americans in Theology and the Church." *Listening: Journal of Religion and Culture* 27, no. 1 (1992): 3-84.

510. **Segovia, Fernando F.** "Two Places and No Place on Which to Stand: Mixture and Otherness in Hispanic American Theology." *Listening: Journal of Religion and Culture* 27, no. 1 (1992): 26-40.

511. **Silva-Gotay, Samuel.** *El Desarrollo del Pensamiento Revolucionario en la Iglesia Latinoamericana Contemporánea y Sus Implicaciones para la Teoría Sociológica de la Religión.* México, D.F.: Universidad Nacional Autónoma de México, 1977.

512. **Silva-Gotay, Samuel.** "Origem e Desemvolvimiento do Pensamento Cristão Revolucionario a Partir da Radicalização da Doutrina Social nas Decadas de 1960 e 1970." In *Historia da Teología na América Latina.* Sao Paulo, Brazil: Edições Paulinas, 1981.

513. **Silva-Gotay, Samuel.** "The Incorporation of Historical Materialism in the Theological Thought of the Theology of Liberation in Latin America and the Caribbean." Presentation given to the Congress on Church and State, the Center for Latin American Studies, Tulane University, New Orleans, April 1982.

514. **Silva-Gotay, Samuel.** *El Pensamiento Cristiano Revolucionario en*

América Latina y el Caribe. 2nd ed. Salamanca: Ediciones Sígueme; San Juan, PR: Editorial Cordillera, 1983. 389 pp.

515. **Silva-Gotay, Samuel.** "La Transformación de la Función Política en el Pensamiento Teológico Caribeño y Latinoamericano." In *Documentos de Trabajo de CISCLA.* San Germán, PR: Universidad Interamericana de San Germán, 1984.

516. **Silva-Gotay, Samuel.** *La Teología de la Liberación: Implicaciones para el Cristianismo y el Marxismo.* 3rd ed. Santo Domingo: Ediciones de CEPAE, 1985. 389 pp.

517. **Silva-Gotay, Samuel.** "El Pensamiento Religioso: La Historización de la Teología Latinoamericana y Sus Consecuencias Políticas." In *América Latina en Sus Ideas,* edited by UNESCO and Siglo XXI. 118-56. México: UNESCO and Siglo XXI, 1986.

518. **Silva-Gotay, Samuel.** "La Incorporación del Instrumental Socio-Analítico del Materialismo Histórico a la Teología de la Liberación." *La Torre, Revista General de la Universidad de Puerto Rico* 34, nos. 131-133 (1986): 89-116.

519. **Silva-Gotay, Samuel.** "La Transformación de la Función Política en el Pensamiento Teológico Caribeño y Latinoamericano." *Revista de Ciencias Sociales de la Universidad de Puerto Rico* 25, nos. 1-2 (1986): 39-78.

520. **Silva-Gotay, Samuel.** *O Pensamento Cristão Revolucionario na América Latina e no Caribe.* Sao Paulo: Editorial Paulinas, 1986. 350 pp.

521. **Silva-Gotay, Samuel.** *El Pensamiento Cristiano Revolucionario en América Latina: Implicaciones de la Teología de la Liberación para la Sociología de la Religión.* 4th ed. Río Piedras, PR: La Editorial Huracán, 1989. 389 pp.

522. **Silva-Gotay, Samuel.** *Christentum und Revolution in Lateinamerika und der Karibik: Die Bedeutung der Theologie der Befreiung für eine Soziologie der Religion.* Vol. 17 of Würzburger Studien zur Fundamentaltheologie, edited by Elmar Klinger. Berlin: Peter Lang, 1995. 465 pp.

523. **Solivan, Samuel.** "Orthopathos: Interlocutor between Orthodoxy and Praxis." *Andover Newton Review* 1, no. 2 (1990): 19-25.

524. **Solivan, Samuel.** "Orthopathos: Prolegomenon for a North American Hispanic Theology." Ph.D. diss., Union Theological Seminary, 1993. 258 pp.

525. **Soliván-Román, Samuel.** "The Need for a North American Hispanic Theology." *Listening: Journal of Religion and Culture* 27, no. 1 (1992): 17-25.

526. **Soltero, Conrado G., ed.** *La Iglesia Hispana en Misión.* New York: National Program Division, General Board of Global Ministries, The United Methodist Church, 1992. 80 pp.

527. **Soltero, Conrado G.** "Nuestra Misión y el Alcance a la Comunidad: Un Modelo Misional." In *La Iglesia Hispana en Misión,* edited by Conrado G. Soltero. 13-23. New York: National Program Division, General Board of Global Ministries, The United Methodist Church, 1992.

528. **Soltero, Conrado G. and Finees Flores.** "Capacitando a los Santos." Paper presented at the "Hispanic Symposium on Ministries of the Hispanic Church," held at Perkins School of Theology, Dallas, TX, November 1978.

529. **Soto, Juan S.** "El Buen Samaritano desde el Margen Hispano." *Apuntes: Reflexiones Teológicas desde el Margen Hispano* 4, no. 2 (1984): 38-40.

530. **Soto, Juan S.** "En Torno a la Transfiguración." *Apuntes: Reflexiones Teológicas desde el Margen Hispano* 6, no. 2 (1986): 40-43.

531. **Statello, Esteban D.** "Towards a Theology for Critical Consciousness." D.Min. Project Report. American Baptist Seminary of the West, 1975.

532. **Stevens-Arroyo, Antonio M., ed.** *Prophets Denied Honor: An Anthology of the Hispanic Church in the United States.* Maryknoll, NY: Orbis Books, 1980. 379 pp.

533. **Stevens-Arroyo, Anthony M. and Gilbert Cadena, eds.** *Old Masks, New Faces: Religion and Latino Identities.* Vol. 2 of PARAL Studies Series. New York: Bildner Center for Western Hemisphere Studies, 1995. 196 pp.

534. **Stevens-Arroyo, Anthony M. and Segundo Pantoja, eds.** *Discovering Latino Religion: A Comprehensive Social Science Bibliography.* Vol. 4 of PARAL Studies Series. New York: Bildner Center for Western Hemisphere Studies, 1995. 142 pp.

535. **Sturni, Gary K.** "Models of Theological Education for Hispanic Candidates for Ordination in the Episcopal Church." D.Min. Project Report. San Francisco Theological Seminary, 1986. 322 pp.

536. **Sylvest, Edwin E.** "The Hispanic American Church: Contextual Considerations/La Iglesia Hispano Americana: Consideraciones

Contextuales." *Perkins Journal* 29, no. 1 (1975): English: 22-31; Spanish: 66-75.

537. **Sylvest, Edwin E., Jr.** "Wesley desde el Margen Hispano." *Apuntes: Reflexiones Teológicas desde el Margen Hispano* 1, no. 2 (1981): 14-18.

538. **Sylvest, Edwin E., Jr.** "Rethinking the 'Discovery' of the Américas: A Provisional Historico-Theological Reflection." *Apuntes: Reflexiones Teológicas desde el Margen Hispano* 7, no. 1 (1987): 3-13.

539. **Sylvest, Edwin E., Jr.** *Amen al Extranjero.* New York: United Methodist Committee on Relief, General Board of Global Ministries and the General Board of Church and Society, The United Methodist Church, 1988.

540. **Sylvest, Edwin E., Jr.** *To Love the Neighbor.* New York: United Methodist Committee on Relief, General Board of Global Ministries and the General Board of Church and Society, The United Methodist Church, 1988.

541. **Támez, Elsa.** *Contra Toda Condena.* San José, Costa Rica: DEI, 1991.

542. **Tinoco, David A.** "Strategies for Effective Hispanic Ministries in Southern California by The United Methodist Church." D.Min Project Report. Fuller Theological Seminary, 1989. 132 pp.

543. **Traverzo, David.** "Towards a Theology of Mission in the U.S. Puerto Rican Migrant Community: From Captivity to Liberation." *Apuntes: Reflexiones Teológicas desde el Margen Hispano* 9, no. 3 (1989): 51-57.

544. **Traverzo, David.** "A Paradigm for Contemporary Latino Thought and Praxis: Orlando E. Costas' Latino Radical Evangelical Approach." *Latino Studies Journal* 5, no. 3 (1994): 103-31.

545. **Traverzo Galarza, David.** "A New Dimension in Religious Education for the Hispanic Evangelical Church in New York City." Master's thesis. New Brunswick Theological Seminary, 1979.

546. **Traverzo Galarza, David.** "The Emergence of a Latino Radical Evangelical Social Ethic in the Work and Thought of Orlando E. Costas: An Ethico-Theological Discourse from the Underside of History." Ph.D. diss., Drew University, 1992. 378 pp.

547. **Trinidad, Saúl.** "Apuntes Hacia una Pastoral Hispana." *Apuntes: Reflexiones Teológicas desde el Margen Hispano* 8, no. 1 (1988): 3-15.

548. **Trinidad, Saúl.** "Perfil Pastoral para el Siglo 21." *Apuntes: Reflexiones Teológicas desde el Margen Hispano* 13, no. 1 (1993): 118-25.

549. **Trovall, Carl C.** "Citizenship and Community: Proposition 187 and the Church." Dallas, TX. Southern Methodist University, 1995. Manuscript.

550. **Vasquez, Raul A.** "Contextualized Theological Education: Development and Implementation of a Basic Pastoral Skills Training Retreat for Texas Hispanics." D.Min Project Report. Golden Gate Baptist Theological Seminary, 1988. 170 pp.

551. **Verkuyl, Johannes.** *Contemporary Missiology: An Introduction.* Translated and edited by Dale Cooper. Grand Rapids, MI: William B. Eerdmans Publishing Co., 1978. References to Orlando E. Costas on pp. 286, 294, 297.

552. **Villafañe, Eldin.** "Toward an Hispanic American Pentecostal Social Ethic, with Special Reference to North Eastern United States." Ph.D. diss., Boston University, 1989. 493 pp.

553. **Villafañe, Eldin.** "An Evangelical Call to a Social Spirituality: Confronting Evil in Urban Society." *Apuntes: Reflexiones Teológicas desde el Margen Hispano* 11, no. 2 (1991): 27-38.

554. **Villafañe, Eldin.** *The Liberating Spirit: Toward an Hispanic American Pentecostal Social Ethic.* Lanham, MD: University Press of America, 1992. 257 pp.

555. **Villafañe, Eldin, and others.** *Seek the Peace of the City: Reflections on Urban Ministry.* Grand Rapids, MI: William B. Eerdmans Publishing Co., 1995.

556. **Weiss, Herold.** "The Theological Task." *Spectrum* 1, no. 4 (1969): 13-22.

557. **Weiss, Herold.** "Are SDAs Protestants?" *Spectrum* 3, no. 2 (1972): 69-78.

558. **Weiss, Herold.** "Genesis, Chapter One: A Theological Statement." *Spectrum* 9, no. 4 (1979): 54-62.

559. **Weiss, Herold.** "Christ Event." In *The Westminster Dictionary of Christian Theology,* edited by Alan Richardson and John Bowden. 93-94. Philadelphia, PA: Westminster Press, 1983.

560. **Weiss, Herold.** "Restoration of All Things." In *The Westminster Dictionary of Christian Theology,* edited by Alan Richardson and John Bowden. 500-501. Philadelphia, PA: Westminster Press, 1983.

561. **Weiss, Herold.** "Adventism as Both/And, not Either/Or." *Spectrum* 23, no. 4 (1994): 28-35.

562. **Weiss, Herold.** "Where the Catholic Church Does its Thinking." *Adventist Today,* vol. 2, no. 4 (1994).

563. **Youngman, Nilah M.** "Affirming Hispanic Women." D.Min Project Report. Austin Presbyterian Theological Seminary, 1993. 125 pp.

564. **Zambrano, Ariel.** "Content and Context of Evangelization: An Hispanic Perspective." D.Min. Project Report. Claremont School of Theology, 1986. 115 pp.

565. **[Hispanic Ecumenical Theological Project in the Américas].** "Final Statement." In *Consultation of the Hispanic Project: Theology in the Américas,* held in New York, 1978.

566. "Report from the Working Group on Racism-Classism-Sexism." In *Women's Spirit Bonding,* edited by Janet Kalven and Mary I. Buckley. 125-36. New York: Pilgrim Press, 1984.

567. "Redescubrimiento: Five Centuries of Hispanic American Christianity 1492-1992 [Symposium I]." A symposium held at Perkins School of Theology, Dallas, TX, January 1987. Working papers published in *Apuntes: Reflexiones Teológicas desde el Margen Hispano* 7, no. 1 (1987): 3-23; 7, no. 3 (1987): 51-70; 8, no. 1 (1988): 3-23; 8, no. 2 (1988): 38-46.

568. "Redescubrimiento: Five Centuries of Hispanic American Christianity 1492-1992 [Symposium II]." A symposium held at Perkins School of Theology, Dallas, TX, October 1989. Working papers published in *Apuntes: Reflexiones Teológicas desde el Margen Hispano* 9, no. 4 (1989): 75-92; 10, no. 1 (1990): 3-16.

569. "Redescubrimiento: Five Centuries of Hispanic American Christianity 1492-1992 [Symposium III]." A symposium held at Perkins School of Theology, Dallas, TX, November 1992. Working papers published in *Apuntes: Reflexiones Teológicas desde el Margen Hispano* 13, no. 1 (1993): 4-131.

570. *Teología de la Evangelización, Bibliografía Selecta.* Seminario Bíblico Latinoamericano. San José, Costa Rica. n.d.

The Hispanic Perspective in Biblical Studies
Francisco García-Treto

The bibliographical list here introduced must be considered a partial and preliminary sketch of a listing of Biblical studies produced by Hispanic Protestants in the United States. This is so in a sense that goes beyond the obvious one in which every bibliography which addresses work in progress must always be considered preliminary. Hispanic Protestantism in the United States is itself very much a work in progress, seeking to define itself even as the community of U.S. Hispanic/Latinos seeks its own definition. Hispanic Protestants include in their identities their diverse national backgrounds, challenges of the several diasporas, and increasingly, their experience as a United States-born generation.

The list of material in this section is partial also in the sense that, even while it seeks to represent works produced by United States Hispanic/Latino Protestants (construed in the wider sense which includes a variety of *evangélicos* from mainline/old line Protestants to Pentecostals), it leaves out the essential contribution and in many cases collaboration, which post-Vatican II Roman Catholic Hispanic/Latino scholars have offered to the Protestant community. The work of Virgilio Elizondo, Ada María Isasi-Díaz, Fernando Segovia, Roberto Goizueta and others too numerous to mention is an important part of the ongoing dialogue in which the authors represented in our list live and move and have their being. That this conversation between Catholic and Protestant authors is truly cooperative needs no more telling example than to look at the composition of the Editorial Board and the Board of Contributing Editors of the *Journal of Hispanic/Latino Theology*. This journal, which is ostensibly a Catholic publication, is the major journal in Hispanic/Latino theological scholarship in the United States today. Yet many of the Protestant authors in our bibliography are contributing editors: Justo L. González, José D. Rodríguez and Samuel Soliván are on the editorial board and Francisco O. García-Treto, Justo L. González, Luis N. Rivera-Pagán, José D. Rodríguez and Eldin Villafañe are contributing editors.

Only a short time ago, a bibliography of this sort would have been short indeed. While things are changing rapidly, there are still relatively few United States Hispanic Protestant scholars in the field of Biblical Studies. Until very recently, academic biblical studies have been the unchallenged ground of Historical-Critical methodologies, which tended to focus more "behind" the text than on the text itself, and have been ruled by the assumption of the universal validity of those so-called scientific approaches. Useful, indeed essential, as the results of the Historical-Critical method have been and continue to be, their ground is no longer unchallenged.

The challenges, diverse as they are, have been almost invariably helpful in increasing the visibility of Hispanic/Latino scholars in the field of Biblical Studies, and in attracting new Hispanic/Latino aspirants to the field. From Latin American Liberation Theology, as well as from Feminist thought, the hegemony of the "culture-neutral, universal validity" approach has been challenged as an Anglo-European white male academic exercise. Readings "from above"—that is, the Academy telling the Church about the Bible—are increasingly regarded as needing to be in dialogue with the kind of readings "from below," which the ecclesial base communities of Latin America taught us to notice. Literary-theoretical analyses of the Bible, using methods now clearly established in the Academy, have provided a needed corrective counterweight to the archaizing and atomizing tendencies of much of the Historical-Critical method. Literary theory has brought a new emphasis on the reader, and of the reader's social location, as crucial in the construction of the meaning of texts, the Bible included. More important for the work of the group of scholars represented in this volume, literary analysis brought hermeneutics to the forefront of an academic field which had for decades distanced itself from it, at least overtly. It is relevant to our discussion to note that, for example, the Society of Biblical Literature now has a section on "The Reading of the Bible in Asia, Africa and Latin America," or that the *New Interpreter's Bible* introductory volume contains substantive articles on "Reading the Bible as..." (African Americans, Asian Americans, Native Americans and Women), including one on "Reading the Bible as Hispanic Americans" by Fernando Segovia.

This paradigm shift in Biblical Studies, in convergence with the rise of what can be called a Hispanic/Latino identity in the United States has already produced theoretical fruit, as can be seen most notably in Justo L. González' proposal of a hermeneutical stance which he calls 'reading the Bible in Spanish." That proposal was presented as part of *Mañana: Christian Theology from a Hispanic Perspective* (1990). In *Santa Biblia: The Bible through Hispanic Eyes* (1996), González surveys several other hermeneutical proposals recently made by United States Hispanic/Latino scholars, both Catholic and Protestant, which complement his own. A salient characteristic of Hispanic/Latino Biblical scholarship, exemplified perhaps most markedly by González' work, is that it often comes from writers who, while provided with impeccable academic credentials in one discipline, tend to transgress the disciplinary borders erected by the Academy; they write both for the Academy and for the Church. While it could be argued that a major reason for this is the relative scarcity of Hispanic/Latino scholars active in any of the traditional academic fields, and the consequently heavier demands placed upon them to meet the needs of both the academic and ecclesial communities, this is not the whole reason. For many, if not most, of the authors here represented, the Bible is immediately foundational to all the "theological' disciplines, a resource which refused to remain pigeonholed in any single academic field. A reading of González' commentary on the Book of Acts (*Hechos: Comentario Bíblico Hispano Americano*) illustrates this point eloquently. *Hechos* is a work of Biblical exegesis by a church historian who manages to comment on the ancient text, expertly reading it while at the same time letting the text "read us," that is, finding at every turn what it has to say to those who would read it "through Hispanic eyes." Or, to use Eldin Villafañe's expression in *Seek the Peace of the City: Reflections on Urban Ministry*, it is critical for the Hispanic/Latino guild of theological scholars that scholarship be always "*Sierva, Santificadora* and *Sanadora*" (servant, sanctifier and healer). *Seek the Peace of the City*, ostensibly a book on urban ministry, belongs in this bibliography of Biblical Studies because it includes a chapter written by New Testament scholar Efraín Agosto ("Paul, Leadership and the Hispanic Church") and is grounded throughout on a contextualized reading of the New Testament.

    Examples could be multiplied that demonstrate that the era when translation—mostly of antiquated conservative English theological literature, in our case usually Bible dictionaries and commentaries—was the major method for attempting to produce resources that could feed the Hispanic churches, is coming to an end. The new scholarship of the Hispanic/Latino community is as bilingual as that community and its churches. But whether written in English or in Spanish, the new work is increasingly the result of reading the Bible "through Hispanic eyes." The vitality of this scholarship and of its products will, it is hoped, continue to increase as the United States Hispanic/Latino community continues to define and to find itself, and as its churches increasingly seek to hear and to speak the gospel to that community "in Spanish." For this reason, the bibliography here presented should indeed be always incomplete, a work in progress for the present and for the foreseeable future.

Biblical Studies Bibliography

571. **Agosto, Efraín.** "Paul, Leadership, and the Hispanic Church." *Urban Mission* 10, no. 4 (1993): 6-20.

572. **Aragón, Rafael J.** "La Realidad Histórica y Existencial del Advenimiento de Jesucristo." *Apuntes: Reflexiones Teológicas desde el Margen Hispano* 2, no. 4 (1982): 85-88.

573. **Armendáriz, Rubén P.** "Estad Pues Firmes: Estudio Bíblico." *Apuntes: Reflexiones Teológicas desde el Margen Hispano* 2, no. 2 (1982): 27-30.

574. **Benko, Stephen.** *Los Evangélicos, los Católicos y la Virgen María.* 4th ed. El Paso, TX: Casa Bautista de Publicaciones, 1993. 165 pp.

575. **Besançon-Spencer, Aida and William David Spencer.** *Joy through the Night: Biblical Resources for Suffering People.* Downers Grove, IL: Intervarsity Press, 1994. 252 pp.

576. **Candelaria, Michael.** "Justice: Extrapolations from the Concept *Mishpat* in the Book of Micah." *Apuntes: Reflexiones Teológicas desde el Margen Hispano* 3, no. 4 (1983): 75-81.

577. **Carcaño, Minerva Garza.** "Una Perspectiva Bíblico-Teológica Sobre la Mujer en el Ministerio Ordenado." *Apuntes: Reflexiones Teológicas desde el Margen Hispano* 10, no. 2 (1990): 27-35.

578. **Carson, Keith.** "The Mission of the Church according to Orlando Costas: A Biblical and Historical Evaluation." Master's thesis. Trinity Evangelical Divinity School, 1984. 104 pp.

579. **Chakarsi, George.** "Bridging the Cultural Gap between Parents and Children of Hispanic Descent Living in the United States." D.Min. Project Report. Talbot School of Theology, Biola University, 1991. 150 pp.

580. **Cintrón-Figueroa, Jorge Nehemías.** "The Use of the Bible in Selected Materials of the Hispanic-American Evangelical Curriculum." Ph.D. diss., Boston University, 1969. 241 pp.

581. **Collinson-Streng, P. and Ismael de la Tejera.** "Bible and Mission in a Hispanic Congregation." In *Bible and Mission: Biblical Foundations and Working Models for Congregational Ministry,* edited by Wayne Stumme. 129-37. Mission in the U.S.A. Minneapolis, MN: Augsburg Publishing House, 1986.

582. **Cook, A. William.** "The Power and the Powerlessness: The Pastoral Vocation of the Hispanic Church in the USA." *Evangelical Review of Theology* 9, no. 2 (1985): 156-65.

583. **Cortés, Luis.** "Seeking the Welfare of the City, Jeremiah 29:5-7: A Study for Hispanic Church Planting and Development." Eastern Baptist Theological Seminary. Philadelphia, PA, 1982.

584. **Cortés-Fuentes, David.** "El Mensaje Apocalíptico de Pablo en Primera de Tesalonicenses como un Medio de Esperanza." *Apuntes: Reflexiones Teológicas desde el Margen Hispano* 13, no. 3 (1993): 190-97.

585. **Cortés-Fuentes, David.** "Reacción al Artículo de Justo L. González." In *Lumbrera a Nuestro Camino,* edited by Pablo A. Jiménez. 119-24. Miami, FL: Editorial Caribe, 1994.

586. **Costas, Orlando, E.** "Contextualization and Incarnation." *Journal of Theology for Southern Africa* 29, no. 29 (1979): 23-30.

587. **Costas, Orlando.** "Evangelism from the Periphery: The Universality of Galilee." *Apuntes: Reflexiones Teológicas desde el Margen Hispano* 2, no. 4 (1982): 75-84.

588. **Costas, Orlando E.** "El Mensaje de los Profetas y la Evangelización de las Naciones." San José, Costa Rica. Seminario Bíblico Latinoamericano, n.d. 7 pp. Mimeographed.

589. **Costas, Orlando E.** "El Llamado de Abrahán y la Evangelización de las Naciones." *En Marcha Internacional* 19 (1972): 14-15.

590. **Costas, Orlando E.** "Aspectos Sobresalientes del Ministerio de Jesús y Sus Implicaciones para la Evangelización." In *Hacia una Teología de la Evangelización,* edited by Orlando E. Costas. 35-44. Buenos Aires, Argentina: Editorial La Aurora, 1973.

591. **Costas, Orlando E.** "El Llamamiento de Israel y la Evangelización de las Naciones." In *Hacia una Teología de la Evangelización,* edited by Orlando E. Costas. 19-23. Buenos Aires, Argentina: Editorial La Aurora, 1973.

592. **Costas, Orlando E.** "El Mensaje de los Profetas y la Evangelización." In *Hacia una Teología de la Evangelización,* edited by Orlando E. Costas. 25-33. Buenos Aires, Argentina: Editorial La Aurora, 1973.

593. **Costas, Orlando E.** "Evangelism as a Total Task: A Look into Jesus' Evangelistic Ministry." 1977. 39 pp. Mimeographed.

594. **Costas, Orlando E.** "Responding to the Challenge of Change (Acts

16:8ff)." Audio recording. Pasadena, CA: Fuller Theological Seminary, 1977.

595. **Costas, Orlando E.** "The Great Commission: History and Horizons." Audiotaped address at Union Theological Seminary, Richmond VA, 15 February 1980.

596. **Costas, Orlando E.** Prólogo a *Opresión, Pobreza y Liberación: Reflexiones Bíblicas,* by Tomás Hanks. San José, Costa Rica: Editorial Caribe, 1982.

597. **Costas, Orlando E.** "Esther: Spokesperson for a Minority (Esther 4:14)." Audiotaped lecture. Pasadena, CA: Fuller Theological Seminary, 1982.

598. **Costas, Orlando E.** "Evangelism as Story-Sharing." Audio recording. Alumnae Lectures. Atlanta GA: Protestant Radio and Television Center, 1982.

599. **Costas, Orlando E.** "Evangelism from the Periphery: A Galilean Model." *Apuntes: Reflexiones Teológicas desde el Margen Hispano* 2, no. 3 (1982): 53-59.

600. **Costas, Orlando E.** "Christian Mission from the Periphery." *Faith and Mission* 1, no. 1 (1983): 1-14.

601. **Costas, Orlando E.** "Witnessing in a Divided World." *International Review of Mission* 72, no. 288 (1983): 631-35.

602. **Costas, Orlando E.** "Wonder, Unbelief, Rejection: Jesus Visits His Home Town." *One World,* no. 96 (June 1984): 18-20.

603. **Costas, Orlando E.** "Waiting on God." In *E. T. Earl Lectures. Sermon on Acts 16:6-10.* Berkeley, CA: Pacific School of Religion, 1985. Video Recording.

604. **Costas, Orlando E.** "The Subversiveness of Faith: Esther as a Paradigm for a Liberating Theology." *The Ecumenical Review* 40, no. 1 (1988): 66-78.

605. **Costas, Orlando E.** "Meditation [Esther 4:14]." *One World,* no. 4 (November 1989): 4.

606. **Costas, Orlando E.** "Evangelism from the Periphery: The Universality of Galilee." In *Voces: Voices from the Hispanic Church,* edited by Justo L. González. 16-23. Nashville, TN: Abingdon Press, 1992.

607. **Cotto-Pérez, Irving.** "The Design and Implementation of a Strategy for a Congregational Mission in Hispanic Churches in the Eastern Pennsylvania Conference of The United Methodist Church." D.Min. Project Report. Eastern Baptist Theological Seminary, 1986. 240 pp.

608. **Elizondo, Javier.** "The Use of the Bible in the Moral Deliberation of Liberation Theologians: An Examination of the Works of Leonardo Boff, José Miguez Bonino, and Porfirio Miranda." Ph.D. diss., Baylor University, 1988. 216 pp.

609. **Elizondo, Virgilio.** *Galilean Journey: The Mexican-American Promise.* Maryknoll, NY: Orbis Books, 1983. 147 pp.

610. **Elizondo, Virgilio P.** *Mestizaje: The Dialectic of Cultural Birth and the Gospel.* San Antonio, TX: Mexican American Cultural Center, 1978.

611. **Escobar, Samuel.** *"Forward in the Fullness of Mission": The 1988 CMS Annual Sermon Preached on 25 October 1988.* London: Church Missionary Society, 1988. 13 pp.

612. **Feliciano, Juan G.** "Gustavo Gutiérrez' Liberation Theology: Toward a Hispanic Epistemology and Theology of the Suffering of the Poor." *Apuntes: Reflexiones Teológicas desde el Margen Hispano* 13, no. 2 (1993): 151-61.

613. **Ferrari, Nilda.** "El Nuevo Rostro de la Mujer Hispana: Agente y Reto Misional." In *La Iglesia Hispana en Misión,* edited by Conrado G. Soltero. 49-58. New York: National Program Division of the General Board of Global Ministries, The United Methodist Church, 1992.

614. **García-Treto, Francisco.** ""El Señor Guarda a los Emigrantes" (Salmo 146:3)." *Apuntes: Reflexiones Teológicas desde el Margen Hispano* 1, no. 4 (1981): 3-9.

615. **Gaud, Carmen.** "La Biblia y el Desarrollo de Materiales Curriculares." In *Lumbrera a Nuestro Camino,* edited by Pablo A. Jiménez. 155-72. Miami, FL: Editorial Caribe, 1994.

616. **Gillett, R.** "The Amnesty Law: A Biblical Imperative." *Episcopal News,* September 1987, 7.

617. **González, Jorge.** "El Estudio del Antiguo Testamento: Ayer, Hoy y Siempre." In *Lumbrera a Nuestro Camino,* edited by Pablo A. Jiménez. 37-51. Miami, FL: Editorial Caribe, 1994.

618. **González, Jorge A.** *Traductor de la Biblia en Español.* México: Sociedades Bíblicas Unidas, 1969.

619. **González, Jorge A.** "[Varios Artículos]." In *Diccionario Ilustrado de la Biblia,* edited by Wilton M. Nelson. Miami, FL: Editorial Caribe, 1974.

620. **González, Jorge A.** "Nuestra Relación con Dios: Estudio Bíblico." In *Recursos para Programas.* 3-6. Cincinnati, OH: Service Center, Board of Global Ministries, The United Methodist Church, 1977.

621. González, Jorge A. "The Liberating God." In *The Upper Room Disciplines,* edited by Tom Page. 254-60. Nashville, TN: General Board of Discipleship, The United Methodist Church, 1981.

622. González, Jorge A. "The Reina-Valera Bible: From Dream to Reality." *Apuntes: Reflexiones Teológicas desde el Margen Hispano* 1, no. 4 (1981): 10-15.

623. González, Jorge A. "The Offices of Christ: Prophet, Priest, King." *Response* 14, no. 11 (1982): 36-37.

624. González, Jorge A. *Daniel: A Tract for Troubled Times.* New York: Mission Education and Cultivation Program Department of the Women's Division, General Board of Global Ministries, The United Methodist Church, 1985. 135 pp.

625. González, Jorge A. "An Introduction to Biblical Exegesis." In *Scripture: The Word Beyond the Word,* edited by Nancy A. Carter. 9-19. New York: Women's Division, General Board of Global Ministries, The United Methodist Church, 1985.

626. González, Jorge A. "The Sovereignty of God." In *The Upper Room Disciplines,* edited by Tom Page. 137-43. Nashville, TN: General Board of Discipleship, The United Methodist Church, 1985.

627. González, Jorge A. "God: Redeemer and Restorer." In *The Upper Room Disciplines,* edited by Tom Page. 306-12. Nashville, TN: General Board of Discipleship, 1991.

628. González, Jorge A. "The Reina-Valera Bible: From Dream to Reality." In *Voces: Voices from the Hispanic Church,* edited by Justo L. González. 46-49. Nashville, TN: Abingdon Press, 1992.

629. González, Jorge A. "What Does the Covenant Demand?" In *The Upper Room Disciplines,* edited by Glenda Webb. 317-23. Nashville, TN: General Board of Discipleship, 1992.

630. González, Jorge A. "God's Gifts are for All." In *The Upper Room Disciplines,* edited by Glenda Webb. 21-27. Nashville, TN: General Board of Discipleship, 1994.

631. González, Jorge A. "Introduction to the Book of Daniel." Videotaped presentation. Nashville, TN: General Board of Discipleship, The United Methodist Church, n.d.

632. González, Jorge A. "Introduction to the Book of Revelation." Videotaped presentation. Nashville, TN: General Board of Discipleship, The United Methodist Church, n.d.

633. González, Justo L. "Interpreting the Scriptures from the Hispanic Perspective." *Engage/Social Action* 6, no. 6 (1978): 13-18.

634. González, Justo L. "Espiritualidad Política." *Apuntes: Reflexiones Teológicas desde el Margen Hispano* 3, no. 1 (1983): 3-9.

635. González, Justo L. "El Espíritu Santo en el Nuevo Testamento." *The Interpreter* 25, no. 3 (1984): 8-10.

636. González, Justo L. "Let the Dead Gods Bury Their Dead." *Apuntes: Reflexiones Teológicas desde el Margen Hispano* 4, no. 4 (1984): 91-95.

637. González, Justo L. *Juntamente con Cristo: Un Comentario Sobre los Textos de Cuaresma y Semana Santa.* Nashville, TN: Ediciones Discipulado, General Board of Discipleship, The United Methodist Church, 1985.

638. González, Justo L. "Sanctuary: Historical, Legal, and Biblical Considerations." *Apuntes: Reflexiones Teológicas desde el Margen Hispano* 5, no. 2 (1985): 36-47.

639. González, Justo L. *Probad los Espíritus: Un Comentario Sobre los Textos de Adviento y Navidad.* Nashville, TN: Ediciones Discipulado, General Board of Discipleship, The United Methodist Church, 1987.

640. González, Justo L. "Why Do Some Suffer and Others Not?" *SEEDS* 11 (1988): 32.

641. González, Justo L. "Reading the Bible in Spanish." *Apuntes: Reflexiones Teológicas desde el Margen Hispano* 9, no. 2 (1989): 39-46.

642. González, Justo L. "Faith and Wealth in the Early Church." *Biblical Literacy Today* 4, no. 2 (1989-90): 14.

643. González, Justo L. "El Pluralismo en la Iglesia." *El Intérprete* 28, no. 4 (1990): 12-13.

644. González, Justo L. *Faith and Wealth: A History of Early Christian Ideas on the Origin, Significance, and Use of Money.* San Francisco: Harper & Row, 1990. 240 pp.

645. González, Justo L. "Pluralismo, Justicia y Misión: Un Estudio Bíblico Sobre Hechos 6:1-7." *Apuntes: Reflexiones Teológicas desde el Margen Hispano* 10, no. 1 (1990): 3-8.

646. González, Justo L. *Hechos.* Comentario Bíblico Hispanoamericano. Miami, FL: Editorial Caribe, 1992.

647. González, Justo L., ed. *Voces: Voices from the Hispanic Church.* Nashville, TN: Abingdon Press, 1992. 171 pp.

648. González, Justo L. "Comfort in God's Promise." In *Whose Birthday Is It, Anyway? Alternatives* Christmas (1993): 12.

649. González, Justo L. "Finding Joy in Christmas." In *Whose Birthday Is It, Anyway? Alternatives* Christmas (1993): 14.

650. González, Justo L. "The Future is God's." In *WhoseBirthday Is It, Anyway? Alternatives* Christmas (1993): 10.

651. González, Justo L. "God's Holy Family." In *Whose Birthday Is It, Anyway? Alternatives* Christmas (1993): 20.

652. González, Justo L. "He Came to His Own." In *Whose Birthday Is It, Anyway? Alternatives* Christmas (1993): 18.

653. González, Justo L. "The Supreme Surprise." In *Whose Birthday Is It, Anyway? Alternatives* Christmas (1993): 16.

654. González, Justo L. "Which King Will We Follow?" In *Whose Birthday Is It, Anyway? Alternatives* Christmas (1993): 22.

655. González, Justo L. "Reading the Bible in Spanish." *Unidad Cristiana/Christian Unity* 1, no. 1 (1993): 5-9.

656. González, Justo L. "Confusion at Pentecost in Latin American Liberation Theology: Scripture as the Foundation for Freedom." In *The Bible in Theology and Preaching,* edited by Donald K. McKim. 146-49. Nashville, TN: Abingdon Press, 1994.

657. González, Justo L. "Historia de la Interpretación Bíblica." In *Lumbrera a Nuestro Camino,* edited by Pablo A. Jiménez. 79-118. Miami, FL: Editorial Caribe, 1994.

658. González, Justo L. "How the Bible Has Been Interpreted in Christian Tradition." In *The New Interpreter's Bible.* 83-106. Vol. 1. Nashville, TN: Abingdon Press, 1994.

659. González, Justo L. *Journey through the Bible.* Vol. 11. Luke. Nashville, TN: Cokesbury, 1994.

660. González, Justo L. *Journey through the Bible, Leader's Guide.* Vol. 11. Luke. Nashville, TN: Cokesbury, 1994.

661. González, Justo L. *Journey through the Bible.* Vol. 13. Acts of the Apostles. Nashville, TN: Cokesbury, 1995.

662. González, Justo L. *Journey through the Bible, Leader's Guide.* Vol. 13. Acts of the Apostles. Nashville, TN: Cokesbury, 1995.

663. González, Justo L. *Lent, Easter 1996: Scriptures for the Church Seasons.* Nashville, TN: Cokesbury, 1995. 74 pp.

664. González, Justo L. "Reading from My Bicultural Place: Acts 6:1-7." In *Reading from This Place.* Vol. 1. Edited by Fernando F. Segovia and Mary Ann Tolbert. 139-47. Minneapolis, MN: Fortress Press, 1995.

665. González, Justo L. "The Story of Christian Beginnings." *Adult Bible Studies Teacher* 4, no. 1 (1995): 16-80.

666. González, Justo L. and Catherine Gonsalus González. *Sus Almas Engrandecieron al Señor.* Miami, FL: Editorial Caribe, 1977.

667. González, Justo L. and Catherine Gunsalus González. *Their Souls Did Magnify the Lord: Studies on Biblical Women.* Atlanta, GA: John Knox, 1977.

668. González, Justo L. and Catherine Gunsalus González. *Rejoice in Your Savior: A Study for Lent-Easter.* Nashville, TN: Graded Press, 1979.

669. González, Justo L. and Catherine Gunsalus González. "Life at the Dawn of the Kingdom: The Readings from Acts for the Easter Season." In *Social Themes of the Christian Year: A Commentary on the Lectionary,* edited by Dieter T. Hessel. 183-88. Philadelphia, PA: The Geneva Press, 1983.

670. González, Justo L. and Catherine Gunsalus González. *Paul: His Impact on Christianity.* Nashville, TN: Graded Press, 1987.

671. González, Justo L. and Catherine Gunsalus González. *A Faith More Precious Than Gold: A Study of I Peter.* Louisville, KY: Horizons, 1989.

672. González, Justo L. and Catherine Gunsalus González. *Vision at Patmos: A Study of the Book of Revelation.* Abingdon Lay Bible Studies. 1978. Reprint, Nashville, TN: Abingdon Press, 1991. 121 pp.

673. González, Justo L. and Catherine Gunsalus González. *The Liberating Pulpit.* Nashville, TN: Abingdon Press, 1994. 123 pp.

674. Guardiola-Sáenz, Leticia A. "Reacción al Artículo de Ediberto López." In *Lumbrera a Nuestro Camino,* edited by Pablo A. Jiménez. 75-78. Miami, FL: Editorial Caribe, 1994.

675. Isasi-Díaz, Ada María. "The Bible and Mujerista Theology." In *Lift Every Voice: Constructing Christian Theologies from the Underside,* edited by Susan Brooks Thistlethwaite and Mary Potter Engel. 261-269. New York: Harper & Row, 1990.

676. Jiménez, Pablo A. "Diálogo Exegético con Mateo y con Ricardo Foulkes." *Vida y Pensamiento* 7, nos. 1-2 (1987): 68-70.

677. Jiménez, Pablo A. "Cristo es Nuestra Paz: Estudio Exegético." *Vida y Pensamiento* 8, no. 1 (1988): 18-24.

678. **Jiménez, Pablo A.** "¿Qué es la Predicación Bíblica?" *El Educador* Tercera Época 1 (February 1990): 4-7.

679. **Jiménez, Pablo A.** "Bases Bíblicas para la Educación para la Paz." *Casabe* 3 (October 1991): 9-12.

680. **Jiménez, Pablo A.** "Creando una Nueva Humanidad: Reflexión Sobre la Tarea Educativa de la Iglesia Basada en Efesios 4:17-32." *Apuntes: Reflexiones Teológicas desde el Margen Hispano* 11, no. 4 (1991): 75-80.

681. **Jiménez, Pablo A.** "La Gran Comisión." *Apuntes: Reflexiones Teológicas desde el Margen Hispano* 12, no. 4 (1992): 150-61.

682. **Jiménez, Pablo A.** "El Modelo del Líder." *La Biblia en las Américas* 48 #204, no. 1 (1993): 9-11.

683. **Jiménez, Pablo A.** "El Desafío de la Mujer Cananea." *La Biblia en las Américas* 49 #211, no. 2 (1994): 13-15.

684. **Jiménez, Pablo A.** "Estudio Bíblico y Hermenéutica: Implicaciones Homiléticas." In *Lumbrera a Nuestro Camino,* edited by Pablo A. Jiménez. 125-48. Miami, FL: Editorial Caribe, 1994.

685. **Jiménez, Pablo A., ed.** *Lumbrera a Nuestro Camino.* Miami, FL: Editorial Caribe, 1994. 179 pp.

686. **Jiménez, Pablo A.** "El Cristo Resucitado en el Apocalipsis." *La Biblia en las Américas* 50 #217, no. 2 (1995): 14-16.

687. **Jiménez, Pablo A.** "In Search of a Hispanic Model of Biblical Interpretation." *Journal of Hispanic/Latino Theology* 3, no. 2 (1995): 44-64.

688. **Jiménez, Pablo A.** "The Use of the Bible in Hispanic Theology." D.Min. Project Report. Columbia Theological Seminary, 1995. 139 pp.

689. **López, Ediberto.** "The Earliest Traditions about Jesus and Social Stratification." Ph.D. diss., Drew University, 1992. 283 pp.

690. **López, Ediberto.** "El Estado Actual de las Investigaciones Sobre el Nuevo Testamento." In *Lumbrera a Nuestro Camino,* edited by Pablo A. Jiménez. 61-74. Miami, FL: Editorial Caribe, 1994.

691. **López, Ediberto.** "Los Métodos Exegéticos." In *Lumbrera a Nuestro Camino,* edited by Pablo A. Jiménez. 17-36. Miami, FL: Editorial Caribe, 1994.

692. **López, Hugo.** "Toward a Theology of Migration." *Apuntes: Reflexiones Teológicas desde el Margen Hispano* 2, no. 3 (1982): 68-71.

693. **Luna, David.** "Patterns of Faith: Woven Together in Life and Mission." *American Baptist Quarterly* 5, no. 4 (1986): 393-97.

694. **Madriz, Esther.** "Nuestra Responsabilidad Social Cristiana: ¿Opción o Mandato Bíblico?" In *La Iglesia Hispana en Misión,* edited by Conrado G. Soltero. 6-12. New York: National Program Division, General Board of Global Ministries, The United Methodist Church, 1992.

695. **Maldonado, David, Jr.** "Faith, Peace, and Courage." In *The Upper Room Disciplines,* edited by Tom Page. 122-28. Nashville, TN: The Upper Room, 1987.

696. **Maldonado, David, Jr.** "Freedom from Barriers." In *Disciplines, 1993,* edited by Glenda Webb. 79-85. Nashville, TN: The Upper Room, 1993.

697. **Mangual Rodríguez, Sandra.** "Reacción al Artículo de Pablo A. Jiménez." In *Lumbrera a Nuestro Camino,* edited by Pablo A. Jiménez. 149-53. Miami, FL: Editorial Caribe, 1994.

698. **Martell-Otero, Loida.** "Lifting Voices, Praising Gifts." *Apuntes: Reflexiones Teológicas desde el Margen Hispano* 13, no. 3 (1993): 171-79.

699. **Martin, Carlos G.** "Evangelistic Strategies of Seventh-Day Adventists to Reach Recent Hispanic Immigrants to Texas: A Critical Evaluation." Ph.D. diss., Southwestern Baptist Theological Seminary, 1992. 300 pp.

700. **Martínez, Aquiles Ernesto.** "El Apóstol Pablo y la Comunidad de Tesalónica: Lecciones Sobre el Uso del Poder." *Apuntes: Reflexiones Teológicas desde el Margen Hispano* 15, no. 1 (1995): 3-13.

701. **Morrison, Aubrey L.** "'El Camino Nuevo de Vida'" (Hebreos 10:20): Estudios Basados en la Epístola a los Hebreos." Master's thesis. Concordia Theological Seminary, 1984. 65 pp.

702. **Mulligan, Joseph E.** "The Good News according to Paul: An Invitation to Community." *Apuntes: Reflexiones Teológicas desde el Margen Hispano* 3, no. 1 (1983): 15-20.

703. **Nieto, Leo D.** "Ethnic Minorities in Ministry: A Prophetic Vision." *Apuntes: Reflexiones Teológicas desde el Margen Hispano* 2, no. 4 (1982): 89-93.

704. **Ortíz, José.** *Una Introducción al Cristianismo del Nuevo Testamento: Guía de Estudio Bíblico.* Guatemala City, Guatemala: Semilla; Santa Fe de Bogotá, Colombia: Clara: 1993. 118 pp.

705. **Pagán, Samuel.** "Ahora es el Tiempo." *La Biblia en las Américas* 42 #174, no. 1 (1987): 4-5.

706. **Pagán, Samuel.** "Exégesis Bíblica y Trabajo Pastoral." *La Biblia en las Américas* 42 #175, no. 2 (1987): 10-11.

707. **Pagán, Samuel.** "From Crisis to Hope." Ph.D. diss., Jewish Theological Seminary, 1988.

708. **Pagán, Samuel.** "La Revisión Valera de la Traducción Reina." *La Biblia en las Américas* 44 #185, no. 1 (1989): 10-11.

709. **Pagán, Samuel.** *Esdras, Nehemías y Ester. Comentario Bíblico Hispanoamericano.* Miami, FL: Editorial Caribe, 1990.

710. **Pagán, Samuel.** "La Muerte de Jesús y la Resurrección de Cristo." *La Biblia en las Américas* 45 #191, no. 2 (1990): 14-15.

711. **Pagán, Samuel.** "Biblia y Estudio: Jesús y los Fariseos." *La Biblia en las Américas* 47 #201, no. 3 (1992): 24-25.

712. **Pagán, Samuel.** "El Apocalipsis de Juan y la Iglesia Hispana." *Apuntes: Reflexiones Teológicas desde el Margen Hispano* 12, no. 1 (1992): 3-12.

713. **Pagán, Samuel.** "El Texto de I Samuel Descubierto en Qumram." *La Biblia en las Américas* 47 #200, no. 2 (1992): 25-26.

714. **Pagán, Samuel.** *Apocalipsis: Visión y Misión.* Miami, FL: Editorial Caribe, 1993.

715. **Pagán, Samuel, ed.** *Biblia Plenitud.* Miami, FL: Editorial Caribe, 1993.

716. **Pagán, Samuel.** "Estudios Bíblicos: Pródigos, Profetas, Siervos y Mesías." *Apuntes: Reflexiones Teológicas desde el Margen Hispano* 13, no. 1 (1993): 4-29.

717. **Pagán, Samuel.** "Itinerario de la Pasión." *La Biblia en las Américas* 48 #205, no. 2 (1993): 10-12.

718. **Pagán, Samuel.** "María...Simplemente María." *Apuntes: Reflexiones Teológicas desde el Margen Hispano* 13, no. 4 (1993): 213-19. Also published in *La Biblia en las Américas* 49 #211, no. 2 (1994): 24-27.

719. **Pagán, Samuel.** "Erudición y Sencillez." *La Biblia en las Américas* 49 #214, no. 5 (1994): 7-10.

720. **Pagán, Samuel.** "Reacción al Artículo de Carmen Gaud." In *Lumbrera a Nuestro Camino,* edited by Pablo A. Jiménez. 173-176. Miami, FL: Editorial Caribe, 1994.

721. **Pagán, Samuel.** "Apocalyptic Poetry: Isaiah 24-27." *Apuntes: Reflexiones Teológicas desde el Margen Hispano* 15, no. 1 (1995): 14-27.

722. **Pagán, Samuel.** "El Evangelio de la Pasión." *La Biblia en las Américas* 50 #217, no. 2 (1995): 21-24.

723. **Pagán, Samuel.** *Palabra Viva. Estudio del Entorno Histórico, Literario y Teológico del Antiguo Testamento.* Miami, FL: Editorial Caribe, 1995.

724. **Pagán, Samuel.** "Traducción Bíblica y Comunicación." *La Biblia en las Américas* 41 #171, no. 3 (1995): 19-24.

725. **Pagán, Samuel.** "Traducción de la Biblia: Una Manifestación del Espíritu." *La Biblia en las Américas* 50 #216, no. 1 (1995): 11-13.

726. **Pankow, Fred J.** "A Scriptural Stance toward Undocumented Hispanics and Selected Methodologies for Reaching Them with the Gospel." Th.D. diss., Concordia Seminary, 1986. 249 pp.

727. **Pazmiño, Roberto W.** *Foundational Issues in Christian Education: An Introduction in Evangelical Perspective.* Grand Rapids, MI: Baker Book House, 1988. 264 pp.

728. **Pereyra, Luis A.** "A Biblical Perspective in a Multicultural Setting." In *Bible and Mission: Biblical Foundations and Working Models for Congregational Ministry,* edited by Wayne C. Stumme. 153-62. Minneapolis, MN: Augsburg Publishing House, 1986.

729. **Quiñones-Ortiz, Javier.** "Psalm 72: On Confronting Rulers in Urban Society." *Apuntes: Reflexiones Teológicas desde el Margen Hispano* 13, no. 3 (1993): 180-89.

730. **Ramírez, Guillermo.** "Perspectivas Apocalípticas: Reto para Hoy." *Apuntes: Reflexiones Teológicas desde el Margen Hispano* 3, no. 3 (1983): 51-57.

731. **Ramírez, Guillermo.** "Reacción al Artículo de Jorge González." In *Lumbrera a Nuestro Camino,* edited by Pablo Jiménez. 53-60. Miami, FL: Editorial Caribe, 1994.

732. **Ramírez, Johnny.** "Five Spanish Lessons on the Spirit of Prophecy in Biblical Times." Alajuela, Costa Rica. Central American Union of Seventh-Day Adventists, 1983. Manuscript.

733. **Ramírez, Johnny.** "Biblical and Ethnopsychological Models for Race Relations." Presentation given to Humans Relations Committee, Atlantic Union Conference of Seventh-Day Adventists, South Lancaster, MA. 1991.

734. **Ramírez, Johnny.** "El Bautismo de Jesús." *El Centinela,* April 1992, 4-5.

735. **Rivera-Pagán, Luis N.** "La Paciencia de la Espera: Exégesis de Santiago 5:1-8." *Apuntes: Reflexiones Teológicas desde el Margen Hispano* 1, no. 2 (1981): 3-9.

736. **Rivera-Pagán, Luis N.** "Paz y Justicia en la Biblia." In *II Congreso Continental de Estudio y Asamblea Plenaria.* 70-88. Matanzas, Cuba: Conferencia Cristiana por la Paz para América Latina y el Caribe, 1982. Reproduced in *Punto y Aparte* 2, no. 3 (1982): 2-9.

737. **Rivera-Pagán, Luis N.** "Peace and Justice in the Bible." In *Peace: A Challenge to the Caribbean,* edited by the Caribbean Conference of Churches. 21-22. Barbados: The Cedar Press, 1982.

738. **Rivera-Pagán, Luis N.** "La Utopía Bíblica, la Amenaza Nuclear y el Problema de la Paz." In *La Esperanza en el Presente de América Latina,* edited by Luis N. Rivera Pagán and Raúl Vidales. 383-407. San José, Costa Rica: DEI, 1983.

739. **Rivera-Pagán, Luis N.** "Biblical Eschatology: Peace, Justice, and Abundance." In *Let Us Win Peace by Defending Life: Continental Consultation of the Latin American and Caribbean Christian Peace Conference.* 5-10. Prague, Czechoslovakia: Christian Peace Conference, 1987.

740. **Rivera-Pagán, Luis N.** "La Utopía Bíblica de la Paz: Anotaciones Críticas a la Hermenéutica Latinoamericana." In *Hacia Una Fe Evangélica Latinoamericanista: Una Perspectiva Bautista,* edited by Jorge Pixley. 183-200. San José, Costa Rica: DEI, 1988. Also published as "Toward a Theology of Peace: Critical Notes on the Biblical Hermeneutic of Latin American Theology of Liberation," in Dow Kirkpatrick, ed., *Faith Born in the Struggle of Life: A Reading of Protestant Faith in Latin America* (Grand Rapids, MI: Wm. B. Eerdmans, 1988), pp. 52-77.

741. **Rivera-Pagán, Luis N.** *Caminos de Esperanza; Cinco Sermones y un Estudio Bíblico.* Río Piedras, PR: Primera Iglesia Bautista de Río Piedras, 1989.

742. **Rivera-Pagán, Luis N.** "Anotaciones Críticas a la Hermenéutica Bíblica de la Teología Latinoamericana de Liberación: Hacia una Teología de la Paz." *Talleres* 3, nos. 3-4 (n.d.): 93-108.

743. **Rodríguez, Angel Manuel.** "Sacrificial Substitution in the Old Testament." In *The Sanctuary and the Atonement,* edited by Arnold Wallenkampf and W. Richard Lesher. 134-56. Washington, DC: Review and Herald Publishing Association, 1981.

744. **Rodríguez, Angel Manuel.** *Substitution in the Hebrew Cultus.* Berrien Springs, MI: Andrews University Press, 1982. 339 pp.

745. **Rodríguez, Angel Manuel.** *La Teología de la Epístola a los Hebreos.* Mayagüez, PR: Antillian College, 1983. 162 pp.

746. **Rodríguez, Angel Manuel.** "Sabbata en Colosenses 2:16." 1983. Manuscript.

747. **Rodríguez, Angel Manuel.** "Romanos 3:21-26: Su Contribución a la Interpretación de la Muerte de Cristo como un Sacrificio." 1985. Manuscript.

748. **Rodríguez, Angel Manuel.** "Levítico 11: Los Animales Puros y los Impuros." *El Ministerio* 34 (March-April 1986): 19-28.

749. **Rodríguez, Angel Manuel.** "Sanctuary Theology in the Book of Exodus." *Andrews University Seminary Studies* 24, no. 2 (1986): 127-45.

750. **Rodríguez, Angel Manuel.** "Significance of the Cultic Language in Daniel 8:9-14." In *Symposium on Daniel,* edited by Frank B. Holbrook. 527-49. Washington, DC: Review and Herald Publishing Association, 1986.

751. **Rodríguez, Angel Manuel.** "Transfer of Sin in Leviticus." In *The Seventy Weeks, Leviticus, and the Nature of Prophecy,* edited by Frank B. Holbrook. 169-97. Washington, DC: Review and Herald Publishing Association, 1986.

752. **Rodríguez, Angel Manuel.** "Cristo: Mediador e Intercesor." *El Ministerio, vol.* 35, nos. 207-208 (1987).

753. **Rodríguez, Angel Manuel.** "El Santuario y Sus Servicios en la Literatura Patrística." *Theologika* 7, no. 1 (1992): 22-79.

754. **Rodríguez, Angel Manuel.** "Salvation by Sacrificial Substitution." *Journal of the Adventist Theological Society* 3, no. 1 (1992): 49-77.

755. **Rodríguez, Angel Manuel.** *El Rapto Secreto de la Iglesia.* Nampa, ID: Pacific Press, 1993. 31 pp.

756. **Rodríguez, Angel Manuel.** "Health and Healing in the Pentateuch." In *Health 2000 and Beyond: A Study Conference of Adventist Theology, Philosophy, and Practice of Health and Healing.* 17-29. Silver Spring, MD: Home Study International Press, 1994.

757. **Rodríguez, Angel Manuel.** "Inspiration and the Imprecatory Psalms." *Journal of the Adventist Theological Society* 5, no. 1 (1994): 40-67.

758. **Rodríguez, Angel Manuel.** *Stewardship Roots—Toward a Theology of Stewardship, Tithe and Offerings.* Silver Spring, MD: Church Ministries, 1994. 69 pp.

759. **Rodríguez, Angel Manuel.** *Esther: A Theological Approach.* Berrien Springs, MI: Andrews University Press, 1995. 162 pp.

760. **Rodríguez, José D., Jr.** "The Parable of the Affirmative-Action Employer." *Apuntes: Reflexiones Teológicas desde el Margen Hispano* 8, no. 3 (1988): 51-57.

761. **Rodríguez, José David.** "The Challenge of Hispanic Ministry (Reflections on John 4)." *Currents in Theology and Mission* 18, no. 6 (1991): 420-26.

762. **Rodríguez, José David.** "Breaking Down Barriers." *Apuntes: Reflexiones Teológicas desde el Margen Hispano* 13, no. 4 (1993): 203-12.

763. **Rosado, Caleb.** "The Significance of Galilee." *Lake Union Ministerial Digest* 3, no. 2 (1985): 11-22.

764. **Rosado, Caleb.** "Hispanics and the Role of Authoritative Documents." Paper presented at the annual meeting of the Andrews Society for Religious Studies in conjunction with the annual meeting of the American Academy of Religion and the Society of Biblical Literature, Boston, MA, December 1987.

765. **Rosado, Caleb.** *What is God Like?* Hagerstown, MD: Review and Herald Publishing Association, 1988. 95 pp.

766. **Rosado, Caleb.** "The Church, the City, and the Compassionate Christ." *Apuntes: Reflexiones Teológicas desde el Margen Hispano* 9, no. 2 (1989): 27-35. Also published in Justo L. González, ed, *Voces: Voices from the Hispanic Church* (Nashville, TN: Abingdon Press, 1992), pp. 72-80.

767. **Rosado, Caleb.** *Broken Walls.* Boise, ID: Pacific Press Publishing Association, 1990. 160 pp.

768. **Rosado, Caleb.** *Women/Church/God.* Riverside, CA: Loma Linda University Press, 1990.

769. **Rosado, Caleb.** "What are You Worth?" *Adventist Review,* 18 March 1993, 24.

770. **Rosado, Caleb.** "The Sin of Saint Peter—Racism." *Ministry* (June 1994): 7-9.

771. **Sanchez, Daniel R.** "An Interdisciplinary Approach to Theological

Contextualisation with Special Reference to Hispanic Americans."
Ph.D. diss., Oxford Centre for Mission Studies, 1991. 466 pp.

772. **Sánchez, Jorge E.** "La Educación Bíblica en Nuestra Iglesia Hispana."
Apuntes: Reflexiones Teológicas desde el Margen Hispano 9, no. 2
(1989): 35-38.

773. **Sandín, Pedro A.** *Cuentos y Encuentros: Hacia una Educación
Cristiana Transformadora.* Bayamón, PR: La Iglesia Cristiana
(Discípulos de Cristo); Davie, FL: Pagán, 1995. 173 pp.

774. **Santillana, Fernando.** "¿Refugiados Económicos, o Víctimas?"
Apuntes: Reflexiones Teológicas desde el Margen Hispano 5, no. 4
(1985): 81-85.

775. **Schkade, Landon.** "The Hispanic Lutheran Cultus: A Bilingual
Exposition of Its Biblical-Theological Bases within a Cultural Setting."
Master's thesis. Concordia Theological Seminary, 1984. 93 pp.

776. **Segovia, Fernando F.** "Hispanic American Theology and the Bible:
Effective Weapon and Faithful Ally." In *We are a People! Initiatives
in Hispanic American Theology,* edited by Roberto S. Goizueta. 21-49.
Minneapolis, MN: Fortress Press, 1992.

777. **Solivan, Samuel.** "Orthopathos: Prolegomenon for a North American
Hispanic Theology." Ph.D. diss., Union Theological Seminary, 1993.
258 pp.

778. **Soltero, Conrado G.** "Nuestra Misión y el Alcance a la Comunidad: Un
Modelo Misional." In *La Iglesia Hispana en Misión,* edited by
Conrado G. Soltero. 13-23. New York: National Program Division,
General Board of Global Ministries, The United Methodist Church,
1992.

779. **Soltero, Conrado G. and Finees Flores.** "Capacitando a los Santos."
Paper presented at the "Hispanic Symposium on Ministries of the
Hispanic Church," held at Perkins School of Theology, Dallas, TX,
November 1978.

780. **Soto, Juan S.** "El Buen Samaritano desde el Margen Hispano." *Apuntes:
Reflexiones Teológicas desde el Margen Hispano* 4, no. 2 (1984): 38-
40.

781. **Soto, Juan S.** "En Torno a la Transfiguración." *Apuntes: Reflexiones
Teológicas desde el Margen Hispano* 6, no. 2 (1986): 40-43.

782. **Sturni, Gary K.** "Models of Theological Education for Hispanic
Candidates for Ordination in the Episcopal Church." D.Min. Project
Report. San Francisco Theological Seminary, 1986. 322 pp.

783. **Villafañe, Eldin.** "Toward an Hispanic American Pentecostal Social Ethic, with Special Reference to North Eastern United States." Ph.D. diss., Boston University, 1989. 493 pp.

784. **Villafañe, Eldin, and others.** *Seek the Peace of the City: Reflections on Urban Ministry.* Grand Rapids, MI: William B. Eerdmans Publishing Co., 1995.

785. **Weiss, Herold.** "The *Pagani* among the Contemporary of the First Christians." *Journal of Biblical Literature* 86, no. 1 (1967): 42-52.

786. **Weiss, Herold.** "History and a Gospel." *Novum Testamentum* 10, Fasc. 2-3 (1968): 81-94.

787. **Weiss, Herold.** "Hebraic and Greek Antecedents of the Johanine 'Word'." In *The Stature of Christ,* edited by V. Carner and G. Stanhiser. 37-44. E. Heppenstall *Festschrift.* Loma Linda, CA: Loma Linda University, 1970.

788. **Weiss, Herold.** "The Law in the Epistle to the Colossians." *Catholic Biblical Quarterly* 34, no. 3 (1972): 294-314.

789. **Weiss, Herold.** "Revelation and the Bible." *Spectrum* 7, no. 3 (1976): 49-54.

790. **Weiss, Herold.** "Footwashing in the Johannine Community." *Novum Testamentum* 21, Fasc. 4 (1979): 298-325.

791. **Weiss, Herold.** "Genesis, Chapter One: A Theological Statement." *Spectrum* 9, no. 4 (1979): 54-62.

792. **Weiss, Herold.** "Uncovering our Heritage: Excavation at Capernaum." *Courier* 54, no. 4 (1980): 18-20.

793. **Weiss, Herold.** "Jesus' Own City." *Ministry* (January 1981).

794. **Weiss, Herold.** "Christ Event." In *The Westminster Dictionary of Christian Theology,* edited by Alan Richardson and John Bowden. 93-94. Philadelphia, PA: Westminster Press, 1983.

795. **Weiss, Herold.** "Gold Hoard Found at Capernaum." *Biblical Archeology Review* 9, no. 4 (1983): 50-53.

796. **Weiss, Herold.** "Lo Asombroso de la Injusticia." *Apuntes: Reflexiones Teológicas desde el Margen Hispano* 5, no. 1 (1985): 3-8.

797. **Weiss, Herold.** "How Can Jeremiah Compare the Migration of Birds to Knowledge of God's Justice?" *Bible Review* 2, no. 3 (1986): 42-45.

798. **Weiss, Herold.** "The Sabbath in Matthew, Mark, and Luke." *Spectrum* 19, no. 1 (1988): 33-39.

799. **Weiss, Herold.** *Paul of Tarsus: His Gospel and Life.* Rev. ed. Berrien Springs, MI: Andrews University Press, 1989. 187 pp.

800. **Weiss, Herold.** "The Sabbath in the Synoptic Gospels." *Journal for the Study of the New Testament* 38, no. 1 (1990): 13-27.

801. **Weiss, Herold.** "The Sabbath in the Fourth Gospel." *Journal of Biblical Literature* 110, no. 2 (1991): 311-21.

802. **Weiss, Herold.** "The Apostle Paul: An Intellectual?" *College and University Dialogue* 4, no. 2 (1992): 14-15, 23.

803. **Weiss, Herold.** "Footwashing." In *The Anchor Bible Dictionary,* edited by David Noel Freedman. 828-29. Vol. 2. New York: Doubleday, 1992.

804. **Weiss, Herold.** "The Sabbath among the Samaritans." *Journal for the Study of Judaism in the Persian, Greek and Roman Period* 25, no. 2 (1994): 252-73.

805. **Weiss, Herold.** "Freedom and Nationalism: A Pauline Perspective." *College and University Dialogue* 7, no. 3 (1995): 15-17.

806. **Weiss, Herold.** "Paul and the Judging of Days." *Zeitschrift fur die Neutestamentliche Wissenschaft und die Kunde der Älteren Kirche* 86, nos. 3-4 (1995): 137-53.

807. **Weiss, Herold.** "Saint Paul on Freedom and Nationalism." In *The Apostle Paul and the Danger of Self-Destruction; Materials of the International Conference Held in Chishinau, Republic of Moldova, 8-15 October, 1994,* edited by Andrei Hropotinschi and Dimitru Tara. 55-61. Chishinau, Republic of Moldova: Moldpress, 1995.

808. **Weiss, Herold.** "San Pablo, la Libertad y el Nacionalismo." *Apuntes: Reflexiones Teológicas desde el Margen Hispano* 15, no. 4 (1995): 115-25.

809. **Youngman, Nilah M.** "Affirming Hispanic Women." D.Min Project Report. Austin Presbyterian Theological Seminary, 1993. 125 pp.

810. **Zackrison, James W.** "Ministry in an Age of Shifting Social Context: A Study Guide on How to Organize and Run Multiethnic/Multicultural Churches in the 1990s." Pasadena, CA. Fuller Theological Seminary, 1991. Manuscript.

811. **Zackrison, James W.** "Multiethnic/Multicultural Ministry in the 1990s: With Special Emphasis on the Seventh-Day Adventist Church in North America." D.Miss. thesis. Fuller Theological Seminary, School of World Mission, 1991. 399 pp.

812. **Zambrano, Ariel.** "In the Depths of the Well, Looking at the Stars." *Apuntes: Reflexiones Teológicas desde el Margen Hispano* 3, no. 4 (1983): 89-93.

The Writing of Religious History in the United States: A Critical Assessment

Daisy Machado

In the September 1993 issue of the journal *Church History*,[1] published by the American Society of Church History, Martin Marty published an article entitled, "American Religious History in the Eighties: A Decade of Achievement." It is a rather extensive article, or rather a detailed bibliography, in which Marty looks at works written by historians of American (meaning U.S.) religion that were published from 1980-1989. Working with a variety of journals up to 1992, Marty presents in his article a survey of those books that became, what he calls, "part of the public record" in the field of Euro-American religious history.

Marty's survey is divided into twelve general topic areas and the fifth one is called "Minorities." In this topic area the last paragraph is on Hispanic-Americans. In seven short sentences we are told that, "[s]adly deficient was the attention paid to the largest non-English speaking group in America, Hispanics... Anyone looking for a dissertation-book area, or who would like to make contributions to a neglected force in the American mix, should explore Hispanic topics."[2] While the invitation Marty makes to church historians is one of great promise, the fact that the religious academy in general, and church historians in particular, continue to pass over the story of Latinos in U.S. religious life seems almost unbelievable. Questions must be asked and how they are asked make all the difference. We can ask, Is it possible that the contributions of Latinos to U.S. Christianity are simply non-existent? or, How can the five centuries that Latinos have been a part of Christianity in North America be so unimportant? However a more accurate set of questions would begin by looking at the religious academy and at the field of church history in the United States and then asking, How can church historians pretend to write the religious history of a nation if they ignore the participation of an entire group of Christians? and, What does this say about how history is used by those who hold positions of power within seminaries and denominations?

Few would deny that history is a powerful lens used to scrutinize and interpret. In the telling of history both events and people are critically examined in their particular space and time. Yet history can also serve to provide the type of historical "evidence" that serves to undergird the political, economic, racial, and social agendas of governments and institutions. If an entire population group has no historical voice, and if that group seems to have occupied no significant historical space, then it is very easy to relegate that group to the margins of a national and religious epic. It is this very marginalization that can then facilitate the claim to hegemony and the advocacy of the ideals of inclusivity, equality, and justice by the churches of that nation. Because there is no written mainstream record to threaten the national epic, be it religious or political, there is also no dissenting historical memory to say it was and is not so. In this manner the non-writing of a people's history finally becomes an act of control and disdain.

History from the Margins

While it may appear from the findings of the survey done in *Church History* that the 1980s was indeed a decade of neglect in the study of the history of the Latino church in the United States, this was not the case. Throughout the decade numerous attempts were made to tell the Latino story, to reaffirm the Latino historical existence as a part of God's church on the North American continent. But if one is to uncover the Latino church, both its past and present, one must recognize that research for this endeavor cannot begin in the center of the established scholarly world. Nor can it begin in the center of denominational structures. Instead, the religious history of Latinos in the United States is researched and written in the margins of both academic and denominational worlds. It is in this other place, this place "outside the gate," where the Latino church can be found and where her history has been made, continues to be made, and is currently being lived and told.

That is why a bibliography of historical writings about the Latino religious experience is so very powerful. The research done for this bibliography brings together a variety of writers, viewpoints, and concerns, many of which often conflict and do not always provide a positive telling of history. Nevertheless, the fact that for the first time students and scholars of North American church history have at their fingertips this very comprehensive bibliography is a reality worth celebrating. It is also a subversive act. Compiling such a large list of books, articles, worship aids from the turn of the century forward is subversive because it affirms, it is proof positive, it is historical evidence, that despite the marginal status to which they have been relegated, Latinos have been, are, and will continue to be a strong and large community of faith in the United States. The publication of this bibliography may mean that professors of church history in many seminaries and universities will no longer be able to use the excuse that they do not teach about Latino religious history because there are no adequate sources of information. This compilation of historical works will be an immense help to those who are serious about discovering the place of Latinos in the U.S. religious landscape.

This bibliography includes many diverse historical narratives. One such telling of history from the margins was published in 1982 by Editora Educativa Dominicana. It is a bilingual, Spanish-English, history of the American Baptist Latino ministry in New York City from 1921-1980. Written by Rev. Soto Fontánez, a well known Baptist leader, it is a voice from those Latino Baptists who struggled to be faithful to their call in the large urban setting of New York City. In 1983 the Mexican American Cultural Center in San Antonio published a collection of essays, edited by Moisés Sandoval, called *Fronteras: A History of the Latin American Church in the USA Since 1513*. Looking at the Latino church from a broader perspective, it too is a voice from the Latino religious community, an affirmation of our presence in North America before the coming of the first British colonists. In 1986 the Herald Press published *The Hispanic Mennonite Church North in America, 1932-1982*, written by Rafael Falcón. In 1987 the Trinity Press published a second edition of the 1978 publication of *Iglesia Presbiteriana, A History of Presbyterians and Mexican Americans in the Southwest*, written by R. Douglas Brackenridge and Francisco García-Treto. The following year, in 1988, the Synod of Southern California and Hawaii of the Presbyterian Church published their history, *Hispanic Presbyterians in Southern California: One Hundred Years of Ministry,* written by Janet Atkins-Vásquez. Also in 1988 Joaquín Vargas, a minister with more than fifty years in the pastorate, wrote *Los Discípulos de Cristo en Puerto Rico, 1899-1987*, which was published by the Departamento Ecuménico de Investigaciones (DEI) in Costa Rica.

While these books represent only a fraction of the histories found in this bibliography, they remind us that the writings about or by Latinos was not as barren as many in the academy or denominations believe. How then do we interpret their invisibility within mainstream U.S. Christianity? Marty explains in his article that the criteria he used for inclusion in his survey of the '80s was that the book had to have been reviewed in at least two of the five major periodicals on religious history such as *Catholic Historical Review, Religious Studies Review*, or *The American Historical Review*, among others. If this was not the case, the book was not included in the survey. The use of those journals as filters for Marty's survey keeps the scholarly community within very defined boundaries. These restricted criteria do not allow for the acknowledgment of the other voices from the margins, even if the scholars might think these voices do exist. The journals cited not only provide guides for acceptable scholarly writings, they also create the boundaries between what is read and what is not read in the classrooms of most of our theological schools.

While the argument here is not against standards for scholarly writings or standards for good historical research, a twofold challenge or appeal must be made. First, there is a need to create a greater awareness of those voices which, because of their marginality, have no access to the better known and established publishing sources. Second, scholars need to promote the utilization of these alternative materials as valid historical records, as worthy of being read and analyzed as any recognized historical account.

Acknowledging the Margins

The issue at hand is not the validity of the histories being written, nor is the issue the worthiness of this alternative historical record. What is important for us to note as Latino historians of the Latino church is that we live and work in the margins of the scholarly world. We find ourselves surrounded by the often over-heard lip-service paid to the need for "inclusivity" and the need to look at "minority issues and concerns." However, the fact remains that the histories of the Latino church are still seen as "special topics" in the majority of seminary settings. The bulk of our Latino Protestant history, and this is true for most denominations, is still to be written. The history which has been recently written has been done so from *la base,* or what some would call from the "bottom-up." This reality is reflected in the authors of some of the books on Latino church history that appear in this bibliography.

The books written by non-scholars bring to us the voices of those who were an integral part of the historical process and played a role in its development, like Soto Fontánez in the Baptist church in New York, or Joaquín Vargas in the Disciples church in Puerto Rico. While these writers do not often carry the pedigree of academia that helps to legitimize their books, they nevertheless provide the Latino community with an historical narrative born of experience. They are in a very real sense eyewitness historical story-tellers. Their histories come from having experienced the battle for existence and recognition from the very margins of North American religious life. In writing their stories they have assured the Latino community in the United States that our story can be told, that our history is being written, that we maintain alive a vivid historical memory. Given the reality that the Latino church in the United States has survived and thrived despite the missionary enterprise, despite neglect, paternalism, attempts at "Americanization," the inadequate funding of new churches, the inheritance of "left over" facilities in rundown, and economically deprived communities, it is no surprise that the histories being written are coming from those who "talked the talk **and** walked the walk."

It is also not surprising that these same books were published by local and/or alternative presses. We hope that this will change in the very near future when church historians use the rubric of "Global perspective" as an opening for the study of the history of the Latino church in seminaries and universities around the country. This in turn may mean that the established and connected publishing houses will seek out more historical material on the Latino church, and this is well and good. In the meantime, what we have to acknowledge and celebrate at this moment are those attempts by both non-academics and academics to tell the Latino faith story. Their voices are worthy of note. This excellent bibliography does them honor.

Endnotes

[1]Martin E. Marty, "American Religious History in the Eighties: A Decade of Achievement," *Church History*, Vol. 62, No 3, September 1993, pp. 335-377.
[2]Marty, p. 353.

History Bibliography

813. **Abel, Theodore.** *Protestant Home Missions to Catholic Immigrants.* New York: Institute of Social and Religious Research, 1933.

814. **Acevedo, Angel.** *Principios Distintivos de la Denominación Bautista.* Puerto Rico, n.d.

815. **Acevedo Delgado, German.** "Hispanic Community Has Reason to Celebrate." *Christian Social Action* 1, no. 7 (1988): 26.

816. **Acosta, Samuel.** "The Hispanic Council of the United Church of Christ: Its History, Impact, and Ability to Motivate Policy." *Chicago Theological Seminary Register* 79, no. 3 (1989): English: 28-41, Spanish: pp. 42-56.

817. **Ad Hoc Committee for the Consultation on Hispanic Theological Education.** "Presentation of the Results of the Consultation on Hispanic Theological Education (held on 18-19 March 1974) to the Theological Schools of Southern California." 1974.

818. **Agnew, Edith and Ruth Barber.** "The Unique Presbyterian School System of New México." *Journal of Presbyterian History* 49, no. 3 (1970): 197-221.

819. **Aldape, Alicia.** *Memorias Orales de Alicia Aldape: Una Entrevista Hecha el 2 de Abril de 1979.* Baylor University Program for Oral History. N.p.: Convención Bautista de Texas, 1979. 10 pp.

820. **Aldape, Eliseo C.** *Memoria Orales de Eliseo C. Aldape: Una Entrevista Hecha el 2 de Abril de 1979.* Baylor University Program for Oral History. N.p.: Convención Bautista Mexicana de Texas, 1980. 23 pp.

821. **Alexander, Neil M., Carolyn M. Marshall, and Robert K. Feaster, eds.** *El Libro de la Disciplina de la Iglesia Metodista Unida.* Translated by Roy Barton. Nashville, TN: Casa Metodista Unida de Publicaciones (United Methodist Publishing House), 1992. 849 pp.

822. **Alicea-Lugo, Benjamín.** "First Black Minister and Congregation in the Reformed Church in America." *NBTS Newsletter, Special Faculty Issue* (Winter 1982): 3-9.

823. **Alicea-Lugo, Benjamín.** "A New Vision for a New Day." In *Two Centuries Plus: The Story of New Brunswick Theological Seminary.* 190-207. The Historical Series of the Reformed Church in America, no. 13. Grand Rapids, MI: William B. Eerdmans Publishing Co., 1984.

824. **Alvarez, Carmelo.** "Protestantismo y Misión: Hacia una Ubicación Histórico-Teológica del Pensamiento de Orlando E. Costas en América Latina y el Caribe." Puerto Rico. 1989. Mimeographed.

825. **Alvarez Pérez, Carmelo.** "Problemas Fundamentales de la Iglesia Evangélica en Puerto Rico." Master's thesis. Seminario Evangélico, 1941.

826. **Alvirez, José Galindo.** "Latin American Methodism in the Southwest: A History of the Río Grande Conference." Master's thesis. Lamar State College of Technology [Lamar University], 1962.

827. **American Baptist Home Mission Societies.** "Proposed Policy for Hispanic Ministry." American Baptist Churches, U.S.A. Valley Forge, PA, 1971.

828. **Aponte, Edwin D.** "Hispanic Protestantism in Philadelphia, 1929-1993: A Case Study in Racial/Ethnic Church History." Paper presented at the annual meeting of the American Society of Church History, San Francisco, CA, January 1994.

829. **Aragón, Rafael J.** "From Los Angeles: Warnings and Spirit." *Church and Society* 82, no. 6 (1992): 111-13.

830. **Aragón, Rafael J.** "El Movimiento de Refugio." *Apuntes: Reflexiones Teológicas desde el Margen Hispano* 5, no. 3 (1985): 65-67.

831. **Aragón, Rafael J. and Donald L. Smith.** "Ecumenical Urban Strategy: A View from Los Angeles." *Church and Society* 83, no. 1 (1992): 117-19.

832. **Arbaugh, William** "Report on Lutheran Work in Puerto Rico." Lutheran Church. N.p., 1954. Manuscript.

833. **Arce Trías, Manuel.** "Consagran Primer Obispo Nativo de la Iglesia Episcopal de P.R." *El Debate,* 6 December 1964, 3.

834. **Arizméndiz, C. P.** "Convención Bautista Mexicana del Norte de California." *Revista Evangélica,* September 1952, 374-75.

835. **Armendáriz, Rubén P.** "Hispanic Heritage and Christian Education." *Alert* (November 1981): 26.

836. **Armendáriz, Rubén P.** "Mexican Presbyterianism and the Dominant Society." Paper presented for a symposium at Austin Presbyterian Theological Seminary, Austin, TX, 1989.

837. **Arrastía, Cecilio.** "Report of Advisory Committee on Hispanic-American Theological Education." 29th Biennial [Meeting], American Association of Theological Schools in the United States and Canada, 1974.

838. **Asociación Bautista Mexicana de West Texas.** *Constitución y Directorio de la Asociación Bautista Mexicana de West Texas.* N.p. 1938.

839. **Asociación Hispana para la Eduación Teológica.** "Rules and Regulations of the Asociación Hispana para la Educación Teológica." 1981. 2 pp. Manuscript.

840. **Athans, S.D., ed.** *Cantos de Alabanza, Pureza y Poder.* Los Angeles, CA: Free Tract Society, 1922. Hymnal.

841. **Athans, S.D., ed.** *Cantos de Alabanza, Pureza y Poder.* 3rd ed. Los Angeles, CA: Free Tract Society, 1930. 256 pp. Hymnal.

842. **Athans, S. D.** *Melodías Evangélicas.* El Paso, TX: Casa Bautista de Publicaciones, [1936]. Hymnal.

843. **Atkins, Carolyn, ed.** *Los Tres Campos. The Three Fields: A History of Protestant Evangelists and Presbyterians in Chimayo, Cordova and Truchas, New México.* Albuquerque, NM: Menaul Historical Library of the Southwest, 1978.

844. **Atkins, Carolyn.** "Menaul School: 1881-1930...Not Leaders, Merely, but Christian Leaders." *Journal of Presbyterian History* 58, no. 4 (1980): 279-98.

845. **Atkins, Jane.** "Who Will Educate: The Schooling Question in Territorial New México, 1846-1911." Ph.D. diss., University of New México, 1982. 460 pp.

846. **Atkins-Vásquez, Jane, ed.** *Hispanic Presbyterians in Southern California: One Hundred Years of Ministry.* Los Angeles, CA: Hispanic Commission, Synod of Southern California and Hawaii, 1988. 216 pp.

847. **Atkins-Vásquez, Jane.** *Manual para una Historia de la Iglesia Local.* Decatur, GA: AETH, 1994. 22 pp.

848. **Atkinson, Ernest E.** *A Selected Bibliography of Hispanic Baptist History.* Nashville, TN: Historical Commission, Southern Baptist Convention, 1981. 88 pp.

849. **Atkinson, Ernest E.** "A Selected Bibliography of Texas Mexican/ Mexican American Baptist History, 1881-1981." Austin, TX. Austin Presbyterian Theological Seminary, 1982. Submitted for the Doctor of Ministry Program.

850. **Aulick, (Mrs.) A. L.** "Paul Bell and the Mexican Bible Institute." *Home and Foreign Fields* 14 (February 1930): 7-10.

851. **Avila de Estrada, Isabel.** *Oral Memoirs of Isabel Avila de Estrada, 10 February, 1981.* Mexican Baptist Oral History Project. [Waco, TX]: Baylor University, Institute for Oral History, 1984. 91 pp.

852. **Báez-Camargo, Gonzalo.** "A New Hispanic-American Curriculum." *World Christian Education,* vol. 5 (July-September 1950).

853. **Bailey, Nanie Lou Tynes.** "Christian Love in Action; A Narrative of Events that Foreshadowed and Culminated in the Establishment of the Mexican Baptist Orphans Home, Located in San Antonio, Texas." Waco, TX. 1957. 87 pp. Manuscript.

854. **Baker, Robert Andrew.** *The Blossoming Desert; a Concise History of Texas Baptists.* Waco, TX: Word Books, 1970. 282 pp.

855. **Baldwin, Deborah J.** *Protestants and the Mexican Revolution.* Chicago, IL: University of Illinois Press, 1990. 205 pp.

856. **Ball, H. C.** *Himnos de Gloria.* San Antonio, TX: Casa de Publicaciones Evangélicas, 1921. Hymnal.

857. **Ball, H. C.** *Cantos de Triunfo.* San Antonio, TX: Casa Evangélica de Publicaciones, 1924. Hymnal.

858. **Ball, H. C.** *Cantor Evangelístico.* San Antonio, TX: Casa Evangélica de Publicaciones, 1934. Hymnal.

859. **Ball, H. C.** *Arpa y Voz de Salmodia.* San Antonio, TX: Casa Evangélica de Publicaciones, 1939.

860. **Ball, H.C., ed.** *Himnos de Gloria.* Rev. ed. Springfield, MO: Editorial Vida, 1949. Hymnal.

861. **Ball, H. C.** *Himnos de Luz.* San Antonio, TX: H. C. Ball, 1968. Hymnal.

862. **Banker, Mark T.** "Presbyterian Missionary Activity in the Southwest: The Careers of John and James Menaul." *The Journal of the West* 23, no. 1 (1984): 55-61.

863. **Banker, Mark T.** "Missionary to His Own People: José Ynes Perea and Hispanic Presbyterianism in New México." In *Religion and Society in the American West: Historical Essays,* edited by Carl Guarneri and David Alvarez. 79-104. Lanham, MD: University Press of America, 1987.

864. **Banker, Mark T.** "They Made Haste Slowly: Presbyterian Mission Schools and Southwestern Pluralism, 1870-1920." Ph.D. diss., The University of New México, 1987. 458 pp.

865. **Banker, Mark T.** *Presbyterian Missions and Cultural Interaction in the*

Far Southwest, 1850-1950. Chicago, IL: University of Illinois Press, 1993. 226 pp.

866. **Bañuelas, Arturo.** "U.S. Hispanic Theology." *Missiology* 20, no. 2 (1992): 275-300.

867. **Bañuelas, Arturo J., ed.** *Mestizo Christianity: Theology from the Latino Perspective.* Maryknoll, NY: Orbis Books, 1995. 278 pp.

868. **Baptist General Convention of Texas.** "Shine Mister?" Motion Picture. Dallas, TX: Baptist General Convention of Texas, n.d.

869. **Baptist Standard.** "Centennial Issue." *Baptist Standard,* 11 June 1936, 126.

870. **Barber, Ruth K. and Edith J. Agnew.** *Sowers Went Forth: The Story of Presbyterian Missions in New México and Southern Colorado.* Albuquerque, NM: Menaul Historical Library of the Southwest, 1981. 171 pp.

871. **Barrera, Mario.** *Beyond Aztlán.* New York: University of Notre Dame Press, 1990.

872. **Barry, David.** "The Protestant Church and Puerto Ricans in United States Cities." *The City Church* 1 (June 1950): 10-11.

873. **Barry, David W.** "Opportunity for Protestant Churches among Puerto Ricans." *National Council Outlook* 9, no. 5 (1959): 9-10.

874. **Barton, Paul.** "Biography of Rev. Abel Gomez." Dallas, Tx. 1988. 17 pp. Manuscript.

875. **Barton, Paul.** "Function and Dysfunction: A Case Study of Mexican American Methodists." *Apuntes: Reflexiones Teológicas desde el Margen Hispano* 14, no. 2 (1994): 35-51.

876. **Baselga, Edward.** "Cultural Change and Protestantism in Puerto Rico, 1945-1966." Ph.D. diss., New York University, 1971. 333 pp.

877. **Bayless, O. L.** *A History of the Colorado Baptist General Convention.* Denver, CO: Rocky Mountain Baptist, 1966.

878. **Beagle, J. W.** "Permanent Homes for Mexican Churches." *Southern Baptist Home Missions* 9 (July 1938): 4-5.

879. **Beagle, J. W.** "Dreams-and More-Realized in Proposed Mission Building." *Southern Baptist Home Missions* 11 (February 1940): 10-11.

880. **Bender, Norman J.** "The Crusade of the Blue Banner: Rocky Mountain Presbyterians, 1870-1900." Ph.D. diss., University of Colorado, 1971. pp. 213-234

881. **Bender, Norman J., ed.** *Missionaries, Outlaws, and Indians: Taylor F. Ealy at Lincoln and Zuni, 1878-1881.* Albuquerque, NM: University of New México Press, 1984. 234 pp.

882. **Bennet, G. Willis.** *Confronting a Crisis: A Depth Study of Southern Baptist Churches in Metropolitan Transitional Areas.* Atlanta, GA: Home Mission Board, Southern Baptist Convention, 1967.

883. **Berg, Clayton L., Jr.** "Larger Than Life." *Latin American Evangelist* 68, no. 3 (1988): 4.

884. **Besançon-Spencer, Aida, et al.** *The Goddess Revival.* Grand Rapids, MI: Baker Book House, 1995. 320 pp.

885. **Bevans, Stephen and Ana María Pineda, eds.** "Columbus and the New World: Evangelization or Invasion?" *Missiology* 20, no. 2 (1992): 133-300.

886. **Bewie, W. H.** "History of Our Spanish Missions in Texas." N.p., 1958. 38 pp. Typescript.

887. **Bidot Pamias, Juan.** "The Origin and Development of Christian Education in Puerto Rico." Master's thesis. Presbyterian College of Christian Education, McCormick Theological Seminary, 1940.

888. **Bisnauth, Dale.** *History of Religions in the Caribbean.* Kingston, Jamaica: Kingston Publishers Limited, 1989.

889. **Blair, Bertha, Anne Lively, and Glen Trimble.** *Spanish Speaking Americans—Mexicans and Puerto Ricans in the United States.* New York: National Council of Churches in the U.S.A., 1959. Reprint, Ann Arbor, MI: University Microfilms, 1970. 242 pp.

890. **Blake, Alice.** "History of Protestant Missions in New México." Menaul Historical Library, Albuquerque, NM, 1935. Manuscript.

891. **Blake, Alice.** "History of Presbyterian Missions in Colorado and New México." 1936. Manuscript.

892. **Blawis, Patricia Bell.** *Tijerina and the Land Grants: Mexican Americans in Struggle for Their Heritage.* New York: International Publishers, 1971. pp. 172-175.

893. **Bonilla, Plutarco A.** "Goodbye, Friend and Compañero [Memorial for Orlando E. Costas]." *Latin American Pastoral Issues* 14, no. 2 (1987): 4-7.

894. **Boots, Nora.** "La Iglesia Hispana en los Estados Unidos y su Relación con la Iglesia en Latinoamérica." In *La Iglesia Hispana en Misión,* edited by Conrado G. Soltero. 30-39. New York: National Program

Division of the General Board of Global Ministries, The United Methodist Church, 1992.

895. **Boots, Nora Quiroga.** "Response." *Apuntes: Reflexiones Teológicas desde el Margen Hispano* 7, no. 3 (1987): 61-65.

896. **Brackenridge, R. Douglas.** *Voice in the Wilderness: A History of the Cumberland Presbyterian Church in Texas.* San Antonio, TX: Trinity University Press, 1968. 192 pp.

897. **Brackenridge, R. Douglas and Francisco O. García-Treto.** "Presbyterians and Mexican Americans: From Paternalism to Partnership." *Journal of Presbyterian History* 55, no. 2 (1977): 161-78.

898. **Brackenridge, R. Douglas and Francisco O. García-Treto.** *Iglesia Presbiteriana: A History of Presbyterians and Mexican Americans in the Southwest.* 2nd ed. San Antonio, TX: Trinity University Press, 1987.

899. **Brackenridge, R. Douglas, Francisco O. Garcia-Treto, and John Stover.** "Presbyterian Missions to Mexican Americans in Texas in the Nineteenth Century." *Journal of Presbyterian History* 49, no. 2 (1971): 103-32.

900. **Brown, Arthur J.** "A Union Missionary Conference." *Public Opinion,* vol. 25 (July-December 1898).

901. **Brown, Milton.** "Presbyterian, U.S.A. Educational Work in New México." N.p., 1957. Mimeographed.

902. **Brown, Robert A., Jr.** "Spanish-Speaking Work in Texas; Opportunities and Problems." United Presbyterian Church, U.S.A. N.p., n.d. Mimeographed report.

903. **Bruce, Keith.** "Ninety Years of Baptist Missionary Administration in Colorado." Th.D. diss., Central Baptist Theological Seminary, 1955. 249 pp.

904. **Buck, Carlos.** "A Study on the History of the Mexican-American Presbyterian Church in Texas." Master's thesis. Austin Presbyterian Theological Seminary, 1969.

905. **Buck, Lucius E.** "An Inquiry into the History of Presbyterian Educational Missions in New México." Master's thesis. University of Southern California, 1949.

906. **Burland, Thelma B.** *Spanish-Speaking Americans; Resource Book for the 1953 Graded Series of Home Mission Studies.* Atlanta, GA: Home Mission Board, Southern Baptist Convention, 1952. 69 pp.

907. **Burset, Victor.** "The First Fifty Years of the Protestant Episcopal Church in Puerto Rico." B.D. thesis. The General Theological Seminary, 1957.

908. **Caballero, Gladys.** "Nuestra Tarea, 1978-80." *Nuestra Tarea,* February 1980, 2.

909. **Cabrera, L. Santiago.** "Como la Religión Evangélica Hizo su Aparición en Puerto Rico en el Año 1860." *Puerto Rico Evangélico,* 10 December 1923, 5.

910. **Campbell, Richard C.** *Los Conquistadores: The Story of the Santa Cruz Evangelical United Brethren Church.* Santa Cruz, NM: n.p., 1968.

911. **Canales, Ferrer.** "Perfil del Ensayista Domingo Marrero." *Revista de Estudios Hispánicos* 1, nos. 3-4 (1971): 69-74.

912. **Caraballo de Silva, Jovita.** *La Iglesia Protestante en Puerto Rico como Agente de Asimilación Cultural.* San Juan, PR: Universidad de Puerto Rico. Biblioteca del Seminario Evangélico, n.d.

913. **Cardoza-Orlandi, Carlos F.** "Nos Llamaron 'Mulatos, Fiesteros, pero Redimibles': Antropología Misionera y Definición del Protestantismo en Puerto Rico." *Apuntes: Reflexiones Teológicas desde el Margen Hispano* 14, no. 4 (1994): 99-111.

914. **Carmona, Juan A.** "The Liberation of Puerto Rico: A Theological Perspective." D.Min. Project Report. Colgate Rochester Divinity School/Bexley Hall/Crozer Theological Seminary, 1982. 93 pp.

915. **Carpenter, Cere C.** *Puerto Rican Disciples: A Personal Narrative of Fifty Years with Christ in the Island of Enchantment.* Tampa, FL: The Christian Press, 1960.

916. **Carrazana, Humberto.** "The Southeastern Jurisdiction." In *Each in Our Own Tongue: A History of Hispanic United Methodism,* edited by Justo L. González. 92-105. Nashville, TN: Abingdon Press, 1991.

917. **Carroll, H. K.** "Religious Question in Porto Rico." *The Independent,* 2 November 1899, 2935-37.

918. **Carroll, H. K.** "Puerto Rico as a Mission Field." *The Missionary Review of the World,* vol. 13, no. 8 (1900).

919. **Carroll, James M.** *Texas Baptist Statistics, 1895.* Houston, TX: J. J. Pastoriza, 1895. 123 pp.

920. **Carroll, James M.** *A History of Texas Baptists.* Dallas, TX: Baptist Standard Publishing, 1923. 1030 pp.

921. **Carson, Keith.** "The Mission of the Church according to Orlando Costas:

A Biblical and Historical Evaluation." Master's thesis. Trinity Evangelical Divinity School, 1984. 104 pp.

922. **Carter, C. G.** "Training Mexican Leaders." *Southern Baptist Home Missions* 22 (February 1951): 11.

923. **Carter, C. G.** "New Mexican Baptist Church Constituted." *Southern Baptist Home Missions* 24 (January 1953): 31.

924. **Carver, E. Earl.** "Evangelical Church Growth in Puerto Rico." Master's thesis. Fuller Theological Seminary, 1972.

925. **Cassese O., Giacomo.** "Sentido y Contrasentido de la Historia: Latinos en Estados Unidos." *Apuntes: Reflexiones Teológicas desde el Margen Hispano* 14, no. 4 (1994): 112-18.

926. **Castañeda, Carlos E.** *Church Views of the Mexican American.* The Mexican American. New York: Arno Press, 1974.

927. **Castellanos, F. Rene.** "African-Hispanic-Cuban Christianity." *Journal of the Interdenominational Theological Center* 16, no. 2 (1989): 259-72.

928. **Cepeda, Rafael.** *José Martí: Perspectivas Eticas de la Fe Cristiana.* San José, Costa Rica: DEI, 1991.

929. **Chavez, Fray Angelico.** "A Nineteenth-Century New México Schism." *New México Historical Review* 58, no. 1 (1983): 35-54.

930. **Chávez, César.** "The Mexican American and the Church." In *Prophets Denied Honor,* edited by Antonio M. Stevens Arroyo. 118-21. Maryknoll, NY: Orbis Books, 1980. First published in Octavio I. Ramano V., ed., *Voices: Readings from El Grito* (Berkeley: Quinto Sol, 1973), 215-18.

931. **Chávez, Guillermo.** "The Recognition of Cuba." *Engage/Social Action* 14, no. 5 (1986): 22-25.

932. **Chávez, Guillermo.** "Los Signos de los Tiempos: Una Mirada hacia el Futuro desde la Perspectiva Latinoamericana y Caribeña." *Apuntes: Reflexiones Teológicas desde el Margen Hispano* 13, no. 1 (1993): 104-17.

933. **Chávez, Tomás.** "Quinceañera: A Liturgy in the Reformed Tradition." *Austin Seminary Bulletin: Faculty Edition* 98, no. 7 (1983): 34-47.

934. **Clark, Elmer Talmage and Harry C. Spencer.** *Latin America, U.S.A.* New York: Joint Division of Education and Cultivation, Board of Missions and Church Extension, The Methodist Church, 1942. 62 pp.

935. **Clear, Val.** *Church Planning in Puerto Rico.* Río Piedras, PR: Evangelical Seminary of Puerto Rico, 1961.

936. **Clercq, Gertrude S.** *Crossroads of the Continents.* New York: ABHMS and WABHMS, 1936. 15 pp.

937. **Coleman, Inabelle Graves.** *For My Countrymen's Salvation.* Greensboro, NC: n.p., 1933. pp. 50-51, 62-66, 91-92.

938. **Commission on Hispanic Ministry.** "Five Year Plan for the Development of the Hispanic Mission and Ministry in the Diocese of Los Angeles." The Episcopal Diocese of Los Angeles, The Episcopal Church. Los Angeles, CA, 1983.

939. **Commission on Hispanic Ministry.** "Extendiendo los Brazos: Five Year Plan for Hispanic Mission and Ministry in the Episcopal Diocese of Los Angeles 1 July 1989-30 June 1994." The Episcopal Diocese of Los Angeles, The Episcopal Church. Los Angeles, CA, 1989.

940. **Cook, A. William.** "The Power and the Powerlessness: The Pastoral Vocation of the Hispanic Church in the USA." *Evangelical Review of Theology* 9, no. 2 (1985): 156-65.

941. **Cook, Guillermo.** "Protestant Mission and Evangelization in Latin America: An Interpretation." In *New Face of the Church in Latin America: Between Tradition and Change,* edited by Guillermo Cook. 41-55. American Society of Missiology Series, no. 18. Maryknoll, NY: Orbis Books, 1994. References to Orlando Costas on pp. 53, 55, 280.

942. **Cook, Guillermo.** "[Untitled]." *Latin American Pastoral Issues* 16, no. 1 (1989): 1-4. [Part 2 of an editorial on Orlando E. Costas].

943. **Cook, Howard Scott.** "Some Sociocultural Aspects of Two Revivalistic Religious Groups in a Puerto Rican Municipio." San Juan, PR. University of Puerto Rico, 1963. Manuscript.

944. **Copass, (Mrs.) Benjamin Andrew.** *Give Ye Them to Eat.* Atlanta, GA: Home Mission Board, Southern Baptist Convention, 1940. pp. 60-66.

945. **Copass, (Mrs.) Benjamin Andrew.** *That They May See.* Dallas, TX: Baptist General Convention of Texas, 1942. 60 pp.

946. **Corder, Loyd.** "From Mexican Official to Baptist Missionary." *Southern Baptist Home Missions* 23 (April 1952): 10-11.

947. **Corder, Loyd.** "Queen Esther of Texas Mexican Baptists." *Southern Baptist Home Missions* 23 (October 1952): 12-13.

948. **Corder, Loyd.** "Through Racial Barriers." *Southern Baptist Home Missions* 24 (April 1953): 8.

949. **Cortés, Carlos, ed.** *Protestantism and Latinos in the United States.* 1963 and 1964. Repint, New York: Arno Press, 1980. 473 (in various pagings).

950. **Costas, Orlando E.** "Baptist Ecclesiology in the 17th Century." Master's thesis. Winona Lake School of Theology, 1967.

951. **Costas, Orlando E.** "En el Camino hacia un Seminario Autóctono, Notas de Viaje: 1970." Misión Latinoamericana. San José, Costa Rica, 1970.

952. **Costas, Orlando E.** "Latin American Revolutions and the Church." *Foundations* 14, no. 2 (1971): 116-27.

953. **Costas, Orlando E.** "Dateline Buenos Aires." *World Vision* 16, no. 5 (1972): 22.

954. **Costas, Orlando E.** "Church Growth as a Goal of In-Depth Evangelism." San José, Costa Rica. Institute of In-Depth Evangelism, 1973.

955. **Costas, Orlando E.** "Dateline Lima." *World Vision* 17, no. 3 (1973): 19.

956. **Costas, Orlando E.** "Influential Factors in the Rhetoric of Augustine." *Foundations* 16, no. 3 (1973): 208-21.

957. **Costas, Orlando E.** "Trabajo Realizado de enero-junio, 1973." Seminario Bíblico Latinoamericano. San José, Costa Rica, 1973.

958. **Costas, Orlando E.** "Viaje a USA 2 al 14 de junio, 1973." Seminario Bíblico Latinoamericano. San José, Costa Rica, 1973.

959. **Costas, Orlando E.** "Dateline Lima." *World Vision* 18, no. 7 (1974): 18-19. Also published in *Occasional Essays [of CELEP]*, vol. 2, no. 2 (1974).

960. **Costas, Orlando E.** "Informe del Director ante la Comisión Administrativa del CELEP." CELEP. Guatemala City, Guatemala, 1974. Mimeographed.

961. **Costas, Orlando E.** "La Realidad de la Iglesia Evangélica Latinoaméricana." In *Fe Cristiana y América Latina Hoy*, edited by C. René Padilla. Buenos Aires, Argentina: Ediciones Certeza, 1974.

962. **Costas, Orlando E.** "Latin American News Front [Comment]." *Latin America Evangelist* 54, no. 1 (1974): 11.

963. **Costas, Orlando E.** "A Sign of Hope: A Latin American Appraisal of Lausanne '74." *Latin America Evangelist* 54, no. 6 (1974): 2-3, 10. Also published as "Een Teken van Hoop. Een Latijns Amerikaanse beschungwing over Lausanne '74." *Wereld en Zendig* (Amsterdam, The Netherlands) 4, no. 4 (1975): 295-304, and "Una Señal de Esperanza: Una Evaluación Latinoamericana de Lausanne '74." *En Marcha Internacional* 10, no. 1 (1975): 3-8, 15.

964. **Costas, Orlando E.** "Depth in Evangelism: An Interpretation of 'In-

Depth Evangelism' Around the World." In *Let the Earth Hear His Voice: Official Reference Volume: International Congress on World Evangelization, Lausanne, Switzerland,* edited by James Dixon Douglas. 675-94. Minneapolis, MN: World Wide Publications, 1975.

965. **Costas, Orlando E.** *El Protestantismo en América Latina Hoy: Ensayos del Camino (1972-1974).* San José, Costa Rica: Publicaciones INDEF, 1975. 175 pp.

966. **Costas, Orlando E.** "In-Depth Evangelism in Latin America." In *Let the Earth Hear His Voice: Official Reference Volume: International Congress on World Evangelization, Lausanne, Switzerland,* edited by James Dixon Douglas. 211-12. Minneapolis, MN: World Wide Publications, 1975.

967. **Costas, Orlando E.** "Informe del Director ante la Comisión Administrativa del CELEP." CELEP. San José, Costa Rica, 1976. Mimeographed.

968. **Costas, Orlando E.** "About This Issue." *Occasional Essays [of CELEP]* 4, no. 3 (1977): 1-2.

969. **Costas, Orlando E.** "Iglesia Evangélica Unida del Ecuador: Una Interpretación Crítica y una Propuesta Constructiva." 1977. 32 pp. Mimeographed.

970. **Costas, Orlando E.** "Informe del Director ante la Junta Directiva de la Región Norte del CELEP." CELEP. San José, Costa Rica, 15 March 1977. Mimeographed.

971. **Costas, Orlando E.** "A Latin American Theologian Looks at the Charismatic Movement—Pros & Cons." *Latin America Evangelist* 57, no. 3 (1977): 10-14.

972. **Costas, Orlando E.** "Responding to the Challenge of Change (Acts 16:8ff)." Audio recording. Pasadena, CA: Fuller Theological Seminary, 1977.

973. **Costas, Orlando E.** "¿Complot Maquiavélico o Soplo del Espíritu?" *Pastoralia* 1, no. 2 (1978): 3-4.

974. **Costas, Orlando E.** "El Camino hacia Oaxtepec—Una Nueva Conciencia Protestante: La III CELA." *Pastoralia* 1, no. 2 (1978): 52-86.

975. **Costas, Orlando E.** *Compromiso y Misión.* Colección CELEP. Miami, FL: Editorial Caribe; San José, Costa Rica: Editorial Caribe: 1979. 159 pp.

976. **Costas, Orlando E.** "In This Issue." *Occasional Essays [of CELEP]* 6, no. 2 (1979): 1-3.

977. **Costas, Orlando E.** "Ecumenical Experiences of an Hispanic Baptist." *Journal of Ecumenical Studies* 17, no. 2 (1980): 118-24. Also published in William Jerry Booney and Glenn A. Ingleheart, eds., *Baptists and Ecumenism* (Valley Forge, PA: Judson Press, 1980).

978. **Costas, Orlando E.** "Foreword to *Renewal Amid Revolution,* by Dean R. Kirkwood." An American Baptist Mission Book. Valley Forge, PA: International Ministries, American Baptist Churches in the USA, 1980.

979. **Costas, Orlando E.** "The Great Commission: History and Horizons." Audiotaped address at Union Theological Seminary, Richmond VA, 15 February 1980.

980. **Costas, Orlando E.** "Report on Thailand 80 (Consultation on World Evangelization)." *TSF Bulletin* 4, no. 2 (1980): 4-7? Also published in *Occasional Essays [of CELEP]* 8, nos. 1-2 (1981): 4-12.

981. **Costas, Orlando E.** "American Baptists Travel to Puerto Rico." *The Christian Century* 98, no. 27 (1981): 872, 874-75.

982. **Costas, Orlando E.** "The Hispanics Next Door." *The Christian Century* 99, no. 26 (1982): 851-56.

983. **Costas, Orlando E.** "A Comment." *International Review of Mission* 72, no. 288 (1983): 595-96.

984. **Costas, Orlando E.** "El CELEP en la Década de los Ochenta: El Legado de los Setenta." *Pastoralia* 6, nos. 12-13 (1984): 81-90.

985. **Costas, Orlando E.** "Origen y Desarrollo del Movimiento de Crecimiento de la Iglesia." *Misión* 3, no. 1 (1984): 6-13.

986. **Costas, Orlando E.** "CELEP in the Decade of the Eighties." *Occasional Essays [of CELEP]* 12, no. 2 (1985): 129-36.

987. **Costas, Orlando E.** "IV International Mission Studies Conference Convened in Zimbabwe." *The Judson Bulletin,* no. 5 (1985): 4-7. Also published as "IV Conferencia de la Asociación Internacional de Estudios Misionales." *Boletín Teológico* 19, no. 28 (1987): 201-18.

988. **Costas, Orlando E.** "The Experience of God in the New China." *The Judson Bulletin,* n.s., 6, no. 1 (1987): 41-47.

989. **Costas, Orlando E.** "A Word from the Editor." *The Judson Bulletin,* n.s., 6, no. 1 (1987): 2.

990. **Costas, Orlando E.** "Forward in Partnership." *Today's Ministry: A*

Report from Andover Newton 2, no. 2 (1988): 4. Also published as "Crezcamos en Compañerismo." *Boletín Teológico* 19, no. 28 (1987): 219-30; *Latin American Pastoral Issues* 16, no. 1 (1989): 61-69; and as "El Ultimo Discurso de Costas Urge a la Unión de la CBA." *Pastoralia* 10, nos. 20-21 (1988): 86-90.

991. **Costas, Orlando E.** "[Varios Artículos]." In *Diccionario de la Historia de la Iglesia,* edited by Wilton M. Nelson. Miami, FL: Editorial Caribe, 1989.

992. **Costas, Orlando E.** "Informe del Viaje a Sur América, Parte B: Barranquilla e Instituticiones Teológicas." *Evangelismo a Fondo/Seminario Bíblico Latinoamericano.* San José, Costa Rica, n.d. 10 pp.

993. **Cotto-Thorner, Alfredo.** "The Northeastern Jurisdiction." In *Each in Our Own Tongue: A History of Hispanic United Methodism,* edited by Justo L. González. 106-22. Nashville, TN: Abingdon Press, 1991.

994. **Craig, Robert M.** *Our Mexicans.* New York: Board of Home Missions of the Presbyterian Church in the U.S.A., 1904. 101 pp.

995. **Cross, Judson L.** "La Iglesia Evangélica de Puerto Rico." New York. American Missionary Association, 1931. Manuscript.

996. **Crow, (Mrs.) G. D.** *A Highway in the Desert: A History of Southern Baptist Work in Arizona.* N.p., 1952. 135 pp.

997. **Crowell, Katherine R.** *Our Mexican Mission Schools.* New York: Women's Board of Home Missions of the Presbyterian Church, 1914.

998. **Cuevas de Jiménez, Noemí.** *Memorias Orales de Noemí Cuevas de Jiménez: Una Entrevista Hecha el 30 de Septiembre de 1978.* Baylor University Program for Oral History. N.p.: Convención Bautista Mexicana de Texas, 1980. 19 pp.

999. **Curl, Robert F.** *Southwest Texas Methodism.* N.p.: Inter-Board Council, Southwest Texas Conference, Methodist Church [1951], 1975. 154 pp.

1000. **Curti, Josafat.** "The Chicano and the Church: Dominant Anglo Institutions Demand Cultural Suicide and Self-Negation as the Price for Chicano's Acceptance." *The Christian Century* 92, no. 9 (1975): 253-57.

1001. **Curtis, S.** "Many Adversaries." *The Church at Home and Abroad* 4, no. 10 (1888): 337.

1002. **Custer, Watson S.** "A Decade of Church-State Relations in Puerto Rico, 1952-1962." Ph.D. diss., Temple University, 1965. 302 pp.

1003. **Daniel, C. D.** "A Message from a Veteran to Mexican Baptists." *Home and Foreign Fields* 21 (March 1937): 6-7.

1004. **Davidson, Donald L.** "A History of Southern Baptists in the Northeastern United States, 1950-1972." Th.D. diss., Southwestern Baptist Theological Seminary, 1974. pp. 149; 153-55; 169-71; 203-4.

1005. **Davis, James H.** *Background Data for Planning for Methodist Ministry to Spanish-Speaking People in Chicago.* Philadelphia, PA: Department of Research and Survey, Division of National Missions of the Board of Missions of the Methodist Church, 1963. 50 pp.

1006. **Davis, James H.** "United Methodists and Minorities." *Response* 2, no. 10 (1970): 5, 6, 49.

1007. **Davis, J. Merle.** *The Church in Puerto Rico's Dilemma: A Study of the Economic and Social Basis of the Evangelical Church in Puerto Rico.* New York: Department of Social and Economic Research and Counsel; London: International Missionary Council, 1942.

1008. **Day, William H.** *Meeting Our Responsibilities in Puerto Rico.* New York: The American Missionary Association, 1980.

1009. **Dávila, Jaime E.** "A Translation of Selected Chapters from an Unpublished History of Baptist Mission Work in Puerto Rico, by Jose L. Delgado." Kansas City, KS. Central Baptist Theological Seminary,

1010. **De La Peña, Elena.** "Faithful Journeys of Hispanic Methodist Women." Master's thesis. Pacific School of Religion, 1987. 138 pp.

1011. **Deck, Allan Figueroa, S.J.** "The Challenge of Evangelical/Pentecostal Christianity to Hispanic Catholicism." In *Hispanic Catholic Culture in the U.S.: Issues and Concerns,* edited by Jay P. Dolan and Allan Figueroa Deck, S.J. 409-39. Notre Dame, IN: University of Notre Dame Press, 1994.

1012. **Deck, Allan Figueroa, S.J.** "Latino Theology: The Year of the 'Boom'." *Journal of Hispanic/Latino Theology* 1, no. 2 (1994): 51-63.

1013. **Delgado, Hector.** "A Strategy for Developing a More Effective Ministry to the Hispanic Community in Southern California." D.Min. Project Report. Fuller Theological Seminary, 1989. 385 pp.

1014. **Delgado, José L.** "Brief History of the Baptist Mission in Puerto Rico." *The Chronicle* 2, no. 3 (1939): 160-70.

1015. **Delgado, Jovita D.** *Memoria Orales de Jovita D. Delgado: Una Entrevista Hecha el 25 de junio de 1975.* Baylor University Program for Oral History. N.p.: Convención Bautista Mexicana de Texas, 1980. 9 pp.

1016. **Department of Church Planning and Research, Protestant Council of the City of New York.** "A Report on the Protestant Spanish Community in New York City." In *Protestantism and Latinos in the United States,* edited by Carlos E. Cortés. New York: Arno Press, 1980. 138 pp.

1017. **Department of Development and Planning, City of Chicago.** "Chicago's Spanish-Speaking Population: Selected Statistics." Chicago, IL. Department of Development and Planning, City of Chicago, 1973.

1018. **Detweiler, Charles S.** *Our Record in Puerto Rico.* New York: ABHMS, 1923. 12 pp.

1019. **Detweiler, Charles S.** *Puerto Rico Outgrowing Her Clothes.* New York: ABHMS, 1926. 12 pp.

1020. **Detweiler, Charles S.** *News from the Caribbean Missions.* New York: ABHMS, 1930.

1021. **Detweiler, Charles S.** *The Waiting Isles.* Philadelphia, PA: The Judson Press, 1930.

1022. **Detweiler, Charles S. and Angel M. Mergal.** *Barranquitas: A Grain of Mustard Seed in Puerto Rico.* New York: ABHMS, 1939. 10 pp.

1023. **Deutsch, Sarah.** *No Separate Refuge: Culture, Class, and Gender on an Anglo-Hispanic Frontier in the American Southwest, 1880-1940.* New York: Oxford University Press, 1987. pp. 63-86.

1024. **Dickinson, James H.** "The Supervision of Religious Education in Latin American Baptist Missions in Texas." D.R.E. thesis. Southwestern Baptist Theological Seminary, 1951. 210 pp.

1025. **Díaz Acosta, Juan.** *Historia de la Iglesia Evangélica Unida de Puerto Rico: Obra Evangélica para el Cincuentenario en Puerto Rico, 1899-1949.* San Juan, PR: n.p., 1950.

1026. **Díaz Alonzo, Maria Mercedes.** "An Approach to Church and State Relations in Puerto Rico." Ph.D. diss., Catholic University of America, 1972. 287 pp.

1027. **Díaz, Ana María.** "Religion in the Melting Pot of the Caribbean: San Juan, Puerto Rico." *New World Outlook,* n.s., 35, no. 9; Whole Series: 65, no. 5 (1975): 8-15. Reprinted in Antonio M. Stevens-Arroyo, ed., *Prophets Denied Honor* (Maryknoll, NY: Orbis Books, 1980), 336-38.

1028. **Díaz, Benjamín.** *Compendio de Historia de la Convención Bautista Mexicana de Texas: Los Bautistas en Texas a través de 50 Años (1910-*

1960) [Compendium of the History of the Mexican Baptist Convention of Texas: The Texas Baptists through 50 Years (1910-1960)]. San Antonio, TX: Casa Evangélica de Publicaciones de los Hermanos Díaz, 1961.

1029. **Dodson, Mamie L.** *History of the Woman's Missionary Union of Austin Association.* Austin, TX: Capital Printing Co, 1936. 38 pp.

1030. **Dohen, Dorothy.** *Two Studies of Puerto Rico: Religion Data. The Background of Consensual Union.* Sondeos, no. 3. Cuernavaca, México: Centro Intercultural de Documentación, 1966. 155 pp.

1031. **Dolan, Jay P. and Gilberto M. Hinojosa, eds.** *Mexican Americans and the Catholic Church, 1900-1965.* The Notre Dame History of Hispanic Catholics in the U.S. Notre Dame, IN: University of Notre Dame Press, 1994. 380 pp.

1032. **Douglass, Harlan P.** *Congregational Missionary Work in Porto Rico.* New York: American Missionary Association, 1910.

1033. **Dresch, Erwin D., ed.** *Himnos y Coros de Palabras Fieles.* St. Louis, MO: Faithful Words Publishing Co, n.d. Hymnal.

1034. **Droste, Mary.** "A Missionary's Vacation in Puerto Rico." *The Spirit of Missions,* June 1923, 350.

1035. **Drury, Marion.** *Mission Triumphs in Puerto Rico and Santo Domingo.* Ponce, P.R.: n.p., 1924.

1036. **Duggan, Janie Prichard.** *An Isle of Eden; A Story of Porto Rico.* Philadelphia, PA: Griffith and Rowland Press, 1912. 346 pp.

1037. **Duggan, Janie P.** *Child of the Sea; A Chronicle of Porto Rico.* Philadelphia, PA: Judson Press, 1920. 237 pp.

1038. **Dunn, Mildred.** "Mexican Mission Takes Root in California." *Southern Baptist Home Missions* 23 (December 1952): 24-25.

1039. **Dunn, Mildred.** "Veteran Missionaries Retire from Board." *Southern Baptist Home Missions* 23 (May 1952): 28-29.

1040. **Dye, Harold E.** *Shining Like the Stars.* Atlanta, GA: Home Mission Board, Southern Baptist Convention, 1947. See chapter four.

1041. **Eastman, Fred.** *Unfinished Business of the Presbyterian Church in America.* Philadelphia, PA: n.p., 1921. pp. 41-78.

1042. **El Departamento de Música y Adoración del Concilio para la Obra Hispano Americana. G. P. Simmonds, editor.** *El Himnario.* Winona Lake, IN: Rodeheaver Company, 1964. Hymnal.

1043. **Elizondo, Virgilio.** *Galilean Journey: The Mexican-American Promise.* Maryknoll, NY: Orbis Books, 1983. 147 pp.

1044. **Elliott, Leslie R., ed.** *Centennial Story of Texas Baptists.* Dallas, TX: The Executive Board of the Baptist General Convention of Texas, 1936. 434 pp.

1045. **Ellis, Martha Thomas.** *Amercans, Too.* Atlanta, GA: Home Mission Board, Southern Baptist Convention, 1953.

1046. **Ellis, Martha Thomas.** "Nuestra Tarea, 1955-1978." *Nuestra Tarea,* February 1980, 17-22.

1047. **Engage/Social Action Forum.** "Hispanic Americans [Interview with Irene Adame and David Nieto]." *Engage/Social Action Forum* 3, no. 7 (1975): 36-37.

1048. **Engage/Social Action Forum.** "Puerto Rico: More Than Vacation Hotels." *Engage/Social Action* 4 (October 1976): 17-48.

1049. **Engh, Michael E.** "Frontier Religion in an Era of Transition: Los Angeles, 1848-1885." Ph.D. diss., The University of Wisconsin, Madison, 1987. 511 pp.

1050. **Escamilla, Roberto.** "MARCHA (Methodist Association Representing the Concerns of Hispanic Americans)." *Engage/Social Action* 6, no. 6 (1978): 18.

1051. **Escobar, Juan Samuel.** "Orlando Costas: In Memoriam." *Transformation* 5, no. 3 (1988): 1.

1052. **Escobar, Samuel.** "Orlando Costas con el Señor [Notice of Death of Orlando E. Costas]." *Enlace Teológico* 3 (November 1987): 3.

1053. **Espino, José.** *Ministerio Dramático.* El Paso, TX: n.p., 1963. 98 pp.

1054. **Espino, José.** *Perfiles.* El Paso, TX: n.p., 1963. 96 pp.

1055. **Espino, José.** *Virutas de Mi Taller.* El Paso, TX: n.p., 1963. 47 pp.

1056. **Espinoza, H. O.** "Response to William H. Bently." In *Evangelical Affirmations,* edited by K. Kantzer and C. Henry. 335-42. Grand Rapids, MI: Academie Books, 1990. pp. 299-333.

1057. **Estrada, Fred L.** "The Second Spanish Baptist Church of Philadelphia: Its Birth and Its Growth." Philadelphia, PA. Eastern Baptist Theological Seminary, 1983. Manuscript.

1058. **Estrada, Isabel A., Ruby H. Vargas, and Judith L. Bishop.** *Fieles al Maestro: Bordadoras del Diseño Misionero.* Dallas, TX: Women's Missionary Union of Texas, 1992. 320 pp.

1059. **Estrada, Leobardo F.** "Doctrine of the Trinity in Recent American and British Thought." Master's thesis. Southwestern Baptist Theological Seminary, 1954. 72 pp.

1060. **Estrada, Leobardo F.** "Limpio de Manos y Puro de Corazón." Audiotaped sermon delivered for "La Hora Bautista," 17 February 1961. Fort Worth, TX: Radio and Television Commission, Southern Baptist Convention, 1961.

1061. **Estrada, Leobardo F.** "Missions Day Chapel." Audiotaped sermon delivered on 22 Frebruary 1961. Fort Worth, TX: Southwestern Baptist Theological Seminary, 1961.

1062. **Estrada, Leobardo F.** "Vida Abundante." Audio recording. Fort Worth, TX: Radio and Television Commission, Southern Baptist Convention, 1961.

1063. **Estrada, Leobardo F.** "Into New York—Puerto Ricans." *Home Missions* 34 (February 1963): 10.

1064. **Estrada, Leobardo F.** *Oral Memoirs of Leobardo Estrada, Sr., 10 February 1981.* Mexican Baptist Oral History Project. [Waco, TX]: Baylor University, Institute for Oral History, 1984. 171 pp.

1065. **Evangelical Council of Churches in Puerto Rico.** "Reports to the Evangelical Council of Churches in Puerto Rico." Puerto Rico Strategy Conference. San Germán: Inter American University, 1959.

1066. **Everett, Harvey A.** "The Spanish-American Baptist Seminary, A Study of Its Work and Future." Valley Forge, PA. 1964. Manuscript.

1067. **Falcón, Rafael.** *The Hispanic Mennonite Church in North America, 1932-1982.* Translated by Ronald Collins. Scottdale, PA: Herald Press, 1986. 223 pp.

1068. **Falls, Anna E.** "The Place of Private and Church Schools in the Education of the State." Master's thesis. University of New México, 1929.

1069. **Faulkenbury, Phyllis.** "Puerto Rico: Special Report." *Home Missions* 50 (June 1979): 12-17.

1070. **Fenton, Jerry F.** *Understanding the Religious Background of the Puerto Rican.* Sondeos, no. 52. Cuernavaca, México: Centro Intercultural de Documentación, 1969.

1071. **Fernandez, Abraham.** "History of the Presbyterian Church, U.S.A., among the Spanish-Speaking People in the Southwest." B.D. thesis. San Francisco Theological Seminary, 1943. 49 pp.

1072. **Fernández, José M.** "The Concept of Central Churches." 1968. Manuscript.

1073. **Fernández, José M.** "Examen, Diagnosis, y Prognosis de Nuestras Congregaciones." The United Methodist Church, 1969. Manuscript.

1074. **Fernández, José M.** "The Relationship between the Brown Community and the Church in the Pomona Valley." Claremont, CA. Claremont School of Theology, 1970. Manuscript.

1075. **Fernández, José M.** "Spanish-American Methodism in the Southern California-Arizona Conference." Claremont, CA. School of Theology, Claremont, 1970. Manuscript.

1076. **Fernández, José M.** "Report of a Survey of the Southern Arizona Hispanic Methodist Churches." Latin American Methodist Action Group, Southern California-Arizona Conference, The United Methodist Church. 1972.

1077. **Fernández, José M.** "The History and Prospects of Hispanic Methodism in the Southern California-Arizona Conference of The United Methodist Church." D.Min. Project Report. Claremont School of Theology, 1973. 206 pp.

1078. **Fernández, José M.** "Un Resumen Breve de la Historia del Metodismo Hispano en California y Arizona." Los Angeles, CA. Latin American Methodist Action Group (LAMAG), 1979. Manuscript.

1079. **Fernández-Calienes, Raúl.** "Who Me? Reflections on an Encounter with Refugees." *International Review of Mission* 78, nos. 311-312 (1989): 455-56.

1080. **Fernández-Calienes, Raúl.** "Celebration or Mourning? 500 Years of Christianity in the Américas." *Presbyterian Outlook* 174, no. 14 (1992): 9.

1081. **Fitzgerald, William A.** "A Survey of Religious Conditions in Puerto Rico, 1899-1934." Ph.D. diss., Fordham University, 1934. 107 pp.

1082. **Fitzpatrick, Joseph P.** "The Dilemma of Social Research and Social Policy: The Puerto Rican Case, 1953-1993." In *Old Masks, New Faces,* edited by Anthony M. Stevens-Arroyo and Gilbert Cadena. 173-81. Vol. 2 of PARAL Studies Series. New York: Bildner Center for Western Hemisphere Studies, 1995.

1083. **Font, Eduardo.** "Porto Rico Association." *The Baptist,* 23 February 1924.

1084. **Foote, Cheryl.** "Alice Blake of Trementina: Mission Teacher of the Southwest." *Journal of Presbyterian History* 60, no. 3 (1982): 228-42.

1085. **Foote, Cheryl Jean.** "'Let Her Works Praise Her': Women's Experiences in the Southwest, 1846-1912." Ph.D. diss., The University of New México, 1986. 285 pp.

1086. **Gadden, Deaconness.** "A Missionary's Vacation in Puerto Rico." *The Spirit of Missions,* August 1922, 532-35.

1087. **Gallego, Daniel T.** "Religiosity as a Coping Mechanism among Hispanic Elderly." In *Hispanic Elderly: A Cultural Signature,* edited by Marta Sotomayor and Herman Curiel. 117-35. Edinburg, TX: Pan American University Press, 1988.

1088. **Galván, Elías.** "Hispanics: Challenge and Opportunity." *Apuntes: Reflexiones Teológicas desde el Margen Hispano* 12, no. 2 (1992): 89-97.

1089. **García, E. Rous.** "Nuestra Obra Médica." *Puerto Rico Evangélico,* 10 September 1914,

1090. **García, E. Rous.** "El Hospital San Lucas de Ponce." *Puerto Rico Evangélico,* 25 July 1937,

1091. **García, Mario T.** *Memories of Chicano History: The Life and Narrative of Bert Corona.* Latinos in American Society and Culture, no. 2. Berkeley, CA: University of California Press, 1994. pp. 14, 36, 38, 41-42, 52, 63-64, 96, 323.

1092. **García, Matías C.** "Faith Tested: Missionary Recovers following United Prayers." *Southern Baptist Home Missions* 10 (May 1939): 5.

1093. **Garcia, Richard A.** "The Catholic Church." In *Rise of the Mexican American Middle Class: San Antonio, 1929-1941,* The Centennial Series of the Association of Former Students, Texas A&M University. College Station, TX: Texas A&M University Press, 1991. pp. 157-58.

1094. **García-Treto, Francisco O.** "Historical Perspectives on Hispanic Missions." *Perkins Journal* 35, no. 1 (1981): 63-72.

1095. **García-Treto, Francisco O. and R. Douglas Brackenridge.** "Hispanic Presbyterians: Life in Two Cultures." In *The Diversity of Discipleship: Presbyterians and Twentieth-Century Christian Witness,* edited by Milton J. Coalter, John M. Mulder, and Louis B. Weeks. 257-79. Presbyterian Presence. Louisville, KY: Westminster/John Knox Press, 1991.

1096. **Garnett, Christine.** "Retired Missionary Finds Cuba in Jacksonville." *Home Missions* 35, no. 2 (1967): 35.

1097. **Garza, Isidro.** "The Development of the Southern Baptist Spanish

Speaking Work in California." Master's thesis. Golden Gate Baptist Theological Seminary, 1954. 56 pp.

1098. **Gay, George A.** "Hispanic Ministries Education at Fuller Theological Seminary." *Theological Education* 13, no. 2 (1977): 85-89.

1099. **General Board of Church and Society of The United Methodist Church.** "Hispanic Americans: A Growing Force." *e/sa forum-99* (December 1983): 72 pp. Articles in Spanish and English.

1100. **General Council on Ministries, The United Methodist Church.** *"Developing and Strengthening the Ethnic Minority Local Church: For Witness and Mission."* 1985-88 Operational Manual. Dayton, OH: General Council on Ministries, The United Methodist Church, 1985.

1101. **Glaze, Michael S.** "A Pilot Study of Southern Baptists' Attitudes towards the Active Use of Art in the Church: A Prelude to Future Research." Ph.D. diss., Florida State University, 1993. 288 pp.

1102. **Godsoe, James E.** "History of Hispanic Work in Illinois." Springfield, IL. Illinois Baptist State Association, 6 pp. Mimeographed.

1103. **González, Jorge A.** *Traductor de la Biblia en Español.* México: Sociedades Bíblicas Unidas, 1969.

1104. **González, Jorge A.** "Día del Estudiante Metodista." *El Intérprete* 12, no. 2 (1974): 4-5, 20.

1105. **González, Jorge A.** "The Reina-Valera Bible: From Dream to Reality." *Apuntes: Reflexiones Teológicas desde el Margen Hispano* 1, no. 4 (1981): 10-15. Also published in Justo L. González, ed., *Voces: Voices from the Hispanic Church* (Nashville, TN: Abingdon Press, 1992), pp. 46-49.

1106. **González, Jorge A.** "La Eucaristía en la Tradición Metodista." *El Intérprete* 21, no. 4 (1983): 5-7.

1107. **González, Jorge A.** "Respuesta: Repensando el Descubrimiento." *Apuntes: Reflexiones Teológicas desde el Margen Hispano* 7, no. 1 (1987): 20-22.

1108. **González, Justo L.** "El Principio de la Reforma como Principio." *El Boletín* 32, no. 3 (1967): 4-7.

1109. **González, Justo L.** "El Cristiano en la Historia." *El Boletín* 34, no. 2 (1969): 3-15.

1110. **González, Justo L.** *The Development of Christianity in the Latin Caribbean.* Grand Rapids, MI: William B. Eerdmans Publishing Co., 1969.

1111. **González, Justo L.** *Ambrosio de Milán.* San José, Costa Rica: Centro de Publicaciones Cristianas, 1970.

1112. **González, Justo L.** *Historia de las Misiones.* Buenos Aires, Argentina: Methopress, 1970.

1113. **González, Justo L.** "La Historia de Occidente: Bosquejo de una Concepción Bibliófila." México. Instituto Internacional de Estudios Superiores (Comunidad Teológica de México), 1972. 7 pp.

1114. **González, Justo L.** "Athens and Jerusalem Revisited: Reason and Authority in Tertullian." *Church History* 43, no. 1 (1974): 17-25. Reprinted in Everett Ferguson, David Scholer and Paul Corby Finney, eds., *The Early Church and Greco-Roman Thought,* Studies in Early Christianity, vol. 8 (New York: Garland Publishing, Inc., 1993).

1115. **González, Justo L.** "Encarnación e Historia." In *Fe Cristiana y Latinoamérica,* edited by René Padilla. 151-67. Buenos Aires, Argentina: Ediciones Certeza, 1974.

1116. **González, Justo L.** "Liturgy and Politics: A Latin American Perspective." *Missiology: An International Review* 2, no. 2 (1974): 175-81.

1117. **González, Justo L.** "Los Ministerios en la Iglesia Protestante." In *Ministerios Eclesiales en América Latina,* edited by CELAM. 106-20. Bogotá, Colombia: CELAM, 1974.

1118. **González, Justo L.** "Inner and Outer Authority in St. Teresa of Avila." *Occasional Essays [of CELEP]* 4, no. 3 (1977): 29-39.

1119. **González, Justo L.** *Luces Bajo el Almud.* San José, Costa Rica: Editorial Caribe, 1977.

1120. **González, Justo L.** *Y Hasta lo Ultimo de la Tierra: Vol. I: La Era de los Mártires.* Miami, FL: Editorial Caribe, 1978.

1121. **González, Justo L.** *Y Hasta lo Ultimo de la Tierra: Vol. II: La Era de los Gigantes.* Miami, FL: Editorial Caribe, 1978.

1122. **González, Justo L.** *Y Hasta lo Ultimo de la Tierra: Vol. III: La Era de las Tinieblas.* Miami, FL: Editorial Caribe, 1978.

1123. **González, Justo L.** *Y Hasta lo Ultimo de la Tierra: Vol. IV: La Era de los Altos Ideales.* Miami, FL: Editorial Caribe, 1978.

1124. **González, Justo L.** *Y Hasta lo Ultimo de la Tierra: Vol. V: La Era de los Sueños Frustrados.* Miami, FL: Editorial Caribe, 1979.

1125. **González, Justo L.** *Y Hasta lo Ultimo de la Tierra: Vol. VI: La Era de los Reformadores.* Miami, FL: Editorial Caribe, 1980.

1126. **González, Justo L.** *Y Hasta lo Ultimo de la Tierra: Vol. VII: La Era de los Conquistadores.* Miami, FL: Editorial Caribe, 1980.

1127. **González, Justo L.** "Towards a New Reading of History." *Apuntes: Reflexiones Teológicas desde el Margen Hispano* 1, no. 3 (1981): 4-14.

1128. **González, Justo L.** *Y Hasta lo Ultimo de la Tierra: Vol. VIII: La Era de los Dogmas y las Dudas.* Miami, FL: Editorial Caribe, 1983.

1129. **González, Justo L.** *The Story of Christianity: Vol. I: Early and Medieval Christianity.* New York: Harper & Row, 1984.

1130. **González, Justo L.** "Sanctuary: Some Historical, Legal, and Theological Considerations." *Exodus,* vol. 3, no. 3 (1985).

1131. **González, Justo L.** *The Story of Christianity: Vol. II: From the Reformation to the Present.* New York: Harper & Row, 1985.

1132. **González, Justo L.** "The Apostles' Creed and the Sanctuary Movement." *Apuntes: Reflexiones Teológicas desde el Margen Hispano* 6, no. 1 (1986): 12-20.

1133. **González, Justo L.** Prologue to *Panorama del Protestantismo en Cuba,* edited by Marcos Antonio Ramos. 9-12. Miami FL: Editorial Caribe, 1986.

1134. **González, Justo L.** *A History of Christian Thought: Vol. I: From the Beginnings to the Council of Chalcedon.* 2nd ed. Nashville, TN: Abingdon, 1987.

1135. **González, Justo L.** *A History of Christian Thought: Vol. II: From Saint Augustine to the Eve of the Reformation.* 2nd ed. Nashville, TN: Abingdon Press, 1987.

1136. **González, Justo L.** *A History of Christian Thought: Vol. III: From the Reformation to the Present.* 2nd ed. Nashville, TN: Abingdon Press, 1987.

1137. **González, Justo L.** "Sanctuary: Part of Our Heritage." *Response Ability,* no. 29 (Winter 1987): 12-13.

1138. **González, Justo L.** "The Two Faces of Hispanic Christianity." *The Judson Bulletin* 6 (1987): 17-26.

1139. **González, Justo L.** *Y Hasta lo Ultimo de la Tierra: Vol. IX: La Era de los Nuevos Horizontes.* Miami, FL: Editorial Caribe, 1987.

1140. **González, Justo L.** "The Crusades: Piety Misguided." In *Cloud of Witnesses. Leader's Guide.* 61-75. Nashville, TN: Graded Press, 1988.

1141. **González, Justo L.** "Monasticism: Patterns of Piety." In *Cloud of Witnesses. Leader's Guide.* 45-59. Nashville, TN: Graded Press, 1988.

1142. **González, Justo L.** *Y Hasta lo Ultimo de la Tierra: Vol. X: La Era Inconclusa.* Miami, FL: Editorial Caribe, 1988.

1143. **González, Justo L.** *Christian Thought Revisited.* Nashville, TN: Abingdon Press, 1989. 185 pp.

1144. **González, Justo L.** "Faith and Wealth in the Early Church." *Biblical Literacy Today* 4, no. 2 (1989-90): 14.

1145. **González, Justo L.** *Faith and Wealth: A History of Early Christian Ideas on the Origin, Significance, and Use of Money.* San Francisco: Harper & Row, 1990. 240 pp.

1146. **González, Justo L., ed.** *Each in Our Own Tongue: A History of Hispanics in United Methodism.* Nashville, TN: Abingdon Press, 1991. 176 pp. Also published in Spanish as *En Nuestra Propia Lengua, Una Historia del Metodismo Unido Hispano.*

1147. **González, Justo L.** Foreword to *A Violent Evangelism: The Politicial and Religious Conquest of the Américas,* by Luis N. Rivera. Louisville, KY: Westminster/John Knox Press, 1992.

1148. **González, Justo L.** *Historia del Pensamiento Cristiano: Vol. I: Desde los Orígenes Hasta el Concilio de Calcedonia.* 2nd ed. Miami, Fl: Editorial Caribe, 1992.

1149. **González, Justo L.** *Historia del Pensamiento Cristiano: Vol II: Desde San Agustín Hasta las Vísperas de la Reforma.* 2nd ed. Miami, FL: Editorial Caribe, 1992.

1150. **González, Justo L.** "Lights in the Darkness." *Christian History* 11, no. 35 (1992): 32-34.

1151. **González, Justo L.** "Setting the Context: The Option for the Poor in Latin American Liberation Theology." In *Poverty and Ecclesiology: Nineteenth-Century Evangelicals in the Light of Liberation Theology,* edited by Anthony L. Dunnavant. 9-26. Collegeville, MN: Liturgical Press, 1992.

1152. **González, Justo L., ed.** *Voces: Voices from the Hispanic Church.* Nashville, TN: Abingdon Press, 1992. 171 pp.

1153. **González, Justo L.** "Voices of Compassion." *Missiology* 20, no. 2 (1992): 163-73.

1154. **González, Justo L.** "América Latina en Perspectiva Histórica." In *Desde el Reverso: Materiales para la Historia de la Iglesia.* 129-41.

Coyoacán, México: Publicaciones el Faro and Academía para la Historia de la Iglesia Latina (APHILA), 1993.

1155. **González, Justo L.** "Globalization in the Teaching of Church History." *ATS Theological Education* 29, no. 2 (1993): 49-71.

1156. **González, Justo L.** *Historia del Pensamiento Cristiano: Tomo 3: Desde la Reforma Protestante Hasta el Siglo Veinte.* Miami, FL: Editorial Caribe, 1993. 491 pp.

1157. **González, Justo L.** "La Enseñanza de la Historia de la Iglesia desde una Perspectiva Global." In *Desde el Reverso: Materiales para la Historia de la Iglesia,* 13-46. El Coyoacán, Mexcio: Publicaciones el Faro and Academía para la Historia de la Iglesia Latina (APHILA), 1993.

1158. **González, Justo L.** "St. Francis Was Right After All." *The Living Pulpit* 2, no. 2 (1993): 21.

1159. **González, Justo L.** "Historia de la Interpretación Bíblica." In *Lumbrera a Nuestro Camino,* edited by Pablo A. Jiménez. 79-118. Miami, FL: Editorial Caribe, 1994.

1160. **González, Justo L.** *Historia del Cristianismo.* Rev. ed. of *Y Hasta lo Ultimo de la Tierra.* 2 Vols. Vol. 1, "Desde la Era de los Martires Hasta la Era de los Sueños Frustrados." Vol. 2, "Desde la Era de la Reforma Hasta la Era Inconclusa." Miami, FL: Editorial Unilit, 1994.

1161. **González, Justo L.** *Historia del Cristianismo I y II.* Rev. ed. Miami, FL: Editorial Unilit, 1994.

1162. **González, Justo L.** "How the Bible Has Been Interpreted in Christian Tradition." In *The New Interpreter's Bible.* 83-106. Vol. 1. Nashville, TN: Abingdon Press, 1994.

1163. **González, Justo L.** "In Remembrance of Me: Present, Past, and Future." In *Hidden Stories: Unveiling the History of the Latino Church,* edited by Daniel R. Rodríguez-Díaz and David Cortés-Fuentes. 159-65. Decatur, GA: AETH, 1994.

1164. **González, Justo L.** "The Religious World of Hispanic Americans." In *World Religions in America: An Introduction,* edited by Jacob Neusner. 111-30. Louisville, KY: Westminster/John Knox Press, 1994.

1165. **González, Justo L.** "Voices of Compassion Yesterday and Today." In *New Face of the Church in Latin America,* edited by Guillermo Cook. 3-12. Maryknoll, NY: Orbis Books, 1994.

1166. **González, Justo L.** *Bosquejo de Historia de la Iglesia.* Decatur, GA: AETH, 1995. 117 pp.

1167. **González, Justo L.** "The Story of Christian Beginnings." *Adult Bible Studies Teacher* 4, no. 1 (1995): 16-80.

1168. **González, Justo L.** *Los Reformistas Españoles.* San Juan, PR: Evangelical Seminary of Puerto Rico, n.d. Separata of *El Boletín* of the Evangelical Seminary of Puerto Rico. Also published in English as "The Spanish Reformers."

1169. **González, Justo L. and Catherine Gunsalus González.** *Paul: His Impact on Christianity.* Nashville, TN: Graded Press, 1987.

1170. **González, Justo L. and Catherine Gunsalus González.** "An Historical Survey." In *The Globalization of Theological Education,* edited by Alice F. Evans, Robert A. Evans, and David A. Roozen. 13-32. Maryknoll, NY: Orbis Books, 1993.

1171. **González, Justo L., Daniel Rodríguez-Díaz, and Eliseo Pérez Alvarez, eds.** *Desde el Reverso: Materiales para la Historia de la Iglesia.* Chicago, IL: Publicaciones el Faro and APHILA, 1993. 141 pp.

1172. **González, (Mrs.) I. E.** "Training Increases Opportunity." *Southern Baptist Home Missions* 12 (November 1941): 11.

1173. **González Peña, Luis M.** "La Misión Hispana de Miami." *La Voz Bautista [Cuba]* 45 (April 1955): 18-19.

1174. **González y Pérez, Belén.** "A Reading of Orlando E. Costas on the Theology of Contextual Evangelization: A Galilean Perspective." Master's thesis. Lutheran Theological Seminary at Gettysburg, 1991. 51 pp.

1175. **Goodykoontz, Colin B.** *Home Missionary Movement and the West.* Cambridge, MA: Harvard University Press, 1921.

1176. **Goodykoontz, Colin B.** *Home Missions on the American Frontier.* Caldwell, ID: Caxton Printers, 1939. 460 pp.

1177. **Grainger, Jane Atkins, ed.** *El Centenario de la Palabra: El Rito Presbyterian Church, 1879-1979.* Albuquerque, NM: Menaul Historical Library of the Southwest, 1980.

1178. **Gray, Elmer L.** *Heirs of Promise: A Chronicle of California Southern Baptists, 1940-1978.* Fresno, CA: Southern Baptist General Convention of California, 1978. 200 pp.

1179. **Grebler, Leo, Joan W. Moore, and Ralph C. Guzmán.** "Protestants and Mexicans." In *The Mexican American People: The Nation's Second Largest Minority,* edited by Leo Grebler, Joan W. Moore, and Ralph C. Guzman. 486-512. New York: The Free Press, 1970.

1180. **Greene, J. Milton.** "What Our Missions are Doing for Porto Ricans." *The Assembly Herald* (May 1910).

1181. **Gregory, Ernest J.** *That They Might Have Life: A Brief History of the First Sixteen Years of the Mexican Baptist Orphans Home.* San Antonio, TX: Board of Directors, Mexican Baptist Orphans Home, n.d. 60 pp.

1182. **Grijalva, Joshua.** *A History of Mexican Baptists in Texas 1881-1981: Comprising an Account of the Genesis, the Progress, and the Accomplishments of the People Called "Los Bautistas de Texas."* Dallas, TX: Office of Language Missions, Baptist General Convention of Texas in cooperation with the Mexican Baptist Convention of Texas, 1982.

1183. **Grijalva, Joshua.** "The Story of Hispanic Southern Baptists." *Baptist History and Heritage* 18, no. 1 (1983): 40-47.

1184. **Grijalva, Joshua and Dorothy Grijalva.** *Heirs of the Soil.* Atlanta, GA: Home Mission Board, Southern Baptist Convention, 1950. 91 pp.

1185. **Groff, G. G.** "Porto Rico, a Mission Field." *The Independent,* 22 December 1898.

1186. **Groff, G. G.** "After Two Year's Work in Porto Rico." *The Independent,* 9 August 1900, 102-5.

1187. **Grose, Howard B.** *Advance in the Antilles: The New Era in Cuba and Porto Rico.* Forward Mission Study Courses. New York: Missionary Education Movement of the United States and Canada; Eaton and Mains, 1910. 259 pp.

1188. **Guajardo, Alcides.** "Brown Like Me." Audiotaped lecture at the "Conference on the Transitional Church," September 1972. Fort Worth, TX: Southwestern Baptist Theological Seminary, 1972.

1189. **Gutiérrez, Félix.** "The Western Jurisdiction." In *Each in Our Own Tongue: A History of Hispanic United Methodism,* edited by Justo L. González. 65-83. Nashville, TN: Abingdon Press, 1991.

1190. **Halbeck, Frank.** "Spanish Ministries." *The California Southern Baptist,* 13 November 1980, 18-19.

1191. **Hall, Bryan, ed.** *Methodist Churches of the New México Conference; a Brief History.* Sacramento, NM: N.p., 1965.

1192. **Hall, E. Edwin.** *Ahab and Naboth: or, The United States and México.* New Haven, CN: A.H. Maltby; J.H. Benham, 1847. 16 pp.

1193. **Hall, George F.** "Problems of Spanish-American Minority Aired for NCC Unit." *The Christian Century* 86, no. 47 (1969): 1498-1500.

1194. **Hallock, Constance Magee.** *Forty-eight Plus!* New York: Friendship Press, 1948. 64 pp.

1195. **Handy, Robert T.** *We Witness Together; a History of Cooperative Efforts in Puerto Rico.* New York: Friendship Press, 1956. 273 pp.

1196. **Harrington, Janette T.** "Puerto Rico: Bridge between the Américas." *Presbyterian Life,* 15 February 1964, 14-21.

1197. **Harrison, David C.** "A Survey of the Administrative and Educational Policies of the Baptist, Methodist, and Presbyterian Churches among Mexican-American People in Texas." Master's thesis. University of Texas, 1952. 148 pp.

1198. **Hartmire, Wayne C., Jr.** "The Church and the Delano Grape Strike-A Partial Report." California Migrant Ministry, 1966. Mimeographed.

1199. **Harvey, Samuel A.** "Roots of California Southern Baptists, 1890-1940." S.T.D. (Doctor of Sacred Theology) thesis. Golden Gate Baptist Theological Seminary, 1973. 147 pp.

1200. **Harwood, Thomas.** "New México Spanish Mission of the Methodist Episcopal Church." *The Gospel in All Lands,* no. 4 (April 1897): 171-72.

1201. **Harwood, Thomas.** *History of Spanish and English Missions of the New México Methodist Episcopal Church from 1850-1910.* Vol. 2. Albuquerque, NM: El Abogado Press, 1908.

1202. **Harwood, Thomas.** *History of New México Spanish and English Missions of the Methodist Episcopal Church. 2 vols.* 2nd ed. Albuquerque, NM: El Abogado Press, 1983. 380 pp.

1203. **Haselden, Kyle.** "Peace and Peril at Ghost Ranch." *Christian Century* 84, no. 31 (1967): 988-90.

1204. **Hawkins, Olga Orozco.** "Hispanic/Latina Women in Agriculture." In *Hidden Stories: Unveiling the History of the Latino Church,* edited by Daniel R. Rodríguez-Díaz and David Cortés-Fuentes. 117-24. Decatur, GA: AETH, 1994.

1205. **Hayne, Coe.** *Old Trails and New: True Life Stories of Baptist Home Mission Fields.* Philadelphia, PA: Judson Press, 1920. pp. 211-221.

1206. **Hernandez, Edwin I. and Charles Teel.** "Missionaries, Revolutionaries, and Visionaries: The Radical Roots of Peruvian Adventism." Paper presented at the annual meeting of the Society for the Scientific Study of Religion, Pittsburgh, PA, November 1991.

1207. **Hernández, Lydia.** "La Mujer Chicana y la Justicia Económica."

Apuntes: Reflexiones Teológicas desde el Margen Hispano 6, no. 4 (1986): 81-83.

1208. **Hernández, Lydia.** "Even Today What Began Five Hundred Years Ago." In *New Face of the Church in Latin America,* edited by Guillermo Cook. 13-20. American Society of Missiology Series, no. 18. Maryknoll, NY: Orbis Books, 1994.

1209. **Herrera, Pedro G.** *Una Mirada a Cristo a través de la Teología Contemporánea: Sermones por Pedro G. Herrera.* San Antonio, TX: n.p., 1971. 188 pp.

1210. **Hill, Charles Edwin.** "Christian Work in Porto Rico, 1898-1918." Master's thesis. Columbia University, 1919. 42 pp.

1211. **Hill, Leonard E.** *Mission: The Northeast.* Atlanta, GA: Home Mission Board, Southern Baptist Convention, 1969.

1212. **Hine, Leland D.** *Baptists in Southern California.* Valley Forge, PA: Judson Press, 1966. 192 pp.

1213. **Hinson, Jackie.** "A History of American Baptist Spanish-Speaking Work in Southern California." 1964. Manuscript.

1214. **Hobart, Charles.** "Census of Protestant Churches in New York City." Report for the Greater New York Federation of Churches. New York, 1937.

1215. **Hobbs, G. Warfield.** "From Cleanliness to Godliness in Porto Rico." *The Spirit of Missions* 89 (January 1924): 15-17.

1216. **Hodges, B. A.** *A History of Mexican Mission Work Conducted...in Synod of Texas.* Waxahachie, TX: n.p., 1931.

1217. **Hodges, B.A.** *Our Mexican Missions in Texas.* Waxahachie, TX: n.p., 1931.

1218. **Hoehn, Richard A.** "Chicano Ethos: An Anglo View." *Lutheran Quarterly* 28, no. 2 (1976): 116-72.

1219. **Holland, Clifton L.** "The Religious Dimension in Hispanic Los Angeles: A Protestant Case Study." Ph.D. diss., South Pasadena, CA: William Carey Library, 1974. 541 pp.

1220. **Holland, Clifton L.** "Anglo-Hispanic Protestant Tensions in Southern California." *Missiology: An International Review* 3, no. 3 (1975): 323-45.

1221. **Holsinger, Justus G.** *Serving Rural Puerto Rico: A History of Eight Years of Service by the Mennonite Church.* Scottdale, PA: Mennonite Publishing House, 1952. 231 pp.

1222. **Home Mission Board, Department of Survey and Special Studies, Southern Baptist Convention.** *A Brief Study for Southern Baptists in Puerto Rico.* Atlanta, GA: Home Mission Board, Southern Baptist Convention, 1968.

1223. **Home Mission Board, Southern Baptist Convention.** "Our Language Friends." Filmstrip. Atlanta, GA: Home Mission Board, Southern Baptist Convention, 1961.

1224. **Horlyk, (Mrs.) Louis K.** "Interview with Rowena O. Horlyk (by Miss. Forman)." 1979.

1225. **Horton, H. G.** "Beginnings of the Mexican Work." *Texas Methodist Historical Quarterly* 1, no. 3 (1910): 289-91.

1226. **Huebert, Lois E.** "A History of Presbyterian Church Schools in New México." Master's thesis. University of New México, 1964. 104 pp.

1227. **Hullum, Everett, Jr.** "Puerto Rico." *Home Missions* 48 (May 1975): 23.

1228. **Hullum, Everett, Jr.** "Puerto Rico: Building Indigenous Churches from Scratch." *Home Missions* 46 (May 1975): 22-37.

1229. **Icaza, Rosa María.** "Spirituality of the Mexican American People." *Worship* 63 (May 1989): 232-46.

1230. **Iglesia Metodista de Puerto Rico.** *Libro de la Disciplina.* San Juan, PR: Iglesia Metodista de Puerto Rico, 1993. 240 pp.

1231. **Iglesia Metodista Episcopal.** *Doctrinas y Disciplina de la Iglesia Metodista Episcopal del Sur.* Matamoros, México: Imprenta de "Ramo de Olivos", 1877. 148 pp.

1232. **Inlow, Eva R.** *Adventuring with God.* Atlanta, GA: Home Mission Board, Southern Baptist Convention, 1952. 112 pp.

1233. **Inman, Samuel G.** *Twenty-five Years of Mission Work in Porto Rico.* Reprint. New York: Committee on Cooperation in Latin America, 1924.

1234. **Inman, Samuel G.** *Evangelicals in Havana.* New York: La Nueva Democracia, 1929.

1235. **Inman, Samuel G.** *Trailing the Conquistadores.* New York: Friendship Press, 1930.

1236. **Inter-Conference Committee on Hispanic Ministry of the Central Texas and Río Grande [Conferences].** "Beginnings, Purposes, and Ministries: Inter-Conference Committee on Hispanic Ministry of the Central Texas and Río Grande [Conferences]." Report presented at the Consultation on Hispanic Ministries, Dallas, TX, November 1985.

1237. **Jackson, Constance.** *Spiritual Outlook in Porto Rico.* New York: Northern Baptist Convention, 1921. 8 pp.

1238. **James, Arthur.** *Twenty Years in Puerto Rico: A Record of Presbyterian Missionary Work since the American Occupation.* New York: Board of Home Missions, Presbyterian Church U.S.A., 1920.

1239. **Japas, Salim.** *Herejía, Colón, y la Inquisición: Se Repitirá la Historia.* Siloam Springs, AR: Creation Enterprises International, 1992. 141 pp.

1240. **Jaramillo, Luis.** "Address Given before the 182nd General Assembly of the United Presbyterian Church U.S.A. during Report of its Standing Committee on Church and Race." In *182nd General Assembly of the United Presbyterian Church U.S.A.,* held on 1970.

1241. **Jervey, Edward Drewry.** *The History of Methodism in Southern California and Arizona.* Nashville, TN: Parthenon Press, 1960.

1242. **Jiménez, Pablo A.,** ed. *Lumbrera a Nuestro Camino.* Miami, FL: Editorial Caribe, 1994. 179 pp.

1243. **Johnston, Julia H.** *Indian and Spanish Neighbors.* ATLA Monograph Preservation Program. New York: Fleming H. Revell, 1905. 194 pp.

1244. **Joint Presbyterian Task Force on Migration Issues in United States-México Relations.** "Mexican Migration to the United States: Challenge to Christian Witness and National Policy." N.d.

1245. **Junta Bautista de Publicaciones.** *Himnos Selectos Evangélicos.* Buenos Aires, Argentina: Junta Bautista de Publicaciones, 1964. 436 pp. Hymnal.

1246. **Junta de Publicaciones de la Convención Evangélica Bautista.** *Himnos Selectos Evangélicos.* 1957. Reprint, Buenos Aires, Argentina: Junta de Publicaciones de la Convención Evangélica Bautista, 1958. 436 pp. Hymnal.

1247. **Kelley, Dean M.** "The Young Lords and the Spanish Congregation [Puerto Rican Revolutionary Group Takes over Church]." *The Christian Century* 87, no. 7 (1970): 208-11.

1248. **Kellogg, Harriet S.** *Life of Mrs. Emily J. Harwood.* Albuquerque, NM: El Abogado Press, 1903. 376 pp.

1249. **Knight, Walker L.,** ed. "The Mexican American in Texas." *Home Missions* 8 (July 1967): 6-29.

1250. **Krehbiel, Adolf J.** *They Worshiped Together.* N.p., 1986. 75 pp.

1251. **LaFontaine, Edith.** "An Image of the Past." *Engage/Social Action* 6, no. 6 (1978): 10-11.

1252. **LAMAG.** "A Proposal for Hispanic Ministry in the California-Pacific Conference of The United Methodist Church." Latin American Methodist Action Group [LAMAG]. N.d.

1253. **Langdale, John W., ed.** *Suplemento a la Disciplina Española de 1920.* New York: The Methodist Book Concern, 1929. 614 pp.

1254. **Langerak de García, Ana.** "In This Issue [Notice of death of Orlando Costas]." *Latin American Pastoral Issues* 14, no. 2 (1987): 4-7.

1255. **Lara-Braud, Jorge.** "The Church's Partnership with Mexican Americans: A Proposal to Anglo Protestant Churchmen." 1967. Manuscript.

1256. **Lara-Braud, Jorge.** "Our Spanish-American Neighbors." *The Christian Century* 85, no. 2 (1968): 43-45.

1257. **Lara-Braud, Jorge.** "Hispanic-Americans and the Crisis in the Nation." *Theology Today* 26, no. 3 (1969): 334-38.

1258. **Lara-Braud, Jorge.** "Hispanic-Americans and the Crisis in the Nation: Background Paper." *Social Progress* 59, no. 6 (1969): 50-60.

1259. **Lara-Braud, Jorge.** "La Raza Unida." *Social Progress* 59, no. 5 (1969): 8-10.

1260. **Lara-Braud, Jorge.** "Problems We Face in the Lower Río Grande Valley." *Social Progress* 59, no. 5 (1969): 22-24.

1261. **Lara-Braud, Jorge, ed.** *Our Claim on the Future, a Controversial Collection from Latin America.* New York: Friendship Press, 1970. 128 pp.

1262. **Lara-Braud, Jorge.** "The Hispanic-American Institute in 1971." Austin, TX. The Hispanic-American Institute, 1971.

1263. **Lara-Braud, Jorge.** "El Pueblo Unido Jamás Será Vencido/Funeral of Archbishop Romero." *Christianity and Crisis* 40, no. 8 (1980): 114, 148-50.

1264. **Lara-Braud, Jorge.** "The Gospel of Justice: 'Monseñor'" among His People." *Christianity and Crisis* 40, no. 8 (1980): 124-31.

1265. **Lara-Braud, Jorge.** "El Salvador: Dilemma for Christian Conscience." *Church and Society* 72, no. 2 (1981): 7-14.

1266. **Lara-Braud, Jorge.** "¿Podemos Creer en Dios Después de Esto?" *Apuntes: Reflexiones Teológicas desde el Margen Hispano* 13, no. 1 (1993): 73-85.

1267. **Lawrence, Una Roberts.** *The Keys of the Kingdom.* 4th ed. Atlanta, GA: Home Mission Board, Southern Baptist Convention, 1934. 128 pp.

1268. **Lawrence, Una Roberts.** "Modern Apostles of the Mexican Border; Men of the Border." *Home and Foreign Fields* 18 (February 1934): 12-15.

1269. **Lawrence, Una Roberts.** "The Story of a Dream and its Realization." *Home and Foreign Fields* 18 (April 1934): 11-13.

1270. **Lawrence, Una Roberts.** *Winning the Border: Baptist Missions among the Spanish-Speaking Peoples of the Border.* Atlanta, GA: Home Mission Board, Souhern Baptist Convention, 1935. 160 pp.

1271. **Lawrence, Una Roberts.** "Death Takes a Mexican Missionary." *Home and Foreign Fields* 20 (December 1936): 13-14.

1272. **Lawrence, Una Roberts.** *The Word of Their Testimony.* 6th ed. Atlanta, GA: Home Mission Board, Southern Baptist Convention, 1947. 128 pp.

1273. **Lawrence, Una Roberts.** *Home Mission Trails; A Study of Home Mission Fields.* Atlanta, GA: Home Mission Board, Southern Baptist Convention, n.d. pp. 36-39.

1274. **Lawrence, Una Roberts.** *Look upon the Fields.* Atlanta, GA: Home Mission Board, Southern Baptist Convention, n.d. pp. 34-53.

1275. **Leach, Milton S., Sr.** "Spanish Mission Work in New México." *Southern Baptist Home Missions* 22 (February 1951): 12.

1276. **Leach, Milton S., Jr.** "Spanish Mission Work in Miami Baptist Association." 1964. 7 pp. Mimeographed.

1277. **Leal, Jesús Hernández.** *Memorias Orales de Rev. & Sra. Hernández Leal: Una Entrevista Hecha el 27 de Febrero de 1979.* Baylor University Program for Oral History. N.p.: Convención Bautista Mexicana de Texas, 1980. 27 pp.

1278. **Lee, Dallas.** "The Puerto Rican in Harlem." *Home Missions* 40 (May 1969): 8-14.

1279. **Lee, Dallas M.** "Puerto Rico." *Home Missions* 40 (April 1969): 6-19.

1280. **Lee, Dallas P.** "The Mexican American in Texas." *Royal Service* 65, no. 11 (1971): 12-14.

1281. **Leigh, (Mrs.) J. E.** "Development and Accomplishments of the Mexican W. M. U. in Texas." *Southern Baptist Home Missions* 9 (June 1938): 10.

1282. **Leija, Juanita.** *Memorias Orales de Juanita Leija: Una Entrevista Hecha el 1 de Marzo de 1979.* Baylor University Program for Oral History. N.p.: Convención Bautista Mexicana de Texas, 1979. 40 pp.

1283. **Liggett, Thomas J.** *Latin America-A Challenge to Protestantism.* San Juan, PR: Evangelical Seminary of Puerto Rico, 1959.

1284. **Liggett, Thomas J.** "Protestantism in Puerto Rico." *The Christian Century* 77, no. 29 (1960): 850-52.

1285. **Lloyd-Sidle, Patricia J., ed.** "Called to the Border: A Paradigm for Mission [in Texas]." *International Review of Mission* 78 (April 1989): 135-220.

1286. **Lockwood, George F.** "Recent Developments in U.S. Hispanic and Latin American Protestant Church Music." D.Min. Project Report. Claremont School of Theology, 1981. 165 pp.

1287. **Loucks, Celeste.** *American Montage: The Human Touch to Language Missions.* Atlanta, GA: Home Mission Board, Southern Baptist Convention, 1976. 191 pp.

1288. **López, Ediberto.** "The Earliest Traditions about Jesus and Social Stratification." Ph.D. diss., Drew University, 1992. 283 pp.

1289. **López, Ike.** "Alcoholism in the Hispanic Community." *Engage/Social Action* 3, no. 10 (1975): 44-46.

1290. **López, Miguel.** "J. G. Sánchez." *El Misionero Bautista* 7, no. 15 (1950): 1-3.

1291. **Lucas, Isidro.** *The Browning of America: The Hispanic Revolution in the American Church.* Chicago IL: Fides/Claretian, 1981. See chapter six for references to Protestantism.

1292. **Luna, David.** "An Historical, Sociological, Theological Analysis of the Hispanic American Baptist in Southern California." D.Min. Project Report. American Baptist Seminary of the West, 1990. 96 pp.

1293. **Machado, Daisy L.** "Daring to Embrace Diversity." *Disciples Theological Digest* 7, no. 2 (1992): 43-49.

1294. **Machado, Daisy L.** "The Latino Protestant Church in the United States: History and Reality." *New Conversations* 14, no. 2 (1992): 21-24.

1295. **Machado, Daisy L.** "A Borderlands Perspective." In *Hidden Stories: Unveiling the History of the Latino Church,* edited by Daniel R. Rodríguez-Díaz and David Cortés-Fuentes. 49-65. Decatur, GA: AETH, 1994.

1296. **Machado, Daisy L.** "Being Ecumenical in the Barrio." *Journal of Hispanic/Latino Theology* 3, no. 2 (1995): 6-13.

1297. **Mackay, Juan A.** *Las Iglesias Latinoamericanas y el Movimiento*

Ecuménico. New York: Comité de Cooperación en América Latina [The Committee on Cooperation in Latin America], 1961.

1298. **Mackey, T. Michael.** "The Roots and Dynamics of Lutheran Hispanic Ministry in Texas." Austin, TX. Lutheran Seminary Program in the Southwest, The Episcopal Theological Seminary of the Southwest, 1989. 74 pp. Manuscript.

1299. **Maldonado, David, Jr.** "The Hispanic Elderly: A Socio-Historical Framework." *Journal of Applied Gerontology* 4, no. 1 (1985): 18-27.

1300. **Maldonado, David, Jr.** "A Historical Framework for Understanding the Hispanic Elderly." In *Cross Cultural Social Work Practice in Aging: A Hispanic Perspective,* edited by David Maldonado, Jr. and Steven Applewhite. I:1-I:17. Arlington, TX: University of Texas at Arlington, 1985.

1301. **Maldonado, David.** "Hispanic Protestantism: Historical Reflections." *Apuntes: Reflexiones Teológicas desde el Margen Hispano* 11, no. 1 (1991): 3-16.

1302. **Maldonado, David.** "Moral Voice Needed on Undocumented Immigrants Issue." *The Dallas Morning News,* 25 March 1995,

1303. **Maldonado, David.** "Religion and Persons of Color." In *Aging, Spirituality, and Religion,* edited by Melvin A. Kimble, *et al.* 119-28. Minneapolis, MN: Fortress Press, 1995.

1304. **Manley, Morton C.** *Kingdom Building in Puerto Rico.* Indianapolis, IN: The United Christian Mission Society, 1949.

1305. **MARCHA.** "The Hispanic Vision for Century III: Presented by MARCHA, The National Hispanic United Methodist Caucus." [Nashville, TN]: Printed by the General Board of Higher Education and Ministry, The United Methodist Church, 1985. 12 pp.

1306. **Mark, Leslie David.** "The Role of Seminary Education in the Development of Spiritual Leadership in the Hispanic American Protestant Church." D.Min. Project Report. Fuller Theological Seminary, School of Theology, 1982.

1307. **Marrero Navarro, Domingo.** "Puerto Rico y Simón el Cananeo." *La Nueva Democracia,* May 1937, 17-18.

1308. **Marrero Navarro, Domingo.** "Crítica de la Ciencia y Concepto de la Filosofía en Ortega." *Homenaje a Ortega, La Torre* 5, nos. 15-16 (1956): 285-303.

1309. **Marrero Navarro, Domingo.** *Los Fundamentos de la Libertad.* San Juan, PR: Talleres Gráficos Ineramericanos, 1970.

1310. **Marrero Navarro, Domingo.** *El Centauro: Persona y Pensamiento de Ortega y Gasset.* Reprint. Río Piedras, PR: Editorial Universitaria, 1974.

1311. **Marrero Navarro, Domingo.** *Meditaciones de la Pasión: Vísperas del Calvario. Las Siete Palabras. El Lirio Sobre la Cruz.* Reprint. Río Piedras, PR: Librería La Reforma, 1984.

1312. **Marrero Navarro, Domingo.** "Notas para Organizar el Estudio de las Ideas en Puerto Rico." *Revista de Estudios Generales* 1, no. 1 (1987): 18-39.

1313. **Martin, Carlos G.** "Evangelistic Strategies of Seventh-Day Adventists to Reach Recent Hispanic Immigrants to Texas: A Critical Evaluation." Ph.D. diss., Southwestern Baptist Theological Seminary, 1992. 300 pp.

1314. **Martínez, Felipe.** "El Quinto Centenario: Perspectivas." *Apuntes: Reflexiones Teológicas desde el Margen Hispano* 11, no. 3 (1991): 51-61.

1315. **Martínez, Jill.** "Worship and the Search for Community in the Presbyterian Church (U.S.A.): The Hispanic Experience." *Church and Society* 76, no. 4 (1986): 42-46.

1316. **Martínez, Juan.** "Mennonite Brethren, Latinos and Mission." *Direction: A Semi-annual Publication of Mennonite Brethren Schools* 23, no. 2 (1994): 43-49.

1317. **Martínez, Joel N.** "La Conferencia Río Grande: Descubriendo Nuestro Cautiverio." Paper presented at a symposium held at Perkins School of Theology, Southern Methodist University, Dallas, TX, November 1979.

1318. **Martínez, Joel N.** "Surviving: The Prelude." *Apuntes: Reflexiones Teológicas desde el Margen Hispano* 1, no. 2 (1981): 10-13.

1319. **Martínez, Joel N.** "The South Central Jurisdiction." In *Each in Our Own Tongue: A History of Hispanic United Methodism,* edited by Justo L. González. 39-64. Nashville, TN: Abingdon Press, 1991.

1320. **Martínez, Miguel E.** "Historia de Puerto Rico Evangélico." *Puerto Rico Evangélico,* Special 50th Anniversary Issue (1949).

1321. **Massa, Mark S.** "Disciples in a Mission Land: The Christian Church in New York." In *A Case Study of Mainstream Protestantism: The Disciples' Relation to American Culture, 1880-1989,* edited by D. Newell Williams. 469-90. Grand Rapids, MI: William B. Eerdmans Publishing Co.; St. Louis, MO: Chalice Press, 1991.

1322. **Matovina, Timothy M.** *Tejano Religion and Ethnicity: San Antonio, 1821-1860.* Austin, TX: University of Texas Press, 1995. pp. 59-64, 66-67.

1323. **Mattel, Raul H.** "Considerations for the Implementation of a Living Curriculum of Christian Education for the Missionary District of the Episcopal Church in Puerto Rico." Bachelor's thesis. University of the South, 1957.

1324. **Maxwell, Harold H.** "The History of the Rocky Mountain Conference, Evangelical United Brethren Church, 1869-1951." Th.D. diss., Iliff School of Theology, 1965.

1325. **Maxwell, (Mrs.) C. B.** *A Highway in the Desert; a History of Southern Baptist Work in Arizona.* El Paso, TX: Baptist Publishing House, 1941. 131 pp.

1326. **McCavran, Donald A.** "A Study of the Life and Growth of the Church of the Disciples of Christ in Puerto Rico in View of the Strategy of World Missions Adopted by the United Christian Missionary Society." United Christian Missionary Society. Indianapolis, IN, 1956. Mimeographed.

1327. **McClellan, Albert.** *The West is Big.* Atlanta, GA: Home Mission Board, Southern Baptist Convention, 1953. 125 pp.

1328. **McCombs, Vernon M.** *From over the Border, a Study of the Mexicans in the United States.* New York: Council of Women for Home Missions and Missionary Education Movement, [1925]. 192 pp.

1329. **McConnell, Harry C.** "The Development of the Hymn among Spanish Speaking Evangelicals." Th.D. diss., The Southern Baptist Theological Seminary, 1953. See pp. 307-17 for a bibliography on Spanish-language hymnals.

1330. **McElroy, Richard.** "World Evangelism: How?—Orlando and Rose Costas Give Themselves to the Needs of Their Seminary Students." *Latin America Evangelist* 51, no. 1 (1971): 10-11.

1331. **McLean, J. H.** *The Living Christ for Latin America.* Philadelphia, PA: The Presbyterian Board of Publication and Sabbath School Work, 1916.

1332. **McLean, Robert N.** *The Northern Mexican.* [San Francisco, R and E Research Associates, 1971]. Reprint, New York: Home Missions Council, 1930, [1971]. 43 pp.

1333. **McLean, Robert N. and Charles A. Thomson.** *Spanish and Mexican in Colorado: A Survey of the Spanish Americans and Mexicans in the State of Colorado.* New York: Department of City, Immigrant, and

Industrial Work, Board of National Missions of the Presbyterian Church in the U.S.A., 1924. 61 pp.

1334. **McLeod, Joseph Alpha, Jr.** "Baptists and Racial and Ethnic Minorities in Texas." Ph.D. diss., North Texas State University [formerly The University of North Texas], 1972. 378 pp.

1335. **McMillin, James.** "Anglo Methodist Missionaries and Mexicans in the Southwest and México." Master's thesis. Southern Methodist University, 1994.

1336. **Mead, Frank.** *On Our Own Doorstep.* New York: Friendship Press, 1948. 167 pp.

1337. **Méndez, Manuel.** "La Iglesia Adventista en Puerto Rico." 1966. Typescript.

1338. **Mendoza, Antonio C.** *Historia de la Educación en el Puerto Rico Colonial (1512-1826).* The Catholic University of America. Studies in American Church History, vol. 27. Washington DC: The Catholic University of America, 1946. 191 pp.

1339. **Mercado, Luis F.** "The Hispanic Urban Center: A Progress Report to the American Baptist Board of Education and Publication." American Baptist Church. Chicago, IL, 1971.

1340. **Mercado, Luis F.** "Walking in the Light." Geneva Point Center, NH. New England Conference, 1987. 20 pp. Manuscript.

1341. **Mercado, Luis F.** "Proyección Misionera Entre los Retos del Futuro." In *Octogégisma Sexta Asamblea de las Iglesias Bautistas de Puerto Rico,* held in Castañer, Lares, PR, 5 March 1988.

1342. **Mergal, Angel M.** "Un Hidalgo Iluminado. Esteban S. Huse. Historia de la Obra del Rev. Stephen S. Huse in Puerto Rico." 1939. 32 pp. Manuscript.

1343. **Mergal, Angel M.** *Puente Sobre el Abismo: Sonetos Espirituales.* N.p.: Academia Bautista, 1941.

1344. **Mergal, Angel M.** *Defensa de la Educación Democrática.* San Juan, PR: Asociación de Iglesias Evangélicas de Puerto Rico, 1946.

1345. **Mergal, Angel M.** *Reformismo Cristiano y Alma Española.* Buenos Aires, Argentina: Editorial La Aurora, 1949.

1346. **Mergal, Angel M.** "Evangelical Catholicism as Represented by Juan de Valdés." In *Spiritual and Anabaptist Writers: Documents Illustrative of the Radical Reformation,* edited by Angel M. Mergal. 297-319. The Library of Christian Classics, vol. 25. Philadelphia, PA: Westminster Press, 1957.

1347. **Mergal, Angel M.** *Puerto Rico: Enigma y Promesa.* San Juan, PR: Editorial Club de la Prensa, 1960. 244 pp.

1348. **Mergal, Angel M.** "Erasmo de Rotterdam (1465-1536)." *Educación* 12 (November 1962): 61-78.

1349. **Mergal Llera, Angel M.** *El Agraz.* Río Piedras, PR: Seminario Evangélico, 1945. 106 pp.

1350. **Merriam, Edumund.** *A History of American Baptist Missions.* Philadelphia, PA: American Baptist Publication Society, 1913. 288 pp.

1351. **Miller, William Bricen.** "Texas Mexican Baptist History: Or, a History of Baptist Work among Mexicans in Texas." Th.D. diss., Southwestern Baptist Theological Seminary, 1981.

1352. **Mills, J. S. and S. S. Hough.** *Our Foreign Missionary Enterprise.* Dayton, OH: United Brethren Publishing House, 1908. pp. 193, 203-6.

1353. **Miranda, Jesse.** "Realizing the Hispanic Dream." *Christianity Today* 33, no. 4 (1989): 37-40.

1354. **Mireles, Santos.** *Memoria Orales de Santos Mireles: Una Entrevista Hecha el 25 de Junio de 1975.* Baylor University Program for Oral History. N.p.: Convención Bautista Mexicana de Texas, 1980. 19 pp.

1355. **Moore, Donald T.** "'Puerto Rico para Cristo': A History of the Progress of the Evangelical Missions on the Island of Puerto Rico." Ph.D. diss., Southwestern Baptist Theological Seminary, 1968. 254 pp.

1356. **Moore, Donald T.** *Puerto Rico para Cristo; A History of the Progress of the Evangelical Missions on the Island of Puerto Rico.* Sondeos, no. 48. Cuernavaca, México: Centro Intercultural de Documentación, 1969. 332 pp.

1357. **Moore, Donald T.** "A History of Southern Baptists in Puerto Rico." Revised and updated. Nashville, TN. Historical Commission, Southern Baptist Convention, 1983. 21 pp. Typescript.

1358. **Moore, Elena Vela.** "Ministry in Puerto Rico." *The Beam* 18 (November 1967): 10.

1359. **Morales, Adam.** *American Baptists with a Spanish Accent.* Chicago, IL: The Judson Press, 1964.

1360. **Morales Hicks, Herminio.** "La Iglesia Evangélica Portorriqueña." *El Día,* 1 February 1917, 6.

1361. **Morehouse, Henry L.** "Porto Rico: A Narrative Sketch of Baptist Missions in the Island." Board of Publications, American Baptist Church. New York, 1904. Typescript.

1362. **Mosqueda, Lawrence J.** *Chicanos, Catholicism, and Political Ideology.* Lanham, MD: University Press of America, 1986. p. 218.

1363. **Mount, Graeme S.** "The Presbyterian Church in the USA and American Rule in Puerto Rico, 1898-1917." *Journal of Presbyterian History* 57, no. 1 (1979): 51-64.

1364. **Mount, Graeme S.** *Presbyterian Missions to Trinidad and Puerto Rico.* Hantsport, N.S.: Lancelot Press, 1983. 356 pp.

1365. **Moye, Esther B.** *Lo, I am with You.* Atlanta, GA: Home Mission Board, Southern Baptist Convention, 1953. 95 pp.

1366. **Moye, Esther B.** "Now They Want to Give." *Southern Baptist Home Missions* 24 (November 1953): 8.

1367. **Moye, J. L.** "Our Hopes are These Young People." *Southern Baptist Home Missions* 12 (April 1941): 6-7.

1368. **Muñoz, Carlos, Jr.** *Youth, Identity, Power: The Chicano Movement.* The Haymarket Series. London; New York: Verso, 1989. pp. 28-29, 35, 53.

1369. **Murray, Andrew E.** *The Skyline Synod: Presbyterianism in Colorado and Utah.* Presbyterian Historical Society Publications, no. 10. Denver, CO: Golden Bell Press, 1971. 151 pp.

1370. **Myers, Lewis A.** *A History of New México Baptists.* 2 Vols. [Albuquerque, NM]: Baptist General Convention of New México, 1965. 683 pp.

1371. **Nail, Olin W.** *The First Hundred Years of the Southwest Texas Conference of the Methodist Church 1858-1958.* San Antonio, TX: The Southwest Texas Conference, The Methodist Church, 1958. 246 pp.

1372. **Náñez, Alfredo.** "Madurando en el Ministerio." 23 pp. Manuscript. [Located in the files of Paul Barton.]

1373. **Náñez, Alfredo, ed.** *Himnario Metodista.* San Antonio, TX: Río Grande Conference Board of Education. Printed by Casa Bautista de Publicaciones, 1955. Hymnal.

1374. **Náñez, Alfredo.** *Ritual de la Iglesia Metodista.* [San Antonio, TX]: Board of Publication of the Methodist Church, Inc., 1965. 76 pp.

1375. **Náñez, Alfredo, ed.** *Himnario Metodista.* Nashville, TN: The United Methodist Publishing House, 1973. 592 pp. Hymnal.

1376. **Náñez, Alfredo.** "Methodism among the Spanish-Speaking People in Texas and New México." In *One in the Lord: A History of Ethnic*

Minorities in the South Central Jurisdiction, The United Methodist Church, edited by Walter N. Vernon. 50-94. Oklahoma City, OK: Commission on Archives and History, South Central Jurisdiction, The United Methodist Church, 1977.

1377. **Náñez, Alfredo.** "Transition from Anglo to Mexican-American Leadership in the Río Grande Conference." *Methodist History* 16, no. 2 (1978): 67-74.

1378. **Náñez, Alfredo.** *History of the Río Grande Conference of The United Methodist Church.* Dallas, TX: Bridwell Library, Southern Methodist University, 1980. 147 pp.

1379. **Náñez, Alfredo.** *Historia de la Conferencia Río Grande de la Iglesia Metodista Unida.* Dallas, TX: Bridwell Library, Southern Methodist University, 1981. 158 pp.

1380. **Náñez, Alfredo and Clotilde Náñez.** "Methodism among the Spanish Speaking People of Texas." In *History of Texas Methodism 1900-1960,* edited by Olin W. Nail. 187-209. Austin, TX: Capital Printing Company, 1961.

1381. **Náñez, Clotilde.** "Hispanic Clergy Wives: Their Contribution to United Methodism in the Southwest, Later Nineteenth Century to the Present." In *Women in New Worlds: Historical Perspectives on the Wesleyan Tradition,* edited by Hilah F. Thomas and Rosemary Kinner Keller. 161-77. Nashville, TN: Abingdon, 1981.

1382. **National Council of Churches of Christ, United States of America.** "Information on Denominational Work in Puerto Rico." National Council of Churches of Christ, United States of America. New York, 1961.

1383. **National Hispanic Caucus of the Lutheran Church in America.** "Hispanic Ministry Profile." Typescript.

1384. **National Hispanic Task Force of the American Lutheran Church.** "A Hispanic Declaration on Ministry Needs and Aspirations Commended to The American Lutheran Church and the Evangelical Lutheran Church in America." The National Hispanic Task Force of the American Lutheran Church. Chicago, IL, 1986.

1385. **Navarro, James.** "Latin American People in Texas." Audiotaped sermon. Fort Worth, TX: Southwestern Baptist Theological Seminary, 1958.

1386. **Neil, Samuel G.** "Baptist Progress in Puerto Rico." *The Baptist,* 9 May 1931,

1387. **Newcomer, E. Kenneth, Jr.** "A Progress Report on the Churchmen's

Committee of Crystal City, Texas." Crystal City, TX, 1970. Manuscript.

1388. **Nieto, Leo D.** "Religious Profile of Spanish Surname Population in Corpus Christi and Nueces County, Texas, 1965 and Agricultural Migrant Labor Statistics for Texas." Study No. 4 of the Texas Council of Churches, Division of Christian Mission, Department of Church Planning and Development and Department of Migrant Ministry, June 1965.

1389. **Nieto, Leo D.** "Religious Profile of Spanish Surname Populations in Austin and Travis County, Texas-1965." Study No. 2 of the Texas Council of Churches, Division of Christian Mission, Department of Church Planning and Development and Department of Migrant Ministry, Austin, TX, March 1965.

1390. **Nieto, Leo D.** "The Chicano Movement and the Churches in the United States/El Movimiento Chicano y las Iglesias en Los Estados Unidos." *Perkins Journal* 29, no. 1 (1975): English: 32-41; Spanish: 76-85.

1391. **Nieto, Leo D.** "Chicano Theology of Liberation." In *Mission Trends No. 4: Liberation Theologies,* edited by Gerald H. Anderson and Thomas F. Stransky. 277-82. New York: Paulist Press, 1979.

1392. **Nieto, Leo D.** "South Bay Hispanic Ministry of Presence, Phase 1: A Report." Pacific and Southwest Annual Conference, The United Methodist Church. Long Beach, CA, 1981.

1393. **Nieto, Leo D.** "The Chicano Movement and the Gospel: Historical Accounts of a Protestant Pastor." In *Hidden Stories: Unveiling the History of the Latino Church,* edited by Daniel R. Rodríguez-Díaz and David Cortés-Fuentes. 143-57. Decatur, GA: AETH, 1994.

1394. **Odell, Edward A.** *New Days in the West Indies.* Board of National Missions of the Presbyterian Church, U.S.A., 1926.

1395. **Odell, Edward A.** *The West Indies and National Missions.* Board of National Missions of the Presbyterian Church, U.S.A., n.d.

1396. **Orozco, E.C.** *Republican Protestantism in Aztlán: The Encounter Between Mexicanism and Anglo-Saxon Secular Humanism in the United States Southwest.* Glendale, CA: Peterins Press, 1980. 261 pp.

1397. **Ortegon, Samuel.** "The Religious Status of the Mexican Population of Los Angeles." Master's thesis. University of Southern California, 1932.

1398. **Ortegon, Samuel.** "Religious Thought and Practice among Mexican Baptists of the United States, 1900-1947." Ph.D. diss., University of Southern California, 1950. 256 pp.

1399. **Ortiz, Manuel.** *The Hispanic Challenge: Opportunities Confronting the Church.* Downers Grove, IL: Intervarsity Press, 1993. 194 pp.

1400. **Ortiz, Manuel.** "My Commitment to Intercultural Christian Community: An Hispanic Pilgrimage." *Urban Mission* 12, no. 2 (1994): 14-24.

1401. **Ortíz, Adan L.** *Historia de la Convención Bautista Mexicana de Texas.* N.p., [1936]. 28 pp.

1402. **Ortíz, José.** *El Año Agradable del '86: Estampas de la Vida de la Iglesia Menonita Hispana.* Goshen, IN: Departamento de Ministerios Hispanos, Goshen College, 1988. 126 pp.

1403. **Ortíz, José and David Graybill.** *Reflections of an Hispanic Mennonite.* Intercourse, PA: Good Books, 1989. 92 pp.

1404. **Padilla, C. René.** "El Legado de Orlando E. Costas (1942-1987)." *Misión* 7, no. 1 (1988): 4-5.

1405. **Pagán, Samuel.** "La Revisión Valera de la Traducción Reina." *La Biblia en las Américas* 44 #185, no. 1 (1989): 10-11.

1406. **Palmer, Gerald B.** *Winds of Change.* Atlanta, GA: Home Mission Board, Southern Baptist Convention, 1964.

1407. **Pantojas Garcia, Emilio.** "La Iglesia Protestante y la Americanización de Puerto Rico, 1898-1917." Bayamón, PR. PRISA, n.d. Manuscript.

1408. **Park, Yong Hak.** "A Study of the Methodist Mexican Mission in Dallas." Master's thesis. Southern Methodist University, 1936. 133 pp.

1409. **Parker, Everett C.** "Hispanic American Churches in New York City." *The Christian Century* 78, no. 15 (1961): 466-68.

1410. **Paschal, George H.** *One Hundred Years of Challenge and Change: A History of the Synod of Texas of the United Presbyterian Church in the U.S.A.* San Antonio, TX: Trinity University Press, 1968. 259 pp.

1411. **Pedraja, Luis G.** "The Destruction of the 'Other' in the Conquest of Latin America." Paper presented at the annual meeting of the Mid-Atlantic Region, American Academy of Religion, Philadelphia, PA., 1993.

1412. **Pérez Alvarez, Eliseo.** "Justo González al Habla: La Historia Se Enseña y Se Escribe a partir del Futuro." *El Faro* (July-August 1992): 124-27.

1413. **Pérez, Isaac V.** "School of Prophets Helps Train Leaders." *Southern Baptist Home Missions* 22 (February 1951): 11.

1414. **Pérez, Orlando.** *Sermones y Biografía de Rudy Hernández.* El Paso: Casa Bautista de Publicaciones, 1970. 115 pp.

1415. **Phillips, J. A.** "English for Aliens, with Special Reference to Mexicans." *Methodist Quarterly Review* 69, no. 4 (1920): 708-18.

1416. **Phillips, Norman D.** "Chicano Workers, Río Grande Farmers Agree to Meet." *Christian Century* 88, no. 3 (1971): 84-86.

1417. **Pierson, Charles C.** *Oral Memoirs of Charles C. Pierson: January 14, 1976-March 1, 1976.* Baylor University Program for Oral History. [Waco, TX]: Baylor University, 1976. 71 pp.

1418. **Pineda, Ana María.** "The Challenge of Hispanic Pluralism for the United States Christians." *Missiology* 21, no. 4 (1993): 437-42.

1419. **Poblete, Renato and Thomas O'Dea.** "Anomie and the 'Quest for Community'—the Formation of Sects among the Puerto Ricans of New York." *American Catholic Sociological Review* 21, no. 1 (1960): 18-36. Also published in Thomas F. O'Dea, *Sociology and the Study of Religion: Theory, Research, Interpretation* (New York: Basic Books, 1970), pp. 180-98.

1420. **Poinsett, Brenda.** "Puerto Rico." *Royal Service* 70 (January 1976): 36.

1421. **Pope-Levison, Priscilla.** "Comprehensive and Contextual: The Evangelism of Orlando Costas." *Journal of the Academy for Evangelism in Theological Education* 4 (1988-1989): 4-14.

1422. **Post, Donald E. and Walter E. Smith.** "Clergy: Outsiders and Adversaries. The Story of Catholic and Protestant Clergy's Attempts to Relate the Gospel in Three South Texas Towns Experiencing Changing Mexicano/Anglo Relationships during the Period of 1945-1975." N.p., n.d. 254 pp. National Endowment for the Humanities Grant, No. RS-26255-531.

1423. **Presbyterian Church in the U.S. Synods. Texas.** *Flying Chips: Latin-American Presbyterianism in Texas. Published for the Executive Committee of Home Missions.* Waco, TX: Wallace Engraving Co., [1947?]. 90 pp.

1424. **Presbyterian Church in the United States.** "Latin American Presbyterian Churches in Texas. A Study Prepared for the Ad Interim Committee on Latin-American Work, Synod of Texas." Synod of Texas, Presbyterian Church in the United States. Austin, TX, 1952.

1425. **Protestant Council of the City of New York.** "A Report on the Protestant Spanish Community in New York City." Protestant Council of the City of New York, Department of Church Planning. New York, 1960.

1426. **Pulido, Alberto L.** "Presbiterianos Mexicanos: Una Perspectiva

Materialista de la Religión y Trabajo en el Sur de Texas." *Cristianismo y Sociedad* 31-32, nos. 4-1 (1994): 19-27.

1427. **Quiróz, Evangelina Grimaldo.** "Daddy Had a Dream." In *We Were There: An Oral History of Illinois Baptist State Convention,* edited by Robert J. Hastings. Springfield, IL: Illinois Baptist State Association, 1976. pp. 234-44.

1428. **Ramírez, Johnny.** "Financial Aid and Minority Representation at Atlantic Union College." South Lancaster, MA, 1991.

1429. **Ramirez, Ricardo.** "Liturgy from the Mexican American Perspective." *Worship* 51, no. 4 (1977): 293-98.

1430. **Ramón de Peña, Noemí.** *Memorias Orales de Noemí Ramón de Peña: Una Entrevista Hecha el 19 de Noviembre de 1978.* Baylor University Program for Oral History. N.p.: Convención Bautista Mexicana de Texas, 1980. 32 pp.

1431. **Ramos, Marcos Antonio.** *Panorama del Protestantismo en Cuba; la Presencia de los Protestantes o Evangélicos en la Historia de Cuba desde la Colonización Española hasta la Revolución.* San José, Costa Rica: Editorial Caribe, 1986. pp. 625-32.

1432. **Ramos, Marcos Antonio.** *Protestantism and Revolution in Cuba.* Coral Gables, FL: Research Institute for Cuban Studies, University of Miami, 1989. pp. 147-50.

1433. **Ramos, Marcos Antonio.** "El Protestantismo Hispanoamericano en la Noticia." *Apuntes: Reflexiones Teológicas desde el Margen Hispano* 12, no. 1 (1992): 21-27.

1434. **Ramos, Norma.** *Memorias Orales de Norma Ramos: Una Entrevista Hecha el 2 de Abril de 1979.* Baylor University Program for Oral History. N.p.: Convención Bautista Mexicana de Texas, 1980. 12 pp.

1435. **Ramos, Santos.** *Memoria Orales de Santos Ramos: Una Entrevista Hecha el 2 de abril de 1979.* Baylor University Program for Oral History. N.p.: Convención Bautista Mexicana de Texas, 1980. 23 pp.

1436. **Ramos, Wilfrido.** "Puerto Rican Perspective—Our Historical Cross-Roads: Towards a New Orientation in Mission." In *Out of the Depths: Papers Presented at Four Missiology Conferences Held in Antigua, Guyana, Jamaica and Trinidad, 1975,* edited by Idriss Hamic. 163-71. San Fernando, Trinidad & Tobago, W.I.: St. Andrew's Theological College, 1977.

1437. **Ramsour, H. B.** *The Oral Memoirs of H. B. Ramsour: A Series of Interviews Conducted November 21, 1978.* Mexican Baptist Oral

History Project. [Dallas, TX]: Baptist General Convention of Texas, 1980. 78 pp.

1438. **Ranck, Lee, ed.** "Hispanic Americans: A Growing Force/Los Hispano Americanos: Una Fuerza Cresciente." *Engage/Social Action [e-sa Forum, 99]* 11, no. 11 (1983): English: 9-49; Spanish: 50-72.

1439. **Rankin, Melinda.** *Twenty Years among the Mexicans: A Narrative of Missionary Labor.* ATLA Monograph Preservation Program; ATLA fiche 1986-0602. Cincinnati, OH: Chase & Hall, Publishers, 1875. 199 pp.

1440. **Read, Benjamin M.** *A History of Education in New México.* Santa Fe, NM: The New México Printing Co., 1911.

1441. **Recinos, Hal.** *Hear the Cry! A Latino Pastor Challenges the Church.* Louisville, KY: Westminter/John Knox Press, 1989. 156 pp.

1442. **Red, William S.** *A History of the Presbyterian Church in Texas.* [Austin, TX: Steck Co.], 1936. 433 pp.

1443. **Reiter, David E.** *History of the Presbyterian Church in the Synod of New México.* [Albuquerque, NM]: n.p., 1963.

1444. **Remy, Martha Caroline Mitchell.** "Protestant Churches and Mexican-Americans in South Texas." Ph.D. diss., University of Texas at Austin, 1970. 356 pp.

1445. **Rendón, Gabino, as told to Edith Agnew.** *Hand on My Shoulder.* New York: Board of National Missions, Presbyterian Church in the U.S.A., 1953. 105 pp.

1446. **Reyes, Marilú Dones de.** "Mis Memorias en Este Lugar Bethel: La Pequeña Jerusalén Monumento de Fe." Canovanas, PR. 1979. Manuscript.

1447. **Reyes, Ruben.** "Prolegomena to Chicano Theology." D.Min. Project Report. Claremont School of Theology, 1974.

1448. **Reza, Honorato and R. W. Stringfield.** *Vida y Solaz.* Kansas City, MO: Lillenas Publishing Company, 1958. Hymnal.

1449. **Rice, Allen B.** *Methodism Frontiers in Puerto Rico.* Cincinnati, OH: Board of Missions of the Methodist Church, 1965.

1450. **Riggs, George A.** *Baptists in Puerto Rico: Brief Historical Notes of Forty Years of Baptist Work, 1899-1939.* Ponce, PR: Puerto Rico Evangélico, 1939. 44 pp.

1451. **Río Grande Conference.** "Nuevas Oportunidades para el Futuro: Report of Research and Planning Process." In *Actas Conferenciales de la Conferencia Anual Río Grande, 1975,* edited by Rubén Salcido. 124-49. Georgetown, TX: Río Grande Annual Conference, The United Methodist Church, 1975.

1452. **Río Grande Conference Study Committee.** "Río Grande Conference Study Committee, The Methodist Church. Report No. 3. Presented to the Río Grande Annual Conference. [Propuesta del Comité de Estudio a la Conference Río Grande]." In *Actas Oficiales de la Conferencia Anual Río Grande de la Iglesia Metodista,* 85-89. Kerrville, TX: Río Grande Annual Conference, 1967.

1453. **Rivas, José.** *Memoria Orales de José Rivas: Una Entrevista Hecha el 28 de Abril de 1978.* Baylor University Program for Oral History. N.p.: Convención Bautista Mexicana de Texas, 1980. 23 pp.

1454. **Rivas, Yolanda.** "I am Cuban, I am Hispanic, I am Woman." *Engage/Social Action* 11, no. 11 (1983): English: 31-35; Spanish: 65-68.

1455. **Rivera, Antonio.** "La Libertad de Cultos Hasta el Establecimiento de la Primera Iglesia Evangélica de Puerto Rico." *Parts 1 and 2. Puerto Rico Evangélico,* 10 July 1952 and 25 July 1952.

1456. **Rivera, Alejandro García.** "Artificial Inelligence, 1992, and Las Casas: The Valladolid Connection." *Apuntes: Reflexiones Teológicas desde el Margen Hispano* 11, no. 2 (1991): 39-43.

1457. **Rivera de Flores, Concepción.** *Memorias Orales de Concepción Rivera de Flores: Una Entrevista Hecha el 22 de Mayo de 1978.* Baylor University Program for Oral History. N.p.: Convención Bautista Mexicana de Texas, 1980. 13 pp.

1458. **Rivera-Pagán, Luis N.** "Unity and Truth: The Unity of God, Man, Jesus Christ, and the Church in Irenaeus." Ph.D. diss., Yale University, 1971.

1459. **Rivera-Pagán, Luis N.** *Domingo Marrero-La Paradoja de la Razón: Filosofía y Religión.* Guaynabo, PR: Editorial Sonador, 1987.

1460. **Rivera-Pagán, Luis N.** "La Conquista de América: Evangelización y Violencia." *"En Rojo," Claridad* Supplement 29, no. 1805 (1987): 22-23.

1461. **Rivera-Pagán, Luis N.** "La Cristianización de América: Reflexión y Desafío." *Apuntes: Reflexiones Teológicas desde el Margen Hispano* 7, no. 1 (1987): 14-19.

1462. **Rivera-Pagán, Luis N.** "Los Tratados de Tlatelolco y Rarotonga: Análisis Comparado." *"En Rojo," Claridad* Supplement 29, no. 1805 (1987): 18, 23.

1463. **Rivera-Pagán, Luis N.** "Respuesta: La Cristianización de América: Reflexión y Desafío." *Apuntes: Reflexiones Teológicas desde el Margen Hispano* 7, no. 1 (1987): 14-19.

1464. **Rivera-Pagán, Luis N.** "Discovery and Conquest of America: Myth and Reality." *Apuntes: Reflexiones Teológicas desde el Margen Hispano* 9, no. 4 (1989): 75-92. Also published as "Descubrimiento y Conquista de América: Mito y Realidad." *Boletín de Antropología Americana* [Instituto Panamericano de Geografía e Historia] 20 (December 1989): 83-98.

1465. **Rivera-Pagán, Luis N.** *Senderos Teológicos: El Pensamiento Evangélico Puertorriqueño.* Río Piedras, PR: Editorial La Reforma, 1989. 197 pp.

1466. **Rivera-Pagán, Luis N.** "Myth and Reality: The Fifth Centennial of the Discovery and Conquest of America." *Christian Social Action* 4, no. 9 (1991): 25-31.

1467. **Rivera-Pagán, Luis N.** "Bartolomé de las Casas y la Esclavitud Africana." In *Sentido Histórico del V Centenario (1492-1992),* edited by Guillermo Meléndez. 63-84. San José, Costa Rica: DEI, 1992. Also published in *Revista de Estudios Generales* 4, no. 4 (1989-1990): 227-251 and in "Publicaciones Ocasionales," in *Proyecto de Historia y Sociología de la Religión en el Caribe,* no. 2, The Caribbean Studies Institute, University of Puerto Rico, 1990.

1468. **Rivera-Pagán, Luis N.** "Conquest and Colonization: The Problem of America." *Apuntes: Reflexiones Teológicas desde el Margen Hispano* 12, no. 2 (1992): 35-48.

1469. **Rivera-Pagán, Luis N.** "Descubrimiento, Conquista y Evangelización." *De Prisa: La Revista Ecuménica* (March 1992): 12-22.

1470. **Rivera-Pagán, Luis N.** "El Descubrimiento y la Conquista de América: Una Empresa Misionera Imperial." *Pasos* segunda época, no. 41 (May-June 1992): 1-10. Also published in *Casabe,* no. 4 (1992): 11-27.

1471. **Rivera-Pagán, Luis N.** *Evangelización y Violencia: La Conquista de América.* 3rd ed. San Juan, PR: Ediciones Cemí, 1992.

1472. **Rivera-Pagán, Luis N.** "La Evangelización de América y la Guerra Justa." *Pasos* segunda época, número especial (1992): 16-18.

1473. **Rivera-Pagán, Luis N.** "La Indígena Raptada y Violada." *Pasos* segunda época, no. 42 (July-August 1992): 7-10.

1474. **Rivera-Pagán, Luis N.** "Libertad y Servidumbre Indígena en la Conquista Española de América." In *Descubrimiento, Conquista y*

Colonización de América: Mito y Realidad. 41-70. Santo Domingo: Centro para la Investigación y Acción Social en el Caribe, 1992. Originally published in *Cuadernos de Teología* [Buenos Aires, Argentina], 10 (2 1989): 41-69.

1475. **Rivera-Pagán, Luis N.** "A New Word and a New Church." *New Conversations* 14, no. 2 (1992): 16-20.

1476. **Rivera-Pagán, Luis N.** "Prophecy and Patriotism: A Tragic Dilemma." *Apuntes: Reflexiones Teológicas desde el Margen Hispano* 12, no. 2 (1992): 49-64.

1477. **Rivera-Pagán, Luis N.** "¿Quién es el Indio? Humanidad o Bestialidad del Indígena Americano." *Pasos* segunda época, no. 43 (1992): 9-18.

1478. **Rivera-Pagán, Luis N.** *A Violent Evangelism: The Political and Religious Conquest of the Américas.* Louisville, KY: Westminster/John Knox Press, 1992. 357 pp.

1479. **Rivera-Pagán, Luis N.** "La Conquista de América: Una Empresa Misionera Imperial." *Revista de Estudios Generales* 7, no. 7 (1993): 13-37.

1480. **Rivera-Pagán, Luis N.** "Las *Capitulaciones de Burgos:* Paradigma de las Paradojas de la Cristiandad Colonial." *Apuntes: Reflexiones Teológicas desde el Margen Hispano* 13, no. 1 (1993): 30-48.

1481. **Rivera-Pagán, Luis N.** "Formation of a Hispanic American Theology: The *Capitulations of Burgos.*" In *Hidden Stories: Unveiling the History of the Latino Church,* edited by Daniel Rodríguez-Díaz and David Cortés-Fuentes. 67-97. Decatur, GA: AETH, 1994. Also published in Spanish as "Las Capitulaciones de Burgos: Paradigma de las Paradojas de la Cristiandad Colonial." *Apuntes: Reflexiones Teológicas desde el Margen Hispano* 13, no. 1 (1993): 30-48 and *Exégesis* (Colegio Universitario de Humacao, Puerto Rico) 6, no. 16 (1993): 2-11.

1482. **Rivera-Pagán, Luis N.** "Migajas Teológicas: Breves Reflexiones Sobre la Producción Teológica Protestante Puertorriqueña." *El Boletín* Special Issue (October 1994): 4-18.

1483. **Rivera-Pagán, Luis N.** "The Penitential Doctrine of Restitution: Its Use by Bartolomé de Las Casas to Liberate Popular Religiosity during the Conquest of America." In *An Enduring Flame: Studies on Latino Popular Religiosity,* edited by Anthony M. Stevens-Arroyo and Ana María Díaz-Stevens. 97-112. Vol. 1 of PARAL Studies Series. New York: Bildner Center for Western Hemisphere Studies, 1994.

1484. **Rivera-Pagán, Luis N.** "Reflexiones Irreverentes y un Almirante Perdido." In *Leer para Escribir,* edited by Julia C. Ortíz and Elsa R. Arroyo. 245-54. Río Piedras: Editorial Plaza Mayor, 1994. Reproduced from *Diálogo* (University of Puerto Rico) October 1992, pp. 12-14.

1485. **Rivera-Pagán, Luis N.** *Entre el Oro y la Fe: El Dilema de América.* San Juan, PR: Editorial de la Universidad de Puerto Rico, 1995. 115 pp.

1486. **Rivera-Pagán, Luis N.** *Los Sueños del Ciervo: Perspectivas Teológicas desde el Caribe.* San Juan, PR: Equipo de Historia y Sociología del Protestantismo en Puerto Rico; Programa de Educación y Teología del Concilio Evangélico de Puerto Rico, 1995. 103 pp.

1487. **Rivera-Pagán, Luis N. and Viola Lugo de Meléndez.** "Una Justa y Honrosa Nominación." *Revista de Estudios Generales* 1, no. 1 (1987): 13-17.

1488. **Rivera-Pagán, Luis N., Raúl Vidales, and Diego Irarrazaval.** *La Esperanza de los Vencidos: Hacia una Visión Crítica del Quinto Centenario.* Guaynabo, PR: Editorial Sonador, 1989. 95 pp.

1489. **Rodríguez, Alfonso.** "Guidelines for a Program Concerning Our Mission among the Spanish Americans in the U.S.A." Division of Church Strategy and Development, Board of National Missions of the United Presbyterian Church in the U.S.A. New York, 28 September 1965.

1490. **Rodríguez, Alfonso.** "The Spanish Americans in the United States: Problems and Opportunities." Working paper, National Committee on Spanish American Ministries, United Presbyterian Church in the U.S.A. New York, 1967.

1491. **Rodríguez, Angel Manuel.** "El Santuario y Sus Servicios en la Literatura Patrística." *Theologika* 7, no. 1 (1992): 22-79.

1492. **Rodriguez, Antonio R. and Angel M. Miguel.** "The Message of the Evangelical Council of Puerto Rico to the Puerto Rican People." 1960. Mimeographed.

1493. **Rodriguez, Daniel.** "Establishing a Community among Hispanic United Methodists: A Critique of MARCHA Origins and Actions." *Engage/Social Action* 11, no. 11 (1983): 47-49.

1494. **Rodriguez, Delia.** *Memoria Orales de Delia Rodriguez: Una Entrevista Hecha el 2 de Abril de 1979.* Baylor University Program for Oral History. N.p.: Convención Bautista Mexicana de Texas, 1980. 24 pp.

1495. **Rodriguez, José Policarpo.** *The Old Guide.* Nashville, TN: Publishing House of the Methodist Episcopal Church, South; Dallas, TX: Smith & Lamar, Agents, n.d. 121 pp.

1496. **Rodríguez, Daniel R.** *La Primera Evangelización Norteamericana en Puerto Rico 1898-1930.* México City, México: Ediciones Borinquen, 1986. 309 pp.

1497. **Rodríguez, José David.** "De 'Apuntes' a 'Esbozo': Diez Años de Reflexión." *Apuntes: Reflexiones Teológicas desde el Margen Hispano* 10, no. 4 (1990): 75-83.

1498. **Rodríguez, José David.** *Introducción a la Teología.* San José, Costa Rica: DEI, 1993.

1499. **Rodríguez, P.A., compiler.** *Himnario Cristiano para Uso de las Iglesias Evangélicas.* 1908. Reprint, Nashville, TN: Methodist Episcopal Church, South, 1915. Hymnal.

1500. **Rodríguez Rivera, J. F.** *Nuestros Males y Su Remedio.* El Paso, TX: Casa Bautista de Publicaciones, 1938.

1501. **Rodríguez Rivera, J. F.** *El Angel de la Bondad: Quince Sermones Evangelísticos de Radio.* San Antonio, TX: Casa Evangélica de Publicaciones, 1940.

1502. **Rodríguez Rivera, J. F.** *El Camino de la Felicidad: Quince Sermones de Radio Que Incluye Profecía y Evangelismo.* El Paso, TX: Casa Bautista de Publicaciones, 1946.

1503. **Rodríguez Rivera, J. F.** *El Privilegio de Llorar y Otros Ensayos.* Madrid: Editorial Irmayol, 1965.

1504. **Rodriguez-Bravo, Enrique.** "Origen y Desarrollo del Movimiento Protestante en Puerto Rico." Ph.D. diss., The George Washington University, 1972. 206 pp.

1505. **Rodríguez-Díaz, Daniel R.** "Los Movimientos Misioneros y el Establecimiento de Ideologías Dominantes: 1800-1940." *Apuntes: Reflexiones Teológicas desde el Margen Hispano* 13, no. 1 (1993): 49-72.

1506. **Rodríguez-Díaz, Daniel R. and David Cortés-Fuentes, eds.** *Hidden Stories: Unveiling the History of the Latino Church.* Decatur, GA: AETH, 1994. 165 pp.

1507. **Rodríguez-Díaz, Daniel.** "Los Movimientos Misioneros y Colonialismo en las Américas." In *Desde el Reverso: Materiales para la Historia de la Iglesia,* 47-95. Coyoacán, México: Publicaciones el Faro and Academia para la Historia de la Iglesia Latina (APHILA), 1993.

1508. **Rodríguez-Díaz, Daniel R.** *Taller de Historia Oral.* Decatur, GA: AETH, 1994. 37 pp.

1509. **Rogers, H. E.** "Report of Work Conducted by Seventh-Day Adventists in Non-Christian and Non-Protestant Countries." Seventh-Day Adventists. 1911.

1510. **Rogers, S. B.** *A Brief History of Florida Baptists, 1825-1925: A Century of Service and Progress.* Jacksonville, FL: Miller Press, n.d. 23 pp.

1511. **Romo, Ricardo.** *East Los Angeles: History of a Barrio.* Austin, TX: University of Texas Press, 1983. pp. 143-48.

1512. **Rosado, Caleb.** "The God of Martin Luther King, Jr." *Message,* January-February 1988, 18-20. Published under Caleb Rosado's pen name, Manuel Sanabria.

1513. **Rosado, Caleb.** "A Christian Response to the L.A. Riots." *Adventist Review,* 18 June 1992, 5.

1514. **Rosado, Caleb.** "Lessons from Waco." *Ministry* (July 1993): 6-11.

1515. **Rosado, Caleb.** "Lessons from Waco II." *Ministry* (August 1993): 14-19.

1516. **Rosales, Raymond S.** "The Experience of the Hispanic Church in the Américas." *Word and World: Theology for Christian Ministry* 12, no. 2 (1992): 129-37.

1517. **Rosario Ramos, Tomás.** "Recordamos." Río Piedras, PR. First Baptist Church, Río Piedras, PR, 1958. Typescript.

1518. **Rosario Ramos, Tomás.** *Ideas, Personas, y Cosas: Libro de Ensayos y Anecdotario.* Río Piedras, PR: Editorial Puerto Rico Evangélico, 1967.

1519. **Rosario Ramos, Tomás.** *Los Bautistas en Puerto Rico; Apuntes Históricos.* Santo Domingo, Dominican Republic: Editorial Librería Dominicana, 1969. 176 pp.

1520. **Rosario Ramos, Tomás.** *Obreros de la Segunda Milla: Breves Biografías de los Ejecutivos Bautistas de Puerto Rico.* Carolina, PR: Editorial Librería Evangélica, 1976. 86 pp.

1521. **Rosario Ramos, Tomás.** *Historia de los Bautistas de Puerto Rico.* 2nd Rev. ed. Santo Domingo, Dominican Republic: Editora Educativa Dominicana, 1979. 437 pp.

1522. **Ross, J. Wilson.** *Sowing the Seed.* [A history of the Baptist Spanish Publishing House from 1904 to 1961.] El Paso, TX: Baptist Spanish Publishing House, 1962. 154 pp.

1523. **Rosser, John Leonidas.** *A History of Florida Baptists.* Nashville, TN: Broadman Press, 1949. 351 pp.

1524. **Roundy, Rodney.** "Getting Together in the Southwest." *Home Mission Monthly* 35 (May 1921): 149-50.

1525. **Rudd, Augustus.** *A Decade in Porto Rico.* New York: ABHMS, n.d. 6 pp.

1526. **Ruiz, Donato.** *Memoria Orales de Donato Ruiz: Una Entrevista Hecha el 9 de Junio de 1975.* Baylor University Program for Oral History. N.p.: Convención Bautista Mexicana de Texas, 1980. 18 pp.

1527. **Ruoss, Meryl.** "Mid-Century Pioneers and Protestants: A Survey Report of the Puerto Rican Migration to the U.S. Mainland and in Particular a Study of the Protestant Expression among Puerto Ricans of New York City." 2nd ed. Department of Church Planning and Research of the Protestant Council of the City of New York. New York, 1954.

1528. **Rutledge, Arthur B.** *Mission to America: A Century and a Quarter of Southern Baptist Home Missions.* Nashville, TN: Broadman Press, 1969. pp. 146, 155-161, 163-165.

1529. **Rutledge, Arthur B. and William G. Tanner.** *Mission to America: A History of Southern Baptist Home Missions.* 2nd rev. ed., Nashville, TN: Broadman Press, 1983. pp. 159-171.

1530. **Ruybalid, M. Keith.** "Mission School in the Homeland." *Adventist Heritage* 6, no. 1 (1979): 41-49.

1531. **Rycroft, W. Stanley.** *Latin America and the United Presbyterians.* New York: Commission on Ecumenical Mission and Relations, 1961.

1532. **San Antonio Baptist Association.** *A Baptist Century Around the Alamo, 1858-1958: 100 Years-San Antonio Baptist Association.* San Antonio, TX: San Antonio Baptist Association, 1958. 208 pp.

1533. **San Antonio Baptist Association.** *Survey Report.* San Antonio, TX: San Antonio Baptist Association, 1960. 192 pp.

1534. **Sanchez, Daniel R.** "An Interdisciplinary Approach to Theological Contextualisation with Special Reference to Hispanic Americans." Ph.D. diss., Oxford Centre for Mission Studies, 1991. 466 pp.

1535. **Sáenz, Michael.** "Economic Aspects of Church Development in Puerto Rico: A Study of the Financial Policies and Procedures of the Major Protestant Church Groups in Puerto Rico from 1898 to 1957." Ph.D. diss., University of Pennsylvania, 1962. 180 pp.

1536. **Sánchez, Gildo.** *Un Jirón de Historia Metodista Unida: Testimonio de un Superintendente de Distrito en Puerto Rico durante Su Incumbencia.* N.p., 1981. 91 pp.

1537. **Sánchez, Gildo.** "Puerto Rico." In *Each in Our Own Tongue: A History of Hispanic United Methodism,* edited by Justo L. González. 131-51. Nashville, TN: Abingdon Press, 1991.

1538. **Sánchez, Jorge E.** "Forty Years a Missionary." *Southern Baptist Home Missions* 23 (March 1952): 12-13.

1539. **Sandoval, Moisés, ed.** *Fronteras: A History of the Latin American Church in the USA Since 1513.* General History of the Church in Latin America, Vol. 10, Hispanics in the United States. San Antonio, TX: Mexican American Cultural Center, 1983. 470 pp.

1540. **Sandoval, Moisés.** *On the Move: A History of the Hispanic Church in the United States.* Maryknoll, N.Y.: Orbis Books, 1990. 152 pp.

1541. **Sandoval, Moisés.** "Conquista y Liberación en los Estados Unidos." In *Sentido Histórico del V Centario (1492-1992),* edited by Guillermo Meléndez. 161-70. San José, Costa Rica: DEI, 1992.

1542. **Santana Jiménez, Benjamín.** "La Iglesia y el Estado en Puerto Rico." B.Th. thesis. Seminario Evangélico de Puerto Rico, 1963.

1543. **Santana Jiménez, Benjamín.** *Un Triángulo Pastoral y Otros Pastores y Hechos.* N.p.: Iglesia Metodista de Puerto Rico, 1992. 217 pp.

1544. **Santana Jiménez, Benjamín and Gildo Sánchez Figueroa.** *¡92 Años de Metodismo en Puerto Rico! (1900-1992).* N.p., 1992. 191 pp.

1545. **Santiago, William Fred.** "Un Hidalgo Iluminado." *Teología y Pastoral Puertorriqueña,* 21 January 1984, 23-28.

1546. **Savage, Pedro.** "Mis Ultimas Semanas con Orlando [Memorial for Orlando E. Costas]." México, D.F. FTL, 1988. 7 pp. Mimeographed.

1547. **Savage, Robert C.** *Adelante Juventud No. 2.* Wheaton, IL: Van Kempen Press, 1947. Hymnal.

1548. **Savage, Robert C.** *Adelante Juventud No. 3.* Wheaton, IL: Van Kempen Press, 1948. Hymnal.

1549. **Savage, Robert C.** *Adelante Juventud.* Wheaton, IL: Van Kempen Press, 1953. Hymnal.

1550. **Savage, Robert C.** *Cánticos de Gozo e Inspiración.* Wheaton, IL: Van Kempen Press, 1953. 56 musical selections.

1551. **Savage, Robert C.** *Voces de Júbilo.* Grand Rapids, MI: Zondervan Publishing House, 1955. 62 musical selections.

1552. **Savage, Robert C., ed.** *Himnos de Fe y Alabanza.* Grand Rapids, MI: Zondervan Publishing House, 1968. [400] pp. Hymnal.

1553. **Scopes, Wilfred, ed.** *The Christian Ministry in Latin America and the Caribbean.* New York: Commission on World Mission and Evangelism, World Council of Churches, 1962.

1554. **Seda, Angel L.** "A Statement by the Evangelical Council of Puerto Rico." 1960. Mimeographed.

1555. **Segovia, Fernando F., ed.** "Hispanic Americans in Theology and the Church." *Listening: Journal of Religion and Culture* 27, no. 1 (1992): 3-84.

1556. **Semple, James H.** "A History of the Florida Baptist Convention from 1865 to 1918." Th.D. diss., Southwestern Baptist Theological Seminary, 1962. 250 pp.

1557. **Sherrill, Lewis J.** *Presbyterian Parochial Schools, 1846-1870.* Yale Studies in Religious Education, 4. New Haven, CN: Yale University Press; London: H. Milford, Oxford University Press, 1932. Reprint, New York: Arno Press, 1969. 261 pp.

1558. **Shope, John H.** "Church Planning in Puerto Rico." Report to the Ninth Annual Assembly of the Evangelical Council of Churches in Puerto Rico. 1962.

1559. **Shorris, Earl.** *Latinos: A Biography of the People.* New York: W. W. Norton & Company, 1992. pp. 366, 373-75, 378-80.

1560. **Siebenmann, Bertie A.** *Oral Memoirs of Bertie A. Siebenmann: February 26, 1976-March 4, 1976.* Baylor University Program for Oral History. [Waco, TX]: Baylor University, 1976. 46 pp.

1561. **Siebenmann, (Mrs.) Paul J.** *Another Man Named Paul; Life Story of Paul J. Siebenmann.* Dallas, TX: Tane Press, 1977. 103 pp.

1562. **Silva-Gotay, Samuel.** "Sociological Considerations about the Typologies of 'Sect' and 'Church'." 1963. 20 pp. Mimeographed.

1563. **Silva-Gotay, Samuel.** "Christian Student Work in Puerto Rico under the Council of Churches." Río Piedras, PR. 1964. Mimeographed.

1564. **Silva-Gotay, Samuel.** "Las Iglesias Protestantes Históricos y la Pobreza en Puerto Rico." San Juan, PR. Universidad de Puerto Rico, 1970.

1565. **Silva-Gotay, Samuel.** "Teoría de la Revolución de Camilo Torres: Su Contexto y sus Consecuencias Continentales." *Latinoamérica,* no. 5 (1972): 105-38.

1566. **Silva-Gotay, Samuel.** "El Estado de los Estudios Religiosos en Puerto Rico Hoy." Presentation given at Colegio de Abogados, bajo los Auspicios del Departamento de Humanidades en la Serie: El Estado de las Humanidades en Puerto Rico Hoy, 1979.

1567. **Silva-Gotay, Samuel.** "Génesis de Pensamiento Cristiano Revolucionario a partir de la Radicalización de la Doctrina Social

Cristiana." Paper presented at the congress en Lima, Perú for the anthology *Historia del Pensamiento Político Cristiano en América Latina y el Caribe,* 1980.

1568. **Silva-Gotay, Samuel.** "The Incorporation of Historical Materialism in the Theological Thought of the Theology of Liberation in Latin America and the Caribbean." Presentation given to the Congress on Church and State, the Center for Latin American Studies, Tulane University, New Orleans, April 1982.

1569. **Silva-Gotay, Samuel.** *El Pensamiento Cristiano Revolucionario en América Latina y el Caribe.* 2nd ed. Salamanca: Ediciones Sígueme; San Juan, PR: Editorial Cordillera, 1983. 389 pp.

1570. **Silva-Gotay, Samuel.** "La Iglesia Protestante como Agente de Americanización en Puerto Rico, 1898-1917." In *Politics, Society and Culture in the Caribbean: Selected Papers of the XIV Conference of Caribbean Historians,* edited by Blanca G. Silvestrini. 37-66. San Juan, PR: University of Puerto Rico, 1983.

1571. **Silva-Gotay, Samuel.** "Iglesias Católicas y Protestantes en el Proceso Político de la Americanización, Análisis de Similaridades y Diferencias." Paper presented at the "XII Congress and Symposium of CEHILA," held jointly with the "First International Conference on the Social History of the Church in Latin America," at the Universidad Nacional Autónoma de México, México City, October 1984.

1572. **Silva-Gotay, Samuel.** "La Iglesia en el Caribe desde 1959." Paper presented for the panel "La Iglesia Latinoamericana en la Coyuntura Actual" at the "XII Congress and Symposium of CEHILA," held jointly with the "First International Conference on the Social History of the Church in Latin America," at the Universidad Nacional Autónoma de México, México City, October 1984.

1573. **Silva-Gotay, Samuel.** "Metodología en la Investigación de la Historia Social de las Iglesias en Puerto Rico." Paper presented at the Centro de Investigaciones Sociales of the Universidad Nacional Autónoma de México, México City, October 1984.

1574. **Silva-Gotay, Samuel.** "La Iglesia Católica en el Proceso Político de la Americanización de Puerto Rico, 1898-1930." [Parts 1 and 2] *Revista de Historia* (1985): Part 1: 1, no. 1 (1985): 102-20; Part 2: 1, no. 2 (1985): 168-87. Also published in *Cristianismo y Sociedad* 23, no. 86 (1985) 7-34.

1575. **Silva-Gotay, Samuel.** *La Teología de la Liberación: Implicaciones para el Cristianismo y el Marxismo.* 3rd ed. Santo Domingo: Ediciones de CEPAE, 1985. 389 pp.

1576. **Silva-Gotay, Samuel.** "Las Condiciones Históricas y Teóricas que Hicieron Posible la Incorporación del Materialismo Histórico en el Pensamiento Cristiano en América Latina." *Cristianismo y Sociedad* Segunda Entrega no. 84 (1985): 25-48.

1577. **Silva-Gotay, Samuel.** "Social History of the Churches in Puerto Rico: Preliminary Notes, 1509-1980." In *Towards a History of the Church in the Third World: The Issue of Periodisation,* edited by Lukas Vischer. 53-80. Geneva, Switzerland: Ecumenical Association of Third World Theologians, 1985.

1578. **Silva-Gotay, Samuel.** "El Pensamiento Religioso: La Historización de la Teología Latinoamericana y Sus Consecuencias Políticas." In *América Latina en Sus Ideas,* edited by UNESCO and Siglo XXI. 118-56. México: UNESCO and Siglo XXI, 1986.

1579. **Silva-Gotay, Samuel.** *O Pensamento Cristão Revolucionario na América Latina e no Caribe.* Sao Paulo: Editorial Paulinas, 1986. 350 pp.

1580. **Silva-Gotay, Samuel, ed.** *Escravidao Negra e Historia de Igreja na América Latina e no Caribe.* Sao Paulo: VOZES, 1987.

1581. **Silva-Gotay, Samuel.** "La Lucha Ideológica por el Dominio de la Eduación en Puerto Rico a partir de la Invasión de 1898." 1987. Conference on the 75th Anniversary of the Interamerican University, San Germán, Puerto Rico, February 1987.

1582. **Silva-Gotay, Samuel.** "Social Visions and Political Roles of the Churches in Puerto Rico and the Caribbean." Paper presented at the "Symposium on Twenty-Five Years of Churches and Social Change in Latin America," held at the Institute of the Américas, University of San Diego, California, April 1987.

1583. **Silva-Gotay, Samuel.** *El Pensamiento Cristiano Revolucionario en América Latina: Implicaciones de la Teología de la Liberación para la Sociología de la Religión.* 4th ed. Río Piedras, PR: La Editorial Huracán, 1989. 389 pp.

1584. **Silva-Gotay, Samuel.** "La Iglesia y la Esclavitud en América Latina y el Caribe." *Cristianismo y Sociedad* 27, no. 4 (1989): 77-95.

1585. **Silva-Gotay, Samuel.** "Desarrollo de la Dimensión Religiosa del Nacionalismo en Puerto Rico: 1898-1989." *Estudios Interdisciplinarios de América Latina de la Universidad de Tel Aviv* (Journal of the School of History, the University of Tel Aviv) 1, no. 1 (1990): 59-82.

1586. **Silva-Gotay, Samuel.** "El Partido Acción Cristiana: Trasfondo Histórico y Significado Sociológico del Nacimiento y Muerte de un Partido Político Católico en Puerto Rico." *Cristianismo y Sociedad* 29, no. 2 (1991): 95-116. Orignally published in *Revista de Historia, Asociación Histórica Puertorriqueña,* 7 (January-December 1988): 146-81.

1587. **Silva-Gotay, Samuel.** "Sentido y Proyección de 500 Años de Historia en el Caribe de la América Nuestra." In *Quinientos Años de Historia, Sentido y Proyección,* edited by Leopoldo Zea. México: Fondo de Cultura Económica, 1991.

1588. **Silva-Gotay, Samuel.** "Bedeutung und Perspektive von 500 Jahren Geschichte der Kritik unseres Amerika." In *Nach 500 Jahren, Stimmen aus dem Sueden, Kritik, Analyse und Meinungen zum V. Centenario,* 35-43. Berlin: FDCL, 1992.

1589. **Silva-Gotay, Samuel.** "El Sentido de la Celebración del 5to Centenario: Una Celebración que Desnuda la Postmodernidad en Puerto Rico." Paper presented for the Association of Puerto Rican Students and the Center for Third World Studies, Princeton University, November 1992.

1590. **Silva-Gotay, Samuel.** "Lo 'Científico' en la Historiografía Protestante Sobre las Iglesias: Hacia una Metodología para el Estudio de las Iglesias Latinas en los Estados Unidos, Puerto Rico y Canada." Paper presented at the Seminar of Hispanic Historians, University of Chicago, May 1993.

1591. **Silva-Gotay, Samuel.** "Anti-Colonial Praxis of Christian Movements in Puerto Rico: The Inter-Generational Conflict in Protestant Churches in the 1960 and 1970 Decades." Paper presented at the annual meeting of the Society for the Scientific Study of Religion, held in Albuquerque, NM, November 1994.

1592. **Silva-Gotay, Samuel.** "The Ideological Dimensions of Popular Religiosity and Cultural Identity in Puerto Rico." In *An Enduring Flame: Studies on Latino Popular Religiosity,* edited by Anthony M. Stevens-Arroyo and Ana María Díaz-Stevens. 133-70. Vol. 1 of PARAL Studies Series. New York: Bildner Center for Western Hemisphere Studies, 1994.

1593. **Silva-Gotay, Samuel.** "A Scientific History of the Latino Church." In *Hidden Stories: Unveiling the History of the Latino Church,* edited by Daniel R. Rodríguez-Díaz and David Cortés-Fuentes. 23-47. Decatur, GA: AETH, 1994.

1594. **Simmonds, G. P.** *Cánticos de Esperanza.* Winona Lake, IN: Rodeheaver Hall-Mack Co., 1948.

1595. **Simmonds, G. P.** *Cánticos Especiales, No. 2.* Albuquerque, NM: Cánticos Escogidos, 1967.

1596. **Simmonds, G. P.** *Cánticos Especiales, No. 3.* Albuquerque, NM: Cánticos Escogidos, 1967.

1597. **Simmonds, G. P.** *Cantos Escogidos para Voces Masculinas, No. 1.* El Paso, TX: Baptist Spanish Publishing House, 1968.

1598. **Simmonds, G. P.** *Cantos Escogidos para Voces Masculinas, No. 2.* El Paso, TX: Baptist Spanish Publishing House, 1968.

1599. **Simmonds, G. P.** *Cánticos Especiales, No. 4.* Albuquerque, NM: Cánticos Escogidos, 1969.

1600. **Simmonds, G. P.** *Cánticos Especiales, No. 5.* Albuquerque, NM: Cánticos Escogidos, 1970.

1601. **Skerry, Peter.** *Mexican Americans: The Ambivalent Minority.* New York: The Free Press, 1993. 463 pp.

1602. **Smith, Richard K. and Melvin J. Nelson.** *Datelines and Bylines: A Sketchbook of Presbyterian Beginnings and Growth in Arizona.* Phoeniz, AZ: 1969.

1603. **Solivan, Samuel.** "Puerto Rico, A History of Struggle for Liberation." Paper presented at the "Symposium on the Self-Determination of Puerto Rico," held at the Inter Church Center, New York City, 1981.

1604. **Soto Fontánez, Santiago.** *Misión a la Puerta: Una Historia del Trabajo Bautista Hispano en Nueva York / Mission at the Door: A History of Hispanic Baptist Work in New York.* Santo Domingo, Dominican Republic: Editora Educativa Dominicana, 1982. 403 pp.

1605. **Spice, Byron.** *Discípulos Americanos (Spanish American Disciples): Sixty Five Years of Christian Churches' Ministry to Spanish-Speaking Persons.* Indianapolis, IN: Department of World Outreach Education, United Christian Missionary Society, 1964. 92 pp.

1606. **Stapleton, Ernest.** "The History of the Baptist Missions in New México, 1849-1866." Master's thesis. University of New México, 1954.

1607. **Stevens, Paul.** *New México and Presbyterian Work.* Albuquerque, NM: Synod of New México, 1967.

1608. **Stevens-Arroyo, Antonio M., ed.** *Prophets Denied Honor: An Anthology of the Hispanic Church in the United States.* Maryknoll, NY: Orbis Books, 1980. 379 pp.

1609. **Stevens-Arroyo, Antonio M.** "Puerto Rican Migration to the United

States." In *Fronteras: A History of the Latin American Church in the USA Since 1513*, edited by Moisés Sandoval. 269-76. San Antonio, TX: Mexican American Cultural Center, 1983.

1610. **Stevens-Arroyo, Anthony M. and Gilbert Cadena, eds.** *Old Masks, New Faces: Religion and Latino Identities.* Vol. 2 of PARAL Studies Series. New York: Bildner Center for Western Hemisphere Studies, 1995. 196 pp.

1611. **Stevens-Arroyo, Anthony M. and Ana María Díaz-Stevens, eds.** *An Enduring Flame: Studies on Latino Popular Religiosity.* Vol. 1 of PARAL Studies Series. New York: Bildner Center for Western Hemisphere Studies, 1994. 219 pp.

1612. **Stewart, Willie Jean.** *Heroes of Home Missions.* Atlanta, GA: Home Mission Board, Southern Baptist Convention, 1945. 78-80.

1613. **Stewart, Willie Jean.** *Fellow Helpers to the Truth.* Atlanta, GA: Home Mission Board, Southern Baptist Convention, n.d. 8-20, 27-40.

1614. **Stowell, Jay S.** *A Study of Mexican and Spanish Americans in the United States.* New York: Home Missions Council and Council of Women for Home Missions, 1920. 78 pp.

1615. **Stowell, Jay S.** *The Near Side of the Mexican Question.* New York: George H. Doran, [1921]. pp. 67-84, 95-99.

1616. **Stratton, David H.** "A History of Northern and Southern Baptists of New México, 1849-1950." Master's thesis. University of Colorado, 1953. 166 pp.

1617. **Stratton, David H.** *The First Century of Baptists in New México, 1849-1950.* Albuquerque, NM: Woman's Missionary Union of New México, 1954. 121 pp.

1618. **Sturm, Roy A.** *Río Grande Conference: A Study of Methodism's Ministry to a People in Process of Acculturation.* Philadelphia, PA: Department of Research and Survey, Division of National Missions, Board of Missions of The Methodist Church, 1958. 131 pp.

1619. **Sturm, Roy A. and Robert L. Wilson.** "Methodism in Puerto Rico." Department of Research and Survey, Division of National Missions of the Board of Missions of the Methodist Church. Philadelphia, PA, 1958.

1620. **Sturni, Gary K.** "Models of Theological Education for Hispanic Candidates for Ordination in the Episcopal Church." D.Min. Project Report. San Francisco Theological Seminary, 1986. 322 pp.

1621. **Swander, Constance.** "The Episcopal Church and the Mexican Americans of the Southwest." Paper presented at a meeting of the Presiding Bishop's Committee on Minority Groups, The Episcopal Church, held at Tuskegee Institute, Tuskegee, AL, September 1957.

1622. **Sylvest, Edwin, Jr.** "Hispanic American Protestantism in the United States." In *Fronteras: A History of the Latin American Church in the USA Since 1513,* edited by Moíses Sandoval. 279-338. San Antonio, TX: Mexican American Cultural Center, 1983.

1623. **Sylvest, Edwin E.** "The Hispanic American Church: Contextual Considerations/La Iglesia Hispano Americana: Consideraciones Contextuales." *Perkins Journal* 29, no. 1 (1975): English: 22-31; Spanish: 66-75.

1624. **Sylvest, Edwin E., Jr.** "Wesley desde el Margen Hispano." *Apuntes: Reflexiones Teológicas desde el Margen Hispano* 1, no. 2 (1981): 14-18.

1625. **Sylvest, Edwin E., Jr.** "Rethinking the 'Discovery' of the Américas: A Provisional Historico-Theological Reflection." *Apuntes: Reflexiones Teológicas desde el Margen Hispano* 7, no. 1 (1987): 3-13.

1626. **Sylvest, Edwin E., Jr.** "Hispanic American Protestantism in the United States." In *On the Move: A History of the Hispanic Church in the United States,* edited by Moisés Sandoval. 115-30. Maryknoll, NY: Orbis Books, 1990.

1627. **Sylvest, Edwin E., Jr.** "The Cosmic Race and Cosmic Grace: New Possibilities for Humankind." *Apuntes: Reflexiones Teológicas desde el Margen Hispano* 12, no. 2 (1992): 65-77.

1628. **Tafolla, James, Sr.** "Nearing the End of the Trail: The Autobiography of Rev. James Tafolla, Sr. A Texas Pioneer, 1827 to 1911." 72 pp.

1629. **Tafolla, Olga.** "The North Central Jurisdiction." In *Each in Our Own Tongue: A History of Hispanic United Methodism,* edited by Justo L. González. 123-130. Nashville, TN: Abingdon Press, 1991.

1630. **Tapia, Andrés.** "Growing Pains: Evangelical Latinos Wrestle with the Role of Women, Generation Gaps, and Cultural Divides." *Christianity Today* 39, no. 2 (1995): 38-40, 42.

1631. **Task Force on Racial Inclusiveness.** "Report and Recommendations to the Northeastern Jurisdictional Conference." Northeastern Jurisdictional Conference, The United Methodist Church. 1992.

1632. **Tatum, Inez.** "Mexican Missions in Texas." Master's thesis. Baylor University, 1939. 131 pp.

1633. **Taylor, Clyde W. and Wade T. Coggins, eds.** *Protestant Missions in Latin America: A Statistical Survey.* Washington, DC: Evangelical Foreign Missions Association, 1961. 314 pp.

1634. **Taylor, Soatia M.** "A Visit to Baptist Missionaries in Porto Rico." *Missions* 5 (July 1914): 582-84.

1635. **Terry, Robert H.** "The McCurdy Mission School Story." *Methodist History* 25, no. 2 (1987): 111-26.

1636. **Texas Council of Churches.** "Texas Migrant Ministry. 1958 Program Report." Texas Council of Churches. Austin, TX. Part I. May-September, 1958.

1637. **Texas Council of Churches.** "Texas Migrant Ministry. Report of Evangelism Research Project. Weslaco, Texas." Texas Council of Churches. Austin, TX, 1958.

1638. **The Board of Home Missions of the Presbyterian Church in the U.S.A.** "The Home Board and Cuba and Porto Rico." New York: The Board of Home Missions of the Presbyterian Church in the U.S.A., 1918.

1639. **The Consulting Committee on Hispanic Ministries in the Southwest U.S.A.** "The Historical, Cultural and Religious Experience of Hispanic Presbyterians in the Southwest U.S.A." Office of Racial Justice and Reconciliation, The Presbyterian Church in the U.S.A. Atlanta, GA, 1985.

1640. **The Evangelical Union of Puerto Rico, Medium of Affiliation.** *United for Kingdom Service in Puerto Rico.* Ponce, PR: Puerto Rico Evangélico Press, 1928.

1641. **Thompson, Charles L.** *The Soul of America: The Contribution of Presbyterian Home Missions.* ATLA monograph preservation program; ATLA fiche 1991-2602. New York: Fleming H. Revell Co., 1919. pp. 201-17.

1642. **Traverzo G., David.** "La Religión Latina en Estados Unidos: Luchas Pasadas y Tendencias Presentes." *Cristianismo y Sociedad* 31-32, nos. 4-1 (1993-1994): 79-94.

1643. **Traverzo Galarza, David.** "A New Dimension in Religious Education for the Hispanic Evangelical Church in New York City." Master's thesis. New Brunswick Theological Seminary, 1979.

1644. **Traverzo Galarza, David.** "The Emergence of a Latino Radical Evangelical Social Ethic in the Work and Thought of Orlando E. Costas: An Ethico-Theological Discourse from the Underside of History." Ph.D. diss., Drew University, 1992. 378 pp.

1645. **Troyer, (Mrs.) L. E.** "The Sovereignty of the Spirit. [Revealed in the Opening of Our Mexican Missions of the South-West.]" In *Protestantism and Latinos in the United States,* edited by Carlos E. Cortés. Los Angeles: Students Benefit Publishing Co, 1934. Reprint, New York: Arno Press, 1980.

1646. **Tushar, Olibama López.** *The People of El Valle: A History of the Spanish Colonials in the San Luis Valley.* Pueblo, CO: El Escritorio, 1992. 230 pp.

1647. **United Presbyterian Church, U.S.A.** "Fifty Years of Spanish-Speaking Effort in Texas." United Presbyterian Church, U.S.A., n.d. 5 pp. Mimeographed.

1648. **Urquidí, Benjamín.** "Historia de la Iglesia Bautista Mexicana de Santa Bárbara, California." *El Atalaya Bautista,* 17 August 1922, 517.

1649. **Veitía, P. E.** "The Cuban Lesson: As Seen by a Cuban Exile." In *Our Claim on the Future, A Controversial Collection from Latin America,* edited by Jorge Lara-Braud. New York: Friendship Press, 1970.

1650. **Vélez López, Ramón, ed.** *Evangelización de Puerto Rico.* San Juan, PR: Tipografía Llabres Ramírez, 1914.

1651. **Virgen, Nicolasa.** *Memoria Orales de Nicolasa Virgen: Una Entrevista Hecha el 29 de septiembre de 1978.* Baylor University Program for Oral History. N.p.: Convención Bautista Mexicana de Texas, 1980. 17 pp.

1652. **Visker, Jaime.** "The Nature and Extent of the Protestant Apostolate in Puerto Rico." In *Spiritual Care of Puerto Rican Migrants: Report on the First Conference, Held in San Juan, Puerto Rico, April 11th to 16th, 1955,* edited by Ivan Illich, William Ferree, and Joseph P. Fitzpatrick. 2/36-40. Sondeos, no. 74. Cuernavaca, México: Centro Intercultural de Documentación, 1970.

1653. **Walker, Randi Jones.** "Protestantism in the Sangre de Cristos: Factors in the Growth and Decline of the Hispanic Protestant Churches in Northern New México and Southern Colorado, 1850-1920." Ph.D. diss., Claremont Graduate School, 1983. 341 pp.

1654. **Walker, Randi Jones.** *Protestantism in the Sangre de Cristos, 1850-1920.* Albuquerque, NM: University of New México Press, 1991. 163 pp.

1655. **Walmsley, Myrtle.** *I Remember, I Remember Truchas the Way It Was, 1936-1956.* Albuquerque, NM: Menaul Historical Library of the Southwest, 1981.

1656. **Ware, J. W.** "New Building—Brighter Prospects." *Southern Baptist Home Missions* 19 (October 1948): 9.

1657. **Watson, Kim.** "Miami: Living with the Cuban Influx." *Home Missions* 46 (May 1975): 5-21.

1658. **Weatherby, Lela.** "A Study of the Early Years of the Presbyterian Work with the Spanish-Speaking People of New México and Colorado and Its Development from 1850-1920." Master's thesis. Presbyterian College of Christian Education, 1942.

1659. **Weigle, Marta.** *Brothers of Light, Brothers of Blood: The Penitentes of the Southwest.* Santa Fe, NM: Ancient City Press, 1976. pp. 68-76.

1660. **Weiss, Herold.** "The *Pagani* among the Contemporary of the First Christians." *Journal of Biblical Literature* 86, no. 1 (1967): 42-52.

1661. **Weiss, Herold.** "History and a Gospel." *Novum Testamentum* 10, Fasc. 2-3 (1968): 81-94.

1662. **Weiss, Herold.** "A Native Son Returns: Report from Argentina." *Spectrum* 15, no. 1 (1984): 34-36.

1663. **Weiss, Herold.** "Letter from Managua." *Spectrum* 18, no. 5 (1988): 222-23.

1664. **Weiss, Herold.** "Philo on the Sabbath." In *Heirs of the Septuagint: Philo, Hellenistic Judaism and Early Christianity,* edited by D. T. Runia, D. M. Hay, and D. Winston. 83-105. Earle Hilgert *Festchrift.* Atlanta, GA: Scholars Press, 1991.

1665. **Weiss, Herold.** "Who was Jesus?" *Signs of the Times* 121, no. 12 (1994): 12-13.

1666. **Weiss, Lorel.** *Ten Years of Brethren Service.* N.p.: Brethren Service Commission, 1951.

1667. **Wellman, Coe R.** "A Plan for the In-Service Training of Teachers and Leaders in the Methodist Church Schools of Puerto Rico." Ed.D. thesis. Columbia University, 1936.

1668. **Westrup, T. M.** *Himnos Selectos.* Philadelphia, PA: Baptist Publishing Society, [1890?] Hymnal.

1669. **Whitam, Frederick L.** "New York's Spanish Protestants." *The Christian Century* 79, no. 6 (1962): 162-64.

1670. **White, Charles L.** *A Century of Faith.* Philadelphia, PA: Judson Press, 1932. 320 pp.

1671. **Wicher, Edward A.** *The Presbyterian Church in California 1849-1927.* New York: Frederick H. Hitchcock, 1927.

1672. **Williams, B.** "Centers Launched to Provide Information on New INS Law." *Episcopal News* 38, no. 5 (1987): 1.

1673. **Williams, (Mrs.) Tallie.** "An Apostle Paul of Today." *Home and Foreign Fields* 14 (December 1930): 6-7.

1674. **Williams, Peter.** *Popular Religion in America: Symbolic Change and the Modernization Process in Historical Perspective.* Edgewood Cliffs, NJ: Prentice-Hall, 1980.

1675. **Willis, S. T.** "First Missionaries to Porto Rico." *The Independent,* 15 October 1899, 371.

1676. **Winkelmann, Roy R.** "Texas Churches Suspend Migrant Ministry, Take a New Look at Intercultural Relations." *The Christian Century* 91, no. 28 (1974): 773-74.

1677. **Woman's Missionary Union of Texas.** *Sendas de Luz; Historia de la Unión Femenil Misionera Auxiliar a la Convención Bautista Mexicana de Texas, 1917-1967.* N.p.: Woman's Missionary Union of Texas, n.d. 112 pp.

1678. **Wood, Levi D.** "Oral History Interviews." Audio recording and transcription. Atlanta, GA: Home Mission Board, Southern Baptist Convention, 1974.

1679. **Yates, Alvey A.** "A Study of the Two Major Cults among Hispanics in Light of Their Historical and Doctrinal Relationship to Roman Catholicism and Their Implications for Lutheran Evangelistic Efforts." Master's thesis. Concordia Theological Seminary, 1983. 158 pp.

1680. **Yohn, Susan M.** "Religion, Pluralism, and the Limits of Progressive Reform: Presbyterian Women Home Missionaries in New México, 1870-1930." Ph.D. diss., New York University, 1987. 307 pp.

1681. **Yohn, Susan M.** *A Contest of Faiths: Missionary Women and Pluralism in the American Southwest.* Ithaca, NY: Cornell University Press, 1995. 272 pp.

1682. **Zackrison, James W.** "Multiethnic/Multicultural Ministry in the 1990s: With Special Emphasis on the Seventh-Day Adventist Church in North America." D.Miss. thesis. Fuller Theological Seminary, School of World Mission, 1991. 399 pp.

1683. **Zambrano, Ariel.** "Content and Context of Evangelization: An Hispanic Perspective." D.Min. Project Report. Claremont School of Theology, 1986. 115 pp.

1684. **[Ortíz, José].** *Familias de Nuestra Iglesia. Con Motivo del 50*

Aniversario Concilio Nacional de Iglesias Hispanas Menonitas. N.p., 1982. 44 pp.

1685. **[Protestant Episcopal Church].** *Libro de Oración Común: Administración de los Sacramentos y Otros Ritos y Ceremonias de la Iglesia Conforme al Uso de la Iglesia Protestante Episcopal en los Estados Unidos de América, con el Salterio o Salmos de David.* N.p.: The National Council [The Protestant Episocpal Church], n.d. 579 pp.

1686. "Resolution and Plan of Organization." The Evangelical Church in Porto Rico. Ponce, PR, *Puerto Rico Evangélico.*

1687. "Mexicans-By One of the Teachers." *The Church at Home and Abroad* 3, no. 5 (1888): 452.

1688. "From Our Mexican Evangelist." *The Home Missionary* 63 (March 1890): 488.

1689. *Himnos Evangélicos.* New York: American Tract Society, 1893. Hymnal.

1690. "116 Plans for Cuba and Puerto Rico." *The Missionary Review of the World,* vol. 12 (January 1899).

1691. "Americanizing the Church in Cuba and Puerto Rico." *Harper's Weekly,* 5 August 1899, 777.

1692. "No Church Unity in Porto Rico." *The Independent,* 6 April 1899, 974-75.

1693. "Christian Missions in Porto Rico." *Missionary Review* 23 (March 1900): 205.

1694. *Outline of Mission Fields Entered by Seventh-Day Adventists.* 2nd ed. Washington DC: Mission Board of Seventh-Day Adventists, 1908.

1695. *El Nuevo Himnario Evangélico.* New York: American Tract Society, 1914. 401 pp. Hymnal.

1696. *Himnario Cristiano para Uso de las Iglesias Evangélicas.* 2nd ed. Nashville, TN: Smith and Lamar, 1915. Hymnal.

1697. "El Mítin de Anoche." *El Día,* 21 December 1916, 2.

1698. "Iglesia Evangélica Puertorriqueña Asamblea Constituyente." *El Día,* 9 November 1916, 4.

1699. "Iglesia Evangélica Puertorriqueña: Primera Asamblea." *El Día,* 9 November 1916, 1, 4.

1700. "Regional Conferences in Latin America: The Reports of a Series of Seven Conferences following the Panama Congress in 1916, Which were held in Lima, Santiago, Buenos Aires, Río de Janeiro, Barranquilla, Havana, and San Juan." The Missionary Education Movement. New York, 1917.

1701. "Mexican Baptist Mission School, 1920." Austin, TX. 1920. 16 pp.

1702. *Handbooks of the Missions of the Episcopal Church. No. V. The West Indies.* New York: Department of Missions, The National Council of the Protestant Episcopal Church, 1926.

1703. "Directory of Evangelical Missions in Latin America." Committee on Cooperation in Latin America. 8th ed. New York, 1931.

1704. *El Himnario para el Uso de las Iglesias Evangélicas de Habla Castellana en Todo el Mundo.* New York: American Tract Society, 1931. Hymnal.

1705. "The Annual Report of the National Council for the Year, 1932." The Domestic and Foreign Missionary Society of the Protestant Episcopal Church in the United States of America. New York, 1932.

1706. "The Eighty-Sixth Annual Report." The Department of Missions, the Puerto Ricans, The American Missionary Association. New York, 1932.

1707. *Himnos Selectos.* El Paso, TX: [First Mexican Church], 1936. Hymnal.

1708. "Death Claims a Missionary." *Southern Baptist Home Missions* 9 (February 1938): 5.

1709. *Himnos de la Vida Cristiana.* New York: Christian and Missionary Alliance, 1939.

1710. *Himnario Evangélico.* Buenos Aires, Argentina: Imprenta Metodista, 1943.

1711. "Thirty Year Career Ended as Death Claims Mrs. Ruiz." *Southern Baptist Home Missions* 14 (August 1943): 10.

1712. *Banda de Voluntarios del Estado de Texas. Seguidores de Cristo: Anuario, 1945-46.* Fort Worth, TX: Southwestern Baptist Theological Seminary, 1946.

1713. "El Hospital Presbiteriano." *Puerto Rico Evangélico,* 25 April 1946,

1714. *Himnario Evangélico Luterano.* St. Louis, MO: Concordia Publishing House, 1947. Hymnal.

1715. *Lluvias de Bendición.* Kansas City, MO: Lillenas Publishing Co, 1947. Hymnal.

1716. *Cánticos de Esperanza.* Winona Lake, IN: Rodeheaver, Hall-Mack, 1948. 75 pp. Hymnal.

1717. *Historia Eclesiástica de Puerto Rico Colonial.* Vol. 1. Ciudad Trujillo: Arte y Cine, 1948.

1718. "Convención Cuadragésima Primera: Cincuentenario de las Iglesias de los Discípulos de Cristo en Puerto Rico." Las Iglesias de los Discípulos de Cristo en Puerto Rico. Bayamón, PR: Imprenta Moreno Hijos, 1949.

1719. *Joyas Favoritas: Una Colección Evangélica de Cantos Especiales.* Compiled by Honorato Reza and Robert Stringfield. Kansas City, MO: Lillenas Publishing Company, 1949.

1720. "Faithful Missionaries Retire." *Southern Baptist Home Missions* 21, no. 4 (1950): 16-17.

1721. *Himnos Favoritos.* El Paso, TX: Casa Bautista de Publicaciones, 1951.

1722. *Latin American Churches in Texas.* Austin, TX: Committee on Program, Publicity, and Research, Synod's Council of Texas, Presbyterian Church, U.S., 1952.

1723. "Paul C. Bell Dies in Texas." *Southern Baptist Home Missions* 23 (September 1952): 17.

1724. *Disciples of Christ and Spanish-Speaking Americans: A Symposium.* Indianapolis, IN: Missionary Education Department, the United Christian Missionary Society, 1953. 24 pp.

1725. *Joyas Favoritas: Otra Colección Evangélica de Cantos Especiales. Numero 2.* Compiled by Honorato Reza and Robert Stringfield. Kansas City, MO: Lillenas Publishing Company, 1955.

1726. *Ecos de Victoria.* Grand Rapids, MI: Zondervan Publishing House, 1956. 63 songs with musical notation.

1727. *The Listening Isles: Records of the Caribbean Consultation, Inter American University, San German, Puerto Rico.* Grand Rapids, MI: Printed for the International Missionary Council by Grand Rapids International Publications, 1957.

1728. *Joyas Favoritas: Otra Colección Evangélica de Cantos Especiales. Numero 3.* Compiled by Honorato Reza and Robert Stringfield. Kansas City, MO: Lillenas Publishing Company, 1958.

1729. *Conference on Latin-American Relations in the Southwestern United States.* New York: [The National Council, Protestant Episcopal Church], 1959.

1730. *El Nuevo Himnario Popular.* Revised and corrected ed., El Paso, TX: Baptist Spanish Publishing House, 1959. Hymnal.

1731. "La Primera Iglesia Bautista Mexicana de El Paso, Texas." *El Atalaya Bautista,* 11 May 1959, 295.

1732. "Principles of Political Action: A Statement by the Evangelical Council of Puerto Rico." *The Christian Century* 77, no. 36 (1960): 1030.

1733. "World in Miami." Filmstrip. Atlanta, GA: Home Mission Board, Southern Baptist Convention, 1960.

1734. "Board Names Language Director for New York." *Home Missions,* vol. 33 (January 1962).

1735. *El Himnario Adventista para Uso en el Culto Divino [Adventist Hymnal Book for Use in Worship Service].* Mountain View, CA: Pacific Press Publishing Association, 1962.

1736. *Gracia y Devoción: Himnario para el Uso de las Iglesias Evangélicas.* Kansas City, MO: Lillenas Publishing Co., 1962. Hymnal.

1737. "Pioneer Missionary Work among Spanish-Speaking People Brings Results." *New York Bulletin,* December 1962, 3.

1738. *Spanish American Missions.* Anderson, IN: Board of Church Extension and Home Missions, 1962.

1739. "Proceedings: Church Planning Institute for Puerto Rico." Indianapolis, IN, 1963. Mimeographed.

1740. "Protestants to Aid Catholic Refugees." *The Christian Century* 80, no. 22 (1963): 702.

1741. *Culto Cristiano.* New York: Publicaciones "El Escudo," 1964. Hymnal.

1742. "Leobardo Estrada: SBC Second Vice President." *Maryland Baptist,* 17 June 1965, 3.

1743. *Cantos Infantiles.* 4th ed. El Paso, TX: Baptist Spanish Publishing House, 1966.

1744. *Himnos de Fe y Alabanza.* Grand Rapids, MI: Zondervan Publishing House, 1968. Hymnal.

1745. *Preparing the Way. A History of the First 100 Years of Las Vegas Presbyterian Church.* Las Vegas, NM: First Presbyterian Church, 1970.

1746. *Cantos para Preescolares.* El Paso, TX: Baptist Spanish Publishing House, 1971. 48 songs for pre-school children.

1747. *El Canto de la Niñez.* El Paso, TX: Baptist Spanish Publishing House, 1971. A collection of songs for children ages six to eight.

1748. "Baptists and the Hispanic American." Filmstrip. Nashville, TN: Broadman Films, 1973.

1749. "Welcoming Estrada." *Baptist Standard* [Texas] 85, no. 5 (1973): 18. Photo. See also "Latin American Named Language Work Head" *Baptist Standard* [Texas] 85, no. 5 (1973): 3.

1750. "Primera Consulta Nacional de Educación Teológica para Hispano-Americanos en EEUU." Vandala, OH, April 1974.

1751. "Puerto Ricans." Audio recording and script. Atlanta, GA: Home Mission Board, Southern Baptist Convention, 1975.

1752. *Seminario Evangélico de Puerto Rico.* [San Juan, PR: Seminario Evangélico de Puerto Rico], 1975. 6 pp.

1753. "Final Statement." In *Consultation of the Hispanic Project: Theology in the Américas,* held in New York, 1978.

1754. "Damas Bautistas de Puerto Rico; Jubileo de Oro, 1930-1980." *El Nuevo Evangelista* 13 (December 1979): 2-21.

1755. "Martha Thomas Ellis: Primera Editora de *Nuestra Tarea." Nuestra Tarea,* February 1980, 23.

1756. "Proposal to the Board of National Ministries and the Board of Educational Ministries of the American Baptist Churches." In *Consultation on Hispanic Theological Education,* held in Ventnor, NJ, April 1980.

1757. "Puerto Rican Woman Ordained on Pentecost." *The Witness* 66, no. 8 (1983): 15.

1758. "Deaths [Notice of Death of Orlando E. Costas]." *The Christian Century* 104, no. 35 (1987): 1,057.

1759. "A Distinguished Missiologist Dies: Orlando E. Costas." *Ministerial Formation* 40 (December 1987): 2.

1760. "Líder Hispano Muere/Hispanic Leader Dies [Orlando E. Costas]." *Jornada* 1, no. 3 (1987): 3.

1761. "[Memorial-Issue Dedicated to Orlando E. Costas]." *Boletín Teológico,* vol. 19, no. 23 (1987).

1762. "Redescubrimiento: Five Centuries of Hispanic American Christianity 1492-1992 [Symposium I]." A symposium held at Perkins School of Theology, Dallas, TX, January 1987. Working papers published in

Apuntes: Reflexiones Teológicas desde el Margen Hispano 7, no. 1 (1987): 3-23; 7, no. 3 (1987): 51-70; 8, no. 1 (1988): 3-23; 8, no. 2 (1988): 38-46.

1763. "A Word from the President [Editorial on the Death of Orlando E. Costas]." *The Judson Bulletin,* n.s., 6, no. 2 (1987): 2.

1764. "Costas, Educator and Theologian, Dies." *The American Baptist* 186, no. 1 (1988): 46.

1765. "Demolition of the Old Oak Cliff Church." Video recording. Dallas, TX: Youth Department of the Oak Cliff Spanish Church, 1988.

1766. "Hispanic Congregation Growing at St. Phillip's." *Episcopal News* 39, no. 5 (1988): 5.

1767. "Hispanic Human Rights Movement Traces Roots to Epiphany Church." *Episcopal News* 39, no. 5 (1988): 5.

1768. "In Memoriam-Orlando E. Costas: De la Encrucijada a la Periferia [Special Issue]." *Pastoralia* 10, nos. 20-21 (1988): 1-69.

1769. "[Notice of Death of Orlando E. Costas]." *International Bulletin of Missionary Research* 12, no. 1 (1988): 24-25.

1770. *Principios Sociales de la Iglesia Metodista Unida.* Nashville, TN: Recursos del Discipulado para Iglesia y Sociedad, 1988.

1771. "[Special Issue]." *American Society of Missiology Newsletter* (April 1988): 1-4.

1772. "Triste Noticia...Fallece Orlando Costas [Notice of Death of Orlando Costas]." *El Intérprete* 26 (January-February 1988): 20.

1773. "Bibliography of the Writings of Orlando Costas." *Latin American Pastoral Issues* 16, no. 1 (1989): 70-81.

1774. "Convención Diocesana Acepta Nuevo Plan Hispano de 5 Año." *Episcopal News* 40, no. 1 (1989): 15.

1775. "[Issue Dedicated to Orlando Costas]." *The Judson Bulletin,* vol. n.s., 7, no. 1 (1989).

1776. "Redescubrimiento: Five Centuries of Hispanic American Christianity 1492-1992 [Symposium II]." A symposium held at Perkins School of Theology, Dallas, TX, October 1989. Working papers published in *Apuntes: Reflexiones Teológicas desde el Margen Hispano* 9, no. 4 (1989): 75-92; 10, no. 1 (1990): 3-16.

1777. "Spanish Churches Report 923 Baptisms." *Record,* 9 April 1991, 9.

1778. "Redescubrimiento: Five Centuries of Hispanic American Christianity 1492-1992 [Symposium III]." A symposium held at Perkins School of Theology, Dallas, TX, October 1989. Working papers published in *Apuntes: Reflexiones Teológicas desde el Margen Hispano* 9, no. 4 (1989): 75-92; 10, no. 1 (1990): 3-16.

1779. "Hispanics Turn Evangelical." *The Christian Century* 111, no. 36 (1994): 1183-84.

1780. "Interview with Justo L. González, as Reported by Neil M. Alexander." *Cokesbury's Good Books Catalog* (Fall-Winter 1993-1994): 2-3.

1781. "Conference of the Evangelical Association of Puerto Rico with Mission Board Representatives." Committee on Cooperation in Latin America. New York, n.d. Mimeographed.

1782. *Destellos del Rubí; Es un Boceto de la Historia de la Unión Femenil Misionera del Estado de Texas, junio de 1957.* San Antonio, TX: N.p., n.d. 39 pp.

1783. *Directory of Language Mission Workers, 1980.* Jacksonville, FL: Florida Baptist Convention, n.d. 28 pp.

1784. "Hispanic Theological Center." Brochure. Huntington Park, CA: American Baptist Seminary of the West, n.d.

1785. *Nuevas Melodías Evangélicas.* Judson Press, California, n.d. Hymnal.

1786. *Puerto Rico.* New York: Division of Home Missions and Church Extension of the Methodist Church by the Editorial Department of the Division of Education and Cultivation, n.d.

1787. *Puerto Rico: Operation Bootstrap.* N.p.: Board of Missions of the Methodist Church, n.d.

1788. *60 Aniversario: Sesenta Mujeres en Misión: Ellas Salieron Sin Saber a Donde Iban.* N.p.: Mujeres Metodistas Unidas, Conferencia Río Grande, Iglesia Metodista Unida, [1993]. 80 pp.

The Hispanic Church and Its Ministry:
A Thematic Review
Harold J. Recinos

Congregations are local community organizations responsible for bringing together the beliefs and practices of people and giving shape to individual identity and moral community. Many studies of the church and its ministry emphasize the way people derive a strong sense of belonging, growth in faith identity and support in times of crisis from their congregational experience. Congregational studies also examine how churches build a sense of community in local neighborhoods and contribute to the development of an ethic of service. This section of the bibliography will be helpful for acquiring a better understanding of the theories and perspectives Latino and Latina researchers employ in their investigations of different churches.

Generally, the literature in the section "The Church and Its Ministry" focus on the local church as a center of culturally specific worship, a Bible-based community of interpretation and prayer, and a context from which arises the impulse for a social witness. The introduction to this section of the bibliography focuses on several themes found in the literature: 1) liturgy and Christian education, 2) political action, 3) the role of women in the church and society, 4) congregations as agents of evangelism, 5) Christianity in culture, 6) social ethics, and 7) pastoral care.

Liturgy and Christian Education: Works in this category are partly centered on the concern to enable congregations to understand their worship life and pedagogical programs as active agents of God present in the world. The pluralism of the Latino and Latina religious experience is reflected in references in this particular categories. Hymn books and Christian education material is listed from many denominational traditions ranging from the evangelical to historic Hispanic mainline Protestant churches. Both hymns and educational material reflect Latino and Latina writers' concern to promote theological identity and group solidarity. Roberto Pazmiño's works are an outstanding example of a critical approach to the study of the Hispanic evangelical tradition.

Political Action: Political action strategies are articulated by Latino and Latina authors in this genre of literature from a variety of perspectives. Writers such as Edwin D. Aponte, Rubén Armendáriz, Roy D. Barton, Harold J. Recinos, Elba R. Ireland Caraballo, Leo Nieto, Minerva Garza Carcaño, Daisy Machado, Virgilio Elizondo, Caleb Rosado, Antonio Stevens-Arroyo, and Jorge Laura-Braud discuss the importance of enabling congregations to enter the political arena by learning first to live consciously in their context. Many of these authors intentionally define the political action of the Hispanic Church as a transformational activity directed toward the restructuring of society in light of the gospel.

Other authors are concerned with issues related to church-based leadership development as well with the task of equipping local congregations to understand their context of ministry. For instance, the works of José Ortiz, Manuel Ortiz, Luis Pereyra, José Reyes, Eli S. Rivera, Conrado Soltero, Saúl Trinidad, Fernando Santillana, Consuelo Urquiza, and Meryl Ruoss help us to understand the importance of leadership development and community-building as a political concern of the Hispanic church. These writers would argue that an effective leadership base is required in order for churches to address racism, poverty, urban violence, immigrant/refugees rights, public education or political exclusion.

The Role of Women in Church and Society: That this body of literature is dominated by male authors is evident from the fact that, of the approximately seven-hundred entries, thirty-four are authored by women. Latinas represent an emerging public voice in the Hispanic religious experience. Their voices demand a better hearing from the church and its publishing houses. Works in this category show women claiming their place in the life of the church that God has already provided for them. Latinas' religious understanding relates the concerns of women to larger social and cultural processes of power at work in society.

Authors such as Daisy Machado, Janet Kalven and Mary I. Buckley, Elba Caraballo, Minerva Carcaño, Nilda Ferrari, Catherine González, Gloria Inés Loya, and María Pérez y González point to the critical role that women play in the church and society. These authors deconstruct the androcentricity of the church and its theology by naming aspects of the church's ministry and theology that exclude their faith perspectives and theological voices. I suspect that this area of authorship will increase in the years to come. More entries will articulate their faith and their understanding of the purpose of the church from a *mujerista* perspective.

Congregations as Agents of Evangelism: For most Hispanic churches evangelization is a very important focus of congregational life. One of the most important writers in the area of evangelization is the late Orlando Costas. In such works as *Christ Outside the Gate* and *Liberating News,* Costas examines the theme of evangelization—sharing the gospel of Jesus Christ—in the context of historical, social, political, economic, and cultural struggles. Albert L. Garcia, Salim Japas, and Pablo Jiménez examine this important theme within the crisis-burdened social reality of the Hispanic community. For the most part, evangelization—verbal proclamation, individual transformation, and social witness—means rethinking the purpose of the church.

Christianity in Culture: Latino and Latina scholars are writing about the relationship of culture to Christianity and various types of religious experience. This section of the literature is making an important contribution to issues related to the cultural construction of Christian identity. For instance, Virgilio

Elizondo *(Galilean Journey)*, Orlando Costas *(Liberating News)*, Justo L. González *(Mañana)*, and Harold J. Recinos *(Jesus Weeps)*, demonstrate the importance of cultural understandings for maintaining, shaping, and amending Hispanic theological identity in changing social contexts. Recinos' *Jesus Weeps* promotes a cross-cultural theological approach that interprets Hispanic piety exclusive of attacks on other sacred creeds.

Social Ethics: Latino scholars like Ismael García, Orlando E. Costas, and Edwin I. Hernández are formulating a social ethics based on the moral narratives that come out of the hopes and struggles of specific Hispanic communities. These authors would argue that social ethics is developed from observation of how contextually-mediated social, political, economic, and cultural processes act in concert to give shape to moral concepts in the Hispanic community. Social ethics concepts are being discussed in a variety of denominational contexts, with the emphasis being placed on the cultural and social dynamics facing the Hispanic population.

Pastoral Care: David Maldonado, Jorge Maldonado and Daniel S. Schipani largely represent the work done in pastoral care. There are others such as Pablo Polischuk who are doing important writing in this area that is not reflected in the bibliography. If you share David Maldonado's concern for addressing the pastoral care of the Hispanic elderly or Schipani's interest in the wider Latin American context and its particular challenge to issues of pastoral care, you will find the literature rich with insight.

An examination of this field of literature suggests that no one approach to congregational studies, and to Hispanic ministry, dominates the field. Most of the authors do not limit their writing to a single theme, but cross thematic boundaries. Moreover, the literature reflects a situation of Hispanic cultural pluralism. In other words, authors may approach the themes of their particular field from the particularity of their own national identity—Mexican-American, Puerto Rican, Cuban, Dominican, Colombian, and so forth—or regional identity. In the near future the work of more women, Central Americans, and more progressive young Latino and Latina scholars may be included and reach a larger and different reading public than that of the church.

The Church and Its Ministry Bibliography

1789. **Acosta, Samuel.** "The Hispanic Council of the United Church of Christ: Its History, Impact, and Ability to Motivate Policy." *Chicago Theological Seminary Register* 79, no. 3 (1989): English: 28-41, Spanish: pp. 42-56.

1790. **Acosta, Sam, Lucille S. Groh, Gustavo Hernandez and Barbara Rathbone.** "Counseling Hispanics in the United States." *Journal of Pastoral Care* 44, no. 1 (1990): 33-41.

1791. **Ad Hoc Committee for the Consultation on Hispanic Theological Education.** "Presentation of the Results of the Consultation on Hispanic Theological Education (held on 18-19 March 1974) to the Theological Schools of Southern California." 1974.

1792. **Agosto, Efraín.** "Paul, Leadership, and the Hispanic Church." *Urban Mission* 10, no. 4 (1993): 6-20.

1793. **Alfaro, Humberto.** "Iglesia de Dios en Vineland: Un Análisis de Su Crecimiento Integral." Philadelphia, PA. Eastern Baptist Theological Seminary, 1983. Manuscript.

1794. **American Baptist Home Mission Societies.** "Proposed Policy for Hispanic Ministry." American Baptist Churches, U.S.A. Valley Forge, PA, 1971.

1795. **Aponte, Edwin D.** "A Report to Lehigh Presbytery on the Establishment of a Hispanic Congregation in the City of Reading, PA." 1992.

1796. **Aponte, Edwin D.** "Towards Understanding Hispanic Protestant Ministry in Philadelphia: A Progress Report." Paper presented at the Hispanic Summer Program, Pacific School of Religion, Berkeley, CA, 1992.

1797. **Aponte, Edwin D.** "Popular Theology in Song: A Hispanic Case Study." Paper presented at "The Church Speaks to the CHURCH," a theological symposium held at Moravian Theological Seminary, February 1994.

1798. **Aponte, Edwin D., David Bartelt, Luis A Cortés, Jr. and John C. Raines.** *The Work of Latino Ministry: Hispanic Protestant Churches in Philadelphia.* Philadelphia, PA: The Pew Charitable Trusts and Temple University, 1994.

1799. **Appleby, Jerry L.** *Missions Have Come to America: The Church's*

Cross-Cultural Ministry to Ethnics. Kansas City, MO: Beacon Hill Press of Kansas City, 1986. 120 pp.

1800. **Aragón, Rafael J.** "From Los Angeles: Warnings and Spirit." *Church and Society* 82, no. 6 (1992): 111-13.

1801. **Aragón, Rafael J. and Donald L. Smith.** "Ecumenical Urban Strategy: A View from Los Angeles." *Church and Society* 83, no. 1 (1992): 117-19.

1802. **Arias, Mortimer.** *Announcing the Reign of God: Evangelization and the Subversive Memory of Jesus.* Philadelphia, PA: Fortress Press, 1984. 155 pp.

1803. **Armendáriz, Rubén P.** "An Ethnic Ministry Geared for Change." Austin, TX. 1974. Manuscript.

1804. **Armendáriz, Rubén P.** "Theological Education within the Context of the Spanish Speaking Community." Paper presented for the pre-assembly meeting of the Council on Hispanic American Ministries (COHAM), San Antonio, Texas, 25 March 1974.

1805. **Armendáriz, Rubén P.** "Issues of Teaching Latinos Preaching." N.p. Academy of Homiletics, 1977. Manuscript.

1806. **Armendáriz, Rubén P.** "Hispanic Heritage and Christian Education." *Alert* (November 1981): 26.

1807. **Armendáriz, Rubén P.** "An Hispanic Theological Education Association—A Possible Reality." In *Consultation on Global Solidarity in Theological Education, World Council of Churches.* Toronto, Canada: n.p., 1981.

1808. **Armendáriz, Rubén P.** "The Preparation of Hispanics for the Ministry of the Church." *Theological Education* 20, no. 1 (1983): 53-57.

1809. **Armendáriz, Rubén P.** "Las Posadas." *Reformed Liturgy and Music* 22, no. 3 (1988): 142-43.

1810. **Arrastía, Cecilio.** *Jesucristo, Señor del Panico: Sermones.* México, D.F.: Casa Unida de Publicaciones, 1964. 109 pp.

1811. **Arrastía, Cecilio.** "Report of Advisory Committee on Hispanic-American Theological Education." 29th Biennial [Meeting], American Association of Theological Schools in the United States and Canada, 1974.

1812. **Arrastía, Cecilio.** *Itinerario de la Pasion: Meditaciones para la Semana Santa.* El Paso, TX: Casa Bautista de Publicaciones, 1978. Second edition published by Casa Bautista de Publicaciones, Buenos Aires, Argentina, 1980.

1813. **Arrastía, Cecilio.** "La Iglesia como Comunidad Hermeneutica." *Apuntes: Reflexiones Teológicas desde el Margen Hispano* 1, no. 1 (1981): 7-13.

1814. **Arrastía, Cecilio.** "The Eucharist: Liberation, Community, and Commitment." *Apuntes: Reflexiones Teológicas desde el Margen Hispano* 4, no. 4 (1984): 75-81.

1815. **Arrastía, Cecilio.** *Teoría y Práctica de la Predicación.* Comentario Bíblico Hispanoamericano. Miami, FL: Editorial Caribe, 1992. 243 pp.

1816. **Arrunategui, Herbert.** "Evaluation of the Development and Implementation of Hispanic Ministries Programs in the Episcopal Church and the Role of the National Hispanic Officer." D.Min. Project Report. Drew University, 1985. 100 pp.

1817. **Ascher, George P.** "Looking Back in Order to Reach Out: An Experiment in Ministry to Aid One Culture in Reaching Another with the Gospel." D.Min. Project Report. Concordia Theological Seminary, 1987. 155 pp.

1818. **Asociación Hispana para la Eduación Teológica.** "Rules and Regulations of the Asociación Hispana para la Educación Teológica." 1981. 2 pp. Manuscript.

1819. **Athans, S.D., ed.** *Cantos de Alabanza, Pureza y Poder.* Los Angeles, CA: Free Tract Society, 1922. Hymnal.

1820. **Athans, S.D., ed.** *Cantos de Alabanza, Pureza y Poder.* 3rd ed. Los Angeles, CA: Free Tract Society, 1930. 256 pp. Hymnal.

1821. **Athans, S. D.** *Melodías Evangélicas.* El Paso, TX: Casa Bautista de Publicaciones, [1936]. Hymnal.

1822. **Atkins-Vásquez, Jane.** *Manual para una Historia de la Iglesia Local.* Decatur, GA: AETH, 1994. 22 pp.

1823. **Atkinson, Ernest E.** "Hispanic Baptist Worship Patterns in San Antonio, Texas." *Austin Seminary Bulletin: Faculty Edition* 98, no. 7 (1983): 11-18.

1824. **Ayala, Silvester.** "Pastoral Counseling the Mexican American Evangelical wthin His/Her Cultural Context." D.Min. Project Report. San Francisco Theological Seminary, 1980. 215 pp.

1825. **Báez-Camargo, Gonzalo.** "A New Hispanic-American Curriculum." *World Christian Education,* vol. 5 (July-September 1950).

1826. **Baker, Susan S.** "A Study of the Role of the Christian Church in Community Development in North Philadelphia's Hispanic Community." Master's thesis. Temple University, 1991.

1827. **Ball, H. C.** *Himnos de Gloria.* San Antonio, TX: Casa de Publicaciones Evangélicas, 1921. Hymnal.

1828. **Ball, H. C.** *Cantos de Triunfo.* San Antonio, TX: Casa Evangélica de Publicaciones, 1924. Hymnal.

1829. **Ball, H. C.** *Cantor Evangelístico.* San Antonio, TX: Casa Evangélica de Publicaciones, 1934. Hymnal.

1830. **Ball, H. C.** *Arpa y Voz de Salmodia.* San Antonio, TX: Casa Evangélica de Publicaciones, 1939.

1831. **Ball, H.C., ed.** *Himnos de Gloria.* Rev. ed. Springfield, MO: Editorial Vida, 1949. Hymnal

1832. **Ball, H. C.** *Himnos de Luz.* San Antonio, TX: H. C. Ball, 1968. Hymnal.

1833. **Barry, David.** "The Protestant Church and Puerto Ricans in United States Cities." *The City Church* 1 (June 1950): 10-11.

1834. **Barry, David W.** "Opportunity for Protestant Churches among Puerto Ricans." *National Council Outlook* 9, no. 5 (1959): 9-10.

1835. **Barton, Paul.** "¿Dónde Están Nuestros Jóvenes?" *El Intérprete* 23, no. 3 (1990): 6.

1836. **Barton, Roy D.** "Training for Ministry." *Engage/Social Action* 6, no. 6 (1978): 19-23.

1837. **Basso, Teresita.** "Ministry to Hispano Mexicano-Chicano Youth." In *Resources for Youth Ministry,* edited by Michael Warren. 190-201. New York: Paulist Press, 1978.

1838. **Belury, William R.** "Creating an Independent Episcopal Congregation in the Neighborhood of an Existing Episcopal Parish." D.Min Project Report. Brite Divinity School, 1984. 62 pp.

1839. **Bengtson, William C.** "Preaching for Spiritual Nurturing in the Anglo-Hispanic Parish Setting." D.Min Project Report. Lutheran School of Theology at Chicago, 1992. 53 pp.

1840. **Bennet, G. Willis.** *Confronting a Crisis: A Depth Study of Southern Baptist Churches in Metropolitan Transitional Areas.* Atlanta, GA: Home Mission Board, Southern Baptist Convention, 1967.

1841. **Betancourt, Esdras.** "Profile of a Puerto Rican Man, the Ministry of a Double Minority Man." D.Min Project Report. New York Theological Seminary, 1976. 266 pp.

1842. **Bongers, Harvey.** "Congregations Responding to Transitional Neighborhoods." D.Min. Project Report. Austin Presbyterian Theological Seminary, 1994. 158 pp.

1843. **Bonilla, Plutarco A.** "Viaje de Ida y Vuelta: Evangelización y Misión—Apuntes Sobre el Pensamiento Misionológico de Orlando E. Costas." Puerto Rico. 1989. Mimeographed.

1844. **Bonilla, Victor and Jesse Miranda.** "Respuestas a Sedillo y Trinidad." *Apuntes: Reflexiones Teológicas desde el Margen Hispano* 8, no. 2 (1988): 38-46.

1845. **Bower, Peter, C., ed.** "Hispanic Hymns in the New Hymnal." *Reformed Liturgy and Music,* vol. 24, no. 2 (1990).

1846. **Brackenridge, R. Douglas and Francisco O. García-Treto.** *Iglesia Presbiteriana: A History of Presbyterians and Mexican Americans in the Southwest.* 2nd ed. San Antonio, TX: Trinity University Press, 1987.

1847. **Braley, Grace.** *Gifts Given/Gifts Received: A Handbook of Resources for Hispanic Ministry.* Port Chester, NY: The Hispanic Ministry Committee of the Episcopal Diocese of New York, 1992.

1848. **Brister, C. W.** "Cultural Factors in Mexican Family Ministry: Helping Families in Crisis and Transition." Audiotaped lecture. Fort Worth, TX: Southwestern Baptist Theological Seminary, 1980.

1849. **Brister, C. W.** "El Cuidado Pastoral en la Iglesia [Pastoral Care in the Church]: Lectures in Pastoral Ministries Class." Audiotaped lecture in Spanish, 3 June 1980. Fort Worth, TX: Southwestern Baptist Theological Seminary, 1980.

1850. **Brown, Milton.** "Presbyterian, U.S.A. Educational Work in New México." 1957. Mimeographed.

1851. **Brunold, William L.** "Directions of Hispanic Ministries of the Lutheran Church—Missouri Synod in the United States." Master's thesis. Concordia Theological Seminary, 1978. 92 pp.

1852. **Bryan, Jesse D.** "Developing a Pilot Baptist Men's Missionary Unit in a Hispanic Church." D.Min. Project Report. New Orleans Baptist Theological Seminary, 1980.

1853. **Butterfield, Robert A.** "Los Natán de Esta Epoca Somos Nosotros." *Apuntes: Reflexiones Teológicas desde el Margen Hispano* 10, no. 3 (1990): 70-72.

1854. **Caloca-Rivas, Rigoberto.** "Hermeneutics for a Theology of Integration: Components for an Understanding of the Role of the Hispanic Church in the United States." Master's thesis. Graduate Theological Union, 1982.

1855. **Camacho, José D.** *El Ministerio de los Santos: Grupos Familiares para el Crecimiento de la Iglesia.* Miami, FL: Editorial Unilit, 1993. 224 pp.

1856. **Camacho-Vásquez, Eliu.** "Safe Teams: Development, Implementation, and Evaluation of a Pilot for an Evangelism Strategy for Hispanics in Florida." D.Min. Project Report. Golden Gate Baptist Theological Seminary, 1989. 105 pp.

1857. **Caraballo Ireland, Elba R.** "The Role of the Pentecostal Church as a Service Provider in the Puerto Rican Community Boston, Massachusetts: A Case Study." Ph.D. diss., Brandeis University, 1991. 194 pp.

1858. **Caraballo, José A.** "A Certificate Program for Hispanic Clergy and Lay Leaders in an Accredited Theological Seminary: A Case Study with Projections." D.Min. Project Report. Drew University, 1983. 239 pp.

1859. **Carcaño, Minerva.** "Women Together: Relating, Working, Creating." *Wellsprings: A Journal for United Methodist Clergywomen* 8, no. 1 (1995): 10-14.

1860. **Carcaño, Minerva Garza.** "Una Perspectiva Bíblico-Teológica Sobre la Mujer en el Ministerio Ordenado." *Apuntes: Reflexiones Teológicas desde el Margen Hispano* 10, no. 2 (1990): 27-35.

1861. **Carillo, Alberto.** "The Chicano and the Church." *IDOC Internacionale* 43 (March 1972): 10-24.

1862. **Carver, E. Earl.** "Evangelical Church Growth in Puerto Rico." Master's thesis. Fuller Theological Seminary, 1972.

1863. **Casachahua, Oscar D.** "A Ministry Approach to the Undocumented Hispanic in the United States of America." Master's thesis. Concordia Theological Seminary, 1981. 63 pp.

1864. **Castuera, Ignacio.** "The Theology and Practice of Liberation in the Mexican American Context/La Teología y Práctica de Liberación en el Contexto México Americana." *Perkins Journal* 29, no. 1 (1975): English: 2-11; Spanish: 43-53.

1865. **Castuera, Ignacio.** "The Best Administrator is a Poet: Towards a Theology of Administration." *Apuntes: Reflexiones Teológicas desde el Margen Hispano* 3, no. 2 (1983): 33-45.

1866. **Catalá, Rafael.** "Liberation and Education." *Apuntes: Reflexiones Teológicas desde el Margen Hispano* 5, no. 4 (1985): 75-80.

1867. **Chakarsi, George.** "Bridging the Cultural Gap between Parents and Children of Hispanic Descent Living in the United States." D.Min.

Project Report. Talbot School of Theology, Biola University, 1991. 150 pp.

1868. **Chávez, César.** "The Mexican American and the Church." In *Prophets Denied Honor,* edited by Antonio M. Stevens Arroyo. 118-21. Maryknoll, NY: Orbis Books, 1980. First published in Octavio I. Ramano V., ed., *Voices: Readings from El Grito* (Berkeley: Quinto Sol, 1973), 215-18.

1869. **Chávez, Guillermo.** "Subtle Symptoms of Racism." *Christian Social Action* 4, no. 5 (1991): 28-31.

1870. **Chávez, Tomás.** "Quinceañera: A Liturgy in the Reformed Tradition." *Austin Seminary Bulletin: Faculty Edition* 98, no. 7 (1983): 34-47.

1871. **Chávez, Tomás, Jr.** "The Theological Basis for a 'Serviglesia'." *Apuntes: Reflexiones Teológicas desde el Margen Hispano* 6, no. 2 (1986): 44-47.

1872. **Chinula, Don.** "Liberation, Praxis, and Psychotherapy." *Apuntes: Reflexiones Teológicas desde el Margen Hispano* 5, no. 4 (1985): 87-95.

1873. **Church and Society.** "General Assembly, 1979: UPCUSA/PCUS." *Church and Society* 69, no. 5 (1979): 5-79.

1874. **Cintron-Figueroa, Jorge Nehemías.** "The Use of the Bible in Selected Materials of the Hispanic-American Evangelical Curriculum." Ph.D. diss., Boston University, 1969. 241 pp.

1875. **Collins, Victor and Carlos Martin.** "Cursillos Sobre la Familia [Family Seminars]." Berrien Springs, MI. Andrews University, 1985.

1876. **Collinson-Streng, P. and Ismael de la Tejera.** "Bible and Mission in a Hispanic Congregation." In *Bible and Mission: Biblical Foundations and Working Models for Congregational Ministry,* edited by Wayne Stumme. 129-37. Mission in the U.S.A. Minneapolis, MN: Augsburg Publishing House, 1986.

1877. **Colón-Colón, Hector L.** "Iglesia Metodista Unida 'La Resurrección': Estudio de una Congregación en Crecimiento Buscando Servir a una Comunidad en Transición." Philadelphia, PA. Eastern Baptist Theological Seminary, 1983. Manuscript.

1878. **Commission on Hispanic Ministry.** "Five Year Plan for the Development of the Hispanic Mission and Ministry in the Diocese of Los Angeles." The Episcopal Diocese of Los Angeles, The Episcopal Church. Los Angeles, CA, 1983.

1879. **Commission on Hispanic Ministry.** "Extendiendo los Brazos: Five Year Plan for Hispanic Mission and Ministry in the Episcopal Diocese of Los Angeles 1 July 1989-30 June 1994." The Episcopal Diocese of Los Angeles, The Episcopal Church. Los Angeles, CA, 1989.

1880. **Committee on a National Plan for Hispanic Ministry, The United Methodist Church.** *Hispanic Ministries: Challenge and Opportunity. A Report to The United Methodist Church.* [Nashville, Tenn.?]: Office of the Committee of Hispanic Ministries, 1992. 85 pp.

1881. **Conde-Frazier, Elizabeth.** "Hispanic Ministry: Teaching and Healing." In *Hidden Stories: Unveiling the History of the Latino Church,* edited by Daniel R. Rodríguez-Díaz and David Cortés-Fuentes. 131-39. Decatur, GA: AETH, 1994.

1882. **Cook, Guillermo.** "Protestant Mission and Evangelization in Latin America: An Interpretation." In *New Face of the Church in Latin America: Between Tradition and Change,* edited by Guillermo Cook. 41-55. American Society of Missiology Series, no. 18. Maryknoll, NY: Orbis Books, 1994. References to Orlando Costas on pp. 53, 55, 280.

1883. **Cortez, Ernest.** "Response." *Apuntes: Reflexiones Teológicas desde el Margen Hispano* 7, no. 3 (1987): 66-70.

1884. **Cortés, Luis.** "Seeking the Welfare of the City, Jeremiah 29:5-7: A Study for Hispanic Church Planting and Development." Eastern Baptist Theological Seminary. Philadelphia, PA, 1982.

1885. **Costas, Orlando E.** "Educación Teológica y Misión." N.p., n.d. 20 pp. Mimeographed.

1886. **Costas, Orlando E.** "Informe del Viaje a Sur América, Parte B: Barranquilla e Instituticiones Teológicas." Evangelismo a Fondo/Seminario Bíblico Latinoamericano. San José, Costa Rica, n.d. 10 pp.

1887. **Costas, Orlando E.** "La Evangelización en los Años Setenta: La Búsqueda de Totalidad." N.p., n.d. 24 pp. Mimeographed.

1888. **Costas, Orlando E.** "La Iglesia como Agente de Dios para la Evangelización." San José, Costa Rica. Seminario Bíblico Latinoamericano, n.d. 18 pp. Mimeographed.

1889. **Costas, Orlando E.** "O Pastor como Agente Mobilizador." n.d. 15 pp. Mimeographed.

1890. **Costas, Orlando E.** "A Strategy for Third World Christians." San José, Costa Rica. Seminario Bíblico Latinoamericano, n.d. 15 pp. Mimeographed.

1891. **Costas, Orlando E.** "El Pastor como Evangelista." San José, Costa Rica. Seminario Bíblico Latinoamericano, 1970. 43 pp. Mimeographed.

1892. **Costas, Orlando E.** "O Sentido Teológico de Pregação." 1970. 18 pp. Mimeographed.

1893. **Costas, Orlando E.** "El Culto en Su Perspectiva Teológica." San José, Costa Rica. Publicaciones INDEF, 1971. 25 pp. Mimeographed.

1894. **Costas, Orlando E.** *La Iglesia y su Misión Evangelizadora.* Buenos Aires, Argentina: Editorial La Aurora, 1971. 123 pp.

1895. **Costas, Orlando E.** *La Realidad de la Iglesia Evangélica Latinoamericana a través de su Expresión Cultural.* San José, Costa Rica: Seminario Bíblico Latinoamericano, 1972.

1896. **Costas, Orlando E.** "Church Growth as a Goal of In-Depth Evangelism." San José, Costa Rica. Institute of In-Depth Evangelism, 1973.

1897. **Costas, Orlando E.** "El Culto como Indice de la Realidad que Vive la Iglesia." *Vida y Pensamiento,* vol. 1, no. 1 (1973).

1898. **Costas, Orlando E.** "From Evangelism-In-Depth to In-Depth Evangelism." *In-Depth Evangelism Around the World* 1, no. 1 (1973): 4-7.

1899. **Costas, Orlando E.** "Influential Factors in the Rhetoric of Augustine." *Foundations* 16, no. 3 (1973): 208-21.

1900. **Costas, Orlando E.** "Mission Out of Affluence." *Missiology* 1, no. 4 (1973): 405-23.

1901. **Costas, Orlando E.** "New Pespectives for In-depth Evangelism." *Parts 1-3. In-Depth Evangelism Around the World* (1973): 1, no. 2 (1973): 17-21; no. 3 (1973): 39, 42-48; no. 4 (1974): 54-55, 58-60.

1902. **Costas, Orlando E.** "¿Qué Significa Evangelizar Hoy?" In *Pastores del Pueblo de Dios en América Latina,* edited and compiled by Emilio Castro. 107-133. Biblioteca de Estudios Teológicos. Buenos Aires, Argentina: Editorial La Aurora, 1973.

1903. **Costas, Orlando E.** *The Church and Its Mission: A Shattering Critique from the Third World.* Wheaton, IL: Tyndale House Publishers; London: Coverdale House Publishers, 1974. 313 pp.

1904. **Costas, Orlando E.** "Depth in Evangelism: A Theological Interpretation of the In-Depth Evangelization Movement." *Occasional Essays [of CELEP],* vol. 2, no. 1 (1974).

1905. **Costas, Orlando E.** "El Pastor como Agente Movilizador." *Psicología Pastoral* 2, no. 8 (1974): 3-10.

1906. **Costas, Orlando E.** "La Realidad de la Iglesia Evangélica Latinoaméricana." In *Fe Cristiana y América Latina Hoy*, edited by C. René Padilla. Buenos Aires, Argentina: Ediciones Certeza, 1974.

1907. **Costas, Orlando E.** "Latin American News Front [Comment]." *Latin America Evangelist* 54, no. 1 (1974): 11.

1908. **Costas, Orlando E.** "A Sign of Hope: A Latin American Appraisal of Lausanne '74." *Latin America Evangelist* 54, no. 6 (1974): 2-3, 10. Also published as "Een Teken van Hoop. Een Latijns Amerikaanse beschungwing over Lausanne '74." *Wereld en Zendig* (Amsterdam, The Netherlands) 4, no. 4 (1975): 295-304, and "Una Señal de Esperanza: Una Evaluación Latinoamericana de Lausanne '74." *En Marcha Internacional* 10, no. 1 (1975): 3-8, 15.

1909. **Costas, Orlando E.** "Depth in Evangelism: An Interpretation of 'In-Depth Evangelism' Around the World." In *Let the Earth Hear His Voice: Official Reference Volume: International Congress on World Evangelization, Lausanne, Switzerland*, edited by James Dixon Douglas. 675-94. Minneapolis, MN: World Wide Publications, 1975.

1910. **Costas, Orlando E.** "In-Depth Evangelism in Latin America." In *Let the Earth Hear His Voice: Official Reference Volume: International Congress on World Evangelization, Lausanne, Switzerland*, edited by James Dixon Douglas. 211-12. Minneapolis, MN: World Wide Publications, 1975.

1911. **Costas, Orlando E.** "Church Growth, In-Depth Evangelization and Human Liberation." *Beautiful Feet/Evangelism for a New Day* Special Joint Issue (1976): 1-7.

1912. **Costas, Orlando E.** "Churches in Evangelistic Partnership." In *The New Face of Evangelicalism: An International Symposium on the Lausanne Covenant*, edited by C. René Padilla. 143-161. Downers Grove, IL: InterVarsity Press, 1976.

1913. **Costas, Orlando E.** *Introducción a la Evangelización I.* San José, Costa Rica: Editorial SEBILA, 1976. 42 pp. Second printing titled *Introducción a la Comunicación.*

1914. **Costas, Orlando E.** "Nuestra Misión y el Crecimiento de la Iglesia: Hacia una Misionología de Masas y Minorías." *Ensayos Ocasionales [de CELEP]* 3, no. 2 (1976): 2-28. Also published as "Our Mission and Church Growth: Towards a Missiology of Masses and Minority Groups." *Theological Fraternity Bulletin* 4 (1976): 3-24.

1915. **Costas, Orlando E.** "On Being a Missionary in the Last Quarter of the Twentieth Century." *Occasional Essays [of CELEP].* Special Supplementary Issue (December 1976): 2-4.

1916. **Costas, Orlando E.** "Evangelism as a Total Task: A Look into Jesus' Evangelistic Ministry." 1977. 39 pp. Mimeographed.

1917. **Costas, Orlando E.** "Evangelism in the 70's: The Quest for Totality." N.p., 1977. 28 pp. Mimeographed.

1918. **Costas, Orlando E.** "A Latin American Theologian Looks at the Charismatic Movement—Pros & Cons." *Latin America Evangelist* 57, no. 3 (1977): 10-14.

1919. **Costas, Orlando E.** "The USA: A Mission Field for Third World Christians?" *Review and Expositor* 74, no. 2 (1977): 183-197.

1920. **Costas, Orlando E.** "El CELEP y la Pastoral." *Pastoralia* 1, no. 1 (1978): 1-12. Also published in *Pastoralia* 6, nos. 12-13 (1984): 81-90, and as "CELEP and Ministry." *Occasional Essays [of CELEP]* 12, no. 2 (1985): 118-28.

1921. **Costas, Orlando E.** "La Empresa Misionera: ¿Un Instrumento de Domesticación?" San José, Costa Rica. Separatas de CELEP, 1978. 20 pp.

1922. **Costas, Orlando E.** "La Misión como Celebración." *La Luz Bautista* (October 1978): 7f?

1923. **Costas, Orlando E.** "La Misión como Discipulado." *La Luz Bautista* (September 1978): 12f?

1924. **Costas, Orlando E.** "La Misión como Proclamación." *La Luz Bautista* (August 1978): 8f.

1925. **Costas, Orlando E.** "Christian Mission in the Américas." *Occasional Essays [of CELEP]* 6, nos. 1-2 (1979): 24-37.

1926. **Costas, Orlando E.** *The Integrity of Mission: The Inner Life and Outreach of the Church.* San Francisco: Harper & Row, 1979. 114 pp.

1927. **Costas, Orlando E.** "La Evangelización en el Contexto de América Latina y el Caribe." *Pastoralia* 2, no. 3 (1979): 8-21.

1928. **Costas, Orlando E.** "Los Protestantes Latinoamericanos y los Derechos Humanos." *Avance Bautista Hispano* (September 1980): 2-3.

1929. **Costas, Orlando E.** "Report on Thailand 80 (Consultation on World Evangelization)." *TSF Bulletin* 4, no. 2 (1980): 4-7? Also published in *Occasional Essays [of CELEP]* 8, nos. 1-2 (1981): 4-12.

1930. **Costas, Orlando E.** "A Strategy for Third World Missions." In *World Missions: Building Bridges or Barriers?,* edited by Theodore Williams. Bangalore, India: WEF Missions Commission, 1980.

Reprint in D. Fraser, ed., *The Church in New Frontiers for Missions* (1983), pp. 223-34.

1931. **Costas, Orlando E.** "The Whole World for the Whole Gospel." *Missiology* 8, no. 4 (1980): 395-405.

1932. **Costas, Orlando E.** "An Awakening Giant: Hispanics in the U.S." Audiotaped address at the "Twelfth Annual National Youth Workers Convention," held in Detroit, MI, November 1981. [Tape Number 40]. El Cajon, CA: Youth Specialties, 1981.

1933. **Costas, Orlando E.** "Christian Faith in the Third World." In *Educating for Christian Missions: Supporting Christian Missions through Education,* edited by Arthur Lonzo Walker, Jr. 73-84. Nashville, TN: Broadman Press, 1981. Originally published in Separatas del *CELEP,* San José, Cost Rica: CELEP, 1979.

1934. **Costas, Orlando E.** "Christian Missions in the 80's: Crisis and Hope." Audiotaped address at Westminster Theological Seminary, Philadelphia, PA, 15 April 1981.

1935. **Costas, Orlando E.** "Church Growth as a Multidimensional Phenomenon: Some Lessons from Chile." *International Bulletin of Missionary Research* 5, no. 1 (1981): 2-8.

1936. **Costas, Orlando E.** "Impressions of Melbourne." *International Review of Mission* 69, nos. 276-277 (1981): 529-31.

1937. **Costas, Orlando E.** "Responding to a World in Need." Audiotaped address at the "Twelfth Annual National Youth Workers Convention," held in Detroit, MI, November 1981. [Tape number 5]. El Cajon, CA: Youth Specialties, 1981.

1938. **Costas, Orlando E.** *Christ Outside the Gate.* Maryknoll, NY: Orbis Books, 1982. 238 pp.

1939. **Costas, Orlando E.** "Dimensiones del Crecimiento Integral de la Iglesia." *Misión* 1, no. 2 (1982): 8-14.

1940. **Costas, Orlando E.** "Evangelism as Story-Sharing." Audio recording. Alumnae Lectures. Atlanta GA: Protestant Radio and Television Center, 1982.

1941. **Costas, Orlando E.** "Evangelism from the Periphery: A Galilean Model." *Apuntes: Reflexiones Teológicas desde el Margen Hispano* 2, no. 3 (1982): 53-59.

1942. **Costas, Orlando. E.** "Evangelism from the Periphery: The Universality of Galilee." *Apuntes: Reflexiones Teológicas desde el Margen Hispano* 2, no. 4.(1982): 75-84.

1943. **Costas, Orlando E.** "Foreword to *Evangelizing Neopagan North America: The Word that Frees,* by Alfred C. Krass." Institute of Mennonite Studies, Missionary Studies, no. 9. Scottsdale, PA and Kitchener, Ontario, Canada: Herald Press, 1982.

1944. **Costas, Orlando E.** "La Misión como Discipulado." *Boletín Teológico* 6 (March-April 1982): 45-59.

1945. **Costas, Orlando E.** "La Misión en el Pueblo de Dios en la Ciudad." *Boletín Teológico* 7 (July-September 1982): 85-96.

1946. **Costas, Orlando E.**, ed. *Predicación Evangélica y Teología Hispana.* San Diego, CA: Publicaciones de las Américas, 1982. 279 pp.

1947. **Costas, Orlando E.** "Predicación Evangélica y Teología Hispana: Los Parámetros del Tema." In *Predicación Evangélica y Teología Hispana,* edited by Orlando E. Costas. 7-19. San Diego, CA: Publicaciones de las Américas, 1982.

1948. **Costas, Orlando E.** "Proclamando a Cristo en los Dos Terceros Mundos." *Boletín Teológico* 8 (October-December 1982): 1-15. Also published as "Proclaiming Christ in the Two-Thirds World." *Theological Fraternity Bulletin* 3 (1982): 1-10.

1949. **Costas, Orlando E.** "The United States as a Mission Field." *TSF Bulletin* 6, no. 2 (1982): 2-4.

1950. **Costas, Orlando E.** "A Comment." *International Review of Mission* 72, no. 288 (1983): 585.

1951. **Costas, Orlando E.** "Crecimiento Integral y Palabra de Dios." N.p. 1983.

1952. **Costas, Orlando E.** *Evangelización Contextual: Fundamentos Teológicos y Pastorales.* San José, Costa Rica: Editorial SEBILA, 1983.

1953. **Costas, Orlando E.** "Interpretación Misionológica del Ministerio." México, D.F. Iglesia Bautista Horeb, 1983. 17 pp. Mimeographed. Also published in *Encuentro y Diálogo* 1 (1 Primer Cuatrimestre 1984): 43-56 and *Diálogo Teológico* no. 25 (1985): 96-115.

1954. **Costas, Orlando E.** "Los Hispanos en los Estados Unidos." *Misión* 2, no. 6 (1983): 6-11.

1955. **Costas, Orlando E.** "A Wholistic Concept of Church Growth." In *Exploring Church Growth,* edited by Wilbert R. Shenk. 95-107. Grand Rapids, MI: William B. Eerdmans Publishing Co., 1983.

1956. **Costas, Orlando E.** "Witnessing in a Divided World." *International Review of Mission* 72, no. 288 (1983): 631-35.

1957. **Costas, Orlando E.** *Comunicación por medio de la Predicación.* 4th ed. Miami, FL: Editorial Caribe, 1984. 255 pp.

1958. **Costas, Orlando E.** "Evangelizing an Awakening Giant: Hispanics in the U.S." In *Signs of the Kingdom in the Secular City,* edited by Helen Ujvarosy. 55-64. Chicago, IL: Covenant Press, 1984.

1959. **Costas, Orlando E.** "Iglecrecimiento, el Movimiento Ecuménico y el Evangelicalismo." *Misión* 3, no. 9 (1984): 56-60.

1960. **Costas, Orlando E.** "Interpretación Misionológica del Ministerio." *Encuentro y Diálogo* 1, no. 1 (1984): 43-56. Also published in *Diálogo Teológico* no. 25 (1985): 96-115.

1961. **Costas, Orlando E.** "Jesucristo el Hombre." In *Creencias Bautistas,* edited by Rolando Gutierrez. 10-20. México: n.p., 1984.

1962. **Costas, Orlando E.** "Origen y Desarrollo del Movimiento de Crecimiento de la Iglesia." *Misión* 3, no. 1 (1984): 6-13.

1963. **Costas, Orlando E.** "The Seminary as Catalyst for Mission." *The Judson Bulletin,* no. 5 (1984): 4-7. Also published in *Latin American Pastoral Issues* 16, no 1 (1989): 49-60.

1964. **Costas, Orlando E.** "Educación Teológica y Misión." Paper presented at the "New Alternatives in Theological Education" conference, sponsored by the Latin American Theological Fraternity, held in Conocoto, Quito, Ecuador, August 1985.

1965. **Costas, Orlando E.** "Waiting on God." In *E. T. Earl Lectures. Sermon on Acts 16:6-10.* Berkeley, CA: Pacific School of Religion, 1985. Video Recording.

1966. **Costas, Orlando E.** *Evangelización Contextual: Fundamentos Teológicos y Pastorales.* San José, Costa Rica: Editorial SEBILA, 1986. 119 pp.

1967. **Costas, Orlando E.** "Internationalizing the Curriculum in Christian Higher Education." In *Internationalizing the Curriculum: Major Presentations at the Faith-Learning Institute Held at Messiah College.* Grantham, PA: The Christian College Consortium, 1986.

1968. **Costas, Orlando E.** "La Iglesia como Comunidad Misionera en la Misionología del Movimiento de Iglecrecimiento." *Misión* 5, no. 2 (1986): 46-53.

1969. **Costas, Orlando.** "Theological Education and Mission." In *Nuevas Alternativas de Educación Teológica,* edited by René Padilla. 9-22. Buenos Aires: Nueva Creación; Grand Rapids, MI: William B. Eerdmans Publishing Co., 1986.

1970. **Costas, Orlando E.** "The Mission of Ministry." *Missiology* 14, no. 4 (1986): 463-72.

1971. **Costas, Orlando E.** "The Gospel and the Poor." In *Evangelism and the Poor: A Third World Study Guide,* edited by Vinay Samuel and Chris Sugden. Rev. ed. 80-85. Oxford, England: Regnum Books, 1987.

1972. **Costas, Orlando E.** "La Estrategia de Iglecrecimiento para la Expansión del Cristianismo." *Misión* 6, no. 1 (1987): 12-16.

1973. **Costas, Orlando E.** "Forward in Partnership." *Today's Ministry: A Report from Andover Newton* 2, no. 2 (1988): 4. Also published as "Crezcamos en Compañerismo." *Boletín Teológico* 19, no. 28 (1987): 219-30; *Latin American Pastoral Issues* 16, no. 1 (1989): 61-69; and as "El Ultimo Discurso de Costas Urge a la Unión de la CBA." *Pastoralia* 10, nos. 20-21 (1988): 86-90.

1974. **Costas, Orlando E.** "Una Estrategia para Misiones en el Tercer Mundo." *Misión* 7, no. 1 (1988): 17-23.

1975. **Costas, Orlando E.** "Conversion as a Complete Experience: A Hispanic Case Study." *Latin American Pastoral Issues* 14, no. 1 (1989): 8-32.

1976. **Costas, Orlando, E.** "Cristo Nuestra Paz." In *Voces del Púlpito Hispano,* edited by Angel Luis Gutiérrez. 20-25. Valley Forge, PA: Judson Press, 1989.

1977. **Costas, Orlando E.** *Liberating News: A Theology of Contextual Evangelization.* Grand Rapids, MI: William B. Eerdmans Publishing Co., 1989. 182 pp.

1978. **Costas, Orlando E.** "[Varios Artículos]." In *Diccionario de la Historia de la Iglesia,* edited by Wilton M. Nelson. Miami, FL: Editorial Caribe, 1989.

1979. **Cotto, Pablo.** *Corazón Adentro.* New York: Riverside Church, Ministerio Hispano-Americano, 1966. 191 pp.

1980. **Cotto-Pérez, Irving.** "The Design and Implementation of a Strategy for a Congregational Mission in Hispanic Churches in the Eastern Pennsylvania Conference of The United Methodist Church." D.Min. Project Report. Eastern Baptist Theological Seminary, 1986. 240 pp.

1981. **Cotto-Thorner, Alfredo.** "The Northeastern Jurisdiction." In *Each in Our Own Tongue: A History of Hispanic United Methodism,* edited by Justo L. González. 106-22. Nashville, TN: Abingdon Press, 1991.

1982. **Curl, Robert F.** *Southwest Texas Methodism.* N.p.: Inter-Board Council, Southwest Texas Conference, Methodist Church [1951], 1975. 154 pp.

1983. **Curti, Josafat.** "The Chicano and the Church: Dominant Anglo Institutions Demand Cultural Suicide and Self-Negation as the Price for Chicano's Acceptance." *The Christian Century* 92, no. 9 (1975): 253-57.

1984. **Davis, James H.** *Background Data for Planning for Methodist Ministry to Spanish-Speaking People in Chicago.* Philadelphia, PA: Department of Research and Survey, Division of National Missions of the Board of Missions of the Methodist Church, 1963. 50 pp.

1985. **Davis, Kenneth G.** "A.A.: Making it User Friendly." *Apuntes: Reflexiones Teológicas desde el Margen Hispano* 10, no. 2 (1990): 36-43.

1986. **Davis, Kenneth G.** "Child Abuse in the Hispanic Community: A Christian Perspective." *Apuntes: Reflexiones Teológicas desde el Margen Hispano* 12, no. 3 (1992): 127-36.

1987. **De Jesús, José A.** *Toward a Model of Evangelism for the 1980s.* St. Louis, MO: The United Church Board for Homeland Ministries, Division of Evangelism and Church Extension, 1983. 10 pp.

1988. **Deck, Allan Figueroa, S.J.** "A Hispanic Perspective on Christian Family Life." *America* 145, no. 20 (1981): 400-402.

1989. **Deck, Allan Figueroa, S.J.** *The Second Wave: Hispanic Ministry and the Evangelization of Cultures.* Isaac Hecker Studies in Religion and American Culture. New York: Paulist Press, 1989. 191 pp.

1990. **Deck, Allan Figueroa, S.J.** "The Spirituality of United States Hispanics." In *An Annotated Bibliography on Hispanic Spirituality,* edited by Verónica Méndez, R.C.D. and Allan Figueroa Deck, S.J. 4-22. Berkeley, CA: The Jesuit School of Theology at Berkeley, 1989.

1991. **Deck, Allan Figueroa, S.J.** "The Challenge of Evangelical/Pentecostal Christianity to Hispanic Catholicism." In *Hispanic Catholic Culture in the U.S.: Issues and Concerns,* edited by Jay P. Dolan and Allan Figueroa Deck, S.J. 409-39. Notre Dame, IN: University of Notre Dame Press, 1994.

1992. **Deiros, Pablo A.** *Día de Bodas.* Miami, FL: Editorial Caribe, 1987. 174 pp.

1993. **Delgado, Hector.** "A Strategy for Developing a More Effective Ministry to the Hispanic Community in Southern California." D.Min. Project Report. Fuller Theological Seminary, 1989. 385 pp.

1994. **Department of Church Planning and Research, Protestant Council of the City of New York.** "A Report on the Protestant Spanish

Community in New York City." In *Protestantism and Latinos in the United States,* edited by Carlos E. Cortés. New York: Arno Press, 1980. 138 pp.

1995. **Díaz, Frank.** "Looking at Hispanic Ministry in 1987." *Austin Seminary Bulletin: Faculty Edition* 103 (October 1987): 37-42.

1996. **Dodrill, Mark Andrew.** "Christian Youth Ministry in Hispanic Chicago and Barcelona: An Inquiry into Similarities, Dissimilarities and Cross-Cultural Themes." Ed.D thesis. Trinity Evangelical Divinity School, 1991. 351 pp.

1997. **Douglass, Harlan P.** *Congregational Missionary Work in Porto Rico.* New York: American Missionary Association, 1910.

1998. **Dresch, Erwin D., ed.** *Himnos y Coros de Palabras Fieles.* St. Louis, MO: Faithful Words Publishing Co, n.d. Hymnal.

1999. **Duran, Boris.** "A Field Education Program for Hispanic Ministers/Un Programa de Entrenamiento Ministerial Practico." D.Min. Project Report. American Baptist Seminary of the West, 1987. 101 pp.

2000. **Eastern Baptist Theological Seminary.** "Hispanic Studies Programs." Philadelphia, PA: 1980.

2001. **Eastman, Fred.** *Unfinished Business of the Presbyterian Church in America.* Philadelphia, PA: n.p., 1921.

2002. **El Departamento de Música y Adoración del Concilio para la Obra Hispano Americana. G. P. Simmonds, editor.** *El Himnario.* Winona Lake, IN: Rodeheaver Company, 1964. Hymnal.

2003. **Elizondo, Virgilio.** "The Mexican American Religious Education Experience." In *Ethnicity in the Education of the Church.* Nashville, TN: Scarritt Press, 1987.

2004. **Elizondo, Virgilio P.** *Christianity and Culture: An Introduction to Pastoral Theology and Ministry for the Bicultural Community.* Huntington, IN: Our Sunday Visitor, Inc., 1975. 199 pp.

2005. **Engage/Social Action Forum.** "Puerto Rico: More Than Vacation Hotels." *Engage/Social Action* 4 (October 1976): 17-48.

2006. **Erdman, Daniel.** "Liberation and Identity: Indo-Hispano Youth." *Religious Education* 78, no. 1 (1983): 76-89.

2007. **Escamilla, Roberto.** "Worship in the Context of the Hispanic Culture." *Worship* 51, no. 4 (1977): 290-93.

2008. **Escamilla, Roberto.** "Toward a Hispanic Liturgy." Paper presented at the

"Hispanic Symposium on Ministries of the Hispanic Church," held at Perkins School of Theology, Dallas, TX, November 1978.

2009. **Escamilla, Roberto, ed.** *Celebremos, Primera Parte: Colección de Coritos.* Musical arrangements by Esther Frances. Nashville, TN: Discipleship Resources, The United Methodist Church, 1979. 32 pp. Hymnal.

2010. **Escamilla, Roberto, ed.** *Celebremos, Segunda Parte: Colección de Himnos, Salmos y Cánticos.* Rev. ed. Nashville, TN: Discipleship Resources, 1983. Hymnal.

2011. **Escamilla, Roberto.** *Prisioneros de la Esperanza: Ensayos Sobre la Jornada de la Vida.* English translation: *Prisoners of Hope: Essays on Life's Journeys.* Nashville, TN: The Upper Room, 1983. 123 pp.

2012. **Espino, José.** *Virutas de Mi Taller.* El Paso, TX: n.p., 1963. 47 pp.

2013. **Espinoza, H. O.** "Response to William H. Bently." In *Evangelical Affirmations,* edited by K. Kantzer and C. Henry. 335-42. Grand Rapids, MI: Academie Books, 1990. pp. 299-333.

2014. **Espinoza, Marco A.** "Pastoral Care of Hispanic Families in the United States: Socio-Cultural, Psychological, and Religious Considerations." D.Min. Project Report. Andover Newton Theological School, 1982. 246 pp.

2015. **Espinoza, Rodolfo and Daniel Rodríguez-Díaz, eds.** *Púlpito Cristiano y Justicia Social.* México City: El Faro & Ediciones Borinquen, 1995.

2016. **Estrada, Fred L.** "The Second Spanish Baptist Church of Philadelphia: Its Birth and Its Growth." Philadelphia, PA. Eastern Baptist Theological Seminary, 1983. Manuscript.

2017. **Estrada, Leobardo F.** "Vida Abundante." Audio recording. Fort Worth, TX: Radio and Television Commission, Southern Baptist Convention, 1961.

2018. **Estrada, Leobardo F.** "Shape of Families." Audio recording. Dallas, TX: Christian Life Commission, Baptist General Convention of Texas, 1984.

2019. **Evangelical Lutheran Church in America.** "Report on Hispanic Ministry." Hispanic Ministries Program, Commission for Multicultural Ministries, Evangelical Lutheran Church in America. Chicago, IL, 1993.

2020. **Evangelista, Ramón A.** "A Theology of Liberation as a Basis for Ministry in the First Hispanic United Methodist Church of Buffalo." D.Min. Project Report. Drew University, 1987. 201 pp.

2021. **Evans, J. Claude.** "Discord Along the Río Grande [Controversial Ministry of Texas Council of Churches among Mexican-American Farm Workers]." *The Christian Century* 86, no. 31 (1969): 397-400.

2022. **Everett, Harvey A.** "The Spanish-American Baptist Seminary, A Study of Its Work and Future." Valley Forge, PA. 1964. Manuscript.

2023. **Executive Committee of the Commission on the Ministry, American Baptist Church.** "Provisional Ordination Standards for Hispanics 1980-85." American Baptist Churches in the U.S.A. 1980.

2024. **Fann, Delbert.** "Hispanic Church Growth: An Eight-Year Study of Hispanic Congregations." Home Mission Board of the Southern Baptist Convention. Atlanta, GA, 1989.

2025. **Fernández, José M.** "The Concept of Central Churches." 1968. Manuscript.

2026. **Fernández, José M.** "Examen, Diagnosis, y Prognosis de Nuestras Congregaciones." The United Methodist Church, 1969. Manuscript.

2027. **Fernández, José M.** "The Relationship between the Brown Community and the Church in the Pomona Valley." Claremont, CA. Claremont School of Theology, 1970. Manuscript.

2028. **Fernández, José M.** "Spanish-American Methodism in the Southern California-Arizona Conference." Claremont, CA. Claremont School of Theology, 1970. Manuscript.

2029. **Fernández, José M.** "Report of a Survey of the Southern Arizona Hispanic Methodist Churches." Latin American Methodist Action Group, Southern California-Arizona Conference, The United Methodist Church. 1972.

2030. **Fernández, José M.** "Un Resumen Breve de la Historia del Metodismo Hispano en California y Arizona." Los Angeles, CA. Latin American Methodist Action Group (LAMAG), 1979. Manuscript.

2031. **Fernández-Calienes, Raúl.** "Who Me? Reflections on an Encounter with Refugees." *International Review of Mission* 78, nos. 311-312 (1989): 455-56.

2032. **Ferrari, Nilda.** "El Nuevo Rostro de la Mujer Hispana: Agente y Reto Misional." In *La Iglesia Hispana en Misión,* edited by Conrado G. Soltero. 49-58. New York: National Program Division of the General Board of Global Ministries, The United Methodist Church, 1992.

2033. **Ferree, William, Ivan Illich, and Joseph P. Fitzpatrick, eds.** *Spiritual Care of Puerto Rican Migrants: Report on the First Conference, Held* *in San Juan, Puerto Rico, April, 1955.* Sondeos, no. 74. Cuernavaca, México: Centro Intercultural de Documentación, 1970. 235 pp.

2034. **Flores, Finees.** "What is Needed from the Denomination." *Engage/Social Action* 6, no. 6 (1978): 26-29.

2035. **Font, Eduardo.** "Hispanic Theological Education: Western States." Paper presented at the meeting of the Hispanic Theological Consultation, Ventnor, NJ, April 1980.

2036. **Fransen, Paul S.** "Raising Up Indigenous Leadership: What's at Stake for the Churches." *Word & World* 5, no. 1 (1985): 60-67.

2037. **Furlow, Elaine S.** *California Journey.* Atlanta, GA: Home Mission Board, Southern Baptist Convention, 1978. pp. 41-45.

2038. **Galván, Elías.** "A Study of the Spanish-Speaking Protestant Church and Her Mission to the Mexican American Minority." Rel. D. thesis. Claremont School of Theology, 1969.

2039. **Galván, Elías.** "Hispanics: Challenge and Opportunity." *Apuntes: Reflexiones Teológicas desde el Margen Hispano* 12, no. 2 (1992): 89-97.

2040. **Gant, Edwin P.** "Evangelism Explosion: A Tool God is Using in Many Cities." *Urban Mission* 3, no. 2 (1985): 32-36.

2041. **Garcia, Alberto L., with the collaboration of Enrique Carcas and Moraima Y. García.** *Conozca a Cristo.* St. Louis, Mo: International Lutheran Laymen's League: 1977. 88 pp.

2042. **Garcia, Albert L.** "Educating Hispanic Americans for Pastoral Ministry." 1981. 10 pp. Manuscript.

2043. **Garcia, Albert L.** *El Arte y Función de la Predicación Evangélica.* Fort Wayne, IN: Concordia Theological Seminary Press, 1983. 34 pp.

2044. **Garcia, Albert L.** *Evangelismo en el Contexto Hispánico.* Fort Wayne, IN: Concordia Theological Seminary Press, 1983. 136 pp.

2045. **Garcia, Albert L.** "Prof. Garcia." Videotaped lecture. Ft. Wayne, IN: Concordia Theological Seminary, 1983.

2046. **Garcia, Albert L.** *Evangelismo y Liberación.* Ft. Wayne, IN: Concordia Theological Seminary Press, 1985. 64 pp.

2047. **Garcia, Albert L.** "Evangelismo y Liberación." 8 audio cassettes. [Fort Wayne, IN: Concordia Theological Seminary], n.d.

2048. **Garcia, Albert L.** *A Cross-cultural Workshop in Hispanic Ministries [presented by A.L. Garcia].* Fort Wayne, IN: Concordia Theological Seminary Press, [c198-?]. [63] pp.

2049. **García, Ismael.** "Reflections on the Ethics of AIDS." *Austin Seminary Bulletin* (Fall 1989): 37-45.

2050. **Garcia, Osvaldo.** "Ministry to the Hispanic Community of the Pomona Valley." D.Min. Project Report. Claremont School of Theology, 1982. 229 pp.

2051. **García-Treto, Francisco O. and R. Douglas Brackenridge.** "Hispanic Presbyterians: Life in Two Cultures." In *The Diversity of Discipleship: Presbyterians and Twentieth-Century Christian Witness,* edited by Milton J. Coalter, John M. Mulder, and Louis B. Weeks. 257-79. Presbyterian Presence. Louisville, KY: Westminster/John Knox Press, 1991.

2052. **Garzon, Fernando and Siang-Yan Tan.** "Counseling Hispanics: Cross-Cultural and Christian Perspectives." *Journal of Psychology and Christianity* 11, no. 4 (1992): 378-90.

2053. **Gaud, Carmen.** "La Biblia y el Desarrollo de Materiales Curriculares." In *Lumbrera a Nuestro Camino,* edited by Pablo A. Jiménez. 155-72. Miami, FL: Editorial Caribe, 1994.

2054. **Gay, George A.** "Hispanic Ministries Education at Fuller Theological Seminary." *Theological Education* 13, no. 2 (1977): 85-89.

2055. **General Board of Church and Society of The United Methodist Church.** "Hispanic Americans: A Growing Force." *e/sa forum-99* (December 1983): 72 pp. Articles in Spanish and English.

2056. **General Council on Ministries, The United Methodist Church.** *"Developing and Strengthening the Ethnic Minority Local Church: For Witness and Mission." 1985-88 Operational Manual.* Dayton, OH: General Council on Ministries, The United Methodist Church, 1985.

2057. **Gillett, Richard W.** "Hispanics and Latin America: Moving Center Stage." *The Witness* 63, no. 9 (1980): 4-8.

2058. **Gimenez, Roman V.** "A Manual for Training Lay Leaders for Youth Ministry in the Hispanic Churches." D.Min. Project Report. Fuller Theological Seminary, School of Theology, 1985.

2059. **Glaze, Michael S.** "A Pilot Study of Southern Baptists' Attitudes towards the Active Use of Art in the Church: A Prelude to Future Research." Ph.D. diss., Florida State University, 1993. 288 pp.

2060. **Gomez, Julio.** "Evangelism among Hispanic American People." Paper presented at the "Hispanic Symposium on Ministries of the Hispanic Church," held at Perkins School of Theology, Southern Methodist University, Dallas, TX, November 1978.

2061. **Gómez, Roberto.** "Mestizo Spirituality: Motifs of Sacrifice, Transformation, Thanksgiving, and Family in Four Mexican American Rituals." *Apuntes: Reflexiones Teológicas desde el Margen Hispano* 11, no. 4 (1991): 81-92.

2062. **Gómez, Roberto L.** "Pastoral Care and Counseling in a Mexican American Setting." *Apuntes: Reflexiones Teológicas desde el Margen Hispano* 2, no. 2 (1982): 31-39.

2063. **González, Jorge A.** "Día del Estudiante Metodista." *El Intérprete* 12, no. 2 (1974): 4-5, 20.

2064. **González, Jorge A.** "La Eucaristía en la Tradición Metodista." *El Intérprete* 21, no. 4 (1983): 5-7.

2065. **González, Justo L.** "Como Escogidos de Dios." In *Diversos Dones, Un Espiritu,* 3-4. Women's Division, General Board of Global Ministries, The United Methodist Church, 1974.

2066. **González, Justo L.** "Cuida de Mis Ovejas." In *Diversos Dones, Un Espiritu,* 45-46. Women's Division, General Board of Global Ministries, The United Methodist Church, 1974.

2067. **González, Justo L.** "Liturgy and Politics: A Latin American Perspective." *Missiology: An International Review* 2, no. 2 (1974): 175-81.

2068. **González, Justo L.** "Los Ministerios en la Iglesia Protestante." In *Ministerios Eclesiales en América Latina,* edited by CELAM. 106-20. Bogotá, Colombia: CELAM, 1974.

2069. **González, Justo L.** "Ni Frío Ni Caliente." In *Diversos Dones, Un Espiritu,* 31-32. Women's Division, General Board of Global Ministries, The United Methodist Church, 1974.

2070. **González, Justo L.** "Un Cuerpo-Diferentes Funciones." In *Diversos Dones, Un Espíritu,* 13-14. Women's Division, General Board of Global Ministries, The United Methodist Church, 1974.

2071. **González, Justo L.** "The Church's Hispanic Presence." *The Interpreter* 23, no. 5 (1979): 31.

2072. **González, Justo L.** "Wanted: Minority Ministers: How can the Church Expect to Reach the Whole World When Almost All Its Ministers are Alike?" *Presbyterian Survey* 70, no. 2 (1980): 43-44.

2073. **González, Justo L.** "Celebrating Our Unity in Cultural Diversity." *The Interpreter* 25, no. 3 (1981): 8-10.

2074. **González, Justo L.** "Guía Para el Pastor Hispano." *El Intérprete* 19, no. 1 (1981): 18-23.

2075. **González, Justo L., ed.** *Proclaiming the Acceptable Year: Sermons from a Perspective of Liberation.* Valley Forge, PA: Judson Press, 1982.

2076. **González, Justo L.** "The Things That Make for Peace." *Handles for Action* 4 (1984): 3-14.

2077. **González, Justo L.** *The Hispanic Ministry of The Episcopal Church in the Metropolitan Area of New York and Environs.* New York: Trinity Grants Board, 1985.

2078. **González, Justo L.** "U.S. Basic Communities." *SEEDS* 9, no. 4 (1986): 3.

2079. **González, Justo L.** "Hacia un Redescubrimiento de Nuestra Misión." *Apuntes: Reflexiones Teológicas desde el Margen Hispano* 7, no. 3 (1987): 51-60.

2080. **González, Justo L.** "Of Figs and Grapes." *Bread for the World in Louisiana,* vol. 6, no. 3 (1987).

2081. **González, Justo L.** "Of Fishes and Wishes: Confronting a Hunger Myth!" *Vanguard* (March-April 1987): 4.

2082. **González, Justo L.** *Probad los Espiritus: Un Comentario Sobre los Textos de Adviento y Navidad.* Nashville, TN: Ediciones Discipulado, General Board of Discipleship, The United Methodist Church, 1987.

2083. **González, Justo L.** "Beyond 'Pocketbook' Voting." *Alternatives* 14, no. 3 (1988): 4.

2084. **González, Justo L.** *The Theological Education of Hispanics.* New York: Fund for Theological Education, 1988. 124 pp.

2085. **González, Justo L.** "El Pluralismo en la Iglesia." *El Intérprete* 28, no. 4 (1990): 12-13.

2086. **González, Justo L.** "Piety and Mercy: Working with Christ." *Covenant Discipleship Quarterly* 5, no. 2 (1990): 1, 24.

2087. **González, Justo L.** "The Theological Education of Hispanics." *Religious Studies Review* 17 (April 1991): 101-9.

2088. **González, Justo L.** "Loving the Enemy I Can't Forgive." *The Living Pulpit* 1, no. 3 (1992): 20-21.

2089. **González, Justo L.** *Mentors as Instruments of God's Call.* Nashville, TN: General Board of Higher Education and Ministry, The United Methodist Church, 1992.

2090. **González, Justo L., ed.** *Voces: Voices from the Hispanic Church.* Nashville, TN: Abingdon Press, 1992. 171 pp.

2091. **González, Justo L.** "St. Francis Was Right After All." *The Living Pulpit* 2, no. 2 (1993): 21.

2092. **González, Justo L.** "View from the Crossroads." *Perspectives* (Fall 1993): 1-3.

2093. **González, Justo L.** "Confusion at Pentecost in Latin American Liberation Theology: Scripture as the Foundation for Freedom." In *The Bible in Theology and Preaching,* edited by Donald K. McKim. 146-49. Nashville, TN: Abingdon Press, 1994.

2094. **González, Justo L.** "Experiences at the Interface." In *Philanthrophy and Religion in a Civil Society: Experiences at the Interface.* 26-28. Washington, DC: Council on Foundations, 1995.

2095. **González, Justo L.** "Hispanic Theological Education." *Ministerial Formation,* no. 70 (July 1995): 27-28.

2096. **González, Justo L.** *Lent, Easter 1996: Scriptures for the Church Seasons.* Nashville, TN: Cokesbury, 1995. 74 pp.

2097. **González, Justo L.** "A Letter from Outer Space." *The Living Pulpit* 4, no. 4 (1995): 36-37.

2098. **González, Justo L.** "Minority Preaching in a Postmodern Age." In *Sharing Heaven's Music: The Heart of Christian Preaching,* edited by Barry L. Callen. 183-90. Nashville, TN: Abingdon Press, 1995.

2099. **González, Justo L. and Catherine Gunsalus González.** "How Total is 'Total'?" *Learning With* 5, no. 1 (1977): 18-21.

2100. **González, Justo L. and Catherine Gunsalus González.** *In Accord: Let Us Worship.* New York: Friendship Press, 1981. 63 pp.

2101. **González, Justo L. and Catherine Gunsalus González.** "Life at the Dawn of the Kingdom: The Readings from Acts for the Easter Season." In *Social Themes of the Christian Year: A Commentary on the Lectionary,* edited by Dieter T. Hessel. 183-88. Philadelphia, PA: The Geneva Press, 1983.

2102. **González, Justo L. and Catherine Gunsalus González.** "The Many Faces of United Methodists." In *Broadly Graded Elective.* Nashville, TN: Graded Press, 1983.

2103. **González, Justo L. and Catherine Gunsalus González.** "The Larger Context." In *Preaching as a Social Act: Theology and Practice,* edited by Arthur van Seters. 29-54. Nashville, TN: Abingdon Press, 1988.

2104. **González, Justo L. and Catherine G. González.** "Babel and Empire: Pentecost and Empire." *Journal for Preachers* 16, no. 4 (1993): 22-26.

2105. **González, Justo L. and Catherine Gunsalus González.** *The Liberating Pulpit.* Nashville, TN: Abingdon Press, 1994. 123 pp.

2106. **González, Justo L. and Catherine Gunsalus González.** "Liberation Preaching." In *Concise Encyclopedia of Preaching,* edited by William H. Willimon and Richard Lischer. 307-8. Louisville, KY: Westminster/John Knox Press, 1995.

2107. **Grebler, Leo, Joan W. Moore, and Ralph C. Guzman.** "Protestants and Mexicans." In *The Mexican American People: The Nation's Second Largest Minority,* edited by Leo Grebler, Joan W. Moore, and Ralph C. Guzman. 486-512. New York: The Free Press, 1970.

2108. **Guajardo, Alcides.** "Brown Like Me." Audiotaped lecture at the "Conference on the Transitional Church," September 1972. Fort Worth, TX: Southwestern Baptist Theological Seminary, 1972.

2109. **Gutiérrez, Angel Luis.** "Marilú Dones de Reyes." In *Wise Women Bearing Gifts: Joys and Struggles of their Faith,* edited by Suzan D. Johnson. 24-28. Valley Forge, PA: Judson Press, 1988.

2110. **Gutiérrez, Angel Luis, ed.** *Voces del Púlpito Hispano.* Valley Forge, PA: Judson Press, 1989.

2111. **Halbeck, Frank.** "Spanish Ministries." *The California Southern Baptist,* 13 November 1980, 18-19.

2112. **Harrison, David C.** "A Survey of the Administrative and Educational Policies of the Baptist, Methodist, and Presbyterian Churches among Mexican-American People in Texas." Master's thesis. University of Texas, 1952. 148 pp.

2113. **Haselden, Kyle.** "Death of a Myth: New Locus for Spanish American Faith." In *Protestantism and Latinos in the United States,* edited by Carlos E. Cortés. New York: Friendship Press, 1964. Reprint, New York: Arno Press, 1980. 172 pp.

2114. **Hatch, James D.** "Juan and James: Pointers Toward Solutions? [Ministry Training]." *Presbyterion* 15, no. 2 (1989): 39-47.

2115. **Hawkins, Wayne R.** "Hispanic and Anglo Christians: A Model for Shared Life." D.Min. Project Report. San Francisco Theological Seminary, 1985. 156 pp.

2116. **Hernandez, Edwin I.** "Factores Que Contribuyen a la Vida Religiosa del Joven." *En Contacto* Tercer Trimestre, no. 2 (1987): 11-12.

2117. **Hernandez, Edwin I.** "Selected Variables Related to Religious Commitment among Church Related Hispanic Seventh-day Adventist Youth." Master's thesis. University of Notre Dame, 1987.

2118. **Hernandez, Edwin I.** "An Assessment of the Problems, Needs, and Challenges of Ministry to and with Hispanics." Paper presented at a Hispanic Consultation in the Religion Division of the Lilly Endowment, January 1992.

2119. **Hernandez, Edwin I.** "Hung Between Two Worlds." *Insight,* 8 February 1992, 15.

2120. **Hernandez, Edwin I.** "Jesus, The Mestizo." *Insight* Special Hispanic Issue 23 (8 February 1992): 12-14. Also published as "Jesus el Mestizo" in *Revista Adventista* 8, no. 2 (1992): 6-7.

2121. **Hernandez, Edwin I.** "The Social Ethics of the Coming Generation." Paper presented at the meeting of the Andrews Society for Religious Studies, San Francisco, CA, November 1992.

2122. **Hernandez, Edwin I.** "Research among Latino Congregations: Issues and Challenges." Paper presented at the annual meeting of the Religious Research Association, Raleigh, NC, October 1993.

2123. **Hernandez, Edwin I.** "Recapturing the Prophetic Imagination." *Adventist Review,* 17 February 1994, 8-10.

2124. **Hernandez, Edwin I.** "Sobreviviendo la Adolescencia de sus Hijos." *Revista Adventista* 10, no. 1 (1994): 8-13.

2125. **Hernandez, Edwin I., et al.** "Religious Institutions as Sources of AIDS Information for Street Injection Drug Users." *Review of Religious Research* 35, no. 4 (1994): 324-34.

2126. **Herrera, Pedro G.** *Una Mirada a Cristo a través de la Teología Contemporánea: Sermones por Pedro G. Herrera.* San Antonio, TX: n.p., 1971. 188 pp.

2127. **Hintze, Otto and Carlos Puig, eds.** *Cantad al Señor.* St. Louis, MO: Editorial Concordia, 1991. Hymnal.

2128. **Hispanic Theological Center, American Baptist Seminary of the West.** "Programs." Los Angeles, CA. 1980.

2129. **Holsinger, Justus G.** *Serving Rural Puerto Rico: A History of Eight Years of Service by the Mennonite Church.* Scottdale, PA: Mennonite Publishing House, 1952. 231 pp.

2130. **Hurt, Hubert Olyn.** "The Establishment of Hispanic Congregations in the Bird Road and Riviera Baptist Churches, Miami, Florida." D.Min. Project Report. New Orleans Baptist Theological Seminary, 1978. 166 pp.

2131. **Icaza, Rosa María.** "Spirituality of the Mexican American People." *Worship* 63 (May 1989): 232-46.

2132. **Iglesia Metodista de Puerto Rico.** *Libro de la Disciplina.* San Juan, PR: Iglesia Metodista de Puerto Rico, 1993. 240 pp.

2133. **Inter-Conference Committee on Hispanic Ministry of the Central Texas and Río Grande [Conferences].** "Beginnings, Purposes, and Ministries: Inter-Conference Committee on Hispanic Ministry of the Central Texas and Río Grande [Conferences]." Report presented at the Consultation on Hispanic Ministries, Dallas, TX, November 1985.

2134. **Japas, Salim.** *Fuego de Dios en la Evangelización [God's Fire in Evangelization].* Mayagüez, PR: Departamento de Teología, Antillian Adventist College, 1971.

2135. **Japas, Salim.** *Llama Divina: Respuesta al Problema de la Evangelización Contemporanea [Divine Flame: Answers to the Problem of Contemporary Evangelization].* Coral Gables, FL: Asociación Publicadora Interamericana, 1989. 122 pp.

2136. **Jiménez, Pablo A.** "Religión Electrónica y Predicación Protestante." *Pasos* no. 13 (September 1987): 10-13.

2137. **Jiménez, Pablo A.** "Apúntes Bibliográficos para la Predicación." *El Educador* Tercera Epoca 1 (February 1990): 22-24.

2138. **Jiménez, Pablo A.** "¿Qué es la Predicación Bíblica?" *El Educador* Tercera Época 1 (February 1990): 4-7.

2139. **Jiménez, Pablo A.** "La Gran Comisión." *Apuntes: Reflexiones Teológicas desde el Margen Hispano* 12, no. 4 (1992): 150-61.

2140. **Jiménez, Pablo A.** "Cómo Preparar un Sermón con la Biblia de Estudio." *La Biblia en las Américas* 49 #214, no. 2 (1994): 11-12.

2141. **Jiménez, Pablo A.** "Estudio Bíblico y Hermenéutica: Implicaciones Homiléticas." In *Lumbrera a Nuestro Camino,* edited by Pablo A. Jiménez. 125-48. Miami, FL: Editorial Caribe, 1994.

2142. **Jiménez, Pablo A.** "Nuevos Horizontes en la Predicación." In *Púlpito Cristiano y Justicia Social,* edited by Daniel R. Rodríguez and Rodolfo Espinosa. 63-79. México: Publicaciones El Faro, 1994.

2143. **Jiménez, Pablo A.** "In Search of a Hispanic Model of Biblical Interpretation." *Journal of Hispanic/Latino Theology* 3, no. 2 (1995): 44-64.

2144. **Johnson, Douglas W.** "Racial/Ethnic Minority Membership in The United Methodist Church." National Program Division, General Board of Global Ministries, The United Methodist Church. New York, 1987.

2145. **Joint Presbyterian Task Force on Migration Issues in United States-**

México Relations. "Mexican Migration to the United States: Challenge to Christian Witness and National Policy." N.d.

2146. **Junta Bautista de Publicaciones.** *Himnos Selectos Evangélicos.* Buenos Aires, Argentina: Junta Bautista de Publicaciones, 1964. 436 pp. Hymnal.

2147. **Junta de Publicaciones de la Convención Evangélica Bautista.** *Himnos Selectos Evangélicos.* 1957. Reprint, Buenos Aires, Argentina: Junta de Publicaciones de la Convención Evangélica Bautista, 1958. 436 pp. Hymnal.

2148. **Kelley, Dean M.** "The Young Lords and the Spanish Congregation [Puerto Rican Revolutionary Group Takes over Church]." *The Christian Century* 87, no. 7 (1970): 208-11.

2149. **Knight, Robert Drew.** "A Study of the Role of the Episcopal Diocese of Los Angeles in Meeting the Psychosocial Needs of Hispanics." Master's thesis. California State University, Long Beach, 1989.

2150. **Krause, James H.** "Why do Mexican-American Lutherans in Corpus Christi Seek the Help of Curanderos/Curanderas?" D.Miss. thesis. Trinity Evangelical Divinity School, 1992. 359 pp.

2151. **Lacayo, Carmela G.** "The Hispanic Elderly: Hope that Belies Their Condition." *Engage/Social Action* 9, no. 6 (1981): 38-39.

2152. **LAMAG.** "A Proposal for Hispanic Ministry in the California-Pacific Conference of The United Methodist Church." Latin American Methodist Action Group [LAMAG]. N.d.

2153. **Langston, Maxine M.** "Profiles of Ministry." *Engage/Social Action* 6, no. 6 (1978): 29-37.

2154. **Langston, Maxine M.** "Sharing the Vision of a Growing Church." *Engage/Social Action* 6, no. 6 (1978): 23-25.

2155. **Lara-Braud, Jorge.** "The Church's Partnership with Mexican Americans: A Proposal to Anglo Protestant Churchmen." 1967. Manuscript.

2156. **Lara-Braud, Jorge.** "Monseñor Romero: Model Pastor for the Hispanic Diaspora." *Apuntes: Reflexiones Teológicas desde el Margen Hispano* 1, no. 3 (1981): 15-21.

2157. **Lara-Braud, Jorge.** "Latin-American Liberation Theology: Pastoral Action as the Basis for the Prophetic Task." In *The Pastor as Prophet,* edited by Earl E. Shelp and Ronald H. Sunderland. 135-68. New York: Pilgrim Press, 1985.

2158. **Lara-Braud, Jorge.** "Authenticity before the Altar as Affirmation and Celebration of Cultural Diversity and Spiritual Oneness." *Church and Society,* vol. 76, no. 4 (1986).

2159. **Lara-Braud, Jorge.** "Hispanic Ministry: Fidelity to Christ." *Pacific Theological Review,* vol. 19, no. 2 (1986).

2160. **Lee, Dallas P.** "The Mexican American in Texas." *Royal Service* 65, no. 11 (1971): 12-14.

2161. **Lloyd–Sidle, Patricia J., ed.** "Called to the Border: A Paradigm for Mission [in Texas]." In *International Review of Mission.* 78 (April 1989): 135-220.

2162. **Lockwood, George F.** "Recent Developments in U.S. Hispanic and Latin American Protestant Church Music." D.Min. Project Report. Claremont School of Theology, 1981. 165 pp.

2163. **López, Carlos A.** "Hymn Singing in the Hispanic Tradition." *Reformed Liturgy and Music* 21, no. 3 (1987): 156-57.

2164. **López, Hugo.** "Toward a Theology of Migration." *Apuntes: Reflexiones Teológicas desde el Margen Hispano* 2, no. 3 (1982): 68-71.

2165. **López, Ike.** "Alcoholism in the Hispanic Community." *Engage/Social Action* 3, no. 10 (1975): 44-46.

2166. **López, Rosa María.** "Salud y Bienestar: La Misión Sanadora de la Congregación Local." In *La Iglesia Hispana en Misión,* edited by Conrado G. Soltero. 40-43. New York: National Program Division, General Board of Global Ministries, The United Methodist Church, 1992.

2167. **Loucks, Celeste.** *American Montage: The Human Touch to Language Missions.* Atlanta, GA: Home Mission Board, Southern Baptist Convention, 1976. 191 pp.

2168. **Loya, Gloria Inés.** "The Hispanic Woman: Pasionaria and *Pastora* of the Hispanic Community." In *Frontiers of Hispanic Theology in the United States,* edited by Allan Figueroa Deck, S.J. 124-33. Maryknoll, NY: Orbis Books, 1992.

2169. **Lucas, Isidro.** *The Browning of America: The Hispanic Revolution in the American Church.* Chicago, IL: Fides/Claretian, 1981. See chapter six for references to Protestantism.

2170. **Luna, David.** "Patterns of Faith: Woven Together in Life and Mission." *American Baptist Quarterly* 5, no. 4 (1986): 393-97.

2171. **Lutheran Church-Missouri Synod. Board of Mission Services.** "Our

Hispanic Friends." Filmstrip, cassette, and script. [St. Louis, MO.]: Lutheran Church—Missouri Synod, [1984].

2172. **Machado, Daisy L.** "A Powerful Gospel." In *And Blessed is She, Sermons by Women,* edited by David Albert Farmer and Edwina Hunter. 188-95. San Francisco, CA: Harper & Row, 1990.

2173. **Machado, Daisy L.** "Jesús Libertador." In *Púlpito y Justicia Social,* edited by Daniel Rodríguez and Rodolfo Espinoza. 221-27. So. Holland, IL: Ediciones Borinquen, 1994.

2174. **Mackey, T. Michael.** "The Roots and Dynamics of Lutheran Hispanic Ministry in Texas." Austin, TX. Lutheran Seminary Program in the Southwest, The Episcopal Theological Seminary of the Southwest, 1989. 74 pp. Manuscript.

2175. **Madriz, Esther.** "Nuestra Responsabilidad Social Cristiana: ¿Opción o Mandato Bíblico?" In *La Iglesia Hispana en Misión,* edited by Conrado G. Soltero. 6-12. New York: National Program Division, General Board of Global Ministries, The United Methodist Church, 1992.

2176. **Maldonado, David, Jr.** "Ministerio con Personas Mayores Hispanas." *El Intérprete* 25, no. 4 (1987): 5, 7.

2177. **Maldonado, David, Jr.** "El Barrio: Perceptions and Utilization of the Neighborhood." In *Hispanic Elderly in Transition,* edited by Steven Applewhite. 135-42. New York: Greenwood Press, 1988.

2178. **Maldonado, David, Jr.** "A Framework for Understanding the Minority Elderly." In *Low-Income, Minority and Rural Adult Populations: Issues for the Future,* edited by E.O. Schuster. 7-29. Ypsilanti, MI: Geriatric Education Center of Michigan, 1989.

2179. **Maldonado, David, Jr.** "The Latino Elderly Living Alone: The Invisible Poor." *California Sociologist* 12, no. 1 (1989): 8-21.

2180. **Maldonado, David, Jr.** "The Minority Church: Its Roles and Significance for the Minority Elderly." In *Ethnicity and Aging: Mental Health Issues,* edited by E. Percil Stanford, Shirley A. Lockery, and Susan A. Schoenrock. 25-32. San Diego, CA: San Diego State University, 1990.

2181. **Maldonado, David, Jr.** "La Iglesia en Misión." In *Salud Para Todos: Manual de Programa,* edited by Conrado Soltero, Nilda Ferrari, and Rosa López. 23-27. New York: Health and Welfare Ministries, General Board of Global Ministries, The United Methodist Church, 1991.

2182. **Maldonado, David, Jr.** "¿Qué es la Salud?" In *Salud para Todos:*

Manual de Programa, edited by Conrado Soltero, Nilda Ferrari, and Rosa López. 1-7. New York: Health and Welfare Ministries, General Board of Global Ministries, The United Methodist Church, 1991.

2183. **Maldonado, David.** "Hispanic and African American Elderly: Religiosity, Religious Participation, and Attitudes toward the Church." *Apuntes: Reflexiones Teológicas desde el Margen Hispano* 14, no. 1 (1994): 3-18.

2184. **Maldonado, Jorge E.** "My Basic Assumptions in Pastoral Counseling of Hispanic Families." *The Covenant Quarterly* 52, no. 2 (1994): 19-28.

2185. **Mangual Rodríguez, Sandra.** "Reacción al Artículo de Pablo A. Jiménez." In *Lumbrera a Nuestro Camino,* edited by Pablo A. Jiménez. 149-53. Miami, FL: Editorial Caribe, 1994.

2186. **Mangual-Rodriguez, Sandra.** "The Training of Hispanic Protestant Preachers in the United States: An Indigenous Approach to Homiletics." D.Min. Project Report. Andover Newton Theological School, 1988. 157 pp.

2187. **MARCHA.** "The Hispanic Vision for Century III: Presented by MARCHA, The National Hispanic United Methodist Caucus." [Nashville, TN]: Printed by the General Board of Higher Education and Ministry, The United Methodist Church, 1985. 12 pp.

2188. **Mark, Leslie David.** "The Role of Seminary Education in the Development of Spiritual Leadership in the Hispanic American Protestant Church." D.Min. Project Report. Fuller Theological Seminary, School of Theology, 1982.

2189. **Marrero Navarro, Domingo.** *Meditaciones de la Pasión: Vísperas del Calvario. Las Siete Palabras. El Lirio Sobre la Cruz.* Reprint. Río Piedras, PR: Librería La Reforma, 1984.

2190. **Martell Otero, Loida.** "En las Manos del Señor. Ministry in the Hispanic American Context." *The Apple Seed* 1 (Winter 1994): 1:14-20.

2191. **Martin, Carlos G.** "Un Ministerio Compartido." *El Ministerio* 56 (October 1987): 13-15.

2192. **Martin, Gary E.** "A Study of Curanderismo for an Effective Ministry to the Mexican-Americans." Master's thesis. Concordia Theological Seminary, 1974. 70 pp.

2193. **Martínez, David L., Jr.** "The Wesleyan Way to Spiritual Formation: Teaching an Adult Sunday School Class." D.Min. Project Report. Nazarene Theological Seminary, 1989. 66 pp.

2194. **Martínez, Homer T.** "[Mexican American Elderly are Still] Fighting the Alamo." *Engage/Social Action* 1, no. 2 (1973): 43-51.

2195. **Martínez, Jill.** "Worship and the Search for Community in the Presbyterian Church (U.S.A.): The Hispanic Experience." *Church and Society* 76, no. 4 (1986): 42-46.

2196. **Martínez, Juan.** "Hispanics in California: Myth and Opportunity." *Direction: A Semi-Annual Publication of Mennonite Brethren Schools* 16, no. 1 (1987): 47-56.

2197. **Martínez, Juan.** "Mennonite Brethren, Latinos and Mission." *Direction: A Semi-Annual Publication of Mennonite Brethren Schools* 23, no. 2 (1994): 43-49.

2198. **Martínez, Juan and Dale Warkentin.** "[Two Responses to Henry Schmidt]: Diverse Models/Strategies of Church Planting/Growth among Mennonite Brethren." *Direction: A Semi-Annual Publication of Mennonite Brethren Schools* 20, no. 2 (1991): 45-49.

2199. **Martínez, Juan F.** "Ministry among United States Hispanics by an Ethno-Religious Minority: A Mennonite Brethren Case Study." Master's thesis. Fuller Theological Seminary, School of World Mission, 1988. 234 pp.

2200. **Martínez, Joel N.** "A Challenge for the Future." *Engage/Social Action* 6, no. 6 (1978): 37-40.

2201. **Martínez, Joel N.** "La Conferencia Río Grande: Descubriendo Nuestro Cautiverio." Paper presented at a symposium held at Perkins School of Theology, Southern Methodist University, Dallas, TX, November 1979.

2202. **Martínez, Joel N.** "The Southwest Border Region: Area of Conflict and Hope." *Engage/Social Action* 11, no. 11 (1983): English: 22-27; Spanish: 60-64.

2203. **Martínez, Joel N.** "Conspiracy Along the Border: The Church's Response." Paper presented at the meeting of the Southwest Border Continuing Committee, National Division, General Board of Global Ministries, The United Methodist Church, held in Tuscon AZ, August 1986.

2204. **Martínez, Joel N.** "Hispanic Ministry: More than 'Add-on.'" *Christian Social Action* 7, no. 2 (1994): 34-35.

2205. **Martínez, Joel N.** "The People on the Go: The Church on the Way." *Apuntes: Reflexiones Teológicas desde el Margen Hispano* 15, no. 2 (1995): 58-71.

2206. **Martinez, Lydia.** "Brown on Brown: Like Water for Chocolate." *Wellsprings: A Journal for United Methodist Clergywomen* 8, no. 1 (1995): 48-49.

2207. **Mata, Michael A.** "The Post-Immigrant Hispanic Generation: Challenges and Leadership Development." Paper presented at a meeting of the advisory council to the Office of Hispanic Ministry, National Division, General Board of Global Ministries, The United Methodist Church, held in Seattle, WA, 1995.

2208. **Maust, John.** "The Exploding Hispanic Minority: A Field in our Back Yard." *Christianity Today* 24, no. 14 (1980): 12-14, 39.

2209. **Maust, John.** "Hispanics Eye Mission Role: But Diversity and Lack of Experience Pose Problems." *Christianity Today* 37, no. 12 (1993): 25.

2210. **McCavran, Donald A.** "A Study of the Life and Growth of the Church of the Disciples of Christ in Puerto Rico in View of the Strategy of World Missions Adopted by the United Christian Missionary Society." United Christian Missionary Society. Indianapolis, IN, 1956. Mimeographed.

2211. **McConnell, Harry C.** "The Development of the Hymn among Spanish Speaking Evangelicals." Th.D. diss., The Southern Baptist Theological Seminary, 1953. See pp. 307-17 for a bibliography on Spanish-language hymnals.

2212. **McElroy, Richard.** "World Evangelism: How?—Orlando and Rose Costas Give Themselves to the Needs of Their Seminary Students." *Latin America Evangelist* 51, no. 1 (1971): 10-11.

2213. **Mergal, Angel M.** *Arte Cristiano de la Predicación.* Río Piedras, PR: Comité de Literatura de la Asociación de Iglesias Evangélicas de Puerto Rico, 1951.

2214. **Mergal, Angel M.** *De Semántica Musical y Otros Estudios.* San Juan, PR: Editorial del Departamento de Instrucción Pública, 1963.

2215. **Miranda, Jesse.** "Los Nuevos Samaritanos: Un Sermón Modelo." In *Predicación Evangélica y Teología Hispana,* edited by Orlando E. Costas. 269-79. San Diego, CA: Publicaciones de las Américas, 1982.

2216. **Miranda, Jesse.** "Realizing the Hispanic Dream." *Christianity Today* 33, no. 4 (1989): 37-40.

2217. **Miranda, Juan Carlos.** "A Church Growth Manual for the Hispanic Community." D.Min. Project Report. Fuller Theological Seminary, School of Theology, 1982.

2218. **Mixon, John.** *The Maywood Hispanic Ministries Project.* Claremont, CA: Church Planning Institute at Claremont, 1970.

2219. **Montoya, Alex D.** *Hispanic Ministry in North America.* Grand Rapids, MI: Zondervan Publishing House, 1987. 155 pp.

2220. **Moore, Elena Vela.** "Ministry in Puerto Rico." *The Beam* 18 (November 1967): 10.

2221. **Morrison, Aubrey L.** "'El Camino Nuevo de Vida' (Hebreos 10:20): Estudios Basados en la Epístola a los Hebreos." Master's thesis. Concordia Theological Seminary, 1984. 65 pp.

2222. **Moseley, J. Edward, ed.** *The Spanish-Speaking People of the Southwest.* N.p.: Council on Spanish-American Work, 1966. 85 pp.

2223. **Müller, Emilio E.** *Cada Celebración: Un Anuario Litúrgico y Algo Más para la Iglesia de Habla Hispana.* Nashville, TN: Discipleship Resources, 1991. 67 pp.

2224. **Müller, Emilio E.** "La Iglesia Local y su Presupuesto Misional." In *La Iglesia Hispana en Misión,* edited by Conrado G. Soltero. 68-78. New York: National Program Division, General Board of Global Ministries, The United Methodist Church, 1992.

2225. **Muñiz-Rocha, William.** "Sí Hay Judíos y Griegos, Esclavos y Libres." *Apuntes: Reflexiones Teológicas desde el Margen Hispano* 8, no. 4 (1988): 88-90.

2226. **Muñoz-Rivera, Brindice.** "A Pastoral Counseling Program for Mexican Immigrant Families." D.Min. Project Report. Claremont School of Theology, 1989. 76 pp.

2227. **Náñez, Alfredo.** "Madurando en el Ministerio." 23 pp. Manuscript. [Located in the files of Paul Barton.]

2228. **Náñez, Alfredo, ed.** *Himnario Metodista.* San Antonio, TX: Río Grande Conference Board of Education. Printed by Casa Bautista de Publicaciones, 1955. Hymnal.

2229. **Náñez, Alfredo.** *Ritual de la Iglesia Metodista.* [San Antonio, TX]: Board of Publication of the Methodist Church, Inc., 1965. 76 pp.

2230. **Náñez, Alfredo, ed.** *Himnario Metodista.* Nashville, TN: The United Methodist Publishing House, 1973. 592 pp. Hymnal.

2231. **National Hispanic Caucus of the Lutheran Church in America.** "Hispanic Ministry Profile." Typescript.

2232. **National Hispanic Task Force of the American Lutheran Church.** "A Hispanic Declaration on Ministry Needs and Aspirations Commended to The American Lutheran Church and the Evangelical Lutheran Church in America." The National Hispanic Task Force of the American Lutheran Church. Chicago, IL, 1986.

2233. **Nelson, Edward Warren.** "Problems of Compiling a Hymnal for Spanish-Speaking Evangelical Churches." Ph.D. diss., New Orleans Baptist Theological Seminary, 1972. 195 pp.

2234. **Nelson G., Eduardo, ed.** *Himnario Bautista.* El Paso, TX: Casa Bautista de Publicaciones, 1978. Hymnal.

2235. **Nieto, Leo D.** "Spanish-Speaking Texans." Department of Migrant Ministry, Department of Church Planning and Development, Texas Council of Churches, 1964. 28 pp.

2236. **Nieto, Leo D.** "South Bay Hispanic Ministry of Presence, Phase 1: A Report." Pacific and Southwest Annual Conference, The United Methodist Church. Long Beach, CA, 1981.

2237. **Nieto, Leo D.** "Ethnic Minorities in Ministry: A Prophetic Vision." *Apuntes: Reflexiones Teológicas desde el Margen Hispano* 2, no. 4 (1982): 89-93.

2238. **Nieto, Leo D.** "The Chicano Movement and the Gospel: Historical Accounts of a Protestant Pastor." In *Hidden Stories: Unveiling the History of the Latino Church,* edited by Daniel R. Rodríguez-Díaz and David Cortés-Fuentes. 143-57. Decatur, GA: AETH, 1994.

2239. **Nieto, Leo D.** "Spanish-Speaking Texans." Department of Migrant Ministry, Texas Council of Churches, [1965?]. 28 pp.

2240. **Nyborg, Scott.** "Latin American Mission at Miami." *Urban Mission* 8, no. 4 (1991): 56-61.

2241. **Office of the General Assembly, Presbyterian Church (U.S.A.).** "Hispanic Ministries in the Southwest: Directions for the Future: A Statement of Policy Directions in the 80's." Office of the General Assembly, Presbyterian Church (U.S.A.). Atlanta, GA and New York, 1984.

2242. **Ogilby, Barbara.** "Philadelphia Story: Tenacious Outlook, Ups and Downs Mark an Emerging Ministry of Solid Integrity." In *Our Hispanic Ministry II: How Latin Americans Consolidate Their Growth in The Episcopal Church.* New York: The Episcopal Church Center, 1991.

2243. **Ortiz Green, José M.** "A Teaching Module for Integration of New Members into the Spanish Mennonite Church." D.Min. Project Report. McCormick Theological Seminary, 1979.

2244. **Ortíz, José.** "A Program Proposal for Spanish-Speaking Mennonite Theological Training." 1977. 12 pp. Typescript.

2245. **Ortíz, José.** *El Año Agradable del '86: Estampas de la Vida de la Iglesia Menonita Hispana.* Goshen, IN: Departamento de Ministerios Hispanos, Goshen College, 1988. 126 pp.

2246. **Ortíz, José.** "Su Iglesia es Administrable." Video recording. Goshen IN: Centro Distribucion, Goshen College, 1988.

2247. **Ortíz, José.** *Ven! Camina con Nosotros: Una Afirmación y una Invitación a Ser Parte de la Iglesia Anabautista-Menonita.* Scottdale, PA: Mennonite Publishing House, 1988. 86 pp.

2248. **Ortíz, José.** "De Como: Ensamblar un Mensaje Bíblico; Ensemblar un Estudio Bíblico; Dirigir un Culto Publico." Video recording. Goshen, IN: Centro de Distribución, Goshen College, 1989.

2249. **Ortíz, José.** "Identificando, Reclutando y Reteniendo Lideres en la Iglesia Actual." Video recording. Goshen, IN: Centro de Distribución, Goshen College, [1991].

2250. **Ortíz, José and David Graybill.** *Reflections of an Hispanic Mennonite.* Intercourse, PA: Good Books, 1989. 92 pp.

2251. **Ortiz, José L.** "Grow by Caring among Hispanic Congregations in the United States and Puerto Rico." *American Baptist Quarterly* 8, no. 3 (1989): 202-12.

2252. **Ortiz, Manuel.** "'Spirit and Truth' in Humboldt Park, Chicago." In *The Gospel and Urbanization: A Workbook for Participants in a Seminar Held April 22-26, 1985, at the Overseas Ministries Study Center,* edited by Robert Coote. Rev. and enl. ed. 59-60. Ventnor, NJ: Overseas Ministries Study Center, 1985.

2253. **Ortiz, Manuel.** "Circle Church: A Case Study in Contextualization." *Urban Mission* 8, no. 3 (1991): 8-18.

2254. **Ortiz, Manuel.** *The Hispanic Challenge: Opportunities Confronting the Church.* Downers Grove, IL: Intervarsity Press, 1993. 194 pp.

2255. **Ortiz, Manuel.** "Insights into the Second Generation Hispanic." *Urban Mission* 10, no. 4 (1993): 21-33.

2256. **Ortiz, Manuel, ed.** "[Pastoral Needs of Hispanic American Churches]." *Urban Mission* 10, no. 4 (1993): 3-59.

2257. **Ortiz, Manuel.** "My Commitment to Intercultural Christian Community: An Hispanic Pilgrimage." *Urban Mission* 12, no. 2 (1994): 14-24.

2258. **Ortiz, Manuel, ed.** "[Race and Reconciliation in the US]." *Urban Mission* 12, no. 2 (1994): 3-63.

2259. **Ortiz, Manuel.** "Reconciliation—Still God's Concern." *Urban Mission* 12, no. 2 (1994): 3.

2260. **Ostrander, Paul C. and Stephen R. Weston.** *Our Hispanic Ministry.* New York: National Episcopal Office of The Episcopal Church, 1989. 50 pp.

2261. **Pagán, Samuel.** "Exégesis Bíblica y Trabajo Pastoral." *La Biblia en las Américas* 42 #175, no. 2 (1987): 10-11.

2262. **Pagán, Samuel.** *Púlpito, Teología y Esperanza.* Miami, FL: Editorial Caribe, 1988.

2263. **Pagán, Samuel.** "Reacción al Artículo de Carmen Gaud." In *Lumbrera a Nuestro Camino,* edited by Pablo A. Jiménez. 173-176. Miami, FL: Editorial Caribe, 1994.

2264. **Page, James T.** "The Development and Implementation of a Basic Spanish Model for Equipping Hispanic Pastors to Lead a Marriage Enrichment Experience." D.Min. Project Report. Golden Gate Baptist Theological Seminary, 1992. 226 pp.

2265. **Pallmeyer, Dwight.** *Our Neighbors in Hiding: A Resource Book for Congregations Engaged in a Ministry with Undocumented Persons.* Minneapolis MN: Augsburg Publishing House; Philadelphia, PA: Board of Publication, Lutheran Church in America; St. Louis, MO: Concordia Publishing House, 1981. 40 pp.

2266. **Palos, José [Interviewer].** "Hispanic Writer Challenges Denomination [An Interview with Justo González]." *Committee on Hispanic Ministries Newsletter* 3, no. 1 (1995): 1-2.

2267. **Palos, José L.** "El Plan Nacional como una Respuesta Práctica a la Pastoral." *Apuntes: Reflexiones Teológicas desde el Margen Hispano* 13, no. 1 (1993): 126-31.

2268. **Pankow, Fred J.** "A Scriptural Stance toward Undocumented Hispanics and Selected Methodologies for Reaching Them with the Gospel." Th.D. diss., Concordia Seminary, 1986. 249 pp.

2269. **Pazmiño, Roberto W.** *Foundational Issues in Christian Education: An Introduction in Evangelical Perspective.* Grand Rapids, MI: Baker Book House, 1988. 264 pp.

2270. **Pazmiño, Roberto W.** *Principles and Practices of Christian Education: An Evangelical Perspective.* Grand Rapids, MI: Baker Book House, 1992. 176 pp.

2271. **Pearce, Guy E.** "Latino, Come!" D.Min. Project Report. Austin Presbyterian Theological Seminary, 1993. 107 pp.

2272. **Pereyra, Héctor.** *Hacia la Elocuencia.* El Paso, TX: Casa Bautista de Publicaciones, 1963.

2273. **Pereyra, Luis A.** "A Biblical Perspective in a Multicultural Setting." In *Bible and Mission: Biblical Foundations and Working Models for Congregational Ministry,* edited by Wayne C. Stumme. 153-62. Minneapolis, MN: Augsburg Publishing House, 1986.

2274. **Perez, Darlene J.** "A Correlational Study of Baptist Groups in Puerto Rico and Youth Curriculum Variables." Ed.D. thesis. Southwestern Baptist Theologial Seminary, 1991. 138 pp.

2275. **Pérez y González, María E.** "Latinas in Ministry: A Pioneering Study on Women Ministers, Educators and Students of Theology." Rev. ed. New York City Mission Society. New York, 1994.

2276. **Pineda, Ana María.** "The Challenge of Hispanic Pluralism for the United States Christians." *Missiology* 21, no. 4 (1993): 437-42.

2277. **Plowman, Edward E.** "Hispanic Christians in the United States." *Christianity Today* 30, no. 1 (1986): 44-45.

2278. **Poethig, Richard P. and Tim Andeersen.** "The Church and Immigration." *Justice Ministries* 11-12 (Winter-Spring 1981): 1-76.

2279. **Pope-Levison, Priscilla.** "Comprehensive and Contextual: The Evangelism of Orlando Costas." *Journal of the Academy for Evangelism in Theological Education* 4 (1988-1989): 4-14.

2280. **Presbyterian Church (U.S.A.), 1986 General Assembly.** "The Church in United States Society." *Church and Society* 76, no. 6 (1986): 48-82.

2281. **Presbyterian Church in the U.S. and United Presbyterian Church, U.S.A.** "Mexican Migration to the United States: Challenge to Christian Witness and National Policy." *Church and Society* 72 (May-June 1982): 29-46.

2282. **Protestant Council of the City of New York.** "A Report on the Protestant Spanish Community in New York City." Protestant Council of the City of New York, Department of Church Planning. New York, 1960.

2283. **Quesada, Milagros Agostini.** "With Güiros and Maracas: Hispanic Christian Music in a Charismatic Church." *Hymn* 41, no. 2 (1990): 30-33.

2284. **Quintanilla, Raúl, as told to Justo L. González.** "My Best Christmas Gift." *Alternatives* 13, no. 4 (1987): 13. Also published in *Mennonite Brethren Herald* 30, no. 23 (1991): 6.

2285. **Radillo, Rebeca.** "The Migrant Family." *Apuntes: Reflexiones Teológicas desde el Margen Hispano* 5, no. 1 (1985): 16-19.

2286. **Ramírez, Johnny.** "The Atlantic Union Hispanic Church: A Church in Development." Presentation given to the Hispanic Education Advisory Board, North American Division of Seventh-Day Adventist, Silver Spring, MD, 1991.

2287. **Ramírez, Johnny.** "Social Ministry for the Year 2000." Presentation given to the Workers' Meeting of the Northeastern Regional Conference of Seventh-Day Adventist, South Lancaster, MA. 1992.

2288. **Ramírez, Johnny.** "La Iglesia y la Sociedad." *El Centinela,* January 1994, 11-12.

2289. **Ramirez, Ricardo.** "Liturgy from the Mexican American Perspective." *Worship* 51, no. 4 (1977): 293-98.

2290. **Ramírez, Ricardo, Bishop.** "The Challenge of Ecumenism to Hispanic Christians." *Ecumenical Trends* 21, no. 8 (1992): 117/1, 127/11-130/14.

2291. **Ramos, Jovelino, ed.** "Authenticity before the Altar: A Racial-Ethnic Colloquium." *Church and Society* 76, no. 4 (1986): 3-71.

2292. **Ranck, Lee.** "Adequate Health Services for Hispanic Americans." *Engage/Social Action* 7, no. 9 (1979): 4-7.

2293. **Ranck, Lee, ed.** "Hispanic Americans: A Growing Force/Los Hispano Americanos: Una Fuerza Cresciente." *Engage/Social Action [e-sa Forum, 99]* 11, no. 11 (1983): English: 9-49; Spanish: 50-72.

2294. **Recinos, Hal.** *Hear the Cry! A Latino Pastor Challenges the Church.* Louisville, KY: Westminter/John Knox Press, 1989. 156 pp.

2295. **Recinos, Harold.** "Mission: A Latino Pastoral Theology." *Apuntes: Reflexiones Teológicas desde el Margen Hispano* 12, no. 3 (1992): 115-26.

2296. **Recinos, Harold.** "The Politics of Salvadoran Popular Religion." Ph.D. diss., The American University, 1993.

2297. **Recinos, Harold J.** *The Student Pastor Track Manual.* Washington, DC: Wesley Theological Seminary, 1987. 30 pp.

2298. **Recinos, Harold J.** "Un Modelo de Ministerio de Alcance." *El Intérprete* 25, no. 4 (1987): 6.

2299. **Recinos, Harold J.** "On the Way." In *Orientation '88,* edited by Terri J. Hiers. 14-18. Nashville, TN: General Board of Higher Education and Ministry, The United Methodist Church, 1988.

2300. **Recinos, Harold J.** "Walking with Christ in the Barrio." *The Other Side* 25, no. 2 (1989): 30-32.

2301. **Recinos, Harold J.** "God's Sacred Place: The City." *Christian Social Action* 3, no. 6 (1990): 31-33.

2302. **Recinos, Harold J.** *The Handbook for the Urban Ministry Track Program.* Washington, DC: Wesley Theological Seminary, 1990. 40 pp.

2303. **Recinos, Harold J.** *Jesus Weeps: Global Encounters on Our Doorstep.* Nashville, TN: Abingdon Press, 1992. 142 pp.

2304. **Recinos, Harold J.** "Racism and Drugs in the City: The Church's Call to Ministry." In *Envisioning the New City,* edited by Eleanor Scott Meyers. 98-108. Louisville, KY: Westminster/John Knox Press, 1992.

2305. **Recinos, Harold J.** "Commentary on the Changing Face of the Parish." In *Globalization of Theological Education,* edited by David A. Roozen, Robert A. Evans and Alice F. Evans. 84-89. Maryknoll, NY: Orbis Books, 1993.

2306. **Recinos, Harold J.** "El Ministerio Urbano en un Contexto de Pobreza y Violencia." *El Intérprete* 32, no. 2 (1994): 4-5.

2307. **Recinos, Harold J.** "Mission: A Latino Pastoral Theology." In *Mestizo Christianity: Theology from the Latino Perspective,* edited by Arturo Bañuelas. 132-45. Maryknoll, NY: Orbis Books, 1995.

2308. **Reyes, José A.** *The Hispanics in the United States.* Cleveland, TN: White Wing Publishing House and Press, 1991. 146 pp.

2309. **Reza, Honorato and R. W. Stringfield.** *Vida y Solaz.* Kansas City, MO: Lillenas Publishing Company, 1958. Hymnal.

2310. **Río Grande Conference Study Committee.** "Río Grande Conference Study Committee, The Methodist Church. Report No. 3. Presented to the Río Grande Annual Conference. [Propuesta del Comité de Estudio a la Conference Río Grande]." In *Actas Oficiales de la Conferencia Anual Río Grande de la Iglesia Metodista,* 85-89. Kerrville, TX: Río Grande Annual Conference, 1967.

2311. **Rivas, Michael G.** "Finding the Right Words." *Engage/Social Action* 6, no. 6 (1978): 22.

2312. **Rivas, Michael G.** "The Hispanic Church and the Future: A Discussion Starter." Paper presented at the annual meeting of Hispanic Instructors, Perkins School of Theology, Dallas, TX, December 1994. Published in *Apuntes: Reflexiones Teológicas desde el Margen Hispano* 15, no. 2 (1995): 72-79.

2313. **Rivas-Druck, Michael G.** "The Challenge of Minority Identification and Enlistment of Ministry." *Apuntes: Reflexiones Teológicas desde el Margen Hispano* 5, no. 3 (1985): 51-57.

2314. **Rivera, Elí S.** "Hispanic Americans: So Much to Offer." *Engage/Social Action* 11, no. 11 (1983): English: 10-17; Spanish: 50-56.

2315. **Rivera, Elí S.** "Desarrollo de una Congregación Misional Hispana." In *La Iglesia Hispana en Misión,* edited by Conrado G. Soltero. 1-5. New York: National Program Division, General Board of Global Ministries, The United Methodist Church, 1992.

2316. **Rivera-Pagán, Luis N.** "Libertad y Revolución. La Educación Teológica en la América Latina." *El Boletín* 34, no. 6 (1969): 1-14, 15-22.

2317. **Rivera-Pagán, Luis N.** "New Styles of Theological Education Relevant to the Caribbean Experience—Method of Training and Teaching." In *Theological Education in a New Caribbean: Report of a Consultation of Directors of Theological Institutions and Programmes in the Caribbean.* 13-23. Port of Spain, Trinidad & Tobajo, W.I.: Caribbean Conference of Churches, 1977.

2318. **Rivera-Pagán, Luis N.** *Caminos de Esperanza; Cinco Sermones y un Estudio Bíblico.* Río Piedras, PR: Primera Iglesia Bautista de Río Piedras, 1989.

2319. **Robleto, Adolfo.** *El Sermón Evangelístico y el Evangelista.* El Paso, TX: Casa Bautista de Publicaciones, n.d.

2320. **Rodríguez, Angel Manuel.** *Podemos Hablar con Dios.* Nampa, ID: Pacific Press, 1988. 7 pp.

2321. **Rodríguez, Angel Manuel.** "The Nature and Basis of Christian Service." *Collegiate Quarterly* 13, no. 1 (1990): 62-64.

2322. **Rodríguez, Angel Manuel.** "Ears to the Sky." *Dialogue* 5, no. 1 (1993): 24-25.

2323. **Rodríguez, Angel Manuel.** *Stewardship Roots—Toward a Theology of Stewardship, Tithe and Offerings.* Silver Spring, MD: Church Ministries, 1994. 69 pp.

2324. **Rodríguez, Daniel.** "Respuesta a Trinidad y Sedillo." *Apuntes: Reflexiones Teológicas desde el Margen Hispano* 8, no. 1 (1988): 23, 17.

2325. **Rodriguez, Esdras A.** "Reflections on the Latin American Reality." *Engage/Social Action* 11, no. 11 (1983): 47-49.

2326. **Rodríguez, José A.** "Hispanic Hymns in the New Hymnal." *Reformed Liturgy and Music* 24, no. 2 (1990): 82-83.

2327. **Rodríguez, José David.** "The Challenge of Hispanic Ministry (Reflections on John 4)." *Currents in Theology and Mission* 18, no. 6 (1991): 420-26.

2328. **Rodríguez, P.A., compiler.** *Himnario Cristiano para Uso de las Iglesias Evangélicas.* 1908. Reprint, Nashville, TN: Methodist Episcopal Church, South, 1915. Hymnal.

2329. **Rodriguez, Richard.** "A Continental Shift." *Los Angeles Times,* 13 August 1989, V-1, V-6.

2330. **Rodríguez Rivera, José David.** *El Precio de la Vocación Profética.* México: Publicaciones El Faro, 1994.

2331. **Rodríguez, Steven.** "Los Centros Comunitarios Metodistas Unidos: Institucionales Misionales." In *La Iglesia Hispana en Misión,* edited by Conrado G. Soltero. 44-48. New York: National Program Division, General Board of Global Ministries, The United Methodist Church, 1992.

2332. **Romo, Oscar I., ed.** *The Challenge of American Hispanics.* Atlanta, GA: Language Church Extension Division, Home Mission Board of the Southern Baptist Convention, 1989.

2333. **Romo, Oscar I.** "Ministering with Hispanic Americans." In *Missions in the Mosaic,* edited by M. Wendell Belew. 44-52. Atlanta, GA: Home Mission Board of the Southern Baptist Convention, 1974.

2334. **Romo, Oscar I.** *Global Refugees: A Southern Baptist Perspective.* Atlanta, GA: Language Missions Division, Home Mission Board, Southern Baptist Convention, n.d.

2335. **Romo, Oscar I.** *Missions in Ethnic America.* Atlanta, GA: Home Mission Board, Southern Baptist Convention, n.d.

2336. **Rosado, Caleb.** "The Significance of Galilee to the Mission of the Hispanic Church." Presented at the "First Annual Hispanic Convocation Lectures," Hispanic Studies and Ministry Program, Eastern Baptist Theological Seminary, Philadelphia, PA, October 1983. pp. 13-25.

2337. **Rosado, Caleb.** "The Deceptive Theology of Institutionalism." *Ministry* 60, no. 11 (1987): 9-12.

2338. **Rosado, Caleb.** "The Church, the City, and the Compassionate Christ." *Apuntes: Reflexiones Teológicas desde el Margen Hispano* 9, no. 2 (1989): 27-35. Also published in Justo L. González, ed, *Voces: Voices from the Hispanic Church.* (Nashville, TN: Abingdon Press, 1992), pp. 72-80.

2339. **Rosado, Caleb.** "Multiculturalism: A Challenge for the Church." *Journal of Music Ministry* 16, no. 1 (1989): 3-5.

2340. **Rosado, Caleb.** "The Stewardship of Power." *Ministry* (July 1989): 18-20. Also published in *Health and Development* 11, no. 1 (1991): 20-33.

2341. **Rosado, Caleb.** *Broken Walls.* Boise, ID: Pacific Press Publishing Association, 1990. 160 pp.

2342. **Rosado, Caleb.** "Lessons from Waco." *Ministry* (July 1993): 6-11.

2343. **Rosado, Caleb.** "Lessons from Waco II." *Ministry* (August 1993): 14-19.

2344. **Rosado, Caleb.** "Multicultural Ministry." *Spectrum* 23, no. 5 (1994): 27-34.

2345. **Rosas, Carlos.** "La Música al Servicio del Reino." *Apuntes: Reflexiones Teológicas desde el Margen Hispano* 6, no. 1 (1986): 3-11.

2346. **Ruoss, Meryl.** "Mid-Century Pioneers and Protestants: A Survey Report of the Puerto Rican Migration to the U.S. Mainland and in Particular a Study of the Protestant Expression among Puerto Ricans of New York City." 2nd ed. Department of Church Planning and Research of the Protestant Council of the City of New York. New York, 1954.

2347. **Saenz, Lydia Martinez.** "The Pain of Racism." *Engage/Social Action* 9, no. 9 (1981): 17-22.

2348. **Salomon, Esaul.** "An Experiment in Visitation: A Growing Church in Hispanic Ministry." D.Min Project Report. Concordia Theological Seminary, 1991. 295 pp.

2349. **Salomon, Esaul.** "The Role of Liturgy in Hispanic Lutheran Churches." *Lutheran Forum* 25, no. 2 (1991): 30-31.

2350. **San Antonio Baptist Association.** *Survey Report.* San Antonio, TX: San Antonio Baptist Association, 1960. 192 pp.

2351. **Sanchez, Daniel R.** "How to Reach U.S. Ethnic Groups." *Evangelical Missions Quarterly* 13, no. 2 (1977): 95-103.

2352. **Sanchez, Daniel R.** "Exposing Students to Urban Ministry and Church Extension." In *The Gospel and Urbanization: A Workbook for Participants in a Seminar Held April 22-26, 1985, at the Overseas Ministries Study Center,* edited by Robert Coote. Rev. and enl. ed. 43-44. Ventnor, NJ: Overseas Ministries Study Center, 1985.

2353. **Sáenz, Michael.** "Economic Aspects of Church Development in Puerto Rico: A Study of the Financial Policies and Procedures of the Major Protestant Church Groups in Puerto Rico from 1898 to 1957." Ph.D. diss., University of Pennsylvania, 1962. 180 pp.

2354. **Sánchez, Jorge E.** "La Educación Bíblica en Nuestra Iglesia Hispana." *Apuntes: Reflexiones Teológicas desde el Margen Hispano* 9, no. 2 (1989): 35-38.

2355. **Sandín, Pedro A.** *Cuentos y Encuentros: Hacia una Educación Cristiana Transformadora.* Bayamón, PR: La Iglesia Cristiana (Discípulos de Cristo); Davie, FL: Pagán, 1995. 173 pp.

2356. **Santillana, Fernando.** "La Experiencia Espiritual en el Trabajo de Santuario." *Apuntes: Reflexiones Teológicas desde el Margen Hispano* 5, no. 3 (1985): 68-71.

2357. **Santillana, Fernando.** "¿Refugiados Económicos, o Víctimas?" *Apuntes: Reflexiones Teológicas desde el Margen Hispano* 5, no. 4 (1985): 81-85.

2358. **Savage, Robert C.** *Adelante Juventud No. 2.* Wheaton, IL: Van Kempen Press, 1947. Hymnal.

2359. **Savage, Robert C.** *Adelante Juventud No. 3.* Wheaton, IL: Van Kempen Press, 1948. Hymnal.

2360. **Savage, Robert C.** *Adelante Juventud.* Wheaton, IL: Van Kempen Press, 1953. Hymnal.

2361. **Savage, Robert C.** *Cánticos de Gozo e Inspiración.* Wheaton, IL: Van Kempen Press, 1953. 56 musical selections.

2362. **Savage, Robert C.** *Voces de Júbilo.* Grand Rapids, MI: Zondervan Publishing House, 1955. 62 musical selections.

2363. **Savage, Robert C., ed.** *Himnos de Fe y Alabanza.* Grand Rapids, MI: Zondervan Publishing House, 1968. [400] pp. Hymnal.

2364. **Schipani, Daniel S.** *La Angustia y la Dimensión Trascendente.* Buenos Aires, Argentina: La Aurora, 1969. 153 pp.

2365. **Schipani, Daniel S.** *Orientación Existencial del Adolescente.* Buenos Aires, Argentina: La Aurora, 1971.

2366. **Schipani, Daniel S.** *Nuestros Hijos y Sus Necesidades Básicas.* San Juan, PR: JELAM, 1978.

2367. **Schipani, Daniel S.** "Aproximación para un Pastoral del Matrimonio en Crisis." *Psicología Pastoral,* no. 10 (1981): 47-52.

2368. **Schipani, Daniel S.** *El Arte de Ser Familia.* Bogotá, Colombia: JELAM, 1982.

2369. **Schipani, Daniel S.** *Conscientization and Creativity: Paulo Freire and Christian Education.* Lanham, MD: University Press of America, 1984.

2370. **Schipani, Daniel S.** "Predicación y Consejo Pastoral: Dos Caras del Ministerio." In *La Predicación y la Comunicación del Evangelio hacia el Siglo XXI,* edited by Marjorie T. Carty and James W. Carty, Jr. 31-42. México: CUPSA, 1984.

2371. **Schipani, Daniel S., ed.** *Los Niños y el Reino.* Bogotá, Colombia: CAEBC, 1987.

2372. **Schipani, Daniel S.** *Cuando Se Piensa en el Aborto.* El Paso, TX: Mundo Hispano, 1990.

2373. **Schipani, Daniel S.** *El Reino de Dios y el Ministerio Educativo de la Iglesia.* San José, Costa Rica, Editorial Caribe, 1983. Reprint, Miami, FL: Editorial Caribe, 1992.

2374. **Schipani, Daniel S.** *Teología del Ministerio Educativo: Perspectivas Latinoamericanas.* Grand Rapids, MI: William B. Eerdmans Publishing Co.; Buenos Aires, Argentina: Nueva Creación, 1993.

2375. **Schipani, Daniel S., ed.** *Comunicación con la Juventud: Diseño para una Nueva Pastoral.* San Juan, PR: Seminario Evangélico de Puerto Rico, 1994. 126 pp.

2376. **Schipani, Daniel S. and Dafne S. de Plou.** *¿Y Fueron Felices?* Buenos Aires, Argentina: La Aurora, 1974.

2377. **Schkade, Landon.** "The Hispanic Lutheran Cultus: A Bilingual Exposition of Its Biblical-Theological Bases within a Cultural Setting." Master's thesis. Concordia Theological Seminary, 1984. 93 pp.

2378. **Schlesinger, Wilhelm D.** "The Serving Church in the Hispanic Context." D.Min. Project Report. McCormick Theological Seminary, 1984. 45 pp.

2379. **Schultz, Frederick W.** "A Church Worker's Manual for Cross-Cultural Education Ministry in a Hispanic Context." Master's thesis. Concordia Theological Seminary, 1984. 104 pp.

2380. **Sclafani, Juan M.** "Seeking to Improve the Quality of Marital Communication for Ten Couples of Iglesia Bautista White Road." D.Min. Project Report. Golden Gate Baptist Theological Seminary, 1989. 165 pp.

2381. **Scopes, Wilfred, ed.** *The Christian Ministry in Latin America and the Caribbean.* New York: Commission on World Mission and Evangelism, World Council of Churches, 1962.

2382. **Seabough, Ed.** *New Day on the Hudson.* Atlanta, GA: Home Mission Board, Southern Baptist Convention, 1970. 92 pp.

2383. **Sielk, William A.** "The Importance of Latin American Cultural and Religious Values for the Christian Parochial Educator." Master's thesis. Concordia Theological Seminary, 1985. 68 pp.

2384. **Simmonds, G. P.** *Cánticos de Esperanza.* Winona Lake, IN: Rodeheaver Hall-Mack Co., 1948.

2385. **Simmonds, G. P.** *Cánticos Especiales, No. 2.* Albuquerque, NM: Cánticos Escogidos, 1967.

2386. **Simmonds, G. P.** *Cánticos Especiales, No. 3.* Albuquerque, NM: Cánticos Escogidos, 1967.

2387. **Simmonds, G. P.** *Cantos Escogidos para Voces Masculinas, No. 1.* El Paso, TX: Baptist Spanish Publishing House, 1968.

2388. **Simmonds, G. P.** *Cantos Escogidos para Voces Masculinas, No. 2.* El Paso, TX: Baptist Spanish Publishing House, 1968.

2389. **Simmonds, G. P.** *Cánticos Especiales, No. 4.* Albuquerque, NM: Cánticos Escogidos, 1969.

2390. **Simmonds, G. P.** *Cánticos Especiales, No. 5.* Albuquerque, NM: Cánticos Escogidos, 1970.

2391. **Soltero, Ana María.** "El Cuerpo Pastoral: Mentores en el Servicio Misional." In *La Iglesia Hispana en Misión,* edited by Conrado G. Soltero. 24-29. New York: National Program Division, General Board of Global Ministries, The United Methodist Church, 1992.

2392. **Soltero, Conrado G., ed.** *La Iglesia Hispana en Misión.* New York: National Program Division, General Board of Global Ministries, The United Methodist Church, 1992. 80 pp.

2393. **Soltero, Conrado G.** "Nuestra Misión y el Alcance a la Comunidad: Un Modelo Misional." In *La Iglesia Hispana en Misión,* edited by Conrado G. Soltero. 13-23. New York: National Program Division, General Board of Global Ministries, The United Methodist Church, 1992.

2394. **Soltero, Conrado G. and Finees Flores.** "Capacitando a los Santos." Paper presented at the "Hispanic Symposium on Ministries of the Hispanic Church," held at Perkins School of Theology, Dallas, TX, November 1978.

2395. **Sosa, Pablo, ed.** *Cántico Nuevo: Himnario Evangélico.* Buenos Aires, Argentina: Methopress Editorial y Grafica, 1964. 557 pp. Hymnal.

2396. **Sotomayor-Chavez, Marta.** "Latin American Migration." *Apuntes: Reflexiones Teológicas desde el Margen Hispano* 2, no. 1 (1982): 8-14.

2397. **Sotomayor-Chavez, Marta.** "The Future for Hispanics." *Engage/Social Action* 15, no. 3 (1987): 19-29.

2398. **Sprinkle, Henry C.,** *et al. Spanish Doorways: American Methodists and the Evangelical Mission among Spanish-Speaking Neighbors. A Symposium.* New York: World Outlook Press, 1964. 125 pp.

2399. **Stevens-Arroyo, Antonio M.,** ed. *Prophets Denied Honor: An Anthology of the Hispanic Church in the United States.* Maryknoll, NY: Orbis Books, 1980. 379 pp.

2400. **Steward, David. S. and Margaret S. Steward.** "Cognitive Development and Ethnicity: Problems for Educational Ministry." *Religious Education* 70 (May-June 1975): 308-16.

2401. **Sturni, Gary K.** "Models of Theological Education for Hispanic Candidates for Ordination in the Episcopal Church." D.Min. Project Report. San Francisco Theological Seminary, 1986. 322 pp.

2402. **Sylvest, Edwin E., Jr.** *Amen al Extranjero.* New York: United Methodist Committee on Relief, General Board of Global Ministries and the General Board of Church and Society, The United Methodist Church, 1988.

2403. **Sylvest, Edwin E., Jr.** *To Love the Neighbor.* New York: United Methodist Committee on Relief, General Board of Global Ministries and the General Board of Church and Society, The United Methodist Church, 1988.

2404. **Tapia, Andrés.** "Viva los Evangélicos! [Hispanics Fueling Greatest Growth in North American Protestantism]" *Christianity Today* 35, no. 12 (1991): 16-22.

2405. **Tapia, Andrés.** "Growing Pains: Evangelical Latinos Wrestle with the Role of Women, Generation Gaps, and Cultural Divides." *Christianity Today* 39, no. 2 (1995): 38-40, 42.

2406. **Task Force on Racial Inclusiveness.** "Report and Recommendations to the Northeastern Jurisdictional Conference." Northeastern Jurisdictional Conference, The United Methodist Church. 1992.

2407. **Texas Council of Churches.** "Texas Migrant Ministry. 1958 Program Report." Texas Council of Churches. Austin, TX. Part I. May-September, 1958.

2408. **Tinoco, David A.** "Doing Hispanic Ministry in the Long Beach District." El Segundo, CA. 1987. Manuscript.

2409. **Tinoco, David A.** "Strategies for Effective Hispanic Ministries in

Southern California by The United Methodist Church." D.Min Project Report. Fuller Theological Seminary, 1989. 132 pp.

2410. **Toledo, Reinaldo.** "Cuban-American United Methodists: One Part of the Exile Population." *Engage/Social Action* 11, no. 11 (1983): 36-38.

2411. **Torres, Enrique M.** "A Challenge for the Growth of Baptist Churches in Los Angeles with Emphasis on the Mexican-American Population." D.Miss. thesis. Fuller Theological Seminary, School of World Mission, 1981.

2412. **Traverzo Galarza, David.** "A New Dimension in Religious Education for the Hispanic Evangelical Church in New York City." Master's thesis. New Brunswick Theological Seminary, 1979.

2413. **Treviño, Alejandro.** *El Predicador: Plácticas a mis Estudiantes.* El Paso, TX: Casa Bautista de Publicaciones, 1964.

2414. **Trinidad, Saúl.** "Apuntes hacia una Pastoral Hispana." *Apuntes: Reflexiones Teológicas desde el Margen Hispano* 8, no. 1 (1988): 3-15.

2415. **Trinidad, Saúl.** "Perfil Pastoral para el Siglo 21." *Apuntes: Reflexiones Teológicas desde el Margen Hispano* 13, no. 1 (1993): 118-25.

2416. **Urquiza, Consuelo.** "La División de Mujeres y el Racismo, la Inmigración y la Justicia Criminal." In *La Iglesia Hispana en Misión,* edited by Conrado G. Soltero. 59-67. New York: National Program Division, General Board of Global Ministries, The United Methodist Church, 1992.

2417. **Vasquez, Manuel.** "America's Changing Face and the Church's Changing Voice (The Minority Majority: Preparing to Meet the Challenge)." Seventh-Day Adventist Church. 1992.

2418. **Vasquez, Raul A.** "Contextualized Theological Education: Development and Implementation of a Basic Pastoral Skills Training Retreat for Texas Hispanics." D.Min Project Report. Golden Gate Baptist Theological Seminary, 1988. 170 pp.

2419. **Vázquez, Edmundo E.** "Hispanic Urban Ministry Comes of Age." *Christian Ministry* 20, no. 2 (1989): 20-21.

2420. **Vega, Rolando.** "Requirements for the Area Minister of Northern California." San Francisco, CA. First Spanish Church of San Francisco, 2 pp.

2421. **Velasquez, Roger.** "Theological Education for Hispanic Pastors in the American Baptist Churches, U.S.A." D.Min. Project Report. The Eastern Baptist Theological Seminary, 1982. 233 pp.

2422. **Vigil, James D.** "Human Revitalization: The Six Tasks of Victory Outreach." *Drew Gateway* 52, no. 3 (1982): 49-59.

2423. **Villafañe, Eldin.** "The Role of the Church in the Preservation of Hispanic Culture: A Puerto Rican Perspective." Cambridge, MA. Harvard Divinity School, 1975. Manuscript.

2424. **Villafañe, Eldin.** "An Approach to Winning Ethnic Minorities in the City." *New England Journal of Ministry* 2, no. 2 (1982): 54-60.

2425. **Villafañe, Eldin.** "An Evangelical Call to a Social Spirituality: Confronting Evil in Urban Society." *Apuntes: Reflexiones Teológicas desde el Margen Hispano* 11, no. 2 (1991): 27-38.

2426. **Villafañe, Eldin.** "Scholarship as Sierva, Santificadora, and Sanadora." *Apuntes: Reflexiones Teológicas desde el Margen Hispano* 12, no. 4 (1992): 147-49.

2427. **Villafañe, Eldin.** "The Socio-Cultural Matrix of Intergenerational Dynamics: An Agenda for the 90's." *Apuntes: Reflexiones Teológicas desde el Margen Hispano* 12, no. 1 (1992): 13-20.

2428. **Villarreal, Luis.** "Counseling Hispanics." *Urban Mission* 9, no. 2 (1991): 33-41.

2429. **Waynick, Thomas C.** "Problems and Suggested Solutions in Ministering in the Lutheran Context Cross Culturally to the Mexican-American." Master's thesis. Concordia Theological Seminary, 1982. 69 pp.

2430. **Webber, George W.** "Hispanic Ministry: New York Theological Seminary." *Theological Education* 13, no. 2 (1977): 90-94.

2431. **Wellman, Coe R.** "A Plan for the In-Service Training of Teachers and Leaders in the Methodist Church Schools of Puerto Rico." Ed.D. thesis. Columbia University, 1936.

2432. **Weston, S.** "Hispanics in an Anglo Church." *The Episcopalian* 104, no. 2 (1989): 4.

2433. **Westrup, T. M.** *Himnos Selectos.* Philadelphia, PA: Baptist Publishing Society, 1890? Hymnal.

2434. **Whitam, Frederick L.** "New York's Spanish Protestants." *The Christian Century* 79, no. 6 (1962): 162-64.

2435. **Wilkerson, Larry.** "Developing a Church Growth Manual for Southern Baptist Puerto Rican Churches according to the Principles of Contextualization." D.Min. Project Report. Golden Gate Baptist Theological Seminary, 1983.

2436. **Willard, Francis Burleigh, Sr.** "A Proposal for the Training of Lay Ministers for Hispanic Free Methodist Churches." D.Min. Project Report. Fuller Theological Seminary, School of Theology, 1984.

2437. **Williams, B.** "Centers Launched to Provide Information on New INS Law." *Episcopal News* 38, no. 5 (1987): 1.

2438. **Wilson, Robert L.** *The First Spanish United Methodist Church and the Young Lords.* New York: Department of Research and Survey, National Division, Board of Missions, The United Methodist Church, 1970. 51 pp.

2439. **Youngman, Nilah M.** "Affirming Hispanic Women." D.Min Project Report. Austin Presbyterian Theological Seminary, 1993. 125 pp.

2440. **Zackrison, James W.** "Ministry in an Age of Shifting Social Context: A Study Guide on How to Organize and Run Multiethnic/Multicultural Churches in the 1990s." Pasadena, CA. Fuller Theological Seminary, 1991. Manuscript.

2441. **Zackrison, James W.** "Multiethnic/Multicultural Ministry in the 1990s: With Special Emphasis on the Seventh-Day Adventist Church in North America." D.Miss. thesis. Fuller Theological Seminary, School of World Mission, 1991. 399 pp.

2442. **[Protestant Episcopal Church].** *Libro de Oración Común: Administración de los Sacramentos y Otros Ritos y Ceremonias de la Iglesia Conforme al Uso de la Iglesia Protestante Episcopal en los Estados Unidos de América, con el Salterio o Salmos de David.* N.p.: The National Council [The Protestant Episocpal Church], n.d. 579 pp.

2443. "El Discípulo." Sunday School Curriculum. Bayamón, PR: Iglesia Cristiana (Discípulos de Cristo),

2444. "Fe y Vida." Sunday School Curriculum. King of Prussia, PA: American Baptist Churches, U.S.A.,

2445. "Lecciones Cristianas." Sunday School Curriculum. Nashville, TN: Cokesbury, The United Methodist Church.

2446. *Himnos Evangélicos.* New York: American Tract Society, 1893. Hymnal.

2447. *El Nuevo Himnario Evangélico.* New York: American Tract Society, 1914. 401 pp. Hymnal.

2448. *Himnario Cristiano para Uso de las Iglesias Evangélicas.* 2nd ed. Nashville, TN: Smith and Lamar, 1915. Hymnal.

2449. *El Himnario para el Uso de las Iglesias Evangélicas de Habla Castellana en Todo el Mundo.* New York: American Tract Society, 1931. Hymnal.

2450. *Himnos Selectos.* El Paso, TX: [First Mexican Church], 1936. Hymnal.

2451. *Himnos de la Vida Cristiana.* New York: Christian and Missionary Alliance, 1939.

2452. *Himnario Evangélico.* Buenos Aires, Argentina: Imprenta Metodista, 1943.

2453. *Himnario Evangélico Luterano.* St. Louis, MO: Concordia Publishing House, 1947. Hymnal.

2454. *Lluvias de Bendición.* Kansas City, MO: Lillenas Publishing Co, 1947. Hymnal.

2455. *Cánticos de Esperanza.* Winona Lake, IN: Rodeheaver, Hall-Mack, 1948. 75 pp. Hymnal.

2456. *Joyas Favoritas: Una Colección Evangélica de Cantos Especiales.* Compiled by Honorato Reza and Robert Stringfield. Kansas City, MO: Lillenas Publishing Company, 1949.

2457. *Himnos Favoritos.* El Paso, TX: Casa Bautista de Publicaciones, 1951.

2458. *Joyas Favoritas: Otra Colección Evangélica de Cantos Especiales. Numero 2.* Compiled by Honorato Reza and Robert Stringfield. Kansas City, MO: Lillenas Publishing Company, 1955.

2459. *Ecos de Victoria.* Grand Rapids, MI: Zondervan Publishing House, 1956. 63 songs with music.

2460. *Joyas Favoritas: Otra Colección Evangélica de Cantos Especiales. Numero 3.* Compiled by Honorato Reza and Robert Stringfield. Kansas City, MO: Lillenas Publishing Company, 1958.

2461. *El Nuevo Himnario Popular.* Revised and corrected ed., El Paso, TX: Baptist Spanish Publishing House, 1959. Hymnal.

2462. *El Himnario de la Iglesia Episcopal.* Greenwich, CN: Seabury Press, 1961.

2463. *El Himnario Adventista para Uso en el Culto Divino [Adventist Hymnal Book for Use in Worship Service].* Mountain View, CA: Pacific Press Publishing Association, 1962.

2464. *Gracia y Devoción: Himnario para el Uso de las Iglesias Evangélicas.* Kansas City, MO: Lillenas Publishing Co., 1962. Hymnal.

2465. "Proceedings: Church Planning Institute for Puerto Rico." Indianapolis, IN, 1963. Mimeographed.

2466. "Protestants to Aid Catholic Refugees." *The Christian Century* 80, no. 22 (1963): 702.

2467. *Culto Cristiano.* New York: Publicaciones "El Escudo," 1964. Hymnal.

2468. *Cantos Infantiles.* 4th ed. El Paso, TX: Baptist Spanish Publishing House, 1966.

2469. *Himnos de Fe y Alabanza.* Grand Rapids, MI: Zondervan Publishing House, 1968. Hymnal.

2470. *Cantos para Preescolares.* El Paso, TX: Baptist Spanish Publishing House, 1971. 48 songs for pre-school children.

2471. *El Canto de la Niñez.* El Paso, TX: Baptist Spanish Publishing House, 1971. A collection of songs for children ages six to eight.

2472. "Baptists and the Hispanic American." Filmstrip. Nashville, TN: Broadman Films, 1973.

2473. *Ministering in Changing Ethnic Patterns.* Atlanta, GA: Home Mission Board, Southern Baptist Convention, 1974.

2474. "Primera Consulta Nacional de Educación Teológica para Hispano-Americanos en EEUU." Vandala, OH, April 1974.

2475. "Leadership Within The United Methodist Church." *Engage/Social Action* 6, no. 6 (1978): 23.

2476. "Proposal to the Board of National Ministries and the Board of Educational Ministries of the American Baptist Churches." In *Consultation on Hispanic Theological Education,* held in Ventnor, NJ, April 1980.

2477. "Report from the Working Group on Racism-Classism-Sexism." In *Women's Spirit Bonding,* edited by Janet Kalven and Mary I. Buckley. 125-36. New York: Pilgrim Press, 1984.

2478. *Cancionero para Niños.* El Paso, TX: Casa Bautista de Publicaciones, 1986. 162 pp. Children's hymnal.

2479. "Demolition of the Old Oak Cliff Church." Video recording. Dallas, TX: Youth Department of the Oak Cliff Spanish Church, 1988.

2480. "Hispanic Congregation Growing at St. Phillip's." *Episcopal News* 39, no. 5 (1988): 5.

2481. "Hispanic Human Rights Movement Traces Roots to Epiphany Church." *Episcopal News* 39, no. 5 (1988): 5.

2482. "Hispanics Call U.S. Church to Action." *The Witness* 7, no. 11 (1988): 16-17.

2483. "Convención Diocesana Acepta Nuevo Plan Hispano de 5 Año." *Episcopal News* 40, no. 1 (1989): 15.

2484. *Hispanic Association of Bilingual and Bicultural Ministries [HABBM].* 1989. An interdenominational organization that addresses the spiritual, social, and educational needs of English-dominant Hispanics in the United States and seeks to create leadership for the church and society. Luis Madrigal, executive director. P.O. Box 92045 Pasadena, CA 91109-2045.

2485. "Lecciones Cristianas para Jóvenes/Christian Lessons for Youth Sunday School Curriculum. Nashville, TN: Cokesbury, 1990-1995.

2486. *Celebremos Su Gloria.* Dallas, TX: Celebremos/Libros Alianza, 1992. Hymnal.

2487. "Redescubrimiento: Five Centuries of Hispanic American Christianity 1492-1992 [Symposium III]." A symposium held at Perkins School of Theology, Dallas, TX, November 1992. Working papers published in *Apuntes: Reflexiones Teológicas desde el Margen Hispano* 13 (1 Spring 1993): 4-131.

2488. *Cánticos Evangelísticos.* El Paso, TX: Baptist Spanish Publishing House, n.d. Hymnal.

2489. "Hispanic Theological Center." Brochure. Huntington Park, CA: American Baptist Seminary of the West, n.d.

2490. *Nuevas Melodías Evangélicas.* Judson Press, California, n.d. Hymnal.

2491. *Teología de la Evangelización, Bibliografía Selecta.* Seminario Bíblico Latinoamericano. San José, Costa Rica. n.d.

Social Science Literature on Hispanic Protestantism
Edwin I. Hernández

The social scientific study of religious life among Latino Protestant groups in the United States and Puerto Rico finds it's most complete and comprehensive bibliographic collection in this section. This collection of published and unpublished materials provide rich and diverse sources of information. Some works are meant for denominational policy development, others are popularized forms of social analysis with particular focus on pastoral implications, some are theological reflections using social analysis, yet others present rigorous social scientific analysis and theorizing, a few provide general social and demographic descriptions without any reference to religion per se. When taken together the collection presents a broad perspective of some of the most salient literature on Hispanic Protestantism. I have divided my comments around general topics which group bibliographic entries. Within each grouping I have taken the liberty to mention those works I consider most significant.

There are a few entries that deserve separate mention. One of these is the publication of the PARAL series on the social scientific study of religion among Latinos edited by Anthony Stevens-Arroyo et. al. It represents a milestone achievement which promises to move the study of religion ahead for years to come. One very helpful article in the PARAL series which integrates quantitative with religious studies on Latinos is Gilbert Cadena's "Religious Ethnic Identity: A Socio-Religious Portrait of Latinas and Latinos in the Catholic Church." Although his focus is on Catholicism, it nevertheless is helpful as a benchmark of analysis from which scholars can begin to assess what has been done to date.

For general demographic information on the Latino community, see the work of Frank Bean and Marta Tienda and the various publications of the U.S. Bureau of the Census. A significant research report focusing on the political, social, and cultural values of Latinos is by de la Garza et. al. *Latino Voices.*

Among the most prolific authors in this collection is David Maldonado, Jr., who has made significant contributions in the field of Gerontology and the Latino community. Following him is the distinguished Puerto Rican sociologist of religion, Samuel Silva-Gotay, with an impressive list of works spanning social scientific theory, theological analysis, and social historical analysis of the role that religion has played in the Americanization of Puerto Rican society. Finally the list of notable and significant writers includes the sociologist Caleb Rosado, whose works includes studies on women's issues, a significant analysis on the role of a sectarian religious community within Cuba's revolutionary situation, and various theological essays brilliantly integrating social analysis.

The collection has a good number of dissertations on various topics. Ideally a scholar will use his or her dissertation and spin off a number of scholarly articles. Surprisingly, there is little evidence to show research beyond the dissertation. This could be accounted for in part by the relatively few Latino scholars in academia, together with the commitment to a broader agenda of work among many Latino and Latina scholars in and outside the community. These factors hamper the production of Latino scholarly work.

Literature that assesses the impact of religiosity on Latinos

The serious student in the sociology of religion will recognize a number of entries which explore the consequential dimension of religion which asks, What effect does religion have on a myriad of social, cultural, and political behavior?

Among the more notable are David Alvírez' exploration of religion's impact on fertility patterns among Mexican-Americans, Elba R. Caraballo's work on the role of churches in providing social services in a Puerto Rican community, and José Rivas' work on religious education among Mexican-American Baptists.

Methodological contributions

This collection includes some important theoretical and methodological essays that are key for the future development of the social scientific research among Latinos. These include the works of Meredith McGuire, Edwin Aponte, Patrick H. McNamara, Edwin Hernández, Caleb Rosado, Otto Maduro, and Samuel Silva-Gotay. Many of these authors' essays are included in the PARAL publication series (references 2776-2779) edited by Anthony Stevens-Arroyo et. al.

Community based studies

The section on social science contains some important local studies worth mentioning. They include Edwin Aponte's et. al. work on Hispanic Ministry in Philadelphia, José Arreguín's work on five counties of Los Angeles, the study commissioned by the Archdiocese of New York, "Hispanics in New York: Religious, Social and Cultural Experiences", and David Luna's study on American Baptists in Los Angeles. These studies provide a regional understanding of the religious landscape within Latino communities.

Protestants dealing with syncretic expressions of religion

Very few Latinos have ventured to study syncretistic expressions of religion. Among the few works addressing this topic is the co-edited work of Andrés Pérez y Mena and Anthony Stevens-Arroyo, *Enigmatic Powers: Syncretism with African and Indigenous People's Religions among Latinos.* See also Tomás Atencio's "Curanderismo: Una Vida Buena y Sana," and James Krause's dissertation on why Mexican-American Lutherans seek out Curanderos.

Ethnographic studies/congregational studies

Several studies have used ethnographic approaches effectively to assess the impact of congregational life and rituals in affirming ethnic identity and solidarity. Among them are Edwin Aponte's work on Protestant Coritos as well as Johnny Ramirez' study of one congregation's impact on educational achievement of its congregants. See also Eldin Villafañe's study on the role of the church in preserving Hispanic culture.

Classical treatments

Classical literature on the social scientific study of religion among Latinos is important in any assessment of a bibliography. This section has a number of duly qualified classical literature. They receive a classical standing by virtue of being among the first works published on the topic or because their long-standing insights and influence have remained to this day. Some of these classics are the work of Joséph Fitzpatrick on Puerto Rican religious life, Leo Grebler et. al.'s work on 'Protestants and Mexicans," Jorge Lara-Braud's 'The Status of Religion among Mexican Americans,' Isidro Lucas' *The Browning of America,* and Renato Poblete's work on Puerto Ricans and sects.

Theological works that use social scientific perspectives

One of the important characteristics of Latino(a) theological reflection is the incorporation of social scientific analysis and categories. Theologians who characterize this trend are Justo L. González, Samuel Silva-Gotay, Luis N. Rivera-Pagán, Roberto S. Goizueta, and Orlando E. Costas.

Conversion and church growth literature

The issues of conversion and religious growth are important and emerging concerns in the religious landscape of the Latino community, particularly among conservative Protestant communities. These concerns have been addressed by a number of Roman Catholic authors, including Andrew Greeley, Kenneth Davis, and Allan Figueroa Deck. See also Allan Figueroa the following essay by Allan Figueroa Deck located in the other sections of this bibliography: "The Challenge of Evangelical/Pentecostal Christianity to Hispanic Catholicism," in *Hispanic Catholic Culture in the U.S.: Issues and Concerns.* Among Protestants, the work of Delbert Fann, Manuel Ortiz, Oscar Romo, Roberto Suro, and Carlos G. Martin represent some attempts to address a dimension of the church growth process.

Youth, family, and women's issues

Despite the Latino community being a young population, studies of adolescents have received little attention. The few authors who address this topic are Edwin Hernández, Daniel Schipani, Jesse Montes, and Darlene Pérez. The absence of literature addressing women's and feminist issues is noteworthy. Some of the few works on this subject are by María Pérez y González, Caleb Rosado, Lourdes Morales-Gundmundsson, Pedro Sandín-Fremaint, and Evelyn Jensen.

Ethnic differences
Despite the great ethnic diversity in the Latino community, few studies have addressed the specific ethnic communities. The community with the largest number of entries addressing it is the Puerto Rican. Notable exceptions are the works of theologian and anthropologist Harold Recinos among the Salvadoran community in Washington, Aneris Goris among Dominicans of New York, and Caleb Rosado among Cubans in Cuba.

Many of the authors represented in this bibliography write out of a commitment to religious communities. This undoubtedly shapes the focus and interpretive lens of the scholar. This faith-based research needs to be continued and encouraged. However, attention to the social scientific study of religion should also be given by scholars in academia whether or not they have an explicit faith commitment.

Much of the social scientific literature among and by Protestant Latinos can be found in popular literature, but few works appear in refereed journals and professional publications. At the present time there are few trained social scientists whose research agenda is the religious life of the Latino community. An important recent development has been the organization of PARAL, thanks to generous funding of the Lilly Endowment and The Pew Charitable Trusts. A major objective of PARAL is that of networking and mentoring sociologists of religion. Participants in PARAL, through their thoroughgoing research and reflection, are charting the vast research agenda that lies ahead.

Traditionally, many Latino social scientists have excluded the religious variable from analysis in their research and theorizing. Many of these scholars in the social sciences work under the assumption of the perpetual and inevitable decline of religion in modern societies. They conceive of religion as simply the vestige of a bygone era or the projection of unrealizable dreams of an oppressed community. However, recent and significant research in the sociology of religion has provided significant empirical as well as theoretical insights to seriously question the secularization thesis (See Rodney Stark and William Sims Bainbridge, *The Future of Religion: Secularization, Revival, and Cult Formation.* Berkeley: University of California Press, 1985).

As a result of the pervasive adoption of the secularization thesis among mainstream Latino social scientists, one finds very little attention to religion in the larger social scientific literature. It is as if religion never existed or exists within Latino communities. This, however, is a grave methodological and theoretical mistake. If there is anything that is common and pervasive about Latinos, it is their respect, openness, and inclination towards the sacred. Thus, the full story of the religious impact on the Latino community has only begun, and much remains to be done. The publication of this bibliography indicates the achievements and gaps in the social scientific research agenda. One hopes that this collection of literature will inspire many Latinos(as) to enter the world of scholarship. One expects that works by future scholars will explore more fully the rapidly growing, and eventually the largest, minority population group in the United States.

Social Science Bibliography

2492. **Acosta, Sam, Lucille S. Groh, Gustavo Hernandez and Barbara Rathbone.** "Counseling Hispanics in the United States." *Journal of Pastoral Care* 44, no. 1 (1990): 33-41.

2493. **Alvirez, David.** "The Effects of Formal Church Affiliation and Religiosity in Fertility Patterns of Mexican-Americans in Austin, Texas." Ph.D. diss., University of Texas, Austin, 1971. 200 pp.

2494. **Anderson, Robert W.** *Party Politics in Puerto Rico.* Stanford, CA: Stanford University Press, 1965.

2495. **Aponte, Edwin D.** "Ethnography as a Methodology for the Study of Hispanic Protestants." Paper presented at the annual meeting of the American Academy of Religion, Washington, DC, November 1993.

2496. **Aponte, Edwin D.** "Latino Protestants in Philadelphia: Methodological Approaches for the Study of Racial/Ethnic Religion in the United States." Paper presented at the annual meeting of the Society for the Scientific Study of Religion, Raleigh, NC, October 1993.

2497. **Aponte, Edwin D.** "Hispanic Protestantism in the United States: Recognizing the Agenda, a Response to J. Samuel Escobar." Paper presented at the Third Interamerican Missiological Consultation, "The Social and Religious Significance of the Growth of Latin American Protestantism," held at Eastern Baptist Theological Seminary, October 1994.

2498. **Aponte, Edwin D.** "Beyond the Two Party System: Hispanic Protestantism in Philadelphia." Paper presented at the Chicago-Area Group for the Study of Religious Communities, Chicago, IL, February 1995.

2499. **Aponte, Edwin D.** "*Coritos* as Active Symbol in Latino Protestant Popular Religion." *Journal of Hispanic/Latino Theology* 2, no. 3 (1995): 57-66.

2500. **Aponte, Edwin D.** "Hispanic Protestantism in Philadelphia: A Case Study Beyond the Two Parties." Paper presented at the conference "Re-forming the Center: Are There Two Parties Today? American Protestantism, 1960-Present," held at Messiah College, Grantham, PA, June 1995.

2501. **Aponte, Edwin D.** "Response Paper to *Pilsen's Hispanic Churches: Building Homes, Constructing Ethnicity, Forming Community*." Paper presented by Janise Hurtig at the conference "Religion and Community in a Restructuring Metropolis, Religion in Urban America Program, Office of Social Science Research at the University of Illinois at Chicago, IL, June 1995.

2502. **Aponte, Edwin D., David Bartelt, Luis A. Cortés, Jr. and John C. Raines.** *The Work of Latino Ministry: Hispanic Protestant Churches in Philadelphia.* Philadelphia, PA: The Pew Charitable Trusts and Temple University, 1994.

2503. **Armendáriz, Rubén P.** "Las Posadas." *Reformed Liturgy and Music* 22, no. 3 (1988): 142-43.

2504. **Arreguín, José.** "Proyecto de Estudios Sobre Educación Teológica (Theological Education Study Project): A Research Project on Hispanic Churches in the Los Angeles 5-County Area Sponsored by the Department of Hispanic Studies, Fuller Theological Seminary. (Subreport on Data Relating to Church Growth, by C. Peter Wagner)." Fuller Theological Seminary. Pasadena, CA, 1979.

2505. **Atencio, Tomás.** *"Resolana: A Chicano Pathway to Knowledge."* Third *Annual Ernesto Galarza Commemorative Lecture.* Stanford, CA: Stanford Center for Chicano Research, Stanford University, 1988. 24 pp.

2506. **Atencio, Tomás.** "Welfare Reform in a Society in Transition: The Case of New México." In *Welfare Reform,* edited by Richard Coughlin. Albuquerque, NM: University of New México Press, 1989.

2507. **Atencio, Tomás.** "Curanderismo: Una Vida Buena y Sana." Smithsonian Folklife Festival, 1992.

2508. **Attinasi, John J., Raymundo Flores, and Rufino Osorio.** *Latino Perspectives for 1990: New Numbers, New Leverage.* Chicago, IL: Latino Institute, 1987.

2509. **Barrera, Mario.** *Beyond Aztlán.* New York: University of Notre Dame Press, 1990.

2510. **Baselga, Edward.** "Cultural Change and Protestantism in Puerto Rico, 1945-1966." Ph.D. diss., New York University, 1971. 333 pp.

2511. **Bean, Frank D. and Marta Tienda.** *The Hispanic Population of the United States.* New York: Russell Sage Foundation, 1987. 456 pp.

2512. **Bevans, Stephen and Ana María Pineda, eds.** "Columbus and the New World: Evangelization or Invasion?" *Missiology* 20, no. 2 (1992): 133-300.

2513. **Blair, Bertha, Anne Lively, and Glen Trimble.** *Spanish Speaking Americans-Mexicans and Puerto Ricans in the United States.* New York: National Council of Churches in the U.S.A., 1959. Reprint, Ann Arbor, MI: University Microfilms, 1970. 242 pp.

2514. **Bronson, Louise, F.** "Changes in Personality Needs and Values Following Conversion to Protestantism in a Traditionally Roman Catholic Ethnic Group." Ph.D. diss., University of Arizona, 1966. 167 pp.

2515. **Cadena, Gilbert.** "Religious Ethnic Identity: A Socio-Religious Portrait of Latinas and Latinos in the Catholic Church." In *Old Masks, New Faces,* edited by Anthony M. Stevens-Arroyo and Gilbert Cadena. 33-59. Vol. 2 of PARAL Studies Series. New York: Bildner Center for Western Hemisphere Studies, 1995. Statistical information on pp. 37-39.

2516. **Caraballo de Silva, Jovita.** *La Iglesia Protestante en Puerto Rico como Agente de Asimilación Cultural.* San Juan, PR: Universidad de Puerto Rico. Biblioteca del Seminario Evangélico, n.d.

2517. **Caraballo Ireland, Elba R.** "The Role of the Pentecostal Church as a Service Provider in the Puerto Rican Community Boston, Massachusetts: A Case Study." Ph.D. diss., Brandeis University, 1991. 194 pp.

2518. **Cardenas, Rene.** "The Gospel Movement in the Hispanic Community." In *The Challenge of American Hispanics,* edited by Oscar I. Romo. 47-52. Atlanta, GA: Language Church Extension Division, Home Mission Board, The Southern Baptist Convention, 1989.

2519. **Cardoza-Orlandi, Carlos F.** "Nos Llamaron 'Mulatos, Fiesteros, pero Redimibles': Antropología Misionera y Definición del Protestantismo en Puerto Rico." *Apuntes: Reflexiones Teológicas desde el Margen Hispano* 14, no. 4 (1994): 99-111.

2520. **Castañeda, Carlos E.** *Church Views of the Mexican American.* The Mexican American. New York: Arno Press, 1974.

2521. **Center for Continuing Study of the California Economy.** *Projections of Hispanic Population for the United States 1990 and 2000.* Palo Alto, CA: Center for Continuing Study of the California Economy, 1982.

2522. **Chakarsi, George.** "Bridging the Cultural Gap between Parents and Children of Hispanic Descent Living in the United States." D.Min. Project Report. Talbot School of Theology, Biola University, 1991. 150 pp.

2523. **Chinula, Don.** "Liberation, Praxis, and Psychotherapy." *Apuntes: Reflexiones Teológicas desde el Margen Hispano* 5, no. 4 (1985): 87-95.

2524. **Cook, Howard Scott.** "Some Sociocultural Aspects of Two Revivalistic Religious Groups in a Puerto Rican Municipio." San Juan, PR. University of Puerto Rico, 1963. Manuscript.

2525. **Costas, Orlando E.** "El Pastor como Agente Movilizador." *Psicología Pastoral* 2, no. 8 (1974): 3-10.

2526. **Costas, Orlando E.** "Socialism and the Christian Witness: An Interview with Orlando Costas." *The Other Side* 12, no. 1 (1976): 27-30, 39-43.

2527. **Costas, Orlando E.** "Conversion as a Complex Experience: A Personal Case Study." In *Gospel & Culture: The Papers of a Consultation on the Gospel and Culture, Convened by the Lausanne Committee's Theology and Education Group,* edited by John Stott and Robert T. Coote. 240-62. Pasadena, CA: William Carey Library, 1979. Also published in *Occasional Essays [of CELEP]* 5, no. 1 (1978): 21-44. Revised editions published in Robert T. Coote and John R. Stott, eds., *Down to Earth: Studies in Christianity and Culture: The Papers of the Lausanne Consultation on Gospel and Culture* (Grand Rapids, MI: William B. Eerdman's Publishing Co., 1980), 173-91; *Gospel in Context* 1, no. 3 (1978): 14-24, with reactions and responses on pages 36-39; *Latin American Pastoral Issues* (San José, Costa Rica) 16, no. 1 (1989): 8-32.

2528. **Costas, Orlando E.** "La Empresa Misionera: ¿Un Instrumento de Domesticación?" *Taller de Teología* 5 (1979): 39-53.

2529. **Costas, Orlando E.** "Análisis Sociocultural del Crecimiento en las Comunidades Cristianas." *Misión* 5, nos. 3-4 (1986): 112-15.

2530. **Cotto-Pérez, Irving.** "The Design and Implementation of a Strategy for a Congregational Mission in Hispanic Churches in the Eastern Pennsylvania Conference of The United Methodist Church." D.Min. Project Report. Eastern Baptist Theological Seminary, 1986. 240 pp.

2531. **Daily, Steven Gerald.** "Adventist Adolescents and Addiction: Substance Use/Abuse in an Adventist Population and its Relationship to Religion, Family, Self-Perception, and Deviant Behavior." Ph.D. diss., United States International University, 1991. 309 pp.

2532. **Davis, J. Merle.** *The Church in Puerto Rico's Dilemma: A Study of the Economic and Social Basis of the Evangelical Church in Puerto Rico.* New York: Department of Social and Economic Research and Counsel; London: International Missionary Council, 1942.

2533. **Davis, Kenneth G.** "The Hispanic Shift: Continuity Rather than Conversion?" *Journal of Hispanic-Latino Theology* 1, no. 3 (1994): 68-79.

2534. **De la Garza, Rodolfo O.**, *et al.* *Latino Voices: Mexican, Puerto Rican, and Cuban Perspectives on American Politics.* Boulder, CO: Westview Press, 1992. pp. 37-39, 57-58.

2535. **Deck, Allan Figueroa, S.J.** "A Hispanic Perspective on Christian Family Life." *America* 145, no. 20 (1981): 400-402.

2536. **Deck, Allan Figueroa, S.J.** "The Spirituality of United States Hispanics." In *An Annotated Bibliography on Hispanic Spirituality,* edited by Verónica Méndez, R.C.D. and Allan Figueroa Deck, S.J. 4-22. Berkeley, CA: The Jesuit School of Theology at Berkeley, 1989.

2537. **Department of Development and Planning, City of Chicago.** "Chicago's Spanish-Speaking Population: Selected Statistics." Chicago, IL. Department of Development and Planning, City of Chicago, 1973.

2538. **Dodrill, Mark Andrew.** "Christian Youth Ministry in Hispanic Chicago and Barcelona: An Inquiry into Similarities, Dissimilarities and Cross-Cultural Themes." Ed.D thesis. Trinity Evangelical Divinity School, 1991. 351 pp.

2539. **Dohen, Dorothy.** *Two Studies of Puerto Rico: Religion Data. The Background of Consensual Union.* Sondeos, no. 3. Cuernavaca, México: Centro Intercultural de Documentación, 1966. 155 pp.

2540. **Erdman, Daniel.** "Liberation and Identity: Indo-Hispano Youth." *Religious Education* 78, no. 1 (1983): 76-89.

2541. **Espinoza, Marco A.** "Pastoral Care of Hispanic Families in the United States: Socio-Cultural, Psychological, and Religious Considerations." D.Min. Project Report. Andover Newton Theological School, 1982. 246 pp.

2542. **Estrada, Leobardo F.** "Comunidades Latinas en los Estados Unidos: Su Presente y Futuro." *Apuntes: Reflexiones Teológicas desde el Margen Hispano* 15, no. 2 (1995): 25-44.

2543. **Fann, Delbert.** "Hispanic Church Growth: An Eight-Year Study of Hispanic Congregations." Home Mission Board of the Southern Baptist Convention. Atlanta, GA, 1989.

2544. **Fenton, Jerry F.** *Understanding the Religious Background of the Puerto Rican.* Sondeos, no. 52. Cuernavaca, México: Centro Intercultural de Documentación, 1969.

2545. **Ferree, William, Ivan Illich, and Joseph P. Fitzpatrick, eds.** *Spiritual Care of Puerto Rican Migrants: Report on the First Conference, Held in San Juan, Puerto Rico, April, 1955.* Sondeos, no. 74. Cuernavaca, México: Centro Intercultural de Documentación, 1970. 235 pp.

2546. **Fisher, Edith Maureen, ed.** *Focusing on Mexican/Chicano American Research: A Guide and Annotated Bibliography to Selected Resources in the University of California, San Diego Libararies.* San Diego, CA: Instructional Services Department, University Library, University of California, San Diego, 1976. 70 pp.

2547. **Fitzpatrick, Joseph.** "Faith and Stability among Hispanic Families: The Role of Religion in Cultural Transition." In *Families and Religions: Conflict and Change in Modern Society,* edited by William V. D'Antonio and Joan Aldous. 221-42. Beverly Hills, CA: SAGE Publications, Inc., 1983.

2548. **Fitzpatrick, Joseph P.** "The Dilemma of Social Research and Social Policy: The Puerto Rican Case, 1953-1993." In *Old Masks, New Faces,* edited by Anthony M. Stevens-Arroyo and Gilbert Cadena. 173-81. Vol. 2 of PARAL Studies Series. New York: Bildner Center for Western Hemisphere Studies, 1995.

2549. **Gallego, Daniel T.** "Religiosity as a Coping Mechanism among Hispanic Elderly." In *Hispanic Elderly: A Cultural Signature,* edited by Marta Sotomayor and Herman Curiel. 117-35. Edinburg, TX: Pan American University Press, 1988.

2550. **Galloway, Ronald R.** "Biculturalism in the United States of America: A Study of Hispanics in the Church of the Nazarene." Ph.D. diss., United States International University, 1995. 174 pp.

2551. **Gibson, Delbert Lee.** "Protestantism in Latin American Acculturation." Ph.D. diss., University of Texas, 1959.

2552. **Glaze, Michael S.** "A Pilot Study of Southern Baptists' Attitudes towards the Active Use of Art in the Church: A Prelude to Future Research." Ph.D. diss., Florida State University, 1993. 288 pp.

2553. **Goizueta, Roberto S.** "Nosotros: Toward a U.S. Hispanic Anthropology." *Listening: Journal of Religion and Culture* 27, no. 1 (1992): 55-69.

2554. **Gómez, Roberto.** "Mestizo Spirituality: Motifs of Sacrifice, Transformation, Thanksgiving, and Family in Four Mexican American Rituals." *Apuntes: Reflexiones Teológicas desde el Margen Hispano* 11, no. 4 (1991): 81-92.

2555. **González, Justo L.** "Searching for a Liberating Anthropology." *Theology Today* 34, no. 4 (1978): 386-94.

2556. **González, Justo L.** "Where Frontiers End...And Borders Begin." *Basta!* (February 1990): 19-22.

2557. **González, Justo L.** "Hispanics in the United States." *Listening: Journal of Religion and Culture* 27, no. 1 (1992): 7-16.

2558. **González, Justo L.** "The Religious World of Hispanic Americans." In *World Religions in America: An Introduction,* edited by Jacob Neusner. 111-30. Louisville, KY: Westminster/John Knox Press, 1994.

2559. **Goris, Anneris.** "Rites for a Rising Nationalism: Religious Meaning and Dominican Cultural Identity in New York City." In *Old Masks, New Faces,* edited by Anthony M. Stevens-Arroyo and Gilbert Cadena. 117-41. Vol. 2 of PARAL Studies Series. New York: Bildner Center for Western Hemisphere Studies, 1995.

2560. **Grebler, Leo, Joan W. Moore, and Ralph C. Guzman.** "Protestants and Mexicans." In *The Mexican American People: The Nation's Second Largest Minority,* edited by Leo Grebler, Joan W. Moore, and Ralph C. Guzman. 486-512. New York: The Free Press, 1970.

2561. **Greeley, Andrew.** "Defection among Hispanics." *America* 159, no. 3 (1988): 61-62.

2562. **Gregory, Spencer.** *Projections of the Hispanic Population: 1983 to 2080.* Current Population Reports. Series P-25, Population Estimates and Projections; no. 995. Washington, DC: U.S. Department of Commerce, Bureau of the Census, 1986.

2563. **Grijalva, Joshua.** "Religiosity of the Mexican-Americans." In *The Challenge of American Hispanics,* edited by Oscar I. Romo. 31-46. Atlanta, GA: Language Church Extension Division, Home Mission Board of the Southern Baptist Convention, 1989.

2564. **Haselden, Kyle.** "Death of a Myth: New Locus for Spanish American Faith." In *Protestantism and Latinos in the United States,* edited by Carlos E. Cortés. New York: Friendship Press, 1964. Reprint, New York: Arno Press, 1980. 172 pp.

2565. **Hernandez, Edwin I.** "Relocating the Sacred among Latinos: Reflections on Methodology." In *Old Masks, New Faces,* edited by Anthony M. Stevens-Arroyo and Gilbert R. Cadena. 61-76. Vol. 2 of PARAL Studies Series. New York: Bildner Center for Western Hemisphere Studies, 1995.

2566. **Hernandez, Edwin I.** "Factores Que Contribuyen a la Vida Religiosa del Joven." *En Contacto* Tercer Trimestre, no. 2 (1987): 11-12.

2567. **Hernandez, Edwin I.** "Selected Variables Related to Religious Commitment among Church Related Hispanic Seventh-day Adventist Youth." Paper presented at the annual meeting of the Society for the Scientific Study of Religion, Louisville, KY, 30 October-1 November 1987.

2568. **Hernandez, Edwin I.** "Eschatological Hope and the Hispanic Evangelical Experience." Paper presented at the annual meeting of the Society for the Scientific Study of Religion, Chicago, IL, October 1988.

2569. **Hernandez, Edwin I.** "Religious Commitment and Its Political Consequences among Seventh-Day Adventists in the United States." Ph.D. diss., University of Notre Dame, 1989.

2570. **Hernandez, Edwin I.** "An Assessment of the Problems, Needs, and Challenges of Ministry to and with Hispanics." Paper presented at a Hispanic Consultation in the Religion Division of the Lilly Endowment, January 1992.

2571. **Hernandez, Edwin I.** "A Descriptive Study of Catholic Health System's Mission Effectiveness Programs." Paper presented at the Adventist Health System Sunbelt Mission Conference, February 1992.

2572. **Hernandez, Edwin I.** "Hung Between Two Worlds." *Insight,* 8 February 1992, 15.

2573. **Hernandez, Edwin I.** "Religious Commitment and Drug Usage among Latino Youth." Paper presented at the annual meeting of the Society for the Scientific Study of Religion, Washington, DC, November 1992.

2574. **Hernandez, Edwin I.** "Research among Latino Congregations: Issues and Challenges." Paper presented at the annual meeting of the Religious Research Association, Raleigh, NC, October 1993.

2575. **Hernandez, Edwin I.** "Nutrition Habits of Hispanics." Paper presented at "Nutrition 2000," a convention held at Andrews University, Berrien Springs, MI, June 1994.

2576. **Hernandez, Edwin I., Evelyn R. Barritt, Linda S. Quick and Sonya R. Albury.** "Life and Death Decisions: A Special Study of Community Values: Vols. 1 & 2." Health Council of South Florida. Miami, FL, 1991.

2577. **Hernandez, Edwin I. and Roger L. Dudley.** "Religious Determinants of Political Attitudes among Seventh-Day Adventists." Paper presented at the annual meeting of the Society for the Scientific Study of Religion, Provo, UT, October 1989.

2578. **Hernandez, Edwin I. and Roger L. Dudley.** "[The] Persistence of Religion through Primary Group Ties among Hispanic Seventh-Day Adventist Young People." Paper presented at the annual meeting of the American Sociological Association, Pittsburgh, PA, August 1990. Published in *Review of Religious Research* 32, no. 2 (1990): 157-72.

2579. **Hernandez, Edwin I. and Roger L. Dudley.** "Public Issues: Where Do U.S. Adventists Stand?" *Adventist Review,* 29 March 1990, 14-18.

2580. **Hernandez, Edwin I. and Roger L. Dudley.** "Citizens of Two Worlds." *Dialogue* 3, no. 3 (1992): 14-15.

2581. **Hernandez, Edwin I. and Roger L. Dudley.** *Citizens of Two Worlds: Religion and Politics among American Seventh-Day Adventists.* Berrien Springs, MI: Andrews University Press, 1992. 318 pp.

2582. **Hernandez, Edwin I., Roger L. Dudley, and Sara M. K. Terian.** "Conservative Christians and American Politics: The Case of Seventh-Day Adventists." In *Research in the Social Scientific Study of Religion, vol. 4,* edited by Monty L. Lynn and David O. Moberg. 73-103. Greenwich, CT: JAI Press Inc., 1992.

2583. **Hernandez, Edwin I., Roger L. Dudley, and Sara M. K. Terian.** "Religiosity and Public Issues among Seventh-Day Adventists." *Review of Religious Research* 33, no. 4 (1992): 330-48.

2584. **Hernandez, Edwin I., Roger L. Dudly, and Sara M. K. Terian.** "Do Adventist Voters Lean Left or Right?" *Spectrum: A Journal of the Association of Adventist Forums* 23, no. 3 (1993): 5-13.

2585. **Hernandez, Edwin I. and Roger L. Dudley.** "Personal Religion and the Elections of 1992: The Case of Seventh-Day Adventists." Paper presented at the annual meeting of the Religious Research Association, Albuquerque, NM, November 1994.

2586. **Hernandez, Edwin I. and Lincoln Johnson.** "Batson's Quest for Orientation: Some Empirical Correlates and an Evaluation." Paper presented at the meeting of the American Psychological Association, Washington, DC, August 1986.

2587. **Hernandez, Edwin I., et al.** "Religious Institutions as Sources of AIDS Information for Street Injection Drug Users." *Review of Religious Research* 35, no. 4 (1994): 324-34.

2588. **Hernandez, Edwin I. and Ivonne Segui.** "The Impact of the Family on Drug Usage among Latino Youth." Paper presented at the annual meeting of the Society for the Scientific Study of Religion, Washington, DC, November 1992.

2589. **Hobart, Charles.** "Census of Protestant Churches in New York City." Report for the Greater New York Federation of Churches. New York, 1937.

2590. **Hoehn, Richard A.** "Chicano Ethos: An Anglo View." *Lutheran Quarterly* 28, no. 2 (1976): 116-72.

2591. **Holland, Clifton L.** "The Religious Dimension in Hispanic Los Angeles: A Protestant Case Study." Ph.D. diss., South Pasadena, CA: William Carey Library, 1974. 541 pp.

2592. **Hornor, Louise L., ed.** *Hispanic Americans: A Statistical Sourcebook.* Palo Alto, CA: Information Publications, 1994. 254 pp.

2593. **Jensen, Evelyn E.** "The Hispanic Perspective of the Ideal Woman: A Correlational Study." Ph.D. diss., Fuller Theological Seminary, School of World Mission, 1987. 163 pp.

2594. **Johnson, Douglas W.** "Racial/Ethnic Minority Membership in The United Methodist Church." National Program Division, General Board of Global Ministries, The United Methodist Church. New York, 1987.

2595. **King, Eleace.** *Proselytism and Evangelization: An Exploratory Study.* Washington, DC: Center for Applied Reasearch in the Apostolate, Georgetown University, 1991.

2596. **Knight, Robert Drew.** "A Study of the Role of the Episcopal Diocese of Los Angeles in Meeting the Psychosocial Needs of Hispanics." Master's thesis. California State University, Long Beach, 1989.

2597. **Krause, James H.** "Why do Mexican-American Lutherans in Corpus Christi Seek the Help of Curanderos/Curanderas?" D.Miss. thesis. Trinity Evangelical Divinity School, 1992. 359 pp.

2598. **Lara-Braud, Jorge.** "The Second Largest Ethnic Minority in the USA." *Migration Today* no. 12 (1969): 5-12.

2599. **Lara-Braud, Jorge, ed.** *Our Claim on the Future, a Controversial Collection from Latin America.* New York: Friendship Press, 1970. 128 pp.

2600. **Lara-Braud, Jorge.** "The Status of Religion among Mexican Americans." In *La Causa Chicana: The Movement for Justice,* edited by Margaret M. Mangold. 87-94. New York: Family Service Association of America, 1971.

2601. **Larson, Roy, ed.** *Hispanics in Chicago.* Chicago, IL: The Chicago Reporter and the Center for Community Research and Assistance, 1985.

2602. **Lee, Lewis E.** "Study of the Educative Process in Neo-Thomism and Evidences of its Similarities as Reflected in Baptist Adult Spanish Curriculum Materials, 1968-1971." Ed.D. thesis. Southwestern Baptist Theological Seminary, 1973.

2603. **Lennon, John J.** *A Comparative Study of the Patterns of Acculturation of Selected Puerto Rican-Protestant and Roman Catholic Families in an Urban Metropolitan Area.* San Francisco, CA: R and E Research Associates, Inc., 1976. 148 pp.

2604. **López, Ediberto.** "The Earliest Traditions about Jesus and Social Stratification." Ph.D. diss., Drew University, 1992. 283 pp.

2605. **Lucas, Isidro.** *The Browning of America: The Hispanic Revolution in the American Church.* Chicago IL: Fides/Claretian, 1981. See chapter six for references to Protestantism.

2606. **Luna, David.** "An Historical, Sociological, Theological Analysis of the Hispanic American Baptist in Southern California." D.Min. Project Report. American Baptist Seminary of the West, 1990. 96 pp.

2607. **Lutheran Church-Missouri Synod. Board for Mission Services.** "Hispanic Ministry in the U.S.A.: Statistical Report, 1991." Hispanic Ministry, Board for Mission Services, The Lutheran Church—Missouri Synod. St. Louis, MO, [1992].

2608. **Madsen, William.** "Mexican-Americans of South Texas." In *Case Studies in Cultural Anthropology,* edited by George and Louise Spindler. 62-67. New York: Holt, Rinehart and Winston, 1964.

2609. **Maldonado, David.** "Policy, Planning, and Administration." In *A Model Course Syllabi Compendium: Social Work and Chicano Content,* edited by Norma Benavides and Frederico Souflee, Jr. Houston, TX: Chicano Training Center, 1978.

2610. **Maldonado, David.** "Hispanic and African American Elderly: Religiosity, Religious Participation, and Attitudes toward the Church." *Apuntes: Reflexiones Teológicas desde el Margen Hispano* 14, no. 1 (1994): 3-18.

2611. **Maldonado, David.** "Religion and Persons of Color." In *Aging, Spirituality, and Religion,* edited by Melvin A. Kimble, *et al.* 119-28. Minneapolis, MN: Fortress Press, 1995.

2612. **Maldonado, David, Jr.** "The Chicano Elderly." *Social Work* 20, no. 3 (1975): 213-16. Also published in *The Later Years: Social Applications of Gerontology,* under the title, "The Mexican American Grows Old," and in Jill Quadagno, ed., *Aging in Modern Society* (New York: St. Martin's Press, 1980), pp. 369-75.

2613. **Maldonado, David, Jr.** "Ethnic Self-Identity and Self-Understanding." *Social Casework* 56 (December 1975): 618-22.

2614. **Maldonado, David, Jr.** "The Mexican American Grows Old." In *The Later Years: Social Applications of Gerontology,* edited by Richard Kalish. 37-43. Monterey, CA: Brooks/Cole Publishing, 1977.

2615. **Maldonado, David, Jr.** "Aging in the Chicano Context." In *Ethnicity and Aging,* edited by Donald Gelfand. 175-83. New York: Springer Publishing Company, 1979.

2616. **Maldonado, David, Jr.** ""Chicano Americans." A Manual to Facilitate the Infusion of Ethnic Minority Content into the Base of Social Work Education Curriculum." Council on Social Work Education. New York, 1980.

2617. **Maldonado, David, Jr.** "The Hispanic Elderly: A Heritage of Survival, Self Reliance and Pride." In *The Hispanic Elderly: Public Health Policy Issues.* 100-105. Rockville, MD: U.S. Department of Health and Human Services, Public Health Service, 1982.

2618. **Maldonado, David, Jr.** "Prevention among the Minority Elderly." In *Primary Prevention Approaches to the Development of Mental Health Services for Ethnic Minorities: A Challenge to Social Work Education and Practice,* edited by Samuel O. Miller, et al. 94-109. New York: Council on Social Work Education, 1982.

2619. **Maldonado, David, Jr.** "Social Work Services in Emergency Departments." In *Handbook of Geriatric Emergency Care,* edited by Laura B.Wilson, Sharon P. Simson, and Charles R. Baxter. 234-36. Baltimore, MD: University Park Press, 1984.

2620. **Maldonado, David, Jr.** "The Hispanic Elderly: A Socio-Historical Framework." *Journal of Applied Gerontology* 4, no. 1 September (1985): 18-27.

2621. **Maldonado, David, Jr.** "A Historical Framework for Understanding the Hispanic Elderly." In *Cross Cultural Social Work Practice in Aging: A Hispanic Perspective,* edited by David Maldonado, Jr. and Steven Applewhite. I:1-I:17. Arlington, TX: University of Texas at Arlington, 1985.

2622. **Maldonado, David, Jr.** "Aged." In *The Encyclopedia of Social Work,* 95-106. New York: National Association of Social Workers, 1987.

2623. **Maldonado, David, Jr.** "El Barrio: Perceptions and Utilization of the Neighborhood." In *Hispanic Elderly in Transition,* edited by Steven Applewhite. 135-42. New York: Greenwood Press, 1988.

2624. **Maldonado, David, Jr.** "A Framework for Understanding the Minority Elderly." In *Low-Income, Minority and Rural Adult Populations: Issues for the Future,* edited by E.O. Schuster. 7-29. Ypsilanti, MI: Geriatric Education Center of Michigan, 1989.

2625. **Maldonado, David, Jr.** "The Latino Elderly Living Alone: The Invisible Poor." *California Sociologist* 12, no. 1 (1989): 8-21.

2626. **Maldonado, David, Jr.** "Ethnicity and Gender: The Case of the Hispanic Elderly." In *Ethnicity and Aging: Mental Health Issues,* edited by A. Jarrett and S. King. 56-60. Arlington, TX: University of Texas at Arlington, 1990.

2627. **Maldonado, David, Jr.** "The Hispanic Elderly: Vulnerability in Old Age." Paper presented at "Minority Affairs Initiative Empowerment Conferences, American Association of Retired Persons," Washington, DC, 1990.

2628. **Maldonado, David, Jr.** "The Minority Church: Its Roles and Significance for the Minority Elderly." In *Ethnicity and Aging: Mental Health Issues,* edited by E. Percil Stanford, Shirley A. Lockery, and Susan A. Schoenrock. 25-32. San Diego, CA: San Diego State University, 1990.

2629. **Maldonado, David, Jr.** *Racial and Ethnic Diversity: Policy Questions and Recommendations.* Washington, DC: National Association of State Units on Aging, 1991.

2630. **Maldonado, David, Jr.** "Religiosity and Religious Participation Among Hispanic Elderly." *Journal of Religious Gerontology* 9, no. 1 (1994): 41-61.

2631. **Maldonado, David, Jr.** "El Pueblo Latino and Its Identity: The Next Generation?" *Apuntes: Reflexiones Teológicas desde el Margen Hispano* 15, no. 2 (1995): 45-57.

2632. **Maldonado, David, Jr., and others.** "Senior Volunteering in Minority Communities." *Generations* 5, no. 4 (1981): 14-19.

2633. **Maldonado, David, Jr. and Steven Applewhite, eds.** *Cross Cultural Social Work Practice in Aging: A Hispanic Perspective.* Arlington, TX: University of Texas at Arlington, 1985.

2634. **Maldonado, David, Jr. and Steven Applewhite.** *The Hispanic Elderly: Empowerment through Training.* Arlington, TX: Center for Chicano Aged, University of Texas at Arlington, 1986.

2635. **Maldonado, David, Jr. and John McNeil, eds.** *Service Strategies in Aging: Coping with the Times. [Proceedings of the Third Annual*

Symposium on Minority Aging]. 3rd ed. Arlington, TX: Graduate School of Social Work, University of Texas at Arlington, 1982. 66 pp.

2636. **Maldonado, David Jr. and David Espino.** "Hypertension and Acculturation in Elderly Mexican Americans: Results from 1982-84 Hispanic HANES." *Journal of Gerontology* 45, no. 6 (1990): 209-13.

2637. **Mark, Leslie David.** "The Role of Seminary Education in the Development of Spiritual Leadership in the Hispanic American Protestant Church." D.Min. Project Report. Fuller Theological Seminary, School of Theology, 1982.

2638. **Martin, Carlos G.** "Evangelistic Strategies of Seventh-Day Adventists to Reach Recent Hispanic Immigrants to Texas: A Critical Evaluation." Ph.D. diss., Southwestern Baptist Theological Seminary, 1992. 300 pp.

2639. **Mata, Michael A.** "The Post-Immigrant Hispanic Generation: Challenges and Leadership Development." Paper presented at a meeting of the advisory council to the Office of Hispanic Ministry, National Division, General Board of Global Ministries, The United Methodist Church, held in Seattle, WA, 1995.

2640. **Maust, John.** "The Exploding Hispanic Minority: A Field in our Back Yard." *Christianity Today* 24, no. 14 (1980): 12-14, 39.

2641. **McCready, William.** "Culture and Religion." In *Hispanics in the United States: A New Social Agenda,* edited by Pastora San Juan Cafferty and William C. McCready. 49-61. New Brunswick, NJ: Transaction Publishers, 1985.

2642. **McGuire, Meredith.** "Linking Theory and Methodology for the Study of Latino Religiosity in the United States Context." In *Enduring Flame: Studies on Latino Popular Religiosity,* edited by Anthony M. Stevens-Arroyo and Ana María Díaz-Stevens. 192-203. Vol. 1 of PARAL Studies Series. New York: Bildner Center for Western Hemisphere Studies, 1994.

2643. **McNamara, Patrick H.** "Assumptions, Theories and Methods in the Study of Latino Religion after Twenty-Five Years." In *Old Masks, New Faces,* edited by Anthony M. Stevens-Arroyo and Gilbert Cadena. 23-32. Vol. 2 of PARAL Studies Series. New York: Bildner Center for Western Hemisphere Studies, 1995.

2644. **Mergal, Angel M.** *Puerto Rico: Enigma y Promesa.* San Juan, PR: Editorial Club de la Prensa, 1960. 244 pp.

2645. **Miranda, Jesse.** "La Iglesia Evangélica Hispana en los Estados Norteamericanos: Un Análisis Socioreligioso." D.Min. Project Report. Fuller Theological Seminary, School of Theology, 1979. 190 pp.

2646. **Montes, Jesse.** "The Mexican American Religous Outlook: An Investigation of the Moral Value Systems of Mexican American Youth in East Los Angeles." Master's thesis. The Jesuit School of Theology at Berkeley, 1983. 135 pp.

2647. **Muñoz-Rivera, Brindice.** "A Pastoral Counseling Program for Mexican Immigrant Families." D.Min. Project Report. Claremont School of Theology, 1989. 76 pp.

2648. **National Council of Churches in the U.S.A.** "Churches and Church Membership in the United States: An Enumeration and Analysis by Counties, States, and Regions." Series A-E. National Council of Churches in the U.S.A., Bureau of Research and Survey. New York, 1956-58.

2649. **National Hispanic Caucus of the Lutheran Church in America.** "Hispanic Ministry Profile." Typescript.

2650. **Nida, Eugene A.** *Understanding Latin Americans, with Special Reference to Religious Values and Movements.* Pasadena, CA: William Carey Library, 1975.

2651. **Nieto, Leo D.** "Religious Profile of Spanish Surname Population in Corpus Christi and Nueces County, Texas, 1965 and Agricultural Migrant Labor Statistics for Texas." Study No. 4 of the Texas Council of Churches, Division of Christian Mission, Department of Church Planning and Development and Department of Migrant Ministry, June 1965.

2652. **Nieto, Leo D.** "Religious Profile of Spanish Surname Populations in Austin and Travis County, Texas-1965." Study No. 2 of the Texas Council of Churches, Division of Christian Mission, Department of Church Planning and Development and Department of Migrant Ministry, Austin, TX, March 1965.

2653. **Nogales, Luis G., ed.** *The Mexican American; a Selected and Annotated Bibliography.* 2nd ed. Stanford, CA: Stanford University, 1971. 162 pp.

2654. **Office of Pastoral Research, Archdiocese of New York.** "Hispanics in New York: Religious, Cultural and Social Experiences." 2 vols. Office of Pastoral Research, Archdiocese of New York. New York, 1982.

2655. **Ortiz, Manuel.** *The Hispanic Challenge: Opportunities Confronting the Church.* Downers Grove, IL: Intervarsity Press, 1993. 194 pp.

2656. **Ortiz, Manuel.** "Insights into the Second Generation Hispanic." *Urban Mission* 10, no. 4 (1993): 21-33.

2657. **Pantojas Garcia, Emilio.** "La Iglesia Protestante y la Americanización de Puerto Rico, 1898-1917." Bayamón, PR. PRISA, n.d. Manuscript.

2658. **Perez, Darlene J.** "A Correlational Study of Baptist Groups in Puerto Rico and Youth Curriculum Variables." Ed.D. thesis. Southwestern Baptist Theologial Seminary, 1991. 138 pp.

2659. **Pérez y González, María E.** "Latinas in Ministry: A Pioneering Study on Women Ministers, Educators and Students of Theology." Rev. ed. New York City Mission Society. New York, 1994.

2660. **Pino, Frank.** *Mexican Americans: A Research Bibliography.* East Lansing, MI: Latin American Studies Center, Michigan State University, 1974.

2661. **Poblete, Renato.** "Sociological Approach to the Sects [Puerto Rican Immigrants in New York]." *Social Compass* 7, nos. 5-6 (1960): 383-406.

2662. **Poblete, Renato and Thomas O'Dea.** "Anomie and the 'Quest for Community'—the Formation of Sects among the Puerto Ricans of New York." *American Catholic Sociological Review* 21, no. 1 (1960): 18-36. Also published in Thomas F. O'Dea, *Sociology and the Study of Religion: Theory, Research, Interpretation* (New York: Basic Books, 1970), pp. 180-98.

2663. **Polischuk, Pablo.** "Personality Characteristics and Role Preferences among Hispanic Protestant Ministers." Ph.D. diss., Fuller Theological Seminary, 1980.

2664. **Polischuk, Pablo.** "Hispanic Populations." In *Clergy Assessment and Career Development,* edited by Richard A. Hunt, John E. Hinkle, and H. Newton Malony. 154-57. Nashville, TN: Abingdon Press, 1990.

2665. **Post, Donald E. and Walter E. Smith.** "Clergy: Outsiders and Adversaries. The Story of Catholic and Protestant Clergy's Attempts to Relate the Gospel in Three South Texas Towns Experiencing Changing Mexicano/Anglo Relationships during the Period of 1945-1975." N.p., n.d. 254 pp. National Endowment for the Humanities Grant, No. RS-26255-531.

2666. **Protestant Council of the City of New York.** "A Report on the Protestant Spanish Community in New York City." Protestant Council of the City of New York, Department of Church Planning. New York, 1960.

2667. **Pulido, Alberto L.** "Presbiterianos Mexicanos: Una Perspectiva Materialista de la Religión y Trabajo en el Sur de Texas." *Cristianismo y Sociedad* 31-32, nos. 4-1 (1994): 19-27.

2668. **Ramírez, Johnny.** *Christianity and Self-Esteem: A Cross-Cultural Perspective.* South Lancaster, MA: IMAGE Publications, 1990. 50 pp.

2669. **Ramírez, Johnny.** "Puerto Rican Infant-Mother Attachment Behavior: A Pilot Study." Cambridge, MA. Harvard University Graduate School of Education, 1990. Manuscript.

2670. **Ramírez, Johnny.** "Biblical and Ethnopsychological Models for Race Relations." Presentation given to Human Relations Committee, Atlantic Union Conference of Seventh-Day Adventist, South Lancaster, MA. 1991.

2671. **Ramírez, Johnny.** "Religion, Education, and Success: In the Leominster Puerto Rican Seventh-Day Adventist Church Community." Ed.D. thesis. Harvard University, 1993.

2672. **Ramírez, Johnny.** "Religion, Education, and Success: In the Leominster Puerto Rican Seventh-Day Adventist Church Community." Paper presented at the annual meeting of the Society for the Scientific Study of Religion, Albuquerque, NM, November 1994.

2673. **Ramos, Marcos Antonio.** "El Protestantismo Hispanoamericano en la Noticia." *Apuntes: Reflexiones Teológicas desde el Margen Hispano* 12, no. 1 (1992): 21-27.

2674. **Recinos, Hal.** *Hear the Cry! A Latino Pastor Challenges the Church.* Louisville, KY: Westminster/John Knox Press, 1989. 156 pp.

2675. **Recinos, Harold.** "The Politics of Salvadoran Popular Religion." Ph.D. diss., The American University, 1993.

2676. **Recinos, Harold J.** *The Handbook for the Urban Ministry Track Program.* Washington, DC: Wesley Theological Seminary, 1990. 40 pp.

2677. **Reyes, José A.** *The Hispanics in the United States.* Cleveland, TN: White Wing Publishing House and Press, 1991. 146 pp.

2678. **Rivas, José.** "A Study to Determine the Role of the Ethical and Socio-Cultural Background as Influence Forces in the Religious Education of Baptist Students of Mexican Descent in Texas." D.R.E. thesis. Southwestern Baptist Theological Seminary, 1967. 217 pp.

2679. **Rivas, Michael G.** "The Hispanic Church and the Future: A Discussion Starter." Paper presented at the annual meeting of Hispanic Instructors, Perkins School of Theology, Dallas, TX, December 1994. Published in *Apuntes: Reflexiones Teológicas desde el Margen Hispano* 15, no. 2 (1995): 72-79.

2680. **Rivera, Raymond.** "The Hispanic Context in the United States." In *The Gospel and Urbanization: A Workbook for Participants in a Seminar Held April 22-26, 1985, at the Overseas Ministries Study Center,* edited by Robert Coote. Rev. and enl. ed. 73. Ventnor, NJ: Oveseas Ministries Study Center, 1985.

2681. **Rivera-Pagán, Luis N.** "Aportes del Marxismo." In *Pueblo Oprimido, Señor de la Historia,* edited by Hugo Assmann. 249-53. Montevideo, Uruguay: ISAL, 1972.

2682. **Rivera-Pagán, Luis N.** "Neue Atomskriegsdoktrinen." *Christliche Friedenskonferenz,* nos. 73-74 (1982): 21-27.

2683. **Rivera-Pagán, Luis N.** "Nuevas Doctrinas de Guerra Nuclear." *Talleres* 1, no. 1 (1984): 33-41.

2684. **Rivera-Pagán, Luis N.** "Análisis Crítico de *Nueva Visita al Cuarto Piso.*" *"En Rojo," Claridad* 29, no. 1769 (1986): 14-17.

2685. **Rivera-Pagán, Luis N.** "Estudios Sobre el Militarismo." *Revista de Historia,* no. 7 (1988): 185-92.

2686. **Rivera-Pagán, Luis N.** *Los Sueños del Ciervo: Perspectivas Teológicas desde el Caribe.* San Juan, PR: Equipo de Historia y Sociología del Protestantismo en Puerto Rico; Programa de Educación y Teología del Concilio Evangélico de Puerto Rico, 1995. 103 pp.

2687. **Rodríguez-Díaz, Daniel R. and David Cortés-Fuentes, eds.** *Hidden Stories: Unveiling the History of the Latino Church.* Decatur, GA: AETH, 1994. 165 pp.

2688. **Rodríguez-Díaz, Daniel R.** *Taller de Historia Oral.* Decatur, GA: AETH, 1994. 37 pp.

2689. **Romo, Oscar I., ed.** *The Challenge of American Hispanics.* Atlanta, GA: Language Church Extension Division, Home Mission Board of the Southern Baptist Convention, 1989.

2690. **Romo, Oscar I.** "U.S. Hispanics: Changing the Face of America." Home Mission Board, Southern Baptist Convention. Atlanta, GA, 1989.

2691. **Rosado, Caleb.** "Race, Class and Religious Schism: The Case of Puerto Rican Seventh-Day Adventists in Chicago." Paper presented at the annual meeting of the Society for the Scientific Study of Religion, Knoxville, TN, November 1983.

2692. **Rosado, Caleb.** "Castro and the Churches." *Spectrum: The Journal of Adventist Forums* 15, no. 3 (1984): 24-27.

2693. **Rosado, Caleb.** "Black and African Theologies of Liberation: Marxian and Weberian Perspectives." *Journal of Religious Thought* 42 (Spring-Summer 1985): 22-37.

2694. **Rosado, Caleb.** "Religion under Revolution." *Message,* March-April 1985, 10-13.

2695. **Rosado, Caleb.** "Sect and Party: Religion under Revolution in Cuba." Ph.D. diss., Northwestern University, 1985.

2696. **Rosado, Caleb.** "The Significance of Galilee." *Lake Union Ministerial Digest* 3, no. 2 (1985): 11-22.

2697. **Rosado, Caleb.** "Bridging Ethnic Differences: Insights on Hispanics." *Message,* May-June 1986, 18-21.

2698. **Rosado, Caleb.** "Hispanics and the Role of Authoritative Documents." Paper presented at the annual meeting of the Andrews Society for Religious Studies in conjunction with the annual meeting of the American Academy of Religion and the Society of Biblical Literature, Boston, MA, December 1987.

2699. **Rosado, Caleb.** "Hispanics and Protestantism: A Reciprocal Challenge." Paper presented at the annual meeting of the Society for the Scientific Study of Religion, Chicago, IL, October 1988.

2700. **Rosado, Caleb.** "The Nature of Society and the Challenge to the Mission of the Church." *International Review of Mission* 77 (January 1988): 22-37.

2701. **Rosado, Caleb.** *What is God Like?* Hagerstown, MD: Review and Herald Publishing Association, 1988. 95 pp.

2702. **Rosado, Caleb.** "The Church, the City, and the Compassionate Christ." *Apuntes: Reflexiones Teológicas desde el Margen Hispano* 9, no. 2 (1989): 27-35. Also published in Justo L. González, ed, *Voces: Voices from the Hispanic Church.* (Nashville, TN: Abingdon Press, 1992), pp. 72-80.

2703. **Rosado, Caleb.** "The Sociological Perspectives on Changes in Hispanic Religious Affiliation." Paper presented at the Spring Research Forum, held in Chicago, IL, March 1989.

2704. **Rosado, Caleb.** *Broken Walls.* Boise, ID: Pacific Press Publishing Association, 1990. 160 pp.

2705. **Rosado, Caleb.** "Latinos—The Search of Identity." *El Centinela,* September 1990, 6-8.

2706. **Rosado, Caleb.** *Women/Church/God.* Riverside, CA: Loma Linda University Press, 1990.

2707. **Rosado, Caleb.** "The Challenge of Cross-Cultural Communication." *Health and Development* 11, no. 1 (1991): 3-9.

2708. **Rosado, Caleb.** "Is War Necessary?" *Message,* July-August 1991, 6-7.

2709. **Rosado, Caleb.** "Affluence and the Advent Hope." *Adventist Review,* 2 January 1992, 18-21.

2710. **Rosado, Caleb.** "Identity Crisis: Ethnic Labels Confusing for All in Politically Correct World." *The Lumberjack* (Humboldt State University campus newspaper), 8 April 1992.

2711. **Rosado, Caleb.** "The Role of Liberation Theology on the Social Identity of Latinos." In *Twentieth-Century World Religious Movements in Neo-Weberian Perspective,* edited by W. Swatos, Jr. 195-209. Lewiston, NY: The Edwin Mellen Press, 1992. Also published in *Latino Studies Journal,* vol. 3, no. 3 (1992).

2712. **Rosado, Caleb.** "The Appeal of Cults." *Adventist Review,* 29 July 1993, 15-20.

2713. **Rosado, Caleb.** "El Poder de las Sectas Extremistas." *Revista Adventista,* October-December 1993, 11-13.

2714. **Rosado, Caleb.** "Lessons from Waco." *Ministry* (July 1993): 6-11.

2715. **Rosado, Caleb.** "Lessons from Waco II." *Ministry* (August 1993): 14-19.

2716. **Rosado, Caleb.** "El Papel de la Teología de la Liberación en la Identidad Social de los Latinos." *Cristianismo y Sociedad,* nos. 118-119 (1993-1994): 63-78.

2717. **Rosado, Caleb.** "America the Brutal: How did We Get to Such a State of Madness?" *Christianity Today* 38, no. 9 (1994): 20-25.

2718. **Rosado, Caleb.** "Multicultural Ministry." *Spectrum* 23, no. 5 (1994): 27-34.

2719. **Rosado, Caleb.** "Violence: Power with an Attitude." *Message,* May-June 1994, 32-36.

2720. **Rosado, Caleb.** "Affirmative Action: A Time for Change?" *North Coast Journal* (May 1995): 12.

2721. **Rosado, Caleb.** "Change and the Challenge of Church Mission." In *Makes Us One,* edited by Delber Baker. 39-59. Boise, ID: Pacific Press Publishing Association, 1995.

2722. **Rosado, Caleb.** "The Concept of 'Pueblo' as a Paradigm for Explaining the Religious Experience of Latinos." In *Old Masks, New Faces: Religion and Latino Identities,* edited by Anthony M. Stevens-Arroyo and Gilbert Cadena. 77-91. Vol. 2 of PARAL Studies Series. New York: Bildner Center for Western Hemispheric Studies, 1995.

2723. **Rosado, Caleb.** "God's Affirmative Action." *Christianity Today* 39, no. 13 (1995): 34-35. Also published as "Affirmative Action and the Gospel" in *Message,* July-August 1995.

2724. **Rosado, Caleb and Samuel Betances.** "Hispanic Christians Face the Upcoming Elections." *Apuntes: Reflexiones Teológicas desde el Margen Hispano* 4, no. 3 (1984): 63-68.

2725. **Rosado, Caleb and Lourdes Elena Morales-Gundmundsson.** "Machismo, Marianismo, and the Seventh-Day Adventist Church: Toward a New Gender Paradigm." In *Women and the Church: The Feminine Perspective,* edited by Lourdes Elena Morales-Gundmundsson. 113-34. Berrien Springs, MI: Andrews University Press, 1995.

2726. **Rosado, Caleb and Samuel Olimer, eds.** "Race, Gender and Ethnicity: Global Perspectives." *Humboldt Journal of Social Relations* 19, no. 2 (1993): 416.

2727. **Ruoss, Meryl.** "Mid-Century Pioneers and Protestants: A Survey Report of the Puerto Rican Migration to the U.S. Mainland and in Particular a Study of the Protestant Expression among Puerto Ricans of New York City." 2nd ed. Department of Church Planning and Research of the Protestant Council of the City of New York. New York, 1954.

2728. **San Antonio Baptist Association.** *Survey Report.* San Antonio, TX: San Antonio Baptist Association, 1960. 192 pp.

2729. **Sanchez, Daniel R.** "An Interdisciplinary Approach to Theological Contextualisation with Special Reference to Hispanic Americans." Ph.D. diss., Oxford Centre for Mission Studies, 1991. 466 pp.

2730. **Sandín-Fremaint, Pedro A.** "Hacia una Teología Femenista Puertorriqueña." *Apuntes: Reflexiones Teológicas desde el Margen Hispano* 4, no. 2 (1984): 27-37.

2731. **Sáenz, Michael.** "Economic Aspects of Church Development in Puerto Rico: A Study of the Financial Policies and Procedures of the Major Protestant Church Groups in Puerto Rico from 1898 to 1957." Ph.D. diss., University of Pennsylvania, 1962. 180 pp.

2732. **Schipani, Daniel S.** *Orientación Existencial del Adolescente.* Buenos Aires, Argentina: La Aurora, 1971.

2733. **Schipani, Daniel S. and Daniel E. Tinao.** *Educación y Comunidad.* Buenos Aires, Argentina: El Ateneo, 1973.

2734. **Segovia, Fernando F., ed.** "Hispanic Americans in Theology and the Church." *Listening: Journal of Religion and Culture* 27, no. 1 (1992): 3-84.

2735. **Shope, John H.** *Los Puertorriqueños y la Biblia.* San Germán, PR: Center for Research in Cultural Change, Inter American University, 1962.

2736. **Shope, John H.** *Puerto Ricans and the Bible: A Preliminary Report of the Study of a Stratified Sample of the Population for the Penzotti Institute, The American Bible Society and the Evangelical Council of Puerto Rico.* San German, PR: The Center for Research in Cultural Change, Inter American University, 1962. 86 pp.

2737. **Sielk, William A.** "The Importance of Latin American Cultural and Religious Values for the Christian Parochial Educator." Master's thesis. Concordia Theological Seminary, 1985. 68 pp.

2738. **Silva-Gotay, Samuel.** "Sociological Considerations about the Typologies of 'Sect' and 'Church'." 1963. 20 pp. Mimeographed.

2739. **Silva-Gotay, Samuel.** "Puerto Rico detrás de la Cortina del Silencio." Paper presented at the "Congreso de Difusión Cultural," held in México, 1972.

2740. **Silva-Gotay, Samuel.** "Teoría de la Revolución de Camilo Torres: Su Contexto y sus Consecuencias Continentales." *Latinoamérica,* no. 5 (1972): 105-38.

2741. **Silva-Gotay, Samuel.** *El Desarrollo del Pensamiento Revolucionario en la Iglesia Latinoamericana Contemporánea y Sus Impliacaciones para la Teoría Sociológica de la Religión.* México, D.F.: Universidad Nacional Autónoma de México, 1977.

2742. **Silva-Gotay, Samuel.** "La Función Social de la Religión en un Mundo en Crisis (Sociología de la Religión)." In *Crisis y Planifación.* N.p.: Escuela de Planificación, Ed. Universitaria, 1978.

2743. **Silva-Gotay, Samuel.** "Génesis de Pensamiento Cristiano Revolucionario a partir de la Radicalización de la Doctrina Social Cristiana." Paper presented at the congress en Lima, Perú for the anthology *Historia del Pensamiento Político Cristiano en América Latina y el Caribe,* 1980.

2744. **Silva-Gotay, Samuel.** "La Dimensión Ética de las Ciencias Sociales. Reflexión en torno a la Memoria de Charles Rosario, Profesor y Maestro de Nuestra Facultad." Paper presented at a meeting of the faculty of Social Sciences, the University of Puerto Rico, 1980.

2745. **Silva-Gotay, Samuel.** *La Religión en América Latina: Sociedad y Teoría.* La Habana, Cuba: Centro de Estudios Sobre América, 1980.

2746. **Silva-Gotay, Samuel.** "La Religión en el Proceso de Formación Cultural en Puerto Rico." Paper presented at the Centro de Estudios Avanzados del Caribe y Puerto Rico en Casa Blanca en la Serie Sobre Cultura Puertorriqueña, 1981.

2747. **Silva-Gotay, Samuel.** "Origem e Desemvolvimiento do Pensamento Cristão Revolucionario a Partir da Radicalização da Doutrina Social nas Decadas de 1960 e 1970." In *Historia da Teología na América Latina.* Sao Paulo, Brazil: Edições Paulinas, 1981.

2748. **Silva-Gotay, Samuel.** "Cambios en el Pensamiento Político del Cristianismo Latinoamericano." Paper presented at the Faculty Seminar of the Caribbean Research Center of the Inter American University, held in San Germán, PR, February 1983.

2749. **Silva-Gotay, Samuel.** *El Pensamiento Cristiano Revolucionario en América Latina y el Caribe.* 2d ed. Salamanca: Ediciones Sígueme; San Juan, PR: Editorial Cordillera, 1983. 389 pp.

2750. **Silva-Gotay, Samuel.** "La Iglesia Protestante como Agente de Americanización en Puerto Rico, 1898-1917." In *Politics, Society and Culture in the Caribbean: Selected Papers of the XIV Conference of Caribbean Historians,* edited by Blanca G. Silvestrini. 37-66. San Juan, PR: University of Puerto Rico, 1983.

2751. **Silva-Gotay, Samuel.** "Iglesias Católicas y Protestantes en el Proceso Político de la Americanización, Análisis de Similaridades y Diferencias." Paper presented at the "XII Congress and Symposium of CEHILA," held jointly with the "First International Conference on the Social History of the Church in Latin America," at the Universidad Nacional Autónoma de México, México City, October 1984.

2752. **Silva-Gotay, Samuel.** "La Iglesia en el Caribe desde 1959." Paper presented for the panel "La Iglesia Latinoamericana en la Coyuntura Actual" at the "XII Congress and Symposium of CEHILA," held jointly with the "First International Conference on the Social History of the Church in Latin America," at the Universidad Nacional Autónoma de México, México City, October 1984.

2753. **Silva-Gotay, Samuel.** "Metodología en la Investigación de la Historia Social de las Iglesias en Puerto Rico." Paper presented at the Centro de Investigaciones Sociales of the Universidad Nacional Autónoma de México, México City, October 1984.

2754. **Silva-Gotay, Samuel.** "La Iglesia Católica en el Proceso Político de la

Americanización de Puerto Rico, 1898-1930." [Parts 1 and 2] *Revista de Historia* (1985): Part 1: 1, no. 1 (1985): 102-20; Part 2: 1, no. 2 (1985): 168-87. Also published in *Cristianismo y Sociedad* 23, no. 86 (1985) 7-34.

2755. **Silva-Gotay, Samuel.** *La Tecnologización de la Universidad o el Fin de la Utopía.* Río Piedras, PR: Asociación Puertorriqueña de Profesores Universitarios, 1985. 10 pp.

2756. **Silva-Gotay, Samuel.** *La Teología de la Liberación: Implicaciones para el Cristianismo y el Marxismo.* 3rd ed. Santo Domingo: Ediciones de CEPAE, 1985. 389 pp.

2757. **Silva-Gotay, Samuel.** "Las Condiciones Históricas y Teóricas que Hicieron Posible la Incorporación del Materialismo Histórico en el Pensamiento Cristiano en América Latina." *Cristianismo y Sociedad* Segunda Entrega no. 84 (1985): 25-48.

2758. **Silva-Gotay, Samuel.** "La Incorporación del Instrumental Socio-Analítico del Materialismo Histórico a la Teología de la Liberación." *La Torre, Revista General de la Universidad de Puerto Rico* 34, nos. 131-133 (1986): 89-116.

2759. **Silva-Gotay, Samuel.** "La Transformación de la Función Política en el Pensamiento Teológico Caribeño y Latinoamericano." *Revista de Ciencias Sociales de la Universidad de Puerto Rico* 25, nos. 1-2 (1986): 39-78.

2760. **Silva-Gotay, Samuel.** *O Pensamento Cristão Revolucionario na América Latina e no Caribe.* Sao Paulo: Editorial Paulinas, 1986. 350 pp.

2761. **Silva-Gotay, Samuel.** "La Religión como Ideología Política en el Caribe." Paper presented at the Wilson Center, Smithsonian Institution, Washington, DC, March 1987.

2762. **Silva-Gotay, Samuel.** "Metodología para la Investigación de la Religión en el Proceso Político en Puerto Rico." Paper presented at the "Simposium on Politics in Puerto Rico," held at the University of Puerto Rico, March 1987.

2763. **Silva-Gotay, Samuel.** "Social Visions and Political Roles of the Churches in Puerto Rico and the Caribbean." Paper presented at the "Symposium on Twenty-Five Years of Churches and Social Change in Latin America," held at the Institute of the Américas, University of San Diego, California, April 1987.

2764. **Silva-Gotay, Samuel.** *El Pensamiento Cristiano Revolucionario en*

América Latina: Implicaciones de la Teología de la Liberación para la Sociología de la Religión. 4th ed. Río Piedras, PR: La Editorial Huracán, 1989. 389 pp.

2765. **Silva-Gotay, Samuel.** "Signification de la recherche sur la phénomène Religieux dans la Caraïbe pour CEHILA." In *La Phénomenène Religieux dans la Caraïbe.* Montreal: Les Ed. du CIHIHCA, 1989.

2766. **Silva-Gotay, Samuel.** "La Disolución del Socialismo Europeo de Corte Leninista desde la Perspectiva de un Latinoamericano." Paper presented at the Casa Latinoamericana de Kramer House, Berlin, Germany, July 1990.

2767. **Silva-Gotay, Samuel.** "El Sentido de la Celebración del 5to Centenario: Una Celebración que Desnuda la Postmodernidad en Puerto Rico." Paper presented for the Association of Puerto Rican Students and the Center for Third World Studies, Princeton University, November 1992.

2768. **Silva-Gotay, Samuel.** "Lo 'Científico' en la Historiografía Protestante Sobre las Iglesias: Hacia una Metodología para el Estudio de las Iglesias Latinas en los Estados Unidos, Puerto Rico y Canada." Paper presented at the Seminar of Hispanic Historians, University of Chicago, May 1993.

2769. **Silva-Gotay, Samuel.** "Anti-Colonial Praxis of Christian Movements in Puerto Rico: The Inter-Generational Conflict in Protestant Churches in the 1960 and 1970 Decades." Paper presented at the annual meeting of the Society for the Scientific Study of Religion, held in Albuquerque, NM, November 1994.

2770. **Silva-Gotay, Samuel.** "The Ideological Dimensions of Popular Religiosity and Cultural Identity in Puerto Rico." In *An Enduring Flame: Studies on Latino Popular Religiosity,* edited by Anthony M. Stevens-Arroyo and Ana María Díaz-Stevens. 133-70. Vol. 1 of PARAL Studies Series. New York: Bildner Center for Western Hemisphere Studies, 1994.

2771. **Silva-Gotay, Samuel.** "A Scientific History of the Latino Church." In *Hidden Stories: Unveiling the History of the Latino Church,* edited by Daniel R. Rodríguez-Díaz and David Cortés-Fuentes. 23-47. Decatur, GA: AETH, 1994.

2772. **Silva-Gotay, Samuel.** *Christentum und Revolution in Lateinamerika und der Karibik: Die Bedeutung der Theologie der Befreiung für eine Soziologie der Religion.* Vol. 17 of Würzburger Studien zur Fundamentaltheologie, edited by Elmar Klinger. Berlin: Peter Lang, 1995. 465 pp.

2773. **Simmons, Ozzie G.** *Anglo-Americans and Mexican Americans in South Texas.* The Mexican American. New York: Arno Press, 1974. pp. 84-103, 153-155.

2774. **Skerry, Peter.** *Mexican Americans: The Ambivalent Minority.* New York: The Free Press, 1993. pp. 166-69, 190-91. Notes 21-22 on pp. 410-11.

2775. **Stanford University. Center for Latin American Studies.** *The Mexican American: A Selected and Annotated Bibliography.* 2nd [rev. and enl.] ed. Stanford, CA: Stanford University, 1971. 162 pp.

2776. **Stevens-Arroyo, Anthony M. and Gilbert Cadena, eds.** *Old Masks, New Faces: Religion and Latino Identities.* Vol. 2 of PARAL Studies Series. New York: Bildner Center for Western Hemisphere Studies, 1995. 196 pp.

2777. **Stevens-Arroyo, Anthony M. and Ana María Díaz-Stevens, eds.** *An Enduring Flame: Studies on Latino Popular Religiosity.* Vol. 1 of PARAL Studies Series. New York: Bildner Center for Western Hemisphere Studies, 1994. 219 pp.

2778. **Stevens-Arroyo, Anthony M. and Andrés Pérez y Mena, eds.** *Enigmatic Powers: Syncretism with African and Indigenous People's Religions among Latinos.* Vol. 3 of PARAL Studies Series. New York: Bildner Center for Western Hemisphere Studies, 1995. 208 pp.

2779. **Stevens-Arroyo, Anthony M. and Segundo Pantoja, eds.** *Discovering Latino Religion: A Comprehensive Social Science Bibliography.* Vol. 4 of PARAL Studies Series. New York: Bildner Center for Western Hemisphere Studies, 1995. 142 pp.

2780. **Sturm, Roy A.** *Río Grande Conference: A Study of Methodism's Ministry to a People in Process of Acculturation.* Philadelphia, PA: Department of Research and Survey, Division of National Missions, Board of Missions of The Methodist Church, 1958. 131 pp.

2781. **Sumner, Margaret L.** "Mexican-American Minority Churches, USA." *Practical Anthropology* 10, no. 3 (1963): 115-21. Reprinted in John H. Burma, ed., *Mexican-Americans in the United States: A Reader.* (New York: Schenkman Publishing Company, 1970), 225-33.

2782. **Suro, Roberto.** "Switch by Hispanic Catholics Changes Face of U.S. Religion [to Evangelical Protestant Denominations]." *New York Times,* 14 May 1989, 1, 14.

2783. **Teske, Raymond and Bandin Nelson.** "Religion and the Assimiliation of Mexican Americans." *Review of Religious Research* 19, no. 3 (1977): 243-53.

2784. **The Lutheran Church—Missouri Synod.** "Hispanic Ministry in the U.S.A. and Puerto Rico: Statistical Report 1993." Lutheran Church-Missouri Synod. St. Louis, MO, 1993.

2785. **Traverzo G., David.** "La Religión Latina en Estados Unidos: Luchas Pasadas y Tendencias Presentes." *Cristianismo y Sociedad* 31-32, nos. 4-1 (1993-1994): 79-94.

2786. **Trovall, Carl C.** "Citizenship and Community: Proposition 187 and the Church." Dallas, TX. Southern Methodist University, 1995. Manuscript.

2787. **United States Bureau of the Census.** "U.S. Census of Population: 1960." Government Printing Office. Washington, DC. 1960.

2788. **United States Bureau of the Census.** *Current Population Report.* Series P-20, no. 238. Washington, DC: Government Printing Office, 1972.

2789. **United States Bureau of the Census.** *Current Population Reports. Series P 25. United States Bureau of the Census. Population Estimates and Projections.* Current Population Reports. Series P-25; no. 891. Washington, DC: Department of Commerce, Bureau of the Census, 1980.

2790. **United States Bureau of the Census.** *Condition of Hispanics in America Today.* Washington, DC: U.S. Department of Commerce, Bureau of the Census, 1983.

2791. **United States Bureau of the Census.** *The Hispanic Population in the United States.* Current Population Reports. Series P-250, Population characteristics; no. 422. Washington, DC: U.S. Department of Commerce, Bureau of the Census, 1985.

2792. **United States Bureau of the Census.** "Projections of the Hispanic Population 1983-2080." *Current Population Reports.* Series P-25, no. 995 (1986).

2793. **United States Bureau of the Census.** "The Hispanic Population of the United States: March 1989." *Current Population Reports,* Series P-20, no. 444 (1990).

2794. **United States Bureau of the Census.** "The Hispanic Population in the United States: March 1991." *Current Population Reports,* Series P-20, no. 455 (1991).

2795. **United States Bureau of the Census.** *Hispanic Americans Today.* Current Population Reports. Series P-20, Population characteristics; 183. Washington, DC: U.S. Department of Commerce, Economic and Statistics Administration, Bureau of the Census, [1993].

2796. **Velasquez, Roger.** "Theological Education for Hispanic Pastors in the American Baptist Churches, U.S.A." D.Min. Project Report. The Eastern Baptist Theological Seminary, 1982. 233 pp.

2797. **Villafañe, Eldin.** "The Role of the Church in the Preservation of Hispanic Culture: A Puerto Rican Perspective." Cambridge, MA. Harvard Divinity School, 1975. Manuscript.

2798. **Villafañe, Eldin.** "Toward an Hispanic American Pentecostal Social Ethic, with Special Reference to North Eastern United States." Ph.D. diss., Boston University, 1989. 493 pp.

2799. **Villarreal, Luis.** "Counseling Hispanics." *Urban Mission* 9, no. 2 (1991): 33-41.

2800. **Vlach, Norita.** "America y el Alma: A Study of Families and Adolescents Who are Recent United States Immigrants from Guatemala." Ph.D. diss., University of California, San Francisco, 1984. 354 pp.

2801. **Weedman, William Lee.** "An Analysis of Socio-Economic Factors Affecting Church Ministries with Reference to Selected Minority Groups in Metropolitan Areas." Th.D. diss., The Southern Baptist Theological Seminary, 1968. 343 pp.

2802. **Weigert, Andrew J., William V. D'Antonio, and Arthur J. Rubel.** "Protestantism and Assimilation among Mexican Americans: An Exploratory Study of Ministers' Reports." *Journal for the Scientific Study of Religion* 10, no. 3 (1971): 219-32.

2803. **Williams, Peter.** *Popular Religion in America: Symbolic Change and the Modernization Process in Historical Perspective.* Edgewood Cliffs, NJ: Prentice-Hall, 1980.

2804. **Wright, Robert E.** "Popular and Official Religiosity: A Theoretical Analysis and a Case Study of Laredo-Nuevo Laredo, 1755-1857." Ph.D. diss., Graduate Theological Union, 1992. 698 pp.

2805. **Zackrison, James W.** "Ministry in an Age of Shifting Social Context: A Study Guide on How to Organize and Run Multiethnic/Multicultural Churches in the 1990s." Pasadena, CA. Fuller Theological Seminary, 1991. Manuscript.

2806. **Zackrison, James W.** "Multiethnic/Multicultural Ministry in the 1990s: With Special Emphasis on the Seventh-Day Adventist Church in North America." D.Miss. thesis. Fuller Theological Seminary, School of World Mission, 1991. 399 pp.

2807. "Americanizing the Church in Cuba and Puerto Rico." *Harper's Weekly,* 5 August 1899, 777.

2808. "Latino Perspectives for 1990 [Statistical Report]." Chicago, IL. Latino Institute, 1988.

Archives

2809. **American Baptist Churches, U.S.A.** *Archives.* Valley Forge, PA. Contains records of the original American Baptist Home Missions Society, later called the Board of National Ministries, including their annual reports and periodicals. Records of the American Baptist Home Missions Society's mission work in Puerto Rico are located at the Historical Society and Archives of the American Baptist Churches, U.S.A.

2810. **American Baptist–Samuel Colgate Historical Library.** *Collections on Hispanic American Baptists.* American Baptist-Samuel Colgate Historical Library, Colgate Rochester Divinity School, Rochestor, NY.

2811. **Archives and History Center of The United Methodist Church.** *Hispanic Methodism Collection.* Drew University, Madison, NJ. Contains minutes of the mission societies' and boards' deliberations on its missions in the United States Southwest, Puerto Rico, and Latin America. The archives also contain letters written between officials of the mission boards and the boards' missionaries. In addition, there are periodicals, books, and other items related to Hispanic Methodists.

2812. **Asociación Bautista de Puerto Rico.** *Actas Anuales, 1965-68.* Wolfe City, TX: Southern Baptist Press, 1969.

2813. **Asociación Bautista de Puerto Rico.** *Libro de Actas para 1971-72.* Wolfe City, TX: Southern Baptist Press, [1972]. 116 pp.

2814. **Asociación para la Educación Teológica Hispana (AETH) [Association for Hispanic Theological Education].** *Archives.* Decatur, GA. An interdenominational organization that supports theological education among Hispanics. 1992-.

2815. **Associated Mennonite Biblical Seminary.** *Archives.* Associated Mennonite Biblical Seminary, Elkhart, IN. There is also some published work available in the Mennonite Historical Library, a separate facility near the archives.

2816. **Association of Hispanic Baptist Churches [New York City].** *Archives.* New York, NY. 1969-.

2817. **Austin Presbyterian Theological Seminary.** *Hispanic Presbyterians in Texas.* Stitt Library, Austin Presbyterian Theological Seminary, Austin, TX. Includes records of the Texas-Mexican Presbytery.

2818. **Baptist General Convention of Texas, Southern Baptist Convention.**

Archives. Located at Roberts Library, Southwestern Baptist Theological Seminary, Fort Worth, TX.

2819. **Baptist General Convention of Texas.** *Mexican Baptist Oral History Project.* Baptist General Convention of Texas. [Dallas, TX]. Located at Roberts Library, Southwestern Baptist Theological Seminary, Fort Worth, Texas. 1980.

2820. **Caribbean Synod of the Lutheran Church in America.** *Archives.* Caribbean Synod of the Lutheran Church in America. 1952, 1962–1965.

2821. **Casa Bautista de Publicaciones [Spanish Baptist Publishing House].** *Archives.* The publishing house publishes materials for the Southern Baptist Convention and for Baptist and evangelical churches in the U.S. and Latin America, as well as pamphlets and books by other evangelical authors. Its library contains first-print editions of all of its publications, as well as materials from other Spanish-language publishers. El Paso, TX. 1905–.

2822. **Claremont School of Theology.** *Hispanic Methodism Collection.* Claremont School of Theology, Claremont, CA. Materials cover Spanish-speaking Methodism in California, Nevada, and Arizona, including the Latin American Mission and the Latin American Provisional Annual Conference.

2823. **Conferencia de Puerto Rico de la Iglesia Metodista Unida.** *Anuarios de la Conferencia de Puerto Rico de la Iglesia Metodista Unida [Annuals of the Puerto Rico Conference of The United Methodist Church].* Iglesia Metodista de Puerto Rico. San Juan, PR. 1902–1991.

2824. **Convención Bautista de Puerto Rico.** *Actas de Asambleas Anuales desde 1931-71.* [1977].

2825. **Council on Hispanic-American Ministries, The National Council of Churches.** *Archives.* Presbyterian Historical Society, Philadelphia, PA.

2826. **Episcopal Theological Seminary of the Southwest.** *Archives.* Episcopal Theological Seminary of the Southwest, Austin, TX. Contains records of domestic missions of The Episcopal Church, including mission work in Puerto Rico. See also reference #2861.

2827. **Evangelical Lutheran Church in America.** *Archives.* Chicago, IL. Contains records of Lutheran mission work and documentation on Spanish-speaking Lutherans.

2828. **Evangelical Seminary of Puerto Rico.** *Archives.* San Juan, PR. Contains records of the missionary work of various denominations in Puerto Rico. It also has collections of important historical periodicals, especially *Puerto Rico Evangélico,* and documents of the Evangelical Council of Puerto Rico, formed in 1912.

2829. **Fernández-Calienes, Raúl.** "Bibliography of the Writings of Orlando E. Costas." *Missiology: An International Review* 17, no. 1 (1989): 87-105. 2nd ed. Denver, Co: Editorial Genesis, 1995. A copyrighted bibliography of writings and addresses by Orlando E. Costas and works written about him. A revised version of this bibliography compiled by Fernández-Calienes has been incorporated into this bibliography with his permission.

2830. **General Board of Higher Education, The United Methodist Church.** *Hispanic Resources of the General Board of Higher Education.* Located at the Archives and History Center of The United Methodist Church, Drew University, Madison, NJ. Contains Hispanic Resources packets produced by the General Board of Higher Education between 1967 and 1982 and records from the Hispanic American Institute for 1965–1969.

2831. **Hispanic American Institute, The Methodist Church.** *Archives.* Located at the Archives and History Center of The United Methodist Church, Drew University, Madison, NJ. 1965-.

2832. **Latin American Mission, The Methodist Episcopal Church.** *Journals.* Located in the "Hispanic Methodism" collection at the library of Claremont School of Theology, Claremont, CA. 1920–1939.

2833. **Latin American Provisional Annual Conference, The Methodist Church.** *Journals.* Located in the "Hispanic Methodism" collection at the library of Claremont School of Theology, Claremont, CA. 1940–1955.

2834. **Lawrence, Una Roberts.** *Una Roberts Lawrence Resource Files, Series of the Home Mission Board Records, Southern Baptist Convention.* Located at the Historical Commission of the Southern Baptist Convention, Nashville, TN. 1893–1972.

2835. **Leavenworth, Lynn and Milton Froyd.** "The Spanish-American Baptist Seminary and Its Task; An Appraisal after a Third of a Century of Service." Los Angeles, CA. Approx. 60 pp. Manuscript. Located at the American Baptist Convention, U.S.A. Board of Education and Publication, Division of Christian Higher Eduction, American Baptist Archives Center, Valley Forge, PA. Also located at American Baptist-Samuel Colgate Historical Library. Colgate Rochester Divinity School. Microfilm records of Division of Christian Higher Education. Reel #CHE-26. 1954.

2836. **MARCHA (Metodistas Asociados Representando la Causa de los Hispano Americanos/Methodists Associated Representing the Cause of Hispanic Americans).** *Archives.* Located in the office of the executive director, Rev. José Orlando Rivera. Lakewood, CA. 1971–.

2837. **McCormick Theological Seminary, Department of Hispanic Ministries.** *Documentation Relating to the Development of the Department for Hispanic Ministries, McCormick Theological Seminary.* Located at McCormick Theological Seminary. Chicago, IL.

2838. **Menaul Historical Library of the Southwest.** *Hispanic Presbyterian Collection.* Menaul School. Albuquerque, NM. Contains records and literature related to Presbyterian, and other Protestant, mission work in the Southwest.

2839. **Mexican American Program, Perkins School of Theology.** *Archives.* Perkins School of Theology, Dallas, TX. Contains documentation of the development of the Mexican American Program at Perkins School of Theology and materials produced by the program. Also contains archives of *Apuntes: Reflexiones Teológicas desde el Margen Hispano.*

2840. **Mexican Baptist Bible Institute.** *Archives.* San Antonio, TX. Contains archives related to Southern Baptist Convention work in Texas, including: Convención Bautista Mexicana de Texas and Unión Femenil Misionera de Texas; a photograph collection for both organizations; some congregational histories and asssorted papers; and Actas y Datos Históricos de la Convención Bautista Mexicana de Texas, 1910-20; 1922; 1927–29; 1934-66; 1968–73; 1975–78.

2841. **Mexican Baptist Children's Home.** *The Children's Evangel.* Newsletter published by The Mexican Baptist Children's Home, The Southern Baptist Convention. San Antonio, TX. Located at Roberts Library, Southwestern Baptist Theological Seminary, Fort Worth, TX. 1961-1965.

2842. **Mexican Baptist Children's Home.** *Just Us: Mexican Baptist Children's Home Newsletter.* Mexican Baptist Children's Home, Southern Baptist Convention. San Antonio, TX. Located at Roberts Library, Southwestern Baptist Theological Seminary, Fort Worth, TX. 1978-1986.

2843. **Mexican Baptist Convention of Texas, The Southern Baptist Convention.** *Archives.* Located at Roberts Library, Southwestern Baptist Theological Seminary, Fort Worth, TX. 1910-1960.

2844. **Náñez, Alfredo.** *Archives.* Located at Bridwell Library, Perkins School of Theology, SMU. Bridwell Archives, Box 842-42.

2845. **National Hispanic Caucus of the Baptist Churches.** *Archives.* Consult the Hispanic/Latino/Haitian Ministries, Board of National Ministries, American Baptist Churches, Valley Forge, PA. 1970-.

2846. **Northern Baptist Theological Seminary.** "Official Document of the Hispanic Tracks of the Northern Baptist Theological Seminary Masters Programs." Northern Baptist Theological Seminary, Chicago, IL. 1980.

2847. **Perkins School of Theology.** *Hispanic Methodism Collection.* Bridwell Library, Perkins School of Theology, Dallas, TX. Materials cover Spanish-speaking Methodism in Texas, New México and the Southwest, including records of the Río Grande Annual Conference.

2848. **Presbyterian Church in the U.S.A. Presbytery of Arizona.** *Minutes.* Located at the University of New Mexico, Alburquerque, NM. Microfilim located at the Presbyterian Historical Society, Philadelphia, PA. 1888-1906.

2849. **Presbyterian Church in the U.S.A. Synod of New México.** *Minutes.* [Albuquerque, NM?]: The Synod. Located at the University of New México, Albuquerque, NM. Microfilm located at the Presbyterian Historical Society, Philadelphia, PA. 1889-1958.

2850. **Presbyterian Historical Society.** *Hispanic Presbyterian Collection.* Philadelphia, PA.

2851. **Presbytery of Puerto Rico.** *Minutes.* [N.p.?] 1907-1966.

2852. **Puerto Rico Evangélico Publishing Company.** *Puerto Rico Evangélico Publishing Company.* Puerto Rico. Participating denominations in the non-profit publishing enterprise were Presbyterian, United Brethren, Congregational, American Baptist, Disciples of Christ and Methodist churches. It published materials for each of these denominations, the ecumenical evangelical magazine *Puerto Rico Evangélico,* and books and pamphlets by evangelical authors. 1927-.

2853. **Rembao, Alberto.** *Alberto Rembao Collection.* Located at Princeton Theological Seminary Library. Princeton, NJ.

2854. **Río Grande Annual Conference of The United Methodist Church.** *Journals.* Organized as the Southwest Mexican Conference in 1939, the name was changed in 1948. Located at Bridwell Library, Perkins School of Theology, Dallas, TX. 1939-.

2855. **Saenz, Ruben, Jr.** *Directory of Hispanic Theological Education in Texas.* Dallas, TX: AETH, 1995. 24 pp. Located at the Mexican-American Program, Perkins School of Theology, Dallas, TX and at the administrative office of AETH, Decatur, GA.

2856. **Southern Baptist General Convention of California.** *Annual.* N.p.: Southern Baptist General Convention of California. 1940–.

2857. **Southwestern Baptist Theological Seminary.** *Hispanic Southern Baptist Collection.* Located at Roberts Library, Southwestern Baptist School of Theology, Fort Worth, TX. N.d. Materials cover Spanish-speaking Southern Baptists, especially in Texas and the Southwest. Includes records of the Convención Bautista Mexicana de Texas [Mexican Baptist Convention of Texas].

2858. **Spanish-American Baptist Seminary [Seminario Bautista Hispano Americano].** *Archives.* Located at the American Baptist–Samuel Colgate Historical Library, Rochestor, NY. 1921–1964.

2859. **Texas–Mexican Presbytery, Presbyterian Church in the United States.** *Archives.* Located at Stitt Library, Austin Presbyterian Theological Seminary, Austin, TX. 1908-1955.

2860. **The Episcopal Church.** *Records of the Executive Council's National Commission for Hispanic Affairs and Hispanic Office.* Record Group 163. Research Office: Austin, TX. Administrative Office: Episcopal Church Center, New York: Institutional records less than 30 years old are closed to the public. 1964-1976. See also reference #2826.

2861. **The Episcopal Church.** *Records of the Executive Council's National Mission in Church and Society Hispanic Affairs Office.* Record Group 204. Research Office: Austin, TX. Administrative Office: Episcopal Church Center, New York: Institutional records less than 30 years old are closed to the public. 1977-1982.

2862. **United Presbyterian Church in the U.S.A. Synod of New México.** *Minutes.* [Albuquerque, NM]: The Synod. Minutes located at the University of New México, Albuquerque, NM. Microfilm located at the Presbyterian Historical Society, Philadelphia, PA. 1959-1972.

2863. **United Presbyterian Church in the U.S.A. Synod of the Southwest.** *Mission in the Southwest.* [Synod of the Southwest]. Brochure located at the University of New México, Albuquerque, NM. 1973-1974.

2864. **Vernon, Walter M.** *Some Thoughts on the Historic Methodist Mission to Mexican Americans.* Manuscript located in Walter Vernon's *Papers,* Bridwell Library, Archives, Perkins School of Theology, Dallas, TX.

Publications without Dates

2865. *La Nueva Senda.* An ecumenical periodical. Some copies are located in the Benson Latin American Collection, The University of Texas, Austin, TX.

2866. *Our Mission Field.* A series of quarterly reports of the Ladies' Board of Missions of the Presbyterian Church. The bound series is located in the Jackson Collection of the Presbyterian Historical Society. [1871-1885]

2867. *The Record.* Periodical published by the Southwestern Union, Conference of Seventh–Day Adventists, beginning in the 1940s. Located at Box 4000, Burleson, TX 76097.

2868. *Record/Review.* Periodical published by the Southwestern Union, Conference of Seventh–Day Adventists, beginning in the 1940s. Located at Box 4000, Burleson, TX 76097.

2869. *Records of the Mexican Presbyterian Church of the Divine Redeemer.* Located at Trinity University Library Archives. San Antonio, TX. Microfilm.

2870. *Southwestern Union Record.* Periodical published by the Southwestern Union, Conference of Seventh–Day Adventists, in the 1920s and 1930s. Located at Box 4000, Burleson, TX 76097.

2871. *Spanish-Language Hymnals: Fifty-one Spanish-language hymnals & musical selections.* Located at Kathryn S. Bowld Music Library, Southwestern Baptist Theological Seminary, Fort Worth, TX. Fifty-one Spanish-language hymnals and musical selections.

Publications arranged Chronologically

2872. *Baptist Standard.* Periodical published weekly by the Baptist General Convention of Texas. Dallas, TX. 1883.

2873. *El Expositor Bíblico para Alumnos.* Casa Bautista de Publicaciones. El Paso, TX. 1890–.

2874. *El Expositor Bíblico para Maestros.* Casa Bautista de Publicaciones. El Paso, TX. 1890–.

2875. "Official Minutes." In *The First Annual Meeting of the Porto Rico Mission of the Methodist Episcopal Church,* held in San Juan, PR. San Juan, PR: Press of the San Juan News, 1902.

2876. *El Defensor Cristiano.* Periodical published in Puerto Rico by The Methodist Episcopal Church. Puerto Rico. 1903–1916.

2877. *El Atalaya Bautista.* Periodical published by Casa Bautista de Publicaciones for Baptists in México and the southwestern United States. El Paso, TX. 1908–1930.

2878. *Puerto Rico Evangélico.* Periodical published by Unión Evangélico de Puerto Rico (Evangelical Council of Puerto Rico). Río Piedras, PR. 1912–1966.

2879. *El Mexicano.* Periodical published by the Spanish American Mission and the Latin American Mission of the Methodist Episcopal Church. Gardena, CA. Vols. 1–11. Located in the "Hispanic Methodism" collection at the library at The Claremont School of Theology. 1913–1923.

2880. *El Heraldo Cristiano.* Periodical published by the Texas Mexican Mission and Texas Mexican Conference of the Methodist Episcopal Church, South; Southwest Mexican Conference and the Río Grande Conference of The Methodist Church. Kingsville, TX. Located in the personal collection of Paul Barton and at Bridwell Library, Perkins School of Theology. 1915-1932; 1939-1953.

2881. *La Nueva Democracia.* Periodical published by the Committee on Cooperation in Latin America. New York. Complete collections are located at Princeton University, The University of Texas at Austin and ISEDET in Buenos Aires, Argentina. 1916–1962.

2882. *Lecciones Bíblicas.* Sunday School Curriculum. Casa Bautista de Publicaciones. El Paso, TX. 1931–1984.

2883. *El Mensajero.* Periodical published by the Texas Mexican Conference and the Western Mexican Conference of The Methodist Episcopal Church, South. 1932-1934.

2884. *Revista Evangélica.* Periodical published by Casa Bautista de Publicaciones. El Paso, TX. Vols. 1-20. 1937-1956.

2885. *El Boletín.* The Journal of the Seminario Evangélico de Puerto Rico (Evangelical Seminary of Puerto Rico). San Juan, PR. 1938; 1948; 1954–83; 1994–.

2886. *Southern Baptist Home Missions.* Periodical published monthly by the Home Mission Board, Southern Baptist Convention. Atlanta, GA. 1938–1954.

2887. *El Bautista Mexicano.* Periodical published monthly by the Language Missions Section, Baptist General Convention of Texas. Dallas, TX. 1939–.

2888. *The California Southern Baptist.* The Southern Baptist Convention of California. Fresno, CA. 1942–.

2889. *United Methodist Women's Program Book [Spanish].* New York: General Board of Global Ministries, The United Methodist Church. Located at the Women's Division, General Board of Global Ministries of The United Methodist Church, New York: 1944-.

2890. *Acción Evangélica.* Periodical published by The Church of the Nazarene. 1944–1946.

2891. *Home Missions.* Periodical published monthly by the Home Mission Board, Southern Baptist Convention. Atlanta, GA. 1954–1980.

2892. *Nuestra Tarea.* Periodical published monthly by the Woman's Missionary Union, Southern Baptist Convention. Birmingham, AL. 1955–.

2893. *El Pastor Evangélico.* Periodical published by Casa Bautista de Publicaciones. El Paso, TX. Vols. 1-16. 1957-1972.

2894. *El Hogar Cristiano.* Periodical published by Casa Bautista de Publicaciones. El Paso, TX. Vols. 1-36. 1957-1992.

2895. *Seminario.* Periodical published by Seminario Evangélico de Puerto Rico. San Juan, PR. 1958-.

2896. "Cooperative Planning Conference (Concilio Evangélico de Puerto Rico)." In *Cooperative Planning Conference,* held at the Inter American University, San Germán, PR, April 1959. 2 vols. Mimeographed papers.

2897. *Acción Metodista.* Periodical published by The Methodist Church. Havana, Cuba. 1960. Issues one through twelve for 1960, are located in the Mexican American Program, Perkins School of Theology, Southern Methodist University.

2898. *Edición de la Conferencia Río Grande.* Periodical published by the Río Grande Annual Conference, The United Methodist Church. San Antonio, TX. Issues located at United Methodist Reporter, Dallas, TX. 1965-.

2899. *El Nuevo Evangelista.* Periodical published by Las Iglesias Bautistas de Puerto Rico. Hato Rey, PR. 1967-.

2900. *El Pastor Bautista.* Periodical published by the Baptist Sunday School Board. Nashville, TN. 1967-.

2901. *La Voz Bautista.* Periodical published by Asociación Bautista de Miami. Miami, FL. 1968-.

2902. *Plight of the Hispanic American.* Audio recording from The United Methodist Church's talk show, *Night Call,* broadcast in 1969. Located at the Archives and History Center of The United Methodist Church. Drew University, Madison, NJ. 1969.

2903. *Avance.* Periodical published by American Baptist Churches (U.S.A.). King of Prussia, PA. 1973-

2904. *El Intérprete.* Periodical published by the General Board of Communications, The United Methodist Church. Nashville, TN. 1973-

2905. *El Obrero Cristiano.* Periodical published by Casa Bautista de Publicaciones. El Paso, TX. Vols. 1-12. 1973-1984.

2906. *Apuntes: Reflexiones Teológicas desde el Margen Hispano.* Journal edited by Justo L. González and published quarterly by the Mexican American Program, Perkins School of Theology, Southern Methodist University, Dallas, TX. 1981-.

2907. *Missions USA.* Periodical published by the Home Mission Board, Southern Baptist Convention. Atlanta, GA. 1981-.

2908. *Spiritual Growth Study [Spanish].* An annual Bible study focusing on a book of the Bible, produced by the Mission Education and Cultivation Program Department of the Women's Division, General Board of Global Ministries of The United Methodist Church. Nilda Ferrari, editor. New York, NY. 1983-

2909. *El Discípulo.* Periodical edited by Samuel Pagán and published by ICDC. Bayamón, PR. 1992-1995.

2910. *Encuentro.* Newsletter published by the Asociación para la Educación Teológica Hispana (AETH). Decatur, GA. 1992-.

2911. *Mañana.* Periodical published by the Academia para la Historia de la Iglesia Latina (APHILA). Daniel Rodríguez Díaz, director. McCormick Theological Seminary, Chicago, IL. 1992-.

2912. *Journal of Hispanic/Latino Theology.* Journal edited under the aegis of the Academy of Catholic Hispanic Theologians of the United States (ACHTUS) and published by The Liturgical Press. Collegeville, MN. 1993-.

2913. *La Voz Latina.* Newsletter published by The Hispanic Mission of the California–Pacific Annual Conference of The United Methodist Church. Los Angeles, CA. 1993-.

2914. *Visión Metodista: Por Cristo, por la Iglesia y por Puerto Rico.* Newsletter published by the Iglesia Metodista de Puerto Rico. San Juan, PR. 1995-.

2915. *Ecos de Vida: Selección Especial de Himnos y Canciones Espirituales.* New York: Editorial Ebenezer, n.d.

2916. "Catálogo, 1966-67: Seminario Teológico Bautista Conservador." Puerto Rico, [1966?].

2917. *El Promotor.* Periodical published by Casa Bautista de Publicaciones y Editorial Mundo Hispano. El Paso, TX. [1995].

Addendum for 1996 and 1997

2918. **Alianza de Ministerios Evangélicos Nacionales.** *[Newsletter].* Los Angeles, CA: Alianza de Ministerios Evangélicos Nacionales, 1996.

2919. **Alvarez, Carmelo E.** "Cecilio Arrastía: Elogio a la Elocuencia." *Apuntes: Reflexiones Teológicas desde el Margen Hsipano* 16, no. 2 (1996): 35-39.

2920. **Alvarez, Carmelo E.** "Ecumenism in Transition? Hispanic Responses from the United States." *Journal of Hispanic/Latino Theology* 4, no. 2 (1996): 60-74.

2921. **Cardoza-Orlandi, Carlos F.** "Facing the Dilemma: The Case for Latin America as a Mission Field." *Apuntes: Reflexiones Teológicas desde el Margen Hsipano* 16, no. 1 (1996): 17-29.

2922. **García, Ismael.** *Dignidad: Ethics through Hispanic Eyes.* Nashville, TN: Abingdon Press, 1997. 190 pp.

2923. **Garza, Minerva N.** "The Influence of Methodism on Hispanic Women through Women's Societies." *Methodist History* 34, no. 2 (1996): 78-89.

2924. **González, Justo L.,** ed. *¡Alabadle!: Hispanic Christian Worship.* Nashville, TN: Abingdon Press, 1996. 133 pp.

2925. **González, Justo L.** "Back to Basics." In *Upper Room Disciplines,* edited by Glenda Webb. 379-380. Nashville, TN: Upper Room, 1996.

2926. **González, Justo L.** *Church History: An Essential Guide.* Nashville, TN: Abingdon Press: Decatur, GA: AETH, 1996.

2927. **González, Justo L.,** ed. *Santa Biblia: The Bible through Hispanic Eyes.* Nashville, TN: Abingdon Press, 1996. 123 pp.

2928. **González, Justo L.,** ed. *Tres Meses en la Escuela de Mateo: Estudios Sobre el Evangelio de Mateo.* Nashville, TN: Abingdon Press, 1996. 168 pp.

2929. **González, Justo L.** *When Christ Lives in Us: A Pilgrimage of Faith: Leaders Guide.* Nashville, TN: Abingdon Press, 1996. 64 pp.

2930 **González, Justo L.** "The Year 2016: Where Will We Be by Then?" *Apuntes: Reflexiones Teológicas desde el Margen Hispano* 16, no. 2 (1996): 40-50.

2931. **González, Justo L.,** ed. *Tres Meses en la Escuela de la Prisión: Estudios*

Sobre Filipenses, Colosenses, Filemón y Efesios. Nashville, TN: Abingdon Press, 1997. 168 pp.

2932. **González, Justo L., ed.** *Tres Meses en la Escuela del Espíritu Estudios Sobre Hechos.* Nashville, TN: Abingdon Press, 1997. 168 pp.

2933. **Machado, Daisy L.** "Of Borders and Margins: Hispanic Disciples in Texas, 1888-1945." Ph.D. diss., The University of Chicago, 1996. 239 pp.

2934. **Martínez, Aquiles Ernesto.** "Reflexiones Pastorales Sobre el Poder Comunitario." *Apuntes: Reflexiones Teológicas desde el Margen Hsipano* 16, no. 1 (1996): 3-16.

2935. **Martinez, Juan Francisco.** "Origins and Development among Latinos in the Southwestern United States, 1836–1900." Ph.D. diss., Fuller Theological Seminary, 1996. 491 pp.

2936. **Martínez, Raquel, ed.** *Mil Voces para Celebrar: Himnario Metodista.* Nashville, TN: United Methodist Publishing House, 1996. Hymnal.

2937. **Ortiz, José.** *Curso Programado Sobre Administración de Iglesias.* N.p.: CLARA, 1996.

2938. **Pagán, Samuel.** "Ester." In *Comentario Bíblico Católico.* Dallas, TX: University of Dallas, 1997.

2939. **Pagán, Samuel.** *La Visión de Isaías.* Miami, FL: Editorial Caribe, 1997.

2940. **Pagán, Samuel.** "Obadiah." In *The New Interpreter's Bible.* 433-59. Vol. 7. Nashville, TN: Abingdon Press, 1997.

2941. **Pazmiño, Robert W.** "Designing the Urban Theological Education Curriculum." In *The Urban Theological Education Curriculum: Occasional Papers,* edited by Eldin Villafañe and Bruce W. Jackson. 13-22. N.p.: Gordon-Conwell Theological Seminary, Center for Urban Ministerial Education, Contextualized Urban Theological Education Enablement Program (CUTEEP), 1996.

2942. **Pedraja, Luis G.** "A New Vision: Ministry through Hispanic Eyes." *Apuntes: Reflexiones Teológicas desde el Margen Hispano* 16, no. 2 (1996): 51-58.

2943. **Rivera-Pagán, Luis N.** "El SIDA y la Religión: Desafíos y Respuestas." In *Sexualidad y el VIH/SIDA: Módulos Innovadoras de Enseñanza,* edited by Ineke Cunningham and others. 33-46. Río Piedras, PR: Universidad de Puerto Rico, 1996.

2944. **Rivera-Pagán, Luis N.** "La Evangelización de los Pueblos Americanos: Algunas Reflexiones Históricas." In *Etnias, Culturas y Teologías,* edited by Manuel Quintero. 25-57. Quito, Ecuador: CLAI, 1996.

2945. **Rivera-Pagán, Luis N.** "Libertad y Servidumbre: La Esclavitud Indígena en la Conquista Española del Caribe." In *General History of the Caribbean*. N.P.: UNESCO, 1996.

2946. **Rivera-Pagán, Luis N.** *Mito, Exilio y Demonios: Literatura y Teología en América Latina*. Río Piedras, PR: Publicaciones Puertorriqueñas, 1996.

2947. **Rivera-Pagán, Luis N.** "Mito, Religiosidad e Historia en la Literatura y el Discurso Teológico en América Latina y el Caribe." *Vida y Pensamiento* 16, no. 1 (1996): 5-115.

2948. **Rodríguez, Angel Manuel.** *¿Fin del Mundo o Comienzo de un Mundo Nuevo?* Nampa, ID: Pacific Press, 1996. 129 pp.

2949. **Rodriguez, Jeanette.** *Stories We Live: Hispanic Women's Spirituality/Cuentos que Vivimos*. New York: Paulist Press, 1996.

2950. **Rodríguez, José David and Loida I. Martell-Otero, eds.** *Teología en Conjunto: A Collaborative Hispanic-Protestant Theology*. Louisville, KY: Westminster/John Knox Press, 1997. 171 pp.

2951. **Romero, C. Gilbert.** "On Becoming 'Apiru: An Agenda for Latino Theology." *Apuntes: Reflexiones Teológicas desde el Margen Hsipano* 16, no. 2 (1996): 59-61.

2952. **Schipani, Daniel S.** "Christian Education for Social Transformation." In *Mapping Christian Education: Approaches to Congregational Learning*, edited by Jack L. Seymour. 23-40. Nashville, TN: Abingdon, 1997.

2953. **Schipani, Daniel S. and Pablo A. Jiménez, eds.** *Psicología y Consejo Pastoral: Perspectivas Hispanas*. Decatur, GA: AETH, 1997. 200 pp.

2954. **Silva Gotay, Samuel.** *Protestantism y Política en Puerto Rico, 1898-1930: Hacia una Historia del Protestantismo Evangélico en Puerto Rico*. San Juan, PR: Editorial de la Universidad de Puerto Rico, 1997. 375 pp.

Authors Index

Keywords Index

Chicago - 367, 1006, 1017, 1289, 1984, 1996, 2165, 2252, 2253, 2257, 2537, 2538, 2601, 2603, 2691

Chicanos
Theology - 175, 282, 364, 365, 408, 532
History - 1077, 1091, 1218, 1259, 1362, 1368, 1390, 1391, 1393, 1447, 1608
The Church and Its Ministry - 1837, 1861, 2006, 2048, 2057, 2238, 2399
Social Science - 2505, 2540, 2546, 2590, 2609, 2612, 2615, 2634, 2647, 2653, 2660, 2775

Children - 1867, 2366, 2478, 2522, 2616, 2799, 2841, 2842

Christian Church (Disciples of Christ) - 915, 1042, 1294, 1321, 1326, 1527, 1535, 1605, 1669, 1710, 1718, 1724, 2002, 2210, 2346, 2353, 2434, 2443, 2452, 2504, 2727, 2731, 2933, 2954

Christian Education
Theology - 163, 175, 244, 260, 305, 325, 377 - 381, 413, 498, 499, 501, 503, 504, 526, 545
Biblical Studies - 580, 607, 615, 641, 647, 665, 680, 720, 727, 772, 773
History - 835, 852, 887, 1024, 1152, 1197, 1323, 1378, 1379, 1383, 1533, 1643
The Church and Its Ministry - 1806, 1825, 1874, 1967, 1980, 1996, 2003, 2006, 2053, 2090, 2102, 2112, 2123, 2193, 2231, 2241, 2248, 2263, 2269, 2270, 2274, 2315, 2350, 2354, 2355, 2365, 2366, 2369, 2371, 2373, 2374, 2383, 2392, 2400, 2412, 2443 - 2445, 2485

Social Science - 2530, 2538, 2540, 2602, 2649, 2658, 2728, 2732, 2737
Archives - 2873, 2874, 2882, 2909
Addendum for 1996 and 1997 - 2952

Christian and Missionary Alliance - 1709, 2451, 2954

Christology - 139, 189, 205, 283, 400, 623, 2300

[The] Church and Its Ministry--A field of study (see numbers 1789-2491)

Church and Society
Theology - 22, 27, 28, 31, 39, 43, 45, 62, 116, 148, 190, 192, 193, 232, 233, 235, 236, 260, 261, 281, 287, 290, 291, 310, 311, 313, 321, 334, 364, 394 - 399, 402, 404, 409, 410, 413, 424 - 426, 428, 430, 435, 437, 440, 442, 444, 445, 451, 470, 473, 475, 501, 513, 524, 526 - 528, 532, 536, 539, 540, 546, 549, 552, 553, 555
Biblical Studies - 614, 616, 638, 647, 694, 729, 763, 764, 777 - 779, 783, 784
History - 830, 836, 855, 871, 892, 930 - 932, 938, 939, 952, 961, 982, 1000, 1002, 1026, 1048, 1068, 1074, 1079, 1081, 1091, 1095, 1116, 1130, 1137, 1152, 1179, 1198, 1207, 1210, 1240, 1444, 1247, 1256 - 1260, 1262, 1263, 1265, 1284, 1285, 1302, 1362, 1368, 1388, 1390, 1396, 1399, 1407, 1416, 1422, 1438, 1441, 1468, 1471, 1476, 1478, 1479, 1492, 1496, 1506, 1511 - 1513, 1541, 1542, 1564, 1567, 1568, 1570 - 1574, 1582, 1583, 1585, 1586, 1608, 1622, 1623, 1626, 1636, 1637, 1644, 1672, 1676, 1691, 1732, 1740, 1767, 1770, 1774
The Church and Its Ministry - 1798,

2346, 2373, 2394, 2399, 2404, 2409, 2417, 2420, 2424, 2431, 2475, 2484
Social Science - 2530, 2538, 2559, 2637, 2639, 2649, 2655, 2656, 2727

Leviticus (Book of) - 748, 751

Liberation - 13, 14, 33, 50, 155, 168, 175, 273, 339, 348, 410, 437, 451, 476, 501, 505, 543, 544, 596, 766, 914, 1314, 1454, 1603, 1814, 1866, 1872, 1911, 2006, 2047, 2173, 2338, 2523, 2540, 2702, 2945

Liberation Theology
Theology - 3, 6, 7, 8, 16, 24, 33, 35, 37, 44, 96, 157, 158, 159, 161, 167 - 169, 175, 182, 186, 188, 198, 222, 223, 229, 259, 265, 283, 292 - 301, 317, 320, 324, 339, 365, 414, 417 - 419, 421, 423, 427, 432, 436, 437, 450 - 452, 462, 466, 472, 483, 485, 494, 498, 500, 501, 504, 505, 513 - 522, 533, 537, 541, 543
Biblical Studies - 608, 656, 675, 740, 742
History - 867, 914, 1013, 1151, 1391, 1400, 1441, 1447, 1486, 1498, 1568, 1569, 1575, 1578, 1579, 1583, 1610, 1624
The Church and Its Ministry - 1864, 1977, 1993, 2006, 2020, 2046, 2075, 2093, 2157, 2161, 2257, 2277, 2294, 2303, 2307, 2369, 2373
Social Science - 2540, 2555, 2674, 2681, 2686, 2693, 2711, 2716, 2730, 2749, 2756, 2758 - 2760, 2764, 2772, 2776

Liturgy
Theology - 11, 13, 176, 277, 351, 368, 367, 370, 381, 388, 397, 403, 406, 408, 490, 492, 506, 532, 542

Biblical Studies - 673, 775
History - 933, 1116, 1373 - 1375, 1429, 1499, 1552, 1608, 1685, 1730, 1741
The Church and Its Ministry - 1809, 1812, 1814, 1823, 1870, 2007, 2008, 2067, 2100, 2101, 2105, 2205, 2223, 2228, 2230, 2289, 2328, 2349, 2363, 2377, 2399, 2409, 2442, 2461, 2467
Social Science - 2503
Addendum for 1996 and 1997 - 2924

Los Angeles - 829, 831, 1219, 1511, 1601, 1800, 1801, 2504, 2591, 2596, 2774, 2858

Louisiana - 937, 1273, 2080

Luke (Book of) - 659, 660, 798, 800

Lutheran
Theology - 6, 7, 42, 187, 463, 468, 469, 492
Biblical Studies - 581, 760 - 762
History - 832, 1093, 1298, 1383, 1384, 1516, 1714, 1741
The Church and Its Ministry - 1876, 2019, 2041, 2127, 2150, 2174, 2231, 2232, 2327, 2346, 2348, 2349, 2453, 2467
Social Science - 2597, 2649, 2727

Lutheran Church - 886, 1527, 2504

Lutheran Church in America - 1383, 1384, 2231, 2232, 2504, 2649, 2820

Lutheran Church--Missouri Synod, The - 189, 506, 549, 701, 775, 1679, 1817, 1851, 1863, 2044, 2045, 2048, 2171, 2192, 2208, 2221, 2377, 2379, 2383, 2429, 2504, 2607, 2640, 2737, 2784, 2786